Vol. 14 No. 1
February 1972

JOURNAL OF INTERAMERICAN STUDIES

and WORLD AFFAIRS

A Publication of the Center for Advanced International Studies,
The University of Miami

Journal of
INTERAMERICAN
STUDIES
and WORLD AFFAIRS

Vol. 14
No. 1
February
1972

CONTENTS

The United States, Canada, and the "Market Mentality"
PETER KARL KRESL 3

The Japanese and Central America
C. HARVEY GARDINER 15

Ideological, Political, and Economic Factors in the Cuban Controversy on Material Versus Moral Incentives
CARMELO MESA-LAGO 49

Book Reviews

Emmanuel & Emmanuel, History of the Jews of the Netherland Antilles
SEYMOUR B. LIEBMAN 113

Grebler, Moore, Guzman, The Mexican-American People
NANCIE L. GONZALEZ 118

Carter, New Lands and Old Traditions; Kekchi Cultivators in the Guatemalan Lowlands
RICHARD ADAMS 120

Books Received 125

Beverly Hills *SAGE PUBLICATIONS* *London*

JOURNAL OF INTERAMERICAN STUDIES AND WORLD AFFAIRS is published four times annually—in February, May, August, and November.

Journal of INTERAMERICAN STUDIES and WORLD AFFAIRS

Editor: Ione S. Wright

Associate Editor: Julian I. Weinkle

Editor-Designate: John P. Harrison

Book Editor: Harry W. Hutchinson

Published quarterly by SAGE PUBLICATIONS
Sara Miller McCune, *Publisher*
Connie Greaser, *Editorial Director–Journals*
Rhoda Blecker, *Production Editor*

POLICY: *The Journal of Interamerican Studies and World Affairs* reflects the interests of the scholarly community and interested public concerned with the social, economic, political, and cultural aspects of life in Latin America (including the Caribbean); particularly in those instances where the subject is of concern to more than one of the traditional disciplines. As these concerns change, so will the content of the journal. ¶ Articles which have special relevance for inter-relationships between American nations and of those nations with the rest of the world will be given special consideration. An effort will be made to include occasional articles that state an unusual or even discordant position on a subject of broad interest to be supplemented by critical comments of authorities representing differing positions on the topic. The editors continue to welcome articles by scholars from all parts of the world.

MANUSCRIPTS: Manuscripts should be submitted in duplicate to: Editor, *Journal of Interamerican Studies and World Affairs,* Box 8134, University of Miami, Coral Gables, Florida 33124. ¶ Correspondence regarding book reviews should be sent directly to: Book Review Editor, *Journal of Interamerican Studies and World Affairs,* Box 8123, University of Miami, Coral Gables, Florida 33124.

Subscriptions: Regular institutional rate $15.00 per year. Professionals and teachers may deduct one-third from the regular institutional rate (one-year rate $10.00); full-time college and university students may subscribe at $8.00. Add $1.50 for subscriptions outside the U.S. No discounts outside the U.S. and Canada. Orders from U.K., Europe, the Middle East, and Africa may be placed at £7.00 annually, and should be sent to the London office (address below).

Inquiries: Address all correspondence and permissions requests to SAGE PUBLICATIONS, INC., 275 South Beverly Drive, Beverly Hills, California 90212. Inquiries and subscriptions from U.K., Europe, the Middle East, and Africa should be sent to SAGE PUBLICATIONS, Ltd, St George's House, 44 Hatton Garden, London EC 1. Other orders should be sent to Beverly Hills office. ¶ **Exclusive Advertising Representatives:** R. K. Armstrong & Associates, Inc., 11661 San Vicente Boulevard, Suite 210, Los Angeles, California 90049.

Back Issues: Single copies of issues are available at $5.00 each. Orders for 10 or more copies of a single issue for course adoption will be billed at $2.50 per copy. ¶ **Claims for undelivered copies** must be made no later than three months following month of publication. The publisher will supply missing copies when losses have been sustained in transit and where the reserve stock will permit. ¶ **Change of Address:** Six weeks' advance notice must be given when notifying of change of address. Please send old address label along with the new address to insure proper identification. Please specify name of journal.

PETER KARL KRESL
Department of Economics
Bucknell University
Lewisburg, Pennsylvania

THE UNITED STATES, CANADA, AND THE "MARKET MENTALITY"

Perhaps nowhere else has the popular mentality been so taken with the idea of the market mechanism and automatic adjustment as in the United States. It is rather incredible—although admittedly something of a monument to the model itself—that in spite of two hundred years of Polanyi-type protective reactions to the market system—unions, cartels, counter-cyclical fiscal policy—Americans continue to be held in the grasp of this anachronistic ideology. The "typical American," from migrant worker to President, may be aware of the fact that we do not live in a market economy, but he believes that something approaching perfect competition lurks unseen behind all activity as a guiding force and is therefore relevant, or that this is a system toward which we ought legitimately to be moving.

This ideology manifests itself in the area of the international economic relations of the United States in a rather all-pervasive desire on the part of American policy makers to organize the entire world economy on the basis of "economic rationality." Economic rationalization of patterns of trade, investment, and finance would call for a minimum of regulation and intervention by various levels of government—an open ball game, so to speak—and a consideration of only those values that could be referred to as being quantifiable—material or "economic." Gross national product, on a real and per capita basis, and the real wage are such values, and policy would be directed so as to maximize their sum.

There are two consequences of holding this view of reality. First, the world is, in fact, not set up in such a fashion as to preclude individuals or firms from gaining a share of this material welfare which can only be referred to as excessively large. Second, the market view is not capable of incorporating into its welfare function nonmaterial values. This narrow perception of welfare places the United States at odds with various other parts of the world on a number of policy issues. What is seen as a rational policy position by the foreign power appears to be irrational from the narrower, economic viewpoint of the United States. The result of these factors is that, by allowing individuals to maximize as if they were held in check by those forces which would exist in a competitive setting, the United States, as a collective entity, becomes vulnerable to charges of economic imperialism.

There are a number of aspects of U.S. international economic policy that can be examined with this conflict of ideologies in mind. We can note briefly how this conflict affects our economic relation with Western Europe. In his recent statement with regard to various pieces of tariff or quota legislation before Congress, President Nixon (1969) said:

> I believe that the interests of the United States and the interests of the whole world will best be served by moving toward freer trade rather than toward protection. I take a dim view of this tendency toward quotas and other methods that may become permanent, whether they are applied here or by nations abroad . . . as far as the textile situation is concerned, that is a special problem which has caused very great distress in certain parts of this country.

The words are Nixon's, but they could have been uttered by any President since World War II. The United States believes in a free-trade world. Tariffs, quotas, and other trade impediments are to be used only to aid a particular industry, firm, region, or commodity.

Western Europeans, however, make policy decisions on the basis of a welfare function which is comprised more of arguments than of just real income—they also include less tangible considerations such as a regional identity and a concern for who controls the corporations into which economic activity is organized. This position has found popular expression in books such as Servan-Schreiber (1968) and Claude Julien (1968).

Of more concrete significance is the extent to which these contrasting views have affected tariff structures. In comparison with the Common Market (EEC) external tariff structure, that of the United States is one of higher individual tariff rates placed on fewer commodities (data to support this point are presented in Hinshaw, 1964: ch. 5). In the early 1960s, where over 57% of the EEC's tariffs were at a rate of no more than 15%, this was true of only 36.7% of United States tariffs. On the other hand, while over 24% of United States tariff rates were greater than 25%, only 2.2% of the Common Market's rates went this high. Hence, the conflict when the "Kennedy Round" discussions got under way (for a blow-by-blow recounting of this conflict, see Preeg, 1969: 1-12).

The United States sought a "linear" cut which would have attacked the EEC tariff wall; the EEC countered with the demand that the primary emphasis ought to be that of disproportionate cuts in the higher individual tariff rates of the United States structure. The United States goal was a lowering of a tariff wall, the existence of which could not be justified or rationalized as an exception to a general condition of free trade made necessary by some specific rigidity or misfortune. The goal of the EEC was that of doing away with these single industry or firm protective devices, thus ensuring some adjustment to changing economic reality, but maintaining some form of protective wall within which this adjustment would be localized under the presumption that there exists some overriding communal interest among the countries behind that wall.

This conflict arises as powerfully in the United States' relations with Canada, and it is in this manifestation that I would like to press the argument farthest. The economic rationalization mentality finds expression here in the desire to include the United States and Canada into one North American Free Trade Area (NAFTA), with the eventual political ramifications and extent of rationalization left rather unreassuringly vague. One of the espousers of this view is George Ball, a man who held major administration posts throughout the 1960s and is now an investment banker in New York. As recently as January of last year, Mr. Ball (1970) presented his free trade area thoughts to the Canadians before a committee of the House of Commons. The newspaper account of the speech reported that Mr. Ball stated that (1) "citizens of both Canada and the United States must regard North America as a single economy"; (2) Canada's neutralist foreign policy position makes her appear to Americans as a "dropout"; (3) "multinational corporations could make the most efficient use of Canada's national resources"; and (4) Canada will eventually join the United States because of the price of independence–lower wages. Mr. Ball is, of course, not alone here. David Rockefeller (1967) of the Chase Manhattan Bank, among a number of United States businessmen, has taken a similar position.

The primary intellectual opposition to NAFTA has come from a group of Canadian academics and politicians–the issue generates little interest among their United States counterparts –who are popularly referred to as Canadian Nationalists. The Nationalists are united only in their opposition to dominance of the United States in a great variety of aspects of Canadian life. They range in fervor from the moderate, who would like to see a "code of good corporate behavior" adopted by United States firms operating in Canada, to the radical who would question the foundations of the Canadian political and economic system. The former sees the problem as a lack of awareness on the part of the United States as to how U.S. policies inconvenience Canadians; the latter sees Canada as a neo-colony; in the middle is the widespread view of Canada as a "branch plant economy." Our purpose would not be served by a review of this literature—rather, refer to the following recent additions to the literature: Lumsden (1970); Godfrey (1970); Grant (1965); Levitt (n.d.); Gordon (1966). The basic point made by nationalists of all complexion is that a great and increasing number of fundamental decisions regarding Canadian life are being made, not in Ottawa, Montreal, or Toronto, but in New York, Washington, and Chicago.

In the early 1960s, it was Walter Gordon, Member of Parliament and later minister of finance, who raised the question of "the American presence." Gordon went largely unheeded—but he did manage to interest a number of academics and other politicians in the problem so that now Canadian universities have courses and teach-ins devoted to Canadian-American economic relations, newspapers give over more and more space to coverage of the issue and the government even commissions reports on foreign investment/ownership in Canada. The importance to us of this nationalist activity is that concern in Canada has reached the stage that the Canadian ambassador to the United States now espouses this view publicly. Ambassador Cadieux (1970: 1) stated that:

> In opposition to the thesis that is sometimes advanced that the forces of continental integration are so overwhelming that we will have to accept relatively painless loss of independence, we have every intention of ensuring that what we do have, we will preserve and enrich.

He noted further, that "the mood of the country is one in which any extra costs and difficulties required to ensure that survival would undoubtedly be accepted."

If we contrast the statement of Ambassador Cadieux with those of Mr. Ball and President Nixon, it is apparent that we again have the stuff of which international conflict is made. The situation is aggravated even more if one superimposes on this ideological conflict a general lack of concern over the American presence issue in the United States. In this latter regard, it is worth quoting the paragraph with which a Canadian newspaper closed its coverage of the symposium in New York at which Ambassador Cadieux (1970: 2) made his remarks:

> The [12th Annual Conference on U.S.-Canadian Relations sponsored by Columbia University], whose purpose was to inform Americans about Canada, drew, by the official attendance list, seven Canadian press representatives, 13 from the CBC and one from CTV and only one during the day from a U.S. medium, 11 Canadian Government officials and five representatives of Quebec compared with only one from the U.S. Government, five MPs and no U.S. Senators or Congressmen.

It may be that a posture of benign neglect is the current official and popular American response to awkward issues, but we must never suppose that this will do anything but intensify the frustration of the party being neglected.

The market ideology, however, is not without its supporters in Canada. In fact, until quite recently, economic rationalization of North America was the establishment position among Canadian economists. For example, Harry Johnson (1962: 58) wrote:

> [A U.S.-Canada Free Trade Area] contains all the ingredients usually thought necessary for successful economic integration . . . as well as the potentiality of a substantial net gain in economic efficiency. . . . The main objection to this proposal is, as it always has been, political rather than economic, derived from the fear of political absorption of Canada by the United States. That fear seems to me completely irrational, an anachronism inherited from a historical era that has long since passed away.

Ronald Wonnacott (1967: 85) was able to support the NAFTA in 1967 as a first step toward true multinational economic integration, while H. Edward English (1968) could espouse it one year later as an alternative to multinational tariff-cutting, should the latter not be achieved.

The business community has also given considerable support to NAFTA. Sixty-two of 77 members of the Canadian-American Committee signed (4 with reservation) a Committee report by Paul and Ronald Wonnacott (1968) which concluded that in the long run:

> Tariff elimination would introduce a greater degree of competition —with all its rewards and discipline. It would provide a stimulus for the efficient and pressure on the inefficient. The implied shift of labour and capital from less efficient to more efficient activities would be reflected in a rise in Canadian real income.

Most recently Wilfred N. Hall (1970) retired president of Canada's second largest pulp and paper company, reported to the Society of the Chemical Industry that NAFTA would be desirable for both Canadian political unity and Canadian industry. John V. Clyne (1968) of MacMillan, Bloedel, Ltd., has long been a spokesman for this view. Thus, if the United States is an imperialist power in Canada, the takeover is supported by a rather significant "fifth column."

A sizable number of Canadian Nationalists do, in fact, look upon NAFTA and the economic rationalization of North America in general as a process whereby Canada will lose its national identity and integrity, becoming an economic appendage of the United States. That is to say, they see the whole matrix, manifestations of the American presence in Canada, as simply another exercise in United States economic imperialism.

Imperialism is a very slippery term indeed. For decades, it has been used as a *schlagwort* and has, as can be imagined, taken on a good bit of emotional import. For our purposes, it would be best to stick with a rather straightforward definition—we shall mean economic imperialism to refer to the control of economic activity in a foreign country for the benefit of the home country. Even this definition is not without its rallying points. The basic consideration boils down to the viewpoint of the observer—home country or controlled country? The home country may not feel it has sufficient control in the foreign country to accomplish its goals, while citizens of the controlled country may believe the relationship that exists already to be oppressive.

Additionally, the controlling country, for one reason or another, may not even be aware of its presence in the foreign country. The ignorance on the part of most Americans of the issue of American dominance in Canada is a case in point. The fact of this ignorance does not mean that the United States is any more or less of an imperialist, but it does color very importantly the dialogue between the two parties. The estimation of the good will of the other party is of crucial importance if the issue at hand is to be negotiated to the long-term satisfaction of all concerned.

What are the facts of the economic relationship between the United States and Canada? Virtually every article on this general subject (for example, see Holbik, 1970, or Forbes, 1970) offers the same parade of statistics: roughly 71-73% of Canada's export and import trade is with the United States, over 50% of Canada's industry is controlled by Americans—the figure exceeding 90% in some individual industries, and so on. One can, however, get a better feeling for the magnitude of this American presence from sources other than statistical compendia. From a book such as Lumsden (1970) and Canadian newspapers, one gets an appreciation of the extent to which Americans and America are present, physically or not, in frequently dominant positions or numbers, in Canadian industry, universities, unions, arts, communications, and politics. The rationalizing mentality leads far beyond General Motors of Canada to Americans teaching Canadians history and literature, not as rare an occurrence as it may appear.[1] Simple relative sizes of the two countries, of course, preclude a reciprocal Canadian presence in the United States ever becoming an issue.

Where, then, does this leave us? Just who is the antagonist of Canadian Nationalists, with their demands for "Canadian content" and their insistence on the value of a "Canadian identity"? To say that it is Americans and United States imperialism contains an element of truth, in a tautological sense, but this involves a good bit of simplification. The impact of America on Canada would appear to be far more insidious than most Americans believe, but equally less malevolent than most Canadians imagine. The fundamental threat to any feeling of national or regional identity on the part of Canadians or Western Europeans–or anyone else, for that matter–is not any other national entity, but rather the rationalizing of the market mentality which does not allow consideration of nonmaterial values. Saying this does not put us in the same category with the paranoid who sees evidence everywhere of an international conspiracy of capitalist or any other origin. But it does get us a step beyond the idea that the major threat to Canadian nationalism is simply the United States, and beyond the policy prescription of closing the border.

As an American, I must stop at this point. It would be fatuous and, indeed, something of an extension of intellectual imperialism for an American to proceed to tell the Canadians how they ought to manage their affairs. It is up to Canadian Nationalists to transform their position from one that is held by an elite of academics and politicians to an idea that can be supported or rejected on its merits as an alternative to the market mentality by the majority of the Canadian populace. The fact that the public has continued to subscribe to Reader's Digest and Time/Life magazines after the 1965 flap attests to the accuracy of a suggestion that this has not yet been accomplished.[2]

A market mentality is, again, incapable of taking into account intangibles such as "Canadian content" or a "Canadian identity." It must, of course, be said that economists have, as a group, done much to maintain the prestige of this ideology, both as a policy for the United States and as a prescription for the world economy as a whole. Recently, several thousand American economists signed a petition in opposition to the current import quota legislation before Congress and presented the statement to the administration and individual legislators. The petition stated in part:

> In foreign policy, the time has come for a U.S. invitation to all the industrialized countries of the Free World to come forward with their own initiatives on how all the advanced countries together might program the dismantling of all their artificial trade barriers

> and distortions in accordance with a realistic timetable and the rules of the General Agreement on Tariffs and Trade [American Economics Association, n.d.].

It is one thing to postulate that, in general, freer trade contributes more to material welfare than does less free trade, and to suggest free trade as a policy prescription for the United States; it is quite another to press this policy on the entire industrialized free world, since, as we have noted, the rest of the developed world may find the singular prospect of material gain less than compelling.

NOTES

1. The Americanization of Canadian university faculties is very graphically discussed in Steele and Mathews (1970: 170-178).

2. In this incident, these American publications attempted to be classified as Canadian to avoid payment of new taxes the Canadian government had imposed on foreign magazines. Ensuing State Department pressure and apparent lack of concern for Canadian sovereignty created a rather ugly issue (for details, see Julien, 1968: 234-235).

REFERENCES

American Economics Association (n.d.) "An appeal for freer world trade." (mimeo)

BALL, G. (1970) Article in New York Times (January 16): 7.

CADIEUX, M. (1970) Article in Toronto Globe and Mail (November 18): 1.

CLYNE, J. V. (1968) Article in U.S. News and World Report (January 1): 48-50.

ENGLISH, H. E. (1968) "Transatlantic economic community: Canadian perspectives," pp. 68-70 in World Trade and Trade Policy. Toronto: Univ. of Toronto Press and the Private Planning Association of Canada.

Forbes (1970) Entire issue 106 (December).

GODFREY, D. [ed.] (1970) Gordon to Watkins to You. Toronto: New Press.

GORDON, W. (1966) A Choice for Canada: Independence or Colonial Status. Toronto: McClelland & Stewart.

GRANT, G. (1965) Lament for a Nation. Princeton: D. Van Nostrand.

HALL, W. N. (1970) Article in Toronto Globe and Mail (October 13): B2.

HINSHAW, R. (1964) The European Community and American Trade. New York: Praeger.

HOLBIK, K. (1970) "Canada's economic sovereignty and United States investment." Q. Rev. of Economics and Business 20 (Spring).

JOHNSON, H. G. (1962) Canada in a Changing World Economy. Toronto: Univ. of Toronto Press.

JULIEN, C. (1968) L'Empire american. Paris: Editions Bernard Grasset.

LEVITT, K. (n.d.) Canada: Economic Dependence and Political Disintegration. Winnipeg: Canadian Dimension.

LUMSDEN, I. [ed.] (1970) Close to 49th Parallel, etc. Toronto: Univ. of Toronto Press.

NIXON, R. M. (1969) Article in New York Times (February 7): 16.

PREEG, E. H. (1969) Traders and Diplomats. Washington, D.C.; Brookings Institution.

ROCKEFELLER, D. (1967) Article in U.S. News and World Report (August 21): 88-89.

SERVAN-SCHREIBER, J. J. (1968) The American Challenge. New York: Atheneum.

STEELE, J. and R. MATHEWS (1970) "The universities: takeover of the mind," pp. 170-178 in I. Lumsden (ed.) Close to 49th Parallel, etc. Toronto: Univ. of Toronto Press.

WONNACOTT, R. J. (1967) "Trade arrangements among industrial countries: effects on Canada," in B. Balassa (ed.) Studies in Trade Liberalization. Baltimore: Johns Hopkins Press.

WONNACOTT, P. and R. J. WONNACOTT (1968) U.S.-Canadian Free Trade: The Political Impact on the Canadian Economy. Washington, D.C.: National Planning Assn.

Latin American Urban Policies and the Social Sciences

Edited by JOHN MILLER *and* RALPH A. GAKENHEIMER

Accelerated urbanization and rapid population growth have drawn particular attention to Latin American in recent years. Current statistics on the growth rate of the nations of South America indicate the highest continental growth rate in the world, and there is no evidence that it may decelerate significantly.

Editors Miller and Gakenheimer have addressed various policy issues related to urban development in Latin America at international, national, and local levels from the points of view of different social sciences. The problems and potentials generated by rapid urbanization and the use of the social sciences for understanding and guiding urbanization and the process of national growth are treated extensively.

This volume is based on the Jahuel, Chile, Conference sponsored by the Ford Foundation—at which eminent scholars from both North and South America met to discuss Latin American Urban Policies.

Table of Contents

I. The New Urban Era in Latin America: A Challenge—The Urban Phase: Raison d'étre for Policy, **John Miller**

II. Integrating Urban-Regional Policies Among Nations—The Rapprochement of Nations with Contiguous Regions, **John Miller** / Economic Integration and the Spatial Development of South America, **Paul Ove Pederson** and **Walter Stohr**

III. Urban Growth Policies for the Nation—Channeling National Urban Growth in Latin America, **John Miller** / The Role of Cities in National Development, **John Friedmann** / Planning, History, Politics: Reflections on John Friedmann's 'The Role of Cities in National Development,' **Richard M. Morse** / Rejoinder to Richard M. Morse, **John Friedmann**

IV. Political Development Vis-a-vis Urban Growth—The Distribution of Political and Governmental Power in the Context of Urbanization, **John Miller** / Urbanization Policy and Political Development in Latin America, **Robert T. Daland**

V. Metropolitan Policy for the Squatter Settlements—Three Proposals Regarding Accelerated Urbanization Problems in Metropolitan Areas: The Lima Case, **Carlos Delgado**

VI. A Future Role for the Social Sciences: Policy and Action—The Contribution of the Social Sciences to Urban Policy Formulation in Latin America, **John Miller**

Appendix: Jahuel Seminar Summary, **Kalman H. Silvert**

ISBN 0-8039-0056-2 **1971** **384 pages** **$12.50**
L.C. 70-103481 **Market: World**

SAGE PUBLICATIONS, INC.
275 S. Beverly Dr. / Beverly Hills, CA. 90212

SAGE PUBLICATIONS LTD
44 Hatton Garden, London E C 1

C. HARVEY GARDINER
Department of History
Southern Illinois University
Carbondale, Illinois

THE JAPANESE AND CENTRAL AMERICA

In their identification with Latin America, major foreign powers—including Japan—have always considered the Central American region—the zone of present-day Guatemala, El Salvador, Honduras, Nicaragua, and Costa Rica—of secondary or lesser significance. For more than three centuries Spain attached marginal importance to this area and during the last 150 years, the five states there have played minor, though occasionally dramatic, roles in U.S. relations with Latin America. For Japan, until quite recently, the region has rarely fostered more than the single interest of trade, and that with stuttering results.

Because of its potential as a canal route, Nicaragua first drew Japanese attention to the area, attention that entered the historical record in such roundabout fashion that it raised more questions than it supplied answers. In February 1913, somewhat more than a year before the opening of the Panama Canal and at a time when the Panama Canal Tolls Act of 1912 by the United States was agitating every significant foreign shipping

AUTHOR'S NOTE: This article derives from research, much of it undertaken while a Fulbright lecturer at the University of Tokyo, leading to a volume on the broader theme, *The Japanese and Latin America.* The sources employed, as the notes indicate, are Japanese, Latin American, and United States in origin.

power, Minister Weitzel sent a despatch to his superiors which gave the incoming Wilson administration one thing more to consider. The archives of the Nicaraguan Foreign Office, according to Weitzel, contained a note, dated April 29, 1908, from Foreign Minister Gámez to the Nicaraguan minister in Paris in which the cabinet officer said that the English consul had informed President Zelaya that the Colombian government had invited the Japanese to enter into a treaty for the construction of a canal, but Japan had declined to do so because of an agreement with Great Britain that gave preference to the Nicaraguan route. Gámez instructed the Nicaraguan diplomat in France to discuss the matter discreetly with the Japanese ambassador in Paris and to assure him that Zelaya would cordially receive Japanese agents empowered to treat the matter.[1]

Inasmuch as Japan never seriously interested itself in the construction of any canal, either north or south of Panama, the Weitzel despatch illustrates the manner in which a Japanese factor was exploited in Nicaraguan-United States relations. By 1908, President General José Santos Zelaya, who had imposed fifteen years of arbitrary rule on Nicaragua, had generated mammoth opposition in official circles in Washington. In 1909, conservative elements revolted against him and American support of their efforts quickly assumed a variety of forms. In the ensuing post-Zelaya struggle for power between liberals and conservatives, American aid routinely inclined toward the latter, although they constituted a minority. Succeeding years expanded U.S. involvement in Nicaraguan affairs by way of fiscal arrangement and Marine intervention. When the turmoil of 1909-1912 subsided, Adolfo Díaz, aided and abetted by the United States, entered upon and served a term as president. Owing to American aid, both his position and the prospect of maintaining himself in it against a hostile majority, President Díaz was sufficiently beholden to Washington that he and his aides just might have tried to ingratiate themselves there by digging out archival items that additionally discredited Nicaragua's liberals. If, at the same time, such documents fed

American suspicion of Japan, that coincidence tended to obscure the ulterior motive, Díaz' consolidation of his own authority.

If American hostility toward Japan played any part in U.S. support of Nicaraguan conservatives, one might also wonder if a Japanese factor, real or imagined, influenced the formulation of the Bryan-Chamorro Treaty. Quite possibly, the Nicaraguan overture of mid-December 1912, which eventually led to the treaty of 1916, sparked even more interest in U.S. official circles when followed up, in February 1913, by the "revelation" of Japanese interest in canal construction that included a preference for a Nicaraguan site (for accounts of this phase of Nicaraguan history, see Freeman, 1925: 151-168; de Nogales, 1928: 7-11; Mecham, 1965: 325-327; U.S. Department of State, 1920: 1021-1034).

A decade later, an abortive treaty proposal contributed another question-raising episode in Japanese-Nicaraguan relations. In December 1924, in Mexico City, Ministers Shigetsuna Furuya and Ramón Solórzano drew up a seventeen-article treaty of amity, commerce, and navigation.[2] Unlike a proposal of 1915 to Panama, this document made no reference to interoceanic transit or to leaseholds. Like the Japanese proposal of 1917 to Panama, the Japanese-Nicaraguan document of 1924 emphasized most-favored-nation treatment in reference to commerce and navigation.[3]

Just as the Japanese-Nicaraguan document of 1924 both resembled and differed from earlier proposals to another isthmian state, so too it was like and unlike Japanese proposals of 1924 to two other Latin American states. Like the Japanese-Peruvian treaty of September 30 and the Japanese-Mexican treaty of October 8, 1924, both of which were ratified and put into effect, the December arrangement between Japan and Nicaragua was essentially an effort to promote trade.[4] The treaties with Peru and Mexico, both countries with thousands of Japanese residents, prominently dealt with matters related to those immigrants. Because there were few, if any, Japanese in Nicaragua, the references to immigration were indirect, as in

Article III, which said, "They shall be at full liberty to acquire and possess every description of property," and those articles (V, XII, XIII, and XIV) touching dwellings, access to courts, the operation of companies, and exemption from military service. Even in the wake of the American exclusion legislation of 1924, when Japan hoped to keep other doors open for her emigrants, that government made no significant effort in that regard concerning Nicaragua.

Because immigration to Nicaragua was not expected and Japanese trade with Nicaragua unimportant, one concludes that the negotiation of December 1924 was prompted more by individuals than by governments. Minister Furuya, having concluded in October a treaty with Mexico, readily seized an opportunity to extend his capacity as a treaty maker, reflecting as he did so the general broadening of Japanese world-mindedness in post-World-War-I years. Less obvious, on the other hand, was the motivation behind Minister Solórzano's participation in the negotiation. By the time a five-man Japanese mission carried a copy of the proposed treaty to Managua in December, the Nicaraguan government had dismissed Solórzano from his post, and it was asserted that, despite Japanese belief that he had possessed full powers for the negotiations, the Nicaraguan diplomat had acted on his own responsibility, without instructions from Managua.

At the same time, however, the American diplomatic mission in Nicaragua, judging President Bartolomé Martínez and his advisers to be consistently unfriendly to the United States, believed that the Mexico City negotiation had official Nicaraguan endorsement.[5] Inasmuch as Japanese-Nicaraguan relations per se were inconsequential, it is conceivable that Nicaragua was exploiting Japan to force Washington, for example, to implement the Bryan-Chamorro Treaty of 1916. Supporting this suspicion was publicity attending the mid-1924 visit to Nicaragua by a Japanese student of the proposed Nicaraguan canal route. At any rate, this flurry of Japanese-Nicaraguan relations, engulfed in uncertainty bordering on mystery, proved isolated and unproductive.

Early in the 1930s, military activity and political irregularity accompanying depressed economic conditions served to promote Japanese-Central American relations. A primary focus embraced the creation of Manchukuo in East Asia and the rise of dictator Maximiliano Hernández Martínez in El Salvador, both being desirous of recognition and initially short of friends. In December 1931, General Hernández Martínez brutally crushed a depression-inspired peasant revolt, ousted the elected president and catapulted himself into the presidency of El Salvador, the last act violating the policy of nonrecognition of revolutionary regimes which had derived from a Washington-based conference of Central American states in 1923. Because of U.S. desire to promote equilibrium in Central America, stability in the Caribbean region in general and peace in the Western Hemisphere, Washington led the diplomatic effort to cold-shoulder the new military master of El Salvador. That same year, Japan had initiated its thrust onto mainland Asia. As a result, early in 1932, Japan sought international recognition for Manchukuo at the same time that Hernández Martínez, seeking similar diplomatic approval, was eliciting no favorable response to the autograph notifications of his assumption of office that went out to the world community. However, Japan ignored the diplomatic boycott which, incidentally, had broken down and, early in 1934, recognized the government of Maximiliano Hernández Martínez. Bucking the disapproval of Japanese action inherent in the nonrecognition policy of Secretary of State Stimson, the anti-Japanese resolution of the League of Nations and, in time, the report of the Lytton Commission to that body, El Salvador reciprocated Japan's diplomatic generosity and de facto outlook by officially recognizing Manchukuo (Latin American Society, 1968; U.S. Department of State, 1948: 566-567, 582-583, 1946: 174, 203-204).

The fact that El Salvador was the only state, in addition to Japan, to have recognized Manchukuo induced a number of pro-Salvadoran gestures by the Japanese. A delegation of Japanese residents of Peru journeyed to the Central American state to express gratitude for Salvadoran good will. A few weeks later Yasuto Shudo, commercial attaché of the Japanese legation in Mexico, went to San Salvador to promote trade. In 1935, when President Martínez was formally inaugurated, the presence of a special Japanese diplomatic representative was a prelude to the establishment of normal diplomatic relations. It logically followed that, as Japanese diplomatic gaze fell upon Central America, El Salvador merited and received special attention (New York Times, 1934a, 1934b, 1935a, 1935b; La República, 1935).[6]

As a result of negotiations in 1934, Japan concurrently accredited the minister to Mexico, Yoshiatsu Hori, to each of the five Central American states. In July and August 1935, that diplomat journeyed there, successively presenting his credentials to the chief executives of Guatemala, El Salvador, Honduras, Nicaragua, and Costa Rica. In every instance, he represented the first Japanese envoy to be accredited to the government. Japanese plans, made operative when Minister Hori returned to his diplomatic base in Mexico, called for the naming of a chargé d'affaires to handle Central American issues from a legation in San Salvador. In January 1936, Chargé Yashishi Otani opened the San Salvador legation. In the meantime the Emperor of Manchukuo, visiting Japan, had honored El Salvador by receiving Consul León Sigüenza in special audience. Beyond such political acts, Japan looked toward Central American trade prospects (New York Times, 1935a, 1935c, 1935d, 1935e, 1935f, 1935g, 1935h, 1935i, 1935j, 1936; República de Honduras, 1935: 145).

Prior to the 1930s, Japanese trade with Central America was so inconsequential that it frequently eluded statistical records and accounted for the lack of formal diplomatic relations. The Japanese sold little there and imported virtually nothing from Central America (see, e.g., República de Salvador, annual).

If the diplomatic moves of the mid-1930s were intended to promote trade, the results, for all concerned, proved disappointing. The total trade between Japan and Nicaragua in the period 1935-1941, approximating 7,500,000 yen in value, was quite balanced, being but slightly in favor of Japan. As with Central

America at large, this trade with Nicaragua featured the Japanese export of cotton goods and the importation of raw materials. In some areas of the region, specifically in Honduras and Costa Rica, the trade, while equaling or exceeding that between Japan and Nicaragua, overwhelmingly favored Japan (Japan Year Book, n.d.: 463-464). Many things accounted for the meager trade generated between Japan and Central America during the 1930s. To the general problems posed by economic depression, a wartime economy in Japan, and U.S. dominance in the region must be added problems related to internal transportation in Central America, port facilities, shipping, fluctuating currencies, and tradition that found neither Japan nor Central America particularly aware of the other.

Because of limited political and economic relations with Japan and minimal attention accorded Central America by Japanese emigrants, plus the multifaceted relationship the area had to the United States, Central American decision-making was automatically and completely pro-United States when bombs rained down on Pearl Harbor. On December 8, 1941, every one of the five Central American governments speedily declared war on Japan. President Martínez of El Salvador, the cold-shouldered revolutionary dictator of a decade earlier, telegraphed President Roosevelt, "I consider that the Japanese attack on Hawaii . . . is absolutely unjustified. . . . National Assembly is meeting today to study the unusual case and to declare war on aggressor nation." To that, almost at once, the American diplomatic mission in San Salvador added, "At 1 P.M. today the National Legislative Assembly unanimously declared El Salvador in a state of war with Japan."

In neighboring and similarly dictatorial Guatemala, the rush to the side of Uncle Sam was equally fast. "It gives me pleasure," Guatemalan Foreign Minister Carlos Salazar wrote on December 9 to Secretary of State Hull, "to advise Your Excellency that Legislative Assembly of this Republic last night declared a state of war between Guatemala and Japan."

From dictator-led Honduras came Foreign Minister Salvador Aguirre's word that "the Sovereign National Congress of

Honduras in Decree No. 2 which it has issued today has declared war on Japan."

Nicaragua, Anastasio Somoza's personal patrimony, faced with the prospect of a tardy declaration of war or a circumvention of the constitutional provision which required at least five days of preliminary session before a reconvened Congress might transact war emergency business, achieved the latter by a joint congressional resolution which insisted that since December 8, a state of war had existed between Nicaragua and Japan.

In Costa Rica, the only democratically tinged sector of Central America, the alignment with the United States matched the speedy responses of the quartet of dictators. On the heels of a legislative resolution and an executive decree, Foreign Minister Alberto Echandi informed Cordell Hull, "the Government of Costa Rica . . . has today at 11 o'clock declared the state of war between Costa Rica and Japan" (U.S. Department of State, 1969: 84, 92, 95, 97, 102, 104; Pan-American Union, 1942a: 225-226, 231-233).

The wartime measures of the Central American states, which never in any instance included putting fighting forces into combat zones, varied, yet were basically similar. Under authorizations which permitted the respective governments to take such measures as the emergency required, they suspended constitutional guarantees as regards Axis nationals, froze funds, acceded to the United States "blacklisting" of individuals and firms, and so forth. All five countries were among the twelve Latin American states that sent Japanese nationals to the United States for internment. Costa Rica had accompanied its declaration of war with an order for the arrest of all Japanese in that country. Nicaragua hurried to confine the two Japanese residents in that land.

By late March 1942, the Japanese from Central America and Panama who were destined for internment by the United States Immigration and Naturalization Service boarded the *S. S. Florida* for the voyage to New Orleans and detention in Texas. Among the few from Central America was a 48-year-old bachelor Puntarenas barber who had been living in Costa Rica for four years. Eventually he, like many other internees, took advantage of the American offer to repatriate them via the *Gripsholm* in September 1943. Benjamin Tanabe, deported from El Salvador, transferred the title of his restaurant to his Salvadoran wife for the duration. A Japanese evacuated from Nicaragua insisted, as he protested that indignity, that he had once served in the United States Navy and would like to do so again (Pan-American Union, 1942a: 226, 231, 233-234; 1943a: 236; Barnhart, 1962a, 1962b; New York Times, 1941; U.S. Department of Justice, n.d.; U.S. Department of State, 1969: 102; 1969: 325-326). This removal of the Japanese from Central America, however few their numbers, pleased wartime Washington officials who nervously eyed the security of the Panama Canal and the shipping using that waterway.

Just as the Central American contribution to the war effort was largely economic in nature, so, too, were most Central American activities touching the Japanese. Fiscal controllers and custodians of alien property quickly appeared. In 1944, President Somoza, whose wartime road-building projects also put the squeeze on the United States, announced that an allotment of 1,000,000 córdobas for roads and other public works would be charged against the proceeds from the sale of Axis properties. Earlier in Costa Rica, the government had sold at auction the agricultural machinery left by interned Japanese. The small Japanese colony had, incidentally, gone there at the behest of Costa Rican authorities to produce cotton for export. Failing to do so, they had moved to the Pacific slope to plant rice. There, the nature of their holdings, coupled with nearness to the Panama Canal, fed Costa Rican fears of a clandestine airfield. Accordingly, the willingness to sell the Japanese machinery reflected the same frame of mind that had sent the Japanese off to internment in the United States.

In the economic sphere, however, the amount of Central American and related U.S. attention directed at Japanese nationals was relatively trifling, both in sum and in relation to that accorded Germans. For Guatemala, at a late stage of the war, the Proclaimed ("Black") List that included 382 names contained no Japanese. For El Salvador, that same Proclaimed List of the spring of 1945 contained only two Japanese names, and questions attended the inclusion of both. No Japanese appeared on that list for Honduras. Irregular reporting from Nicaragua concerning the 65 names on the Proclaimed List complicates the separation of the Japanese from other Axis nationals. The Proclaimed List for Costa Rica included among its 164 names only 6 Japanese (Pan-American Union, 1942b: 535, 1943b: 351-352; New York Times, 1943, 1944; U.S. Department of State, 1969: 325-326, 328, 335-342; Inter-American, 1942: 47).

The postwar reestablishment of Japanese-Central American commercial relations enjoyed no priority of concern in Japan, as was evidenced by the failure, in 1949, of the trade mission of the Supreme Commander of the Allied Powers to include that region on its itinerary. Gradually, however, trade resumed and its future prospect, as well as the formality of concluding their political estrangement, took representatives of all five Central American nations to the climax of the peace-making process.

On September 8, 1951, in San Francisco, three Guatemalans, two Salvadorans, three Hondurans, two Nicaraguans, and three Costa Ricans affixed their signatures on behalf of their governments to the treaty of peace with Japan, but more than three years elapsed before all five governments had deposited their ratifications of that document. That preliminary to the reestablishment of normal diplomatic relations occurred as follows: by El Salvador, several of whose declared exceptions were decidedly friendly gestures to Japan, on May 6, 1952; by Costa Rica on September 17, 1952; by Nicaragua on November 4, 1952; by Honduras on September 4, 1953; and by Guatemala on September 23, 1954 (Foreign Commerce Weekly, 1949; United Nations annual).

Expanding trade and commercial optimism prior to the peace treaty and between its signing and ratification, as well as later, paved the way to normal diplomatic relations (see Table 1).

The statistics for this brief interval prior to normal diplomatic relations illustrate both the hopes that attended subse-

TABLE 1
JAPANESE TRADE WITH CENTRAL AMERICA, 1949-1953
(in U.S. thousand $)

Country	*1949*	*1950*	*1951*	*1952*	*1953*
Guatemala					
To	70	51	96	109	151
From	–0–	–0–	152	15	24
El Salvador					
To	22	541	692	885	1,639
From	–0–	–0–	185	2	647
Honduras					
To	59	675	535	775	1,418
From	–0–	–0–	360	–0–	–0–
Nicaragua					
To	4	242	108	692	1,978
From	34	339	2,624	1,433	3,794
Costa Rica					
To	38	558	430	1,071	1,790
From	–0–	12	42	10	345

SOURCE: (anon.), "Sengo ni okeru Nippon no Rabei shokoku to wo bōeki jisseki suii (Japanese Postwar Trade Development with Various Latin American Countries)," *Raten Amerika Jihō (Latin America News),* XII No. 14 (May 11, 1969), 19-24.

quent Japanese-Central American trade and the diversity of that American region. The total trade expanded almost 52-fold in the five-year period, ranging from $227,000 in 1949 to $11,786,000 in 1953. By the latter year, although Japan was still in an early stage of economic recovery, Japanese-Central American trade exceeded the best prewar years in value. As in those earlier years, most of the Central American nations found it difficult to export sizable quantities to Japan with regularity. While three of the countries–El Salvador, Honduras, and Costa Rica–never achieved a favorable trade balance with Japan during the half-decade, Nicaragua never failed to achieve one. Despite fluctuations, the volume of trade so increased as to encourage both commercial optimism and political maneuver.

In the renewal of diplomatic relations, at different moments but generally during the mid-1950s, Japan resumed her prewar practice of having her representative in Mexico serve concurrently as minister to the Central American states. In 1953, as the new diplomatic chapter opened, Ambassador Shunichi Kase played this dual role, first for Costa Rica and El Salvador. In the former country the presentation of his credentials, once planned to coincide with the inaugural ceremonies for President José Figueres, took place instead in the waning days of the administration of President Otilio Ulate. In 1954, Kase's successor in Mexico, Kanichiro Kubota, also assumed the Central American duties which quickly widened to include the remaining states of that region.

During this same period, official Central American representation in Japan varied considerably. El Salvador sent Carlos Azúcar Chávez from the Foreign Ministry to Japan on a special mission following which a consul-general was promptly named to serve in Tokyo. To establish its mission in Tokyo, Costa Rica, in 1953, sent Minister Jorge Zeledón Castro. Possessor of the most sizable slice of Japanese trade with the region, Nicaragua logically launched its mission by naming a consul-general. In due course, recognition of the importance of the Somoza dynasty in Japanese-Nicaraguan trade encouraged Ambassador Kubota's presence in Managua in mid-1957 for the inauguration of Luis Somoza Debayle as President of Nicaragua (Nippon Times, 1953a, 1953b, 1953c, 1953d, 1955a, 1955b, 1955c 1955d, 1955e, 1955f, 1955g, 1955h, 1955i; Japan Times, 1957; Latin American Society, 1968: 431, 528-529, 549, 576, 636).

In the second half of the 1950s, trade, the dominant tie between Japan and Central America, expanded rapidly, accompanied, on occasion, by Japanese investment. In 1956, a Japanese trade mission representing numerous manufacturers and wholesalers spent considerable time in Central America. Other such missions followed. Equivalent firsthand interest in the Japanese economy was rare and, as when a Salvadoran mission spent weeks inspecting industrial facilities, prompted by an invitation from the Japanese government (Nippon Times, 1956; Hispanic American Report, 1956: 229; Japan Times, 1959c).

Early in the postwar era, as in the 1930s, El Salvador became a special focus of Japanese interest in Central America. In 1955,

Kureha Spinning Company, on the way to becoming a giant in the field of textiles, arranged to establish a cotton-spinning company in El Salvador under a joint investment scheme. For its fifty percent investment, Kureha would introduce machinery, while the Salvadoran half of the enterprise called for cash. Japanese technical assistance by more than a score of men would contribute to the construction and operation of the plant which would house 25,296 spindles and 264 weaving machines. Inasmuch as cotton had long been the principal commodity of the region of interest to Japan, this industrial development was exceedingly logical. Even as this factory was being planned, El Salvador was selling most of its bumper 1955-1956 cotton crop to Japan.

When Ambassador Kubota journeyed south from Mexico City to San Salvador to attend the inaugural ceremonies for President José María Lemus in September 1956, that visit coincided with the dedication of the new textile plant which, employing 600 workers and producing tens of thousands of yards of low-quality cotton fabrics, would utilize Salvadoran cotton exclusively. All was not smooth, however, in such an operation. As soon as Salvadoran authorities noted the continuing high import level of Japan-originated cotton cloth, tariff increases were demanded to protect the new domestic industry (Nippon Times, 1955i; Hispanic American Report, 1956: 13, 229, 334; Japan Times, 1956a, 1956b, 1958a).

As a follow-up to the Kureha venture, the Japanese External Trade Rehabilitation Organization (JETRO) urged upon the Ministries of Economy and Foreign Affairs in Tokyo the idea of establishing certain local industries, including a Toyota motor vehicle assembly plant, in El Salvador. This broad-based proposal, which also included a china factory and a food dehydrating plant, won favorable public response in El Salvador where it was hailed for creating employment and advancing the industrial level of the national economy (Japan Times, 1957: 6).

In this period, El Salvador was also looking toward Japan for wider trade opportunities. Minister of Economy Alfonso

Rochac (1956: 961) wrote, "puede citarse al Japón entre los paises que paulatinamente se van convirtiendo en mercados importantes para nuestro café." As a coffee market Japan would continue to receive Salvadoran attention.

Although Japanese investment and technology, introduced into Central America in this period, constituted additions to prior Japanese interest in the area, the basic Japanese-Central American tie remained trade.

During this period, the yearly totals for Japanese-Central American trade increased about three hundred fifty percent from approximately $20,000,000 in 1954 to approximately $70,000,000 in 1959. While Honduras found it difficult to sell to Japan and routinely registered an adverse trade balance with that country, neighboring Nicaragua experienced the opposite, its exports to Japan regularly ranging from two to six times the value of its related imports. In the five-year period ending with 1956, sales to Japan had climbed from one percent to eleven percent of El Salvador's exports (Hispanic American Report,

TABLE 2
JAPANESE TRADE WITH CENTRAL AMERICA, 1954-1959
(in U.S. thousand $)

Country	*1954*	*1955*	*1956*	*1957*	*1958*	*1959*
Guatemala						
To	239	551	641	844	1,340	3,312
From	212	1,130	1,073	639	3,308	4,175
El Salvador						
To	2,191	3,801	6,279	8,004	5,765	5,790
From	2,102	9,796	14,694	7,412	12,968	20,096
Honduras						
To	2,109	2,766	3,614	4,238	4,094	5,074
From	–0–	–0–	57	11	1,613	2,335
Nicaragua						
To	3,881	2,572	1,352	2,122	3,041	3,319
From	8,418	13,126	7,428	5,305	9,675	19,110
Costa Rica						
To	1,147	2,098	1,586	3,178	5,108	5,400
From	52	21	42	84	532	1,385

SOURCE: (anon.), "Sengo . . . bōeki," *Raten Amerika Jihō,* XII No. 14 (May 11, 1969), 19-24.

1957: 179). In 1956, Japanese-Salvadoran trade alone topped $20,000,000, a level that outstripped the region's aggregate trade with Japan in any prewar year. That volume, incidentally, was not unrelated to the above-mentioned industrial-investment programs Japan engineered for El Salvador.

Given the expanding roles of trade and investment in Salvadoran-Japanese relations, it was logical, late in 1958, when the government in Tokyo named former Consul-General Fujio Hayashi as minister to El Salvador, that he be a man with a special talent for economic matters. He also became Japan's first diplomatic appointment directly to a Central American country. Logical, too, soon after Hayashi's arrival in San Salvador, was the Japanese invitation that prompted a visit to Japan by a Salvadoran economic mission led by Ricardo Quiñones, President of the Chamber of Commerce of El Salvador.

When El Salvador, aided by a $3,000,000 loan from the World Bank, planned the expansion of its electrification program, Hitachi won the international bidding to supply turbines and generators. This, at the time, in 1959, when the *Atlas Maru*, Japan's floating exhibition facility, was acquainting Latin Americans with the range of Nipponese industrial products, helped to explode lingering prewar prejudices about the quality and sophistication of Japanese equipment. Another contribution toward the changing image of Japan came when NHK, Japan's radio and television facility, sent experts to El Salvador and elsewhere in Latin America to make recommendations for improved technical training (Japan Times, 1958b, 1959a, 1959b, 1959c; Hispanic American Report, 1959: 259, 314, 371; Japan Report, 1963).

The delegation that descended upon San Salvador in the autumn of 1959, headed by Fumio Miura, who was soon to be named Ambassador to Peru, and representing both Japanese government and industry, went to the Central American capital to promote trade and to explore additional possibilities for Japanese capital investment. Basically this and other searches for opportunities for capital investment in El Salvador amounted to Japanese response to a Salvadoran invitation. Since 1952, that nation's Law for the Promotion of Processing Industries, offering ten years of preferential treatment regarding numerous duties and taxes, constituted a kind of lure that no other Central American country was dangling before the Japanese. Just as Japan had responded to the generous terms of Salvadoran law, and as each had reciprocated the other's commercial missions, so now El Salvador, in appointing its first diplomatic representative to Japan, elevated to that post Walter Beneke Medina, formerly Consul-General in Tokyo.

Shortly after the first Salvadoran minister to Japan had presented his credentials, one of his superiors, Vice Foreign Minister Alfredo Martínez Moreno, visited Japan on a good-will mission. In the course of his ten-day stay, he presented 150 Spanish-language books to each of six universities in Tokyo. This possibly constituted the first significant cultural gesture by any Central American government, although Guatemala was so inclined when Minister of Education Dr. Enrique Quiñonez had expressed a hope for cultural exchanges involving professors and students. However, the realization of such hopes, which the Japanese shared, suffered because of the lack of a Guatemalan diplomat in Tokyo and the handling of Guatemalan affairs by the Japanese Ambassador to Mexico (Japan Times, 1956c, 1959d, 1959e, 1960a, 1960b, 1960c).

Although El Salvador constituted, in terms of both trade and investment, the prime focus of Japanese economic interest in Central America, the volume of trade between Japan and Nicaragua also merited serious attention. As of mid-1959, Japan had replaced the United States as Nicaragua's largest export market, cotton approximating seventy percent of that volume. When General Anastasio Somoza Debayle visited Japan in the spring of 1961 as the good-will representative of the president, his brother Luis, he presented the highest Nicaraguan decoration to Emperor Hirohito. Soon both sons of the founder of the Somoza dynasty received similar honors from Japan. That same year, Humberto Arguello Tefel inaugurated the first Nicaraguan diplomatic mission in Tokyo. Indicating that his labors would emphasize economic matters, Minister Arguello promptly informed the Japanese of the attractions Nicaraguan law offered foreign investors. Soon, too, changed tariff schedules eased the entry of Japanese textiles into Nicaragua (Hispanic American Report, 1959: 595; Japan Times, 1961a, 1961b, 1961c, 1961d, 1962a).

Japanese interest in political stability occasionally suffered shock at Central American developments, but the related Japanese policy of recognizing de facto regimes quickly resolved most of them. The assassination of the senior Anastasio Somoza in 1956 and the quick succession of son Luis had not ruffled Tokyo's relations with Managua.

El Salvador, without benefit of a family dynasty, similarly tested Japanese adherence to its de facto recognition policy. Late in 1960, a bloodless coup toppled the government of President José María Lemus, and Japan promptly recognized the resultant junta. Early in 1961, however, other military dissidents overthrew that six-man junta, and once more Japan accorded a new government recognition (Japan Times, 1960d, 1961e). The recognition of political regimes that achieved power irregularly did not pose the problem encountered three decades earlier in the revolutionary triumph of Maximiliano Hernández Martínez.

Although Japanese economic ties with Central America, as the 1960s dawned, were strongest with El Salvador and Nicaragua, relations with other states of the region were expanding. In the autumn of 1961, Guatemalan President Miguel Ydígoras Fuentes helped to dedicate new refrigeration and packing plants and seven new fishing boats at the Pacific port of Champerico. The boats and the buildings belonged to two joint Japanese-Guatemalan ventures, Compañía Pesquera Guatemalteca and La Pesca, operations geared to shrimp fishing for export. Guatemalan cotton, as did that of the region generally, consistently looked to the Japanese market. In January 1962, Guatemala had already sold most of the crop in futures to Japan and ninety percent of the next year's crop also went to Japan. During the spring of 1962, a trade mission with an extensive Latin American itinerary visited Guatemala in an effort to ease restrictions on Japanese imports. Results favorable to Japan materialized almost at once as Guatemala abolished the discriminatory treatment by which that government was collecting duties raised one hundred percent since 1959 on more than a dozen Japanese articles, including cotton yarn and rayon goods (Hispanic American Report, 1961: 878; 1962: 20, 210; Japan Times, 1962b).

Honduras and Costa Rica, so unlike in many respects, were similar in that their consistently unfavorable trade balances with Japan were synonymous with the smallest volumes of Central American trade with that country. One major penetration of Honduras by Japanese industry came when Oki Electric Industry Company sold telephone and radio equipment for installation in Tegucigalpa. Scheduled to be installed within eighteen months, it would be paid for over a period of eight years. This capacity to extend credit for sizable periods, a reflection of Japanese financial well-being, helped Japan increasingly as it competed with Americans, Britons, West Germans, and others in Central America. In the same period, Honduran lumbermen, losing markets in Cuba and Venezuela, sought Japanese outlets for their product.

Costa Rica, able to sell cotton to Japan, also strove to put bananas into that market. When Costa Rica shipped 10,000 stems there in 1960, the resultant competition for the Taiwan bananas materially lowered the Japanese price of bananas. Although Ecuador, later in the 1960s, would become the principal New World supplier of that fruit to Japan, Costa Rica quite likely did so first. In addition to promoting trade between the two countries, Dr. Germán Gago Pérez, the first postwar Costa Rican consul-general in Tokyo, announced plans for the exchange of journalists and college students. Japan, while listening to his joint-venture proposals, rejoiced that the Costa Rican government had purchased from Tokyo Shibaura Electric Company (Toshiba) power-generating equipment for the Río Macho project south of San José (Hispanic American Report, 1960: 446, 1962: 24, 599; Japan Times, 1960e, 1961f, 1962c).

If, in reference to volume of trade, exchange of commercial missions, joint ventures, and diplomacy, El Salvador and Nicaragua represented a Central American tandem in the Japanese mind, El Salvador persistently played trailblazer. Its resident Japanese minister also served the legation in Managua. Similarly joint ventures involving the Japanese were undertaken first in El Salvador. They, in turn, had followed favorable local legislation which had attracted Japanese capital. Under such circumstances, it was natural for Japan to hope that its first Central American trade agreement would be negotiated with El Salvador.

As a means of coping with the inroads there by members of the European Common Market, as well as serving as an adjustment to the Central American Common Market, Japan felt a need for a trade agreement on the Central American front. Periodically since independence, Central America had attempted various forms of unity, but only in the late 1950s had the area taken meaningful economic steps. In June 1958, the five states had signed a treaty which sought, over a ten-year period, to establish Central America as a free trade area with a developing customs union. In February 1960, a Tripartite Treaty of Economic Association, embracing Guatemala, El Salvador, and Honduras, instituted free trade for almost all goods produced by those countries. Later that same year, the General Treaty of Central American Integration, signed by all five states and put into effect in 1961, constituted a geographical expansion of the tripartite arrangement. Under the circumstances, the Japanese could project their joint-investment ventures on a regional rather than a narrowly national basis. When this is coupled with the statistics which soon stamped El Salvador the possessor of the largest share of the regional trade, it logically followed that any agreement Japan might reach with El Salvador possessed both national and regional significance (for a detailed statement concerning this regional development, see Mohr, 1968).

Motivated by hopes attending trade expansion and investment, as well as uncertainties regarding foreign competition and the economic integration of the Central American region, Japan sought a trade agreement with El Salvador, a desire which El Salvador reciprocated. The resultant negotiation, for all of its specific significance, must also be viewed in light of the general trend of Japanese international relations which, in the Latin American sector alone, had recently produced trade agreements with Cuba, Peru, and Argentina, as well as encouraging negotiations with numerous other Latin American governments. Specifically, in reference to El Salvador, Japan hoped for increased trade once it could induce that government to remove its discriminatory tariff treatment of certain products. During the spring of 1962, a Japanese trade mission spent 25 days in El Salvador and other Central American and Caribbean countries discussing, much of that time, the easing of import restrictions. That mission candidly asserted that, of all Central America, El Salvador offered the most favorable prospects for Japanese industrial investment.

The following year, a 130-member Salvadoran trade and cultural mission, one of the largest groups ever sent to Japan by a foreign government, spent a month there, inspecting industrial operations and holding trade talks. Among other things, the Salvadoran mission sought Japanese cooperation in the advancement of its textile industry. Desirous of more joint industrial projects, the visitors specifically hoped for an operation that would produce Honda motorcycles in El Salvador. Other joint-venture prospects included a fishing company, glass bottle manufacturing, and a ceramics industry. All the more because the trade balance was then heavily in favor of El Salvador, Japan rejoiced to hear of the mission's interest in plastic manufacturing machinery, ironware, farm machinery, paint manufacturing machinery, and semi-finished fishing boats. Before leaving Japan, the mission contracted for various kinds of machinery. While this mission, composed as it was of scholars, doctors, businessmen, and industrialists, acquainted influential sectors of Salvadoran life as never before with Japan, a Japanese sample fair, the first held in Central America, aimed at acquainting stay-at-home Salvadorans with a wide range of

Japanese goods (Hispanic American Report, 1962: 210, 216; Japan Times, 1962d, 1963a, 1963b, 1963c).

Diplomatic achievements soon demonstrated that these enthusiasms and undertakings had the sincere support of both governments. El Salvador, the first Central American state to exchange ministers with Japan, became the first such nation to join Japan in raising their respective diplomatic missions to embassy status. Fujio Hayashi, for years minister, became the first Japanese ambassador in San Salvador. In the same season, Nicaragua and Japan also elevated their missions to embassies and although Nicaragua received special attention when Ambassador Hayashi attended the inauguration of President René Schick, Japan continued to have Hayashi, resident in San Salvador, serve concurrently as its representative to Nicaragua. In Tokyo, Walter Beneke Medina, having previously moved up from consul-general to minister, now presented his credentials as ambassador (Japan Times, 1963d, 1963e, 1963f).

In Tokyo, on July 19, 1963, Japan's Foreign Minister, Masayoshi Ohira, and El Salvador's Minister of Economic Affairs, Salvador Jáuregui, signed a ten-article Agreement on Commerce.[7] Its purpose was "to strengthen and develop the commercial relations between the two countries and to encourage mutually beneficial investments and other types of economic cooperation." Any advantage accorded by either Party to a third country in reference to customs duties, charges of any kind related to importation or exportation, internal taxes, and any other internal charges would automatically be extended to the other Party (Art. I). This provision, which amounted to most-favored-nation treatment without employing that term, was modified by the accompanying protocol, which stated that advantages accorded Panama and the neighboring Central American states constituted an exception. Similarly, the statement (Art. II) that nationals and companies of either Party would be treated no less favorably in their business and financial transactions than those of any third country faced an equivalent exception in the protocol for the zone related to the Central American Common Market. The rights of the nationals of either Party concerning entry, stay, travel, residence, taxes, access to courts, property, economic activity, patents, trade marks, and so forth were stated as equal to those of any third country, subject again to certain preferential treatment for nationals of the American isthmian area. Quite possibly the Castro revolution prompted, in part, the pledge (Art. IV) that the property of alien nationals and companies would not be taken without "just compensation." The merchant vessels of either Party could enter the ports of the other Party with passengers and cargoes on equal terms with any third country (Art. VI). In compliance with Article X, the treaty came into effect on July 1, 1964, one month after the exchange of ratifications at San Salvador.

The life of the agreement, beyond an initial interval of three years, was to be automatically extended indefinitely in three-year periods unless written notice of desire to terminate it was given at least three months before the expiration of a stated period. In the manner of many other Japanese-Latin American agreements, both earlier and contemporaneous, this first one between Japan and a Central American country would be interpreted, in case of confusion of meaning, on the basis of its English-language text. In the meantime, no confusion attended the interpretation of El Salvador's trade statistics for 1963, which indicated that its leading customer, Japan, was absorbing twenty-five percent of the nation's total exports (Comercio Exterior, 1964a).

While ratification of this document was under way, a Salvadoran agricultural mission to Japan developed a joint venture with Satoh Agricultural Machine Company for the manufacture of cultivators in El Salvador. This item of farm machinery represented but one aspect of El Salvador's program of agricultural modernization. In the same season, the government in San Salvador announced that it was considering a national program of televised instruction designed especially to reach rural centers of population. If the plan were implemented, it would call for technical assistance from Japanese consultants. This proposition found Japan going far beyond the simple supply of equipment for television stations and viewers to undertake a significant role in the basic development of television in Central America (Japan Times, 1964a; Hispanic American Report, 1964: 406).

Soon after the signing of the Japanese-Salvadoran agreement, and before it took effect, Japan and Nicaragua also took steps that brought them closer together economically. One indication that the Japanese approached Nicaragua in light of political realities as well as economic possibilities found a Tokyo firm making a substantial investment in the Somoza-controlled metals enterprise Metasa, which was producing galvanized steel tubing in Managua for the Central American market at large. Naturally, most of the steel used by Metasa came from Japan. Private and public motives inspiring it, a large Nicaraguan trade mission, headed by ex-President Luis Somoza Debayle, visited Japan in the autumn of 1963 for ten days of conferences and tours. In February 1964, JETRO sponsored its second industrial fair in Central America—the first having been the one in San Salvador the previous February, this time in Managua. Mitsui and other major companies had exhibits which featured, among other things, textile machinery (Hispanic American Report, 1963: 955, 1964: 218; Japan Times, 1963g, 1963h, 1963i, 1964b). Two things were rather obvious: the sales emanating from the San Salvador fair of 1963 had stamped it a success, and the offering in Managua was intended as the opening of a widened economic push by Japan in Nicaragua. Also, just as the pattern of Japanese-Salvadoran relations, featuring trade missions and fair and agreement, had paved the way for the elevation of diplomatic missions, so, too, had the economic rapprochement, via commercial missions and investment and trade fair, created between Japan and Nicaragua conditions prompting the elevation of their respective diplomatic missions.

In similar fashion, to the lesser degree that found it ranking third among Japan's Central American trading partners, Guatemala drew closer to Japan through a combination of economic and diplomatic moves. In the same season that Japan and Nicaragua were doing so, Guatemala and Japan agreed to set up embassies. Before the promise became reality a Guatemalan economic mission, led by Economic and Labor Minister Enrique Peralta Méndez, visited Japan, hoping for expanded trade and increased Japanese economic and technical assistance. The expectations were well grounded inasmuch as while Guatemalan imports from the United States had dropped from approximately sixty percent to about fifty percent during the previous decade, they had notably increased with reference to Japan.

When the third Japanese Industrial Fair in Central America, that of February 1965, took shape in Guatemala City, it also fit into a standard pattern of Japanese-Central American relations. Incidentally, Guatemala, like El Salvador and Nicaragua, so consistently presented Japan with unfavorable trade balances that these fairs were not only to promote trade but also to rectify, within limits, the trade imbalance. Shortly before the fair, which drew more than 118,000 Guatemalans to the display of radios, television sets, automobiles, motorcycles, industrial machinery, and agricultural and electrical products, Ambassador Carlos Enrique Molina Muñoz had presented his ambassadorial credentials to Emperor Hirohito (Japan Times, 1964c, 1964d, 1964e, 1965a; Hispanic American Report, 1964: 405; Commercio Exterior, 1964b).

Japan's mounting interest, in the mid-1960s, regarding Central America quickly included Costa Rica. By 1965, Costa Rica, never having experienced a favorable postwar trade balance with Japan, sought from the Tokyo authorities a commercial agreement which would balance that limited but expanding trade. During the decade 1954-1964 Japanese-Costa Rican trade had increased about tenfold. A mid-1965 project of the Costa Rican Ministry of Economy, in pursuit of balanced trade, hoped for Japanese investments in Costa Rican industry that would produce commodities for the Japanese market. At that very moment, a new jointly financed Japanese-Costa Rican textile plant was being built, but obviously its products were not among those that might go to Japan. Somewhat akin to the joint venture in Nicaragua which aimed at supplying Central America with galvanized steel tubing was the Costa Rican purchase of a Japanese galvanized sheeting installation, the output from which was also geared to the general Central American market. Climaxing this intensification of Japanese-Costa Rican relations was the trip by Minister of Economy Bernal Jimenez to Tokyo where, on September 18, 1965, he signed a one-year trade agreement which, in its ten articles, concerned itself not only with trade but also with the exchange of scientific information and technology and the simplification of immigration procedures. Following the signing of this agreement, the elevation of the diplomatic missions to embassy status quickly took place. In this manner, as Ambassador Mikitaro Matsuno went to San José, Japan closed out the recent practice whereby the Japanese Ambassador to Panama had served concurrently as Minister to Costa Rica (Latin American Society, 1968: 431; Comercio Exterior, 1965a, 1965b, 1965c; Japan Times, 1965b, 1965c, 1965d, 1965e, 1965f, 1965g).

In due course, Honduras, lacking the political stability of some Central American states and the economic possibilities of others, was nonetheless swept along by the winds of change. Scarcely anything in the economic sphere–volume of trade, trade balance, joint-venture investment possibilities–commended the elevation of the Japanese and Honduran diplomatic missions to embassy status, but nevertheless that happened in 1967 (Latin American Society, 1968: 576). After all, on the world diplomatic front legations were passé and others had done as much, so why not Japan?

Diplomatic missions included, one of the best barometers of Japanese relations with Central America, the trade statistics, suggested noteworthy advance during the first half of the 1960s.

In five years, the annual trade volume had more than doubled, increasing from $65,267,000 (1960) to $144,558,000 (1964). As trading partners of Japan, they ranked in precisely the same order in which the diplomatic missions had been raised: El Salvador, Nicaragua, Guatemala, Costa Rica, and Honduras. The statistics of 1964, for example, illustrate the variation within the region, the trade of Honduras then

TABLE 3
JAPANESE TRADE WITH CENTRAL AMERICA, 1960-1964
(in U.S. thousand $)

Country	*1960*	*1961*	*1962*	*1963*	*1964*
Guatemala					
To	6,310	5,364	6,228	8,610	11,225
From	7,100	9,344	13,664	18,977	22,139
El Salvador					
To	9,658	6,159	8,169	9,238	12,658
From	13,996	21,047	25,391	38,522	37,400
Honduras					
To	4,100	6,080	4,194	7,180	4,681
From	691	846	562	1,706	4,146
Nicaragua					
To	4,520	3,882	5,339	6,485	7,356
From	10,096	17,187	25,616	31,806	33,513
Costa Rica					
To	7,963	5,534	7,996	7,112	10,315
From	833	635	895	1,165	1,125

SOURCE: (anon.), "Sengo . . . bōeki," *Raten Amerika Jihō,* XII No. 14 (May 11, 1969), 19-24 and Jay Webber, "Big Japanese Success in Nicaragua," *Export Trade* (New York), March 23 (p. 15), 1964.

struggling toward $9,000,000 while that of El Salvador topped $50,000,000. Every country exhibited a stubborn trade pattern, three of them—El Salvador, Nicaragua, and Guatemala—routinely posting favorable trade balances with Japan and the other two, Costa Rica and Honduras, routinely registering unfavorable balances in that trade.

In most of Central America, the second half of the 1960s consolidated Japanese economic relations with that region. Long accustomed to buying large quantities of cotton in that market, Japanese merchants began to explore the coffee trade in El Salvador. Japanese initiative, plus the homeland prosperity and changing tastes that increased a demand for coffee, soon found sizable quantities of the Salvadoran product in Japan. That all was not an amiable widening of economic relations, however, witness a furor that found cotton versus synthetic fibers. The Association of Salvadoran Textile Industries accused its government of endangering the future of the domestic cotton industry through its agreement with a Japanese company to build a synthetic fibers plant in El Salvador. Mitsui, the company involved, insisted that its operation would not offer competition, but rather would be producing different kinds of garments, a line of reasoning that failed to impress the worried cotton interests.

El Salvador, the focus of initial attention in Central America in many instances by Japan, became the first Latin American country to receive Japan Overseas Cooperation Volunteers, an oriental version of the Peace Corps. Arranged for by an exchange of diplomatic notes, eight volunteers went to El Salvador late in 1968 to give guidance and offer coaching in sports, specifically in track and field events, swimming, softball, gymnastics, and weight-lifting. This kind of activity by the Japanese, utterly devoid of political or economic implications, tended to increase the warmth of their welcome by a people who had met and known very few Japanese. Quite possibly, in addition to a normal willingness on both sides to indulge cultural exchanges, the presence of the athletic volunteers related to a number of other factors, among them Japanese hospitality at the Tokyo Olympics in 1964 and the achievements of the Japanese in that international competition.

When El Salvador sponsored, late in 1968 in San Salvador, a trade fair, Japan was among the 23 participating countries. Unknown is the degree of influence that Japanese-sponsored trade fairs might have had on the planning and execution of this undertaking (Japan Times, 1965h, 1966a, 1968a, 1968b; Comercio Exterior, 1965d: 654).

Japan and Costa Rica both sought to sustain the surge of friendly cooperation that had characterized the economic policies of the administration of President Orlich. Indicative of that Japanese desire was the sending, in May 1966, of a special envoy for the inauguration of President José Joaquín Trejos. Soon thereafter, a member of the new Costa Rican cabinet visited Japan, to inspect soil conservation projects. A year later, a sizable delegation from the Legislative Assembly inspected various industrial facilities, including Toshiba Electric, during a five-day visit to Japan. A few months later, Toshiba Electric received an order from a Costa Rican firm for television parts to be assembled in Costa Rica into 4,500 sets. The assembly operation by Inelco Company assured Toshiba approximately fifty percent of the Costa Rican market for television sets (Japan Times, 1966b, 1968c, 1968d, 1969a, 1969b).

During the second half of the 1960s, trade, investment, and technical assistance programs characterized Japanese relations with Central America, and of these three the most obvious one continued to be trade.

Shifts and fluctuations, rather than growth, marked the trade of this period, the regional total of $179,159,000 for 1969 being almost a duplication of that of 1965 ($179,956,000). However, as Japanese investment in joint ventures in the area increasingly moved from planning and construction phases into active production, it became difficult to appreciate the total role of Japan in Central American economic life (for a listing of

TABLE 4
JAPANESE TRADE WITH CENTRAL AMERICA, 1965-1969
(in U.S. thousand $)

Country	*1965*	*1966*	*1967*	*1968*	*1969*
Guatemala					
To	13,788	15,983	18,514	18,545	24,032
From	24,054	22,845	18,796	27,938	24,242
El Salvador					
To	16,091	13,783	13,884	14,814	19,586
From	33,836	22,392	16,326	15,949	19,480
Honduras					
To	5,621	4,633	6,613	9,132	10,171
From	5,544	4,429	5,140	10,560	15,864
Nicaragua					
To	11,138	8,308	11,594	12,081	10,901
From	54,494	47,325	51,342	47,294	32,575
Costa Rica					
To	14,357	14,306	12,738	13,436	19,957
From	1,033	1,357	1,843	2,313	2,351

SOURCE: (anon.), "Sengo . . . bōeki," *Raten Amerika Jihō,* XII No. 14 (May 11, 1969), 19-24.

Japanese enterprises and technical assistance programs, see Latin American Society, 1968: 32, 529-530, 549, 577, 637).

In the last years of the decade, 1968 and 1969, sharp increases in Japanese exports to Central America included automobiles, textile machinery, heavy electrical equipment, radio and television receivers, precision instruments, and iron and steel. These products fell into two categories, those for customer consumption and those for industrial development. In the meantime, Japanese imports from Central America continued in unbroken fashion to feature raw materials—cotton generally contributing eighty to ninety percent of it—and foodstuffs, among which coffee, bananas, and cacao led (Japan, External Trade Organization, 1969: 146-147; 1970: 146).

Although Japan, by means of joint-venture investments in industrial operations, had prepared for the impact expected from the economic integration projected by the Central American Common Market, that pinch did not become excessive, due to regional squabbling that reduced the unity and effectiveness of the area operation.

The multifaceted contacts between the peoples of Japan and Central America were almost totally economic in nature. Few Central Americans studied about or visited Japan for other than economic reasons. The same was true of the Japanese with reference to Central America. The relative smallness of the countries, especially vis-à-vis Mexico or Brazil, found them vying unsuccessfully for Japanese attention. Also, the strategic and political considerations related to United States hegemony in the region constituted a brake on Japanese identification with the area.

As in prewar years, few Japanese migrated to and settled in Central America. In 1960, in El Salvador, which was the most attractive portion of Central America to them for a variety of reasons, only 66 Japanese were residing. In Costa Rica that same year, the official record of the movement of aliens indicated that 168 Japanese entered the country and 200 departed from it. The following year, the figures were 215 and 216 respectively. Neither economically interesting El Salvador nor politically stable Costa Rica proved a magnet for Japanese immigrants. When Japan established its embassy in Tegucigalpa in 1967, only one Japanese then resided in Honduras (Japan, Bureau of Statistics, n.d.: 45; Costa Rica, Ministerio de Economía y Hacienda, 1961: 83; 1962: 79). Plainly, the record of the past haunted the future prospect of any considerable number of Japanese migrating to Central America. Recollection of the haste and completeness with which prewar Japanese had been shipped to internment in the United States, plus more favorable personal economic opportunities at home and elsewhere in the postwar years, combined to minimize the movement of Japanese to Central America despite attractive terms in more than one international agreement.

As the present decade dawned, EXPO '70 afforded Central Americans and Japanese another, somewhat different, opportunity to become aware of one another. Central American pavilions and National Days at EXPO '70 invited expressions of friendship and optimism. When General Anastasio Somoza Debayle, President of Nicaragua, went to Osaka in June 1970, accompanied by a sizable entourage, his speech there emphasized hopes for expanded trade between the two countries. His hope was a common one, however uncommon his being the first Central American chief executive to visit Japan. Costa Rica's official representatives at EXPO '70, her Ministers of Industry and Commerce and Foreign Affairs, indicated that their interests went beyond their country's flower-decked pavilion. To EXPO '70 from El Salvador came Education Minister Walter Beneke Medina, who had known Japan during more than a half-dozen years of diplomatic duty. Complimenting the work habits of both his countrymen and his hosts, he told his audience at Osaka on El Salvador's National Day, "We have often been called the Japanese of Central America." He remembered economic lessons learned from Japan. The Japanese spokesman that day remembered and thanked El Salvador for its generous outlook regarding Japanese peace treaty terms of 1951 concerning territories and assets. In El Salvador, and elsewhere in the region of which it was a part, international ties between them and Japan were firmly rooted. In October 1970, a second Central American president visited Japan. Noting great similarity between the two countries as regarded dense population and limited resources, President Fidel Sánchez Hernández of El Salvador discussed economic cooperation. A month later, Japan was participating in the Fourth Biennial International Fair in San Salvador (Japan Times, 1970a, 1970b, 1970c, 1970d, 1970e, 1970f, 1970g).

NOTES

1. This document can be found as Minister George T. Weitzel to Secretary of State, Managua, February 27, 1913, 717.00.

2. Text of Treaty of Amity, Commerce and Navigation between Japan and Nicaragua, December 1924, 710.94/20.

3. Texts of the Japanese-Panamanian documents of 1915 and 1917 are in 719.942/13 and 719.942/2 respectively.

4. Texts of the Japanese-Peruvian and Japanese-Mexican treaties are in League of Nations, Treaty Series 102 (1930): 33-47 and 36 (1925): 275-282, respectively.

5. Walter C. Thurston to Secretary of State, Managua, December 17 and 24 (1924) 710.94/12 and 710.94/20, and New York Times (1924).

6. In 1912, Japan ranked twelfth among El Salvador's suppliers, below such countries as Mexico and China.

7. The text of the agreement, as well as the accompanying protocol and exchange of notes of the same date, are in the United Nations Treaty Series 518 (1964): 156-170.

REFERENCES

BARNHART, E. N. (1962a) "Citizenship and political tests in Latin American republics in World War II." Hispanic Amer. Historical Rev. 42 (August): 297-332.

--- (1962b) "Japanese internees from Peru." Pacific Historical Rev. 31 (May).

Commercio Exterior (1965a) Volume 15 (Mayo): 364-365.

--- (1965b) Volume 15 (Junio).

--- (1965c) Volume 15 (Agosto).

--- (1965d) Volume 15 (Septiembre).

--- (1964a) Volume 14 (Julio): 491-492.

--- (1964b) Volume 14 (Noviembre).

Costa Rica, Ministerio de Economía y Hacienda (1962) Anuario Estadístico de Costa Rica 1961. San Jose: Direccíon General de Estadística y Censo.

--- (1961) Anuario Estadístico de Costa Rica 1960. San Jose: Direccíon General de Estadística y Censo.

DE NOGALES, R. (1928) The Looting of Nicaragua. New York.

Foreign Commerce Weekly (1949) "Japan: tariffs and trade controls: SCAP trade and financial mission to Latin America." Volume 36 (September 19).

FREEMAN, J. (1925) Dollar Diplomacy: A Study of American Imperialism. New York.

Hispanic American Report (1964) Volume 17.

--- (1963) Volume 16.

--- (1962) Volume 15.

--- (1961) Volume 14.

--- (1960) Volume 13.

--- (1959) Volume 12.

--- (1957) Volume 10.

--- (1956) Volume 9.

Inter-American (1942) "Honduras takes Japanese funds." Volume 1 (November).

Japan, Bureau of Statistics (n.d.) Japan Statistical Yearbook 1964. Tokyo: Office of the Prime Minister.

Japan, External Trade Organization (1970) Foreign Trade of Japan 1970.

--- (1969) Foreign Trade of Japan 1969.

Japan Report (1963) Volume 9 (April 15).

Japan Times (1970a) March 20: 12.

--- (1970b) June 4: 3.

--- (1970c) June 5: 10.

--- (1970d) June 6: 4.

--- (1970e) August 6: 4.

--- (1970f) September 8: 4.

--- (1970g) October 4: 4.

--- (1969a) March 8: 8.

--- (1969b) October 17: 9.

--- (1968a) July 28: 3.

--- (1968b) November 11: 9.

--- (1968c) June 29: 4.

--- (1968d) July 2: 4.

--- (1966a) January 24: 10.

--- (1966b) April 13: 4.

--- (1965a) February 11: 10.

--- (1965b) August 22: 6.

--- (1965c) September 2: 4.

--- (1965d) September 12: 6.

--- (1965e) September 19: 6.

--- (1965f) December 22: 1.

--- (1965g) December 29: 3.

--- (1965h) February 24: 10.

--- (1964a) March 7: 10.

--- (1964b) January 28: 10.

--- (1964c) March 18: 1.

--- (1964d) April 11: 1.

--- (1964e) December 17: 17.

--- (1963a) February 18: 10.

--- (1963b) March 8: 1-2.

--- (1963c) March 23: 10.

--- (1963d) April 12: 4.

--- (1963e) April 27: 2.

--- (1963f) May 22: 3.

--- (1963g) September 24: 10.

--- (1963h) October 4: 10.

--- (1963i) November 30: 10.

--- (1962a) April 4: 9.

--- (1962b) May 11: 10.

--- (1962c) August 3: 3.

--- (1962d) March 26: 3.

--- (1961a) April 18: 3.

--- (1961b) April 23: 3.

--- (1961c) September 13: 4.

--- (1961d) September 15: 6.

--- (1961e) February 18: 1.

--- (1961f) May 18: 6.

--- (1960a) March 13: 3.

--- (1960b) April 27: 4.

--- (1960c) May 7: 3.

--- (1960d) December 10: 3.

--- (1960e) December 23: 2.

--- (1959a) January 21: 3.

--- (1959b) February 8: 3.

--- (1959c) May 20: 6.

--- (1959d) September 15: 4.

--- (1959e) November 12: 6.

--- (1958a) September 12: 7.

--- (1958b) December 17: 2.

--- (1957) April 19: 3, 6.

--- (1956a) August 17: 3.

--- (1956b) September 2: 11.

--- (1956c) December 14: 3.

Japan Year Book (n.d.) 1943-1944. Tokyo.
Latin American Society (1968) Latin American Handbook. Tokyo.
MECHAM, J. L. (1965) A Survey of United States-Latin American Relations. New York.
MOHR, A. F. (1968) "The Central American common market," pp. 551-557 in C. Véliz (ed.) Latin America and the Caribbean: A Handbook. New York: Praeger.
New York Times (1944) December 31: 19.
--- (1943) February 15: 6.
--- (1942a) March 7: 5.
--- (1942b) March 22: 40.
--- (1941) December 9: 22.
--- (1936) January 15.
--- (1935a) February 16: 4.
--- (1935b) June 23: 11.
--- (1935c) February 8: 4.
--- (1935d) February 12: 7.
--- (1935e) February 24: 12.
--- (1935f) March 16: 1.
--- (1935g) July 11: 9.
--- (1935h) July 26: 10.
--- (1935i) August 1: 21.
--- (1935j) August 22: 12.
--- (1934a) September 15: 5.
--- (1934b) October 12: 14.
--- (1924) July 29: 5.
Nippon Times (1956) March 26: 6.
--- (1955a) January 3: 1.
--- (1955b) January 17: 3.
--- (1955c) January 23: 4.
--- (1955d) April 16: 3.
--- (1955e) July 10: 3.
--- (1955f) August 11: 4.
--- (1955g) August 21: 2.
--- (1955h) September 15: 5.
--- (1955i) November 25: 1.
--- (1955j) October 21: 10.
--- (1953a) September 1: 3.
--- (1953b) September 8: 3.
--- (1953c) September 15: 3.
--- (1953d) October 1: 2.
Pan-American Union (1943a) Bulletin 77 (April).
--- (1943b) Bulletin 77 (June).
--- (1942a) Bulletin 76 (April).
--- (1942b) Bulletin 76 (September).
La República (1935) February 4: 2-3; February 5: 2. San Salvador.
República de Honduras (1935) Memoria . . . Relaciones Exteriores . . . 1934-1935. Tegucigalpa.
República de Salvador (annual) Memoria de Hacienda y Crédito Pública. San Salvador.
ROCHAC, A. (1956) "Memoria de las labores desarrolladas por el poder ejecutivo en el ramo de economía durante el ejercicio comprendido entre el 15 el septiembre de 1955 y el 14 de septiembre de 1956." Revista de Economía de El Salvador 8 (Enero-Deciembre).
United Nations (annual) Treaty Series, Volumes 136: 46, 126-127; 163: 385; 184: 358; 243: 326.
U.S. Department of Justice (n.d.) Immigration and Naturalization Service File 146-13-2-1153.
U.S. Department of State (1969) Papers Relating to the Foreign Relations of the United States.
--- (1948)
--- (1946)
--- (1941)
--- (1920)

CARMELO MESA-LAGO
Center for Latin American Studies
University of Pittsburgh
Pittsburgh, Pennsylvania

IDEOLOGICAL, POLITICAL, AND ECONOMIC FACTORS IN THE CUBAN CONTROVERSY ON MATERIAL VERSUS MORAL INCENTIVES

This paper discusses the Cuban stand in the socialist controversy on material versus moral incentives, placing emphasis on the role of economic, political, and ideological factors. The controversy is of fundamental importance for Marxist-Leninist theory, as well as for the implementation of such theory in socialist countries. Actually, the reference to "incentives" conveys the impression of a narrower scope than the controversy has been in reality. Internally, the type of incentives chosen affects crucial economic areas such as the method of planning, the allocation of resources, the distribution system, the use of money, the organization of the enterprise, and even the criteria for appointing managers. In the political sphere, the incentive decision affects political control, mass mobilization, people's participation in the decision-making process, and the degree of consensus. In the social sphere, the incentive decision affects social stratification, income equaliza-

AUTHOR'S NOTE: An earlier version of this paper was presented to the Second National Meeting of the Latin American Studies Association (LASA), Washington, D.C., April 17-18, 1970. The paper has been expanded and updated to include events until mid-1971.

tion, and alienation versus solidarity problems. The external policy of the socialist countries is also often related to the internal system of incentives. Usually, material incentives are tied to "construction of socialism in one country," while moral incentives are related to "universal socialism."

In the socialist world, there are three groups of countries actively taking part in the controversy: Yugoslavia, as the leading proponent of material incentives; the Soviet Union and most of Eastern Europe, also in favor of material incentives but in a more moderate position; and Cuba and the Chinese group, stressing moral incentives. The impact of the concentration on material incentives typified by Yugoslavia would imply, initially at least, emphasis on economic over ideological development; higher productivity of capital and labor, but some degree of unemployment; maintenance of social and economic inequalities; some emphasis in quality and assortment of production; better supply of consumer goods; tendency toward decentralization in planning and use of market mechanisms; expertise and training as the main criteria for selecting managers; self-financed enterprise; increasing participation of the public in politics, and labor unions in decision-making and enterprise profits; a freer attitude of the state concerning education and artistic expression; and a foreign policy characterized by respect of the sovereignty of other states and coexistence between different economic systems.

Moral incentives as typified by Cuba would imply, initially at least, emphasis on ideological over economic development; lower capital and labor productivity, but full employment; trend toward equalization; emphasis in quantity of production; bias in favor of capital goods and, often, scarcity and rationing of consumer goods; planning centralization; political loyalty as the main criterion for selecting managers; budgetary enterprise; mass mobilization in support of political and economic plans; more state control over education and artistic expression; and a foreign policy characterized by the commitment to export the socialist revolution. What is most significant about the Cuban experiment is the intensity of the commitment, the desire to implement the model rapidly, and the length of the period in which the government has been pushing this policy forward.

If the Cuban path were successful, a rapid development of this model should be expected in the less-developed countries of the socialist world. The Cuban experiments seem to have a significant appeal to the youth movements throughout the world, and especially in the industrialized countries, such as the U.S. or France, and to the black movement in the U.S. Finally, the feasibility of the Cuban model is also observed with attention by the Third World, particularly Latin America. If unsuccessful, the Cuban experiment will be a landmark in the practice of the international communist movement, and the implications will be profound for the development of Cuban society itself.

Antecedents: Marxist-Leninist Theory

Karl Marx (1936) vaguely distinguished between two stages which would come about after the socialist revolution destroyed the capitalist system. The first stage, characterized by the dictatorship of the proletariat, would be a period of gradual transition between capitalism and communism and, therefore, would maintain shortcomings of the abolished system and would also begin to manifest the evolution of certain communist traits. Among the shortcomings, Marx singled out the existence of money, the scarcity of goods and services, individual interest and selfishness, continuation of labor as a means to earn a living, centralized control by the state, unequal distribution of income and wage differences (each person was paid according to his work, instead of according to his needs), and social conflicts.

In the higher stage of communism, a society purified of the cited defects would appear, and its principal characteristics would be: the absence of money and of the state as an oppressive force in society, the abundance of goods and services, the transformation of labor into a pleasurable activity which permits the self-realization of man, the distribution of income in an egalitarian manner or in accordance with the needs of each person, the disappearance of classes and social conflicts, and the appearance of a "new man" with a superior communist consciousness—that is, stripped of selfish interests and dedicated entirely to serving the community.[1]

Marxist-Leninist theory maintains that the passing from the transition stage, socialism, to the superior stage, communism, ought to be realized by mass education, the transformation of the means of production, and individual self-betterment. The plan consists of gradually replacing individual and material incentives and stimuli typical of the bourgeois society (salaries, enterprise profit, connections between effort and remuneration, and the like) by the so-called social or moral stimuli (the satisfaction of fulfilled social duty, honorary rewards, social services granted directly and gratuitously by the state). Today, there is not a communist country in the world, since all are in the transition, or socialist, stage. In accordance with the theory, the degree of development of communist consciousness in a given country (e.g., the USSR) can be measured partly by the advance of moral incentives over material ones.

In spite of the above theory, one of the more serious difficulties encountered by the governments of the socialist countries has been the substitution of moral incentives for material ones: "Socialism created new moral stimuli for the workers. . . . Nevertheless, the practical construction of socialism has already demonstrated within the first few years, that moral incentives, by themselves, are not enough to deeply interest the workers in the increase and perfection of production. . . . This showed the necessity of using material incentives for the development of the labor activities within the masses" (Shkurko, 1962).

Sino-Soviet Experiments

During the stage of "War Communism" (1919-1920), Trotsky and his followers conducted experiments with communes in factories, trying to skip the transition stage and directly construct a communist society. In said communes, all the workers put their salary into a collective fund, which was invested in the acquisition of consumer goods, which were in turn distributed equally among the members. Outside the communes, Lenin attempted to reduce inequalities in income by means of salary scales with small differences among the different occupations (Shkurko, 1962: 39, see also Felker, 1966: 21-27). But these experiments did not produce the hoped-for results and, facing a decline in production and economic chaos, Lenin stated in 1921: "Not directly upon the enthusiasm, but upon personal interests, upon individual advantages, on the basis of commercial yield [enterprise profit] is it possible to come near communism. . . . Personal interest elevates production" (Lenin, 1950). With a foundation in this new criterion, Lenin inaugurated the New Economic Policy (NEP) which emphasized economic incentives, substantial differences in salaries, enterprise profitability, profit as a means to increase efficiency, free markets, and the importance of private initiative, in order to reconstruct the Soviet economy. In 1927, the results of the Leninist plan had surpassed expectations (see Dobb, 1966: 97-176).

At the end of the 1920s, Stalin was faced with a sharp controversy within the Soviet leadership. One faction, labeled right-wing and led by Bukharin, proposed to maintain the NEP and to develop industry with certain moderation. The other trend, called left-wing and presided over by Trotsky, rejected the plan of the NEP and supported the collectivization of all the means of production as well as accelerating industrialization. With great political astuteness, Stalin liquidated the leaders of both factions and then after a brief apparent flirtation with the right-wing thesis, fervently embraced the left-wing program (see Campbell, 1966: 11-25). The first Five-Year Plan (1928-1932) was characterized by the abandoning of the NEP and the collectivization of agriculture, but Stalin did not completely eradicate the policy of material incentives. Attacking egalitarian ideas as obsolete (typical of French utopian socialism which

Marx so strongly criticized) the Soviet leader substantially augmented differences in salaries and introduced a system of bonuses based on the fulfillment and overfulfillment of output quotas (on Stalin's position against egalitarianism, see Stalin, 1955: 58-59, 120-121, 361-364). However, the use of the market mechanism and the technique of enterprise profitability were abandoned and, in substitution, strict state control of the economy was established, on the basis of centralized planning.

The schism between the USSR and Yugoslavia, occurring in 1948, facilitated in the latter a gradual return to economic decentralization, use of the market mechanism, increases in material incentives, and expansion of private initiative especially in agriculture. After the death of Stalin, the reformist Yugoslavian ideas influenced the economists of Eastern Europe (Bícaníc, 1966). Thus, during the Khrushchev years, a new movement grew in the USSR, headed by the economist Evsei Liberman (Problems of Economics, 1963, 1965a, 1965b, 1965c). Based on the reestablishment of profit as a principal indicator to measure the success of state enterprises, the plan was tested with encouraging results in several enterprises. The new Premier, Kosygin, officially endorsed Libermanism at the end of 1965. One of the reasons, alluded to by the change, was the necessity of revitalizing the Soviet economy, which had shown signs of crisis since the end of the 1950s. Another reason was the increasing complexity of an unmanageable economy. The new program not only reintroduced profit, but also interest and rent (rejected by Marx), while at the same time it gave greater autonomy to the state managers and interested them and the workers in the profit of the enterprise (Joint Economic Committee, 1966). The use of market mechanisms (e.g., profit) does not necessarily imply that the USSR is moving back to capitalism, because the means of production are still owned by the state. Yet it could be argued that the increasing use of economic incentives and the relative negligence of moral stimuli have not helped to develop communist consciousness.

The failure of the Soviet attempt to eliminate economic incentives during War Communism could have been caused in part by other factors such as the disorganization created by the civil war, the brief and limited nature of the experiment, or the lack of experience of the leaders. China offers a shining example of the large-scale establishment of moral incentives. Between 1953 and 1968, three stages in incentives occurred, and one can see a connection between the use of material or moral incentives and the country's economic situation. The first stage coincided with the first Five-Year Plan (1953-1957) and was based on material incentives in the Soviet pattern. In general, the effects of the plan, at least measured by the growth in GNP, were satisfactory.

But the Chinese leadership, especially Mao Tse-tung, wanted more rapid and spectacular results in both ideological and economic development. With this end in mind, they embarked upon an ambitious program, the Great Leap Forward, which replaced the projected second Five-Year Plan (1958-1962) of the Soviet type. Collectivization of industry and especially of agriculture was accelerated, piecework was eliminated, and rural communes were created. In these communes, the Trotskyite experiment was repeated: the connection between work effort and remuneration was broken in order to establish the distribution of the product in accordance with the necessities of the members of the commune. The change in the economic system, together with other factors (e.g., adverse climate, suspension of Soviet aid) brought about an abrupt decline in production levels. An economic depression soon developed. Waves of hungry Chinese people sought refuge in the British port of Hong Kong, and the Chinese government was forced to import large quantities of wheat from Canada and France. Pressured by the failure of the experiment, the leaders interrupted the Great Leap and initiated, at the beginning of 1961, a return to material incentives. This third stage ended the cycle begun in 1953, but at the price of a decade of lag in development (Hoffman, 1964; Li, 1964: 11). When, in 1966, the economy appeared to be recuperating, Mao launched a new campaign, the Great Proletarian Cultural Revolution, based on the enthusiasm of the masses, moral incentives, and the permanent revolution. According to Western experts in 1967, industrial output in China declined by ten to twenty percent (Asia Research Centre, 1969: 47; Hughes, 1970). In 1968, the campaign had been abandoned, and although official silence made it difficult to find out its exact results on the Chinese economy, it was clear that fear of economic deterioration had been a crucial factor in ending the movement.

The Sino-Soviet experiments suggest that the use of moral incentives with priority over material ones has been, at least an important factor, if not an essential one, in the economic stagnation and recession suffered by these countries in certain periods of their history. Cuba has ignored the above experience and, after several vacillations, has chosen the path of moral stimulation, taking the position today as a leader of this tendency within the socialist world.

Cuba: The Stage of Vacillations

Between 1963 and 1965, two antagonistic positions relative to the problem of incentives were outlined in Cuba. One defended material incentives, following the Soviet line of thinking, which is labeled revisionist or right-wing by the Chinese. The other position advocated moral incentives, adopting the Chinese line of thinking of the epoch of the Great Leap, which is tagged left-wing deviation by the USSR (a brief resumé of the controversy in 1963-1965 has been prepared by De Santis, 1965; for more recent information, see Mandel, 1967). The majority of the Cuban leaders, however, did not take part in the controversy, possibly imitating the ambiguous position of Fidel Castro during this period.

THE SOVIET LINE OF THINKING

The members of the prerevolutionary Communist Party (PSP) were the principal defendants of this position. Next follows a relation of the participants in the controversy and of the official posts that they had at the time: Blas Roca

(President of the PSP and Director of the newspaper *Hoy*); Lázaro Peña (Secretary General of the Confederation of Cuban Workers: CTC); Aníbal Escalante (organizer of the first nucleus of the Cuban Party: ORI); Carlos Rafael Rodríguez (President of the National Institute for Agrarian Reform: INRA); Manuel Luzardo (Minister of Domestic Trade); and Ramón Calcines (head of the Agricultural Trade Union). Also included in this group was a small number of young revolutionaries, such as Alberto Mora (Minister of Foreign Trade); Marcelo Fernández (President of the National Bank), Regino Boti (Minister of the Economy); and Augusto Martínez Sánchez (Minister of Labor). Finally, foreign specialists (e.g., the Frenchman Charles Bettelheim) gave scientific backing to this line of thinking. The magazine *Cuba Socialista,* controlled by the PSP until the end of 1965, began in 1962 to publish articles by Soviet specialists defending material incentives (Evenko, 1962; Glezerman, 1964; Shkurko, 1962: 38-54). Other articles signed by Cubans and foreign technicians (e.g., Liberman, Ota Sik, Bettelheim) were also published in the above magazine or in *Comercio Exterior.* The principles of this position (i.e., material rewards, self-financed enterprise, socialist emulation based on economic stimuli) were applied in several government agencies, especially INRA, and were endorsed by the Minister of Foreign Trade and the National Bank.

The controversy began in 1963, with an article written by Mora in which he labeled as unrealistic the idea of doing away with the laws of supply and demand and the use of the market mechanism in the transition stage. For his part, Fernández expanded on the theme defending in two articles the method of self-financed enterprise. This accounting system consists of permitting the state enterprises to retain a large part of their profits with the aim of reinvestment and distribution and allegedly stimulates efficiency, productivity and the interest of the state administrators and workers. The most important theoretical work was written by Bettelheim, trying to demonstrate that the development of consciousness ought not to be advanced more than the system of production has evolved

(Mora, 1963; also Barros, 1963; Fernández, 1964a, 1964b; Bettleheim, 1964; Infante, 1964).

Practical implementation of the above theory was led by Rodríguez, who introduced, during the 1963 sugar harvest, a system of piecework payment with a progressive scale whose object was increasing production. In the harvests of 1965-1966, material rewards in the form of trips to resorts in Cuba or other socialist countries were added, as well as houses, automobiles, motorcycles, and refrigerators. But it must be indicated that only twenty percent of the labor force participated in this program and only between one and 1.7 percent of the workers were benefited by the rewards (CMQ-TV, 1963; Gaceta Oficial, 1964; Castro, 1965a, 1965b).

One of the principal instruments conducive to material incentives in Cuba has been the system of salary scales and rewards for production, of the Soviet type, introduced in 1963 by the Minister of Labor in collaboration with the CTC (Suplemento de la Revista Trabajo, 1963; Sánchez, 1963).[2] The scales shown in Table 1 fixed graduated wage rates (according to the workers skills and the complexity and effort required in their work) for three occupational groups—that is to

TABLE 1
COMPARISON OF WAGE RATES IN CUBA BY MID-1960s
(pesos per month)

Grades	*Agricultural Workers*	*Nonagricultural Workers and Administrative Employees*	*Executive and Technical Personnel*
1st	63.80	85.00	302.60
2nd	72.45	98.60	351.00
3rd	82.80	114.75	408.10
4th	96.60	134.30	478.10
5th	112.10	157.25	559.80
6th	131.10	185.30	659.70
7th	153.50	218.45	777.70
8th	–	263.50	938.05

SOURCE: Carmelo Mesa-Lago, *The Labor Sector and Socialist Distribution in Cuba* (New York, 1968), pp. 94-101, Tables 8-11.

say, agricultural workers (forty-two percent of the labor force), nonagricultural workers and administrative employees (fifty-three percent), and technical and executive personnel (five percent). Information on the percentage distribution by wage rate within the first and third occupational groups is not available. Within the second occupational group, eighty-three percent of the workers fell in the four lowest grades of the salary scale—that is, the worst paid—and the percentage of workers in the highest grade, or the best paid, was only 0.7 percent (for original sources and detailed comments, see Mesa-Lago, 1968: 92-112, and Figures 7 and 8).

The French Marxist, Jacques Vallier (1968), maintains that the salary scales were a step forward in favor of egalitarianism because they reduced the differences in income which existed at the time in Cuba (see also Karol, 1967; Zeitlin, based on isolated observations, made some wrong conclusions about the Cuban wage-salary scale ratios, 1970). This thesis that the introduction of wage scales helped to reduce wage differences has also been maintained by Cuban officials, but these stress that prior to the Revolution wage differences were not as large in Cuba as in most of Latin America due to the development, in the former, of organized labor and minimum wage legislation (Cuba Socialista, 1966a).

In fact, wage differences among occupational groups were still significant in the mid-1960s after the implementation of the wage-scale system, and the Minister of Labor justified such differences by attacking egalitarianism in salary as unjust (Suplemento de la Revista Trabajo, 1963: 3). Table 1 shows that, in 1964, for each peso earned by an agricultural worker of the first grade, a nonagricultural worker of eighth grade earned 4 pesos. If the comparison is made between two extremes in the table—that is, the minimum salary of agricultural workers and the maximum salary of technical personnel—the ratio is 1 to 15. Furthermore, official data suggest that, after a reduction of wage differences in 1964, there was a tendency for widening wage differences in 1965-1966 (Dirección Central de Estadística, n.d.: 26, Table 4). By comparing, within the state sector, the median salary of the worst-paid occupation (cattle-raising) with that of the best-paid occupation (air transport), a ratio has been computed. In 1963, this ratio was 1 to 3.6; in 1964, it had been reduced to 1:3.4, but, in 1965, the ratio increased to 1:3.5, and, in 1966, it was back to 1:3.6. It should be noted that these data compare median wages which do not give the extreme differences (i.e., between the highest and the lowest wages) as Table 1 does.

The above comparisons are made taking cash salary as a base, but if benefits of various types received by one group or another are included, income differences are even greater. Adolfo Gilly (1964), a South American journalist who is sympathetic with the Chinese line of thinking and who was in Cuba in 1964, has said concerning this: "The bureaucratic sectors exert [a permanent pressure] to increase their share by invisible means—these may be a series of privileges which go with the job or which are added on arbitrarily: automobiles, apartments, trips, meals, etc." Zeitlin (1970: 14) has also acknowledged privileges such as cars and chauffeurs, as well as expense accounts, but underestimated the importance of housing, resorts, and travel. Radoslav Selucky (1964), a Czech economist who visited Cuba in 1964, criticized the Cuban salary policy, saying that although he rejected egalitarianism, the wage differences in Cuba were cruelly large, even in comparison with the capitalist countries of Western Europe.

Besides the basic salary fixed by the scale, other economic incentives were: bonuses for overfulfillment of the work quota assigned to each worker (output standard), and the payment for overtime work with a higher salary. Also, the so-called "historical salary" was added—that is, the difference resulting between the salary a worker received before the salary scales were established, and the new remuneration assigned to the same worker by the corresponding grade.

Finally the "socialist emulation" (competition among workers and among state enterprises in order to raise production and productivity), in force in the years 1964 and 1965, offered material rewards consisting of cash bonuses in proportion to the base salary, and paid vacations of 20 to 30 days to tourist centers in Cuba (Gaceta Oficial, 1964; see also PURS, 1963).

It is almost impossible to judge how effective (or ineffective) material incentives were in Cuba. The experiment was tried for three or four years only and in small scale. Even more, a former adviser of the Cuban government, the Chilean economist Albán Lataste maintains that material incentives, when implemented, were actually corrupted or mixed with elements of the moral-incentive model. For example, the state granted capital "gifts" to many of the so-called self-financed enterprises, or subsidized them or covered their deficits, hence making this a disguised budgetary-enterprise system (Lataste, 1968: 36).

THE SINO-GUEVARIST LINE OF THINKING

This position was defended by a select group of the so-called "new communists" *(fidelistas)* led by Ernesto Che Guevara. Although they did not reject the plan of material incentives, they relegated these to a secondary position, giving priority to moral incentives. Technicians and foreign ideologists (e.g., the Americans Leo Huberman and Paul Sweezy, and the Belgian Ernest Mandel) made their contributions to the thesis and publicized it outside Cuba. Two publications controlled by Guevara when he was Minister of Industry, *Nuestra Industria* and *Nuestra Industria Revista Económica,* as well as *Cuba Socialista,* published several articles by Guevara (1964a, 1964b, 1964c, 1963) responding to the arguments of the opposing line of thinking. The first of these magazines criticized the already cited articles of the Soviet technicians, as well as Liberman's theory endorsing material incentives (Nuestra Industria, 1964a, 1964b, 1964c). Other interesting contributions on this topic are those of the Minister of Finance, Luis Alvarez Ron (1963, 1964) and that of Mandel (1964).

According to Guevara (1963: 54), the communist society will be characterized by the existence of a new man, with a superior consciousness, and the excessive use of material incentive in the transition stage does not contribute at all to the development of that consciousness but, on the contrary, delays its evolution:

> We do not deny the objective necessity of material stimulus [but] we reject its use as the fundamental level of the economy [because] it rapidly takes unto itself special powers and afterward imposes its own force on social relations. We must not forget that it proceeds from capitalism and is destined to die in socialism. . . . The society in transition should liquidate its old ties in order to enter quickly into the new stage.

Accepting that material incentive is in opposition to the development of communist consciousness, the problem still remains that the former is the fundamental lever for obtaining increases in production. Guevara himself was faced with the dilemma: "Must one understand that preferential attention to the development of consciousness delays production and economic growth?" His answer (Guevara, 1963), although cautious, was negative:

> In comparative terms, in a given period, it is possible [that the preferential attention to consciousness delays economic development], although no one has made the pertinent calculations. . . . We affirm that in a relatively short time, the development of consciousness will be more favorable to economic development than material incentives. . . . [However], this assertion requires confirmation by experience, which we are now undergoing. If in the course of the experiment it is demonstrated that [this attitude] is a dangerous brake on productive forces, the decision will have to be made to pluck it by the roots and start again on already trodden roads.

The Sino-Guevarist line of thinking emphasizes several aspects: progressive use of moral incentives instead of material ones, enterprise financed through the state budget (instead of the accounting system of self-financing), education through unpaid labor, and strict administrative centralization.

Moral incentives consist of medals, flags, pennants, and diplomas, earned through socialist emulation and granted by the CTC and the Council of Ministers. Also, honorary titles of "Vanguard Worker" and "National Work Hero" are awarded. One form of moral punishment is the selection of the laziest worker (or the least productive) in an enterprise and the exhibition of his name in a visible location (Gaceta Oficial, 1964: articles 40-47).

Another aspect of the system is the gradual reduction of the proportion paid to a worker in cash (monetary salary) and the increase in social services conferred gratuitously by the state (social salary), such as education, housing, medical attention, and social security. Through this mechanism, it is hoped that the worker will less and less associate his work effort with the remuneration that the enterprise pays him and begin to relate his effort to the services that the state gives him in gratuitous form.

Under the budgetary accounting system, the state enterprises are dispossessed of their profit by means of a high tax whose revenue goes to the national treasury. Afterward, the planners decide how to invest this revenue through capital allocation to the enterprises, stipulated in the state budget. These are not bank loans but capital "gifts" that do not have to be repaid; deficits in the enterprise accounts are often cancelled. In the majority of cases, the criterion for investment is not the profitability of the enterprise, but the importance of the development of certain sectors of the economy or regions of the country. Thus, the connection is broken between the effort of managers and workers of the enterprise and the possibility of reinvesting part of the profit in the enterprise and distributing the other part among the managers and workers. For its part, the enterprise depends totally on the state in order to receive the capital grants necessary for its expansion (Guevara, 1963: 50-54).

Education, indoctrination, and political mobilization are, at least in theory, means to produce a change in the attitude of society—that is, a gradual transformation in the set of values which, ultimately, results in communist consciousness.[3] Unpaid labor is conceived as an essential instrument for transforming the consciousness of the masses. This type of labor is realized in a good number of cases by force—e.g., recruits for the compulsory military service, political prisoners, and re-educating bureaucrats. It may also be under strong pressure from mass organizations–e.g., workers under the CTC, students under the Young Communist Union (UJC), and housewives under the Cuban Women's Federation (FMC). But there is a large number of workers who give their labor in a truly voluntary form. The promoters of this system understand that donations of work reinforce the sense of solidarity of the masses with respect to the state and the community, weakening their utilitarian individual interests (for a detailed treatment of this aspect, see Mesa-Lago, 1969a).

Finally, through the centralized planning system, a single agency hierarchically structured in a pyramidal manner (the Central Planning Board: JUCEPLAN) controls most decision-making powers and the allocation of resources. JUCEPLAN concentrates and allocates resources with a macroeconomic view instead of dispersing them among regions or enterprises that could decide according to their own needs and objectives. This planning system is essential for the implementation of the Sino-Guevarist model, which requires a tremendous mobilization, on a national scale, of economical, technical, and human resources.

The latest declarations made by Guevara on this theme were published while he was on a trip through Asia and Africa at the end of 1964 and the beginning of 1965. On the occasion of his visit to the United Arab Republic, Guevara (1965a) criticized the economic revisionism of Yugoslavia, Poland, and Czechoslovakia, contending that due to the excessive use of economic incentives the first of these countries ran the risk of returning to capitalism. A letter sent to the Uruguayan magazine *Marcha* by Guevara (1965b) contained his last admonition: "Pursuing the chimera of achieving socialism with the blunted weapons bequeathed to us by capitalism (profitability, material interest as a lever, etc.) one can end up in a blind alley." On March 14, 1965, Guevara returned unexpectedly to Cuba and after that time was veiled in mystery until, in October 1967, the Bolivian Army announced his capture and death.

THE FLUCTUATING POSITION OF CASTRO

Until the middle of 1966, Castro's position in the controversy was not clear, inclining at times toward material incentives and at times toward moral stimuli. In 1964, the Prime Minister stated in an interview granted to *Nouvelle Critique:* "The problem is to find the equilibrium between material stimulation and moral stimulation" (see Nuestra Industria, 1964d). With this delicate equilibirum, Castro succeeded in controlling the two tendencies within Cuba regarding the matter of incentives. At the same time, he was able to negotiate with the USSR, threatening it with a swing to the Sino-Guevarist tendency.

Nevertheless, in the years 1963-1964, pressure from the Soviets and other socialist countries reached a climax. This coincided with the economic difficulties confronted in the application of the Cuban Four-Year Plan and Castro's two visits to the USSR. The Cuban controversy between the two lines of thinking also climaxed in 1964. Besides this, several technicians and visitors from the socialist bloc, as well as sympathizers with the revolution, began to censor Cuba's excessive emphasis on moral stimulus. The French Marxist and agrarian adviser of Cuba, Dumont (1964: 41, 50, 54-55), attacked Guevara: "to trust in moral stimuli as substitutes for material rewards will lead to the reinitiation, in a voluntary and unuseful way, of the whole cycle of errors perpetrated by other socialist countries . . . disregard the very high price already paid by such mistakes." The American Marxist and economic adviser of the Cuban government, Edward Boorstein, writing in the theoretical magazine of the U.S. Communist Party criticized the excessive administrative centralization, the system of budgetary enterprise, the gigantic proportions of state enterprises, and the financial irresponsibility that the Cubans demonstrated by their scorn of the idea of enterprise profitability: "In many circles of the government, the lessons of the Soviet experience in giving financial autonomy and responsibility to individual enterprises was disregarded" (Bellows, 1964). The Czech economist Selucky (1964: 22) reminded the adherents of the Sino-Guevarist line of thinking of Lenin's statement in the sense that socialism cannot be constructed only on the basis of enthusiasm but that it is necessary to use material interest. It has already been explained how the French planner Bettelheim became involved in a serious controversy with Guevara, in which the former criticized the idea that the development of the communist consciousness could precede the development of the material base. He concluded that the process of state control in Cuba should not be hurried and nonsocialist forms of property organization should be allowed (e.g., cooperatives, private farms).

The strategy employed by Castro under double pressure, internal and external, reminds one of the strategy followed by Stalin during the debate that preceded the first Five-Year Plan. Castro got rid of the leaders of both the right-wing and left-wing tendencies, appearing at first to support the Soviet line of thinking. Later, when he was sure of his power, he adopted the Sino-Guevarist tendency even more emphatically than had Guevara. The Minister of Foreign Trade, Mora, was dismissed in June of 1964, while the Minister of the Economy, Boti, was given the same treatment in July. In December, the Minister of Labor, Martínez Sánchez, was dismissed from his job for having committed "serious administrative errors," and the next day he attempted suicide (El Mundo, 1964). In January of 1965, Castro supported Rodríguez's idea of introducing material rewards in the sugar harvest. Animated by his apparent victory, Rodríguez praised Castro's decision and predicted that the use of material incentives would result in an increase in sugar production. Two weeks later, Rodríguez (1965) was removed from his position and replaced by Castro himself. In March, Guevara in his turn ceased to be an influential figure, at least within Cuba.

In July of 1965, Castro presided over the presentation of material rewards to the cane cutters in the sugar harvest and referred to the controversy over incentives with a clear criticism of the Sino-Guevarist line of thinking:

> We cannot choose idealistic methods that conceive that all men are guided by the concepts of duty, because in actual life, this is not

> so. . . . It would be absurd to expect that the great masses of men who earn their living cutting cane will make a maximum effort just by being told that it is their duty, whether they earn more or less. This would be idealistic [Castro, 1965c].

Immediately, Castro announced that for the sugar harvest of 1966, the number of material rewards would be increased and that other new types of rewards would be established.

Early in October, all the newspapers published the list of the members of the new Central Committee of the Communist Party of Cuba (PCC). The leaders of the Soviet line of thinking were excluded from the Political Bureau and reduced to secondary posts in the Committee. Only two members of the vanished PSP participated in secretarial positions within the Party, Roca and Rodríguez. On the other hand, the name of Guevara was not included. As a justification, a letter attributed to Guevara was published, in which he renounced all his positions within Cuba. On the same day, October 14, 1965, the newspaper of the PSP, *Hoy,* was merged with the newspaper of the July 26 movement, *Revolución,* into a new publication, *Granma,* which was turned over to Castro's most loyal followers. The road was clear by the end of 1965 so that the Prime Minister could make his own decision.

The Adoption and Radicalization of the Sino-Guevarist Line of Thinking

In spite of the slight increase in material rewards, the sugar harvest of 1966 was poor. Only 4.9 million tons of sugar were produced, 1.6 million less than the goal set by the prospective plan. Rodríguez's prediction was not realized, but it is fitting to ask oneself if the insignificant number of rewards granted in this harvest constituted an effective incentive to increase production. Besides this, a large portion of the rewards for 1965 (refrigerators and motorcycles) had not been delivered by the end of that year, due to delays in imports. Finally, the rewards consisting of trips to the socialist countries were apparently not very attractive, since only 80 workers accepted one of the 500 trips offered (El Mundo, 1965; Granma, 1965a).

The Twelfth Congress of the CTC, held at the end of August 1966, set up the bases for the change in the Cuban position in the controversy. Symbolically, Lázaro Peña, a man in the confidence of the USSR, member of the vanished PSP, founder of the CTC and Secretary General of said organization since 1962, was replaced in his position by a young *fidelista,* Miguel Martín. In his official report to Congress, Martín placed great emphasis on the necessity of forging a new man and harshly attacked the line of thinking which favors material incentives. To this end, he exhorted the working class to fight against materialistic formulas and affirmed that the communist consciousness ought to be encouraged with a basis of moral stimuli (Martin, 1966).

Castro's speech terminating the Twelfth Congress was even more categorical. The Prime Minister complained that he was accused of being "a heretic of Marxism-Leninism" because he was against the dogmas and disagreed with the manuals, and asserted that he had his own criterion for the construction of socialism. Indirectly accusing the USSR and other countries of Eastern Europe, the speaker said: "It could easily happen that a country would believe that it is constructing communism and in reality be constructing capitalism. We want to construct [at the same time] socialism and communism. . . . The socialist society is not going to create a man so that he can be guided by the same criteria as the capitalist man." Castro (1966a) announced that the first Congress of the PCC, to be held in 1967, would decide the question of material versus moral incentives. The announced Party Congress never took place.

Proving that Castro's decision was a fact, several administrative and political agencies hastened to support the new line of thinking. Thus, the Minister of Education, José Llanusa warned that in the teaching profession all kinds of material stimuli would be eliminated, and that there would only be room for teachers whose goal was the formation of the new man. A plan for socialist emulation, developed by the Party and the CTC was released two weeks after the termination of the Congress of the CTC. Said plan, in effect today, has eliminated every kind of material reward and has increased moral rewards (El Mundo, 1966a, 1966b).

At the end of September 1966, Castro made his decision official, announcing before thousands of representatives of the Committees for the Defense of the Revolution (CDR: an association in charge of vigilance in the cities) that in Cuba they would not develop socialist and communist consciousness with a dollar sign on the brain. Castro's formula would be to expand moral stimulus and the enthusiasm of the masses; all those who disagreed with this formula would be comparable to counter-revolutionaries and combatted by the CDR: "He who strives for material gains is a reactionary, an obstacle to the creation of the superior consciousness. . . . We revolutionaries will not cease to combat individualistic and selfish tendencies" (Castro, 1966b).

In December, Carlos Rafael Rodríguez was interviewed by the magazine *Marcha* on the subject, and explained that, although the official position of Cuba was to give "absolute preference" to moral incentives, there was not, nor could there be unanimity among the leaders with respect to said controversy (Rodríguez, 1966; Monthly Review, 1967).[4] With the argument that, due to the lack of ideological maturity, it was not possible to discuss publicly the problems of the nation, the magazine *Cuba Socialista* which had taken the Soviet side during the controversy over incentives, was closed down in February of 1967 (Cuba Socialista, 1967). During the following months, all the magazines which had taken part in the controversy (e.g., *Nuestra Industria, Nuestra Industria Revista Económica,* and *Comercio Exterior*) were also closed down.

The year 1967 witnessed a gradual elimination of those material incentives that still remained in the system of production. In January, the workers of the state farms were deprived of the small family parcels of land (where they could cultivate their own crops and do with them as they wished) with the allegation that they were dedicating more time to said parcels of land than to the state's land (Granma, 1967a). In the sugar harvest, material rewards were not offered. The planning system was centralized even more, erasing all traces of self-financing in the enterprises. A pilot plan of six months' duration was tried in an important cement factory in order to cut back the payment of bonuses for the overfulfillment of the work quotas. Later it was announced that said bonuses, as well as payment for overtime hours, were in the process of being eliminated (El Mundo, 1967; London Times, 1968). The trade unions began to exhort workers to renounce the "historical salary," with the aim of reducing wage inequalities.

In an interview which Castro granted to Herbert Matthews (1967), the Prime Minister harshly attacked the Soviet line of thinking: "Communist countries like Russia are becoming more capitalistic because they are relying on material incentives more and more." Next, Castro explained that Cuba was developing its own Marxist-Leninist system, different from that of Eastern Europe:

> Our economic system is being planned, gradually and with much success, to create a society in which money will become unnecessary except for certain things that cannot be acquired in other ways. It will take a long time, but we do not believe in the materialistic concepts of capitalism or other types of communism in which money is the incentive. Men live for more things than money. . . . [The workers] must learn that their work is a contribution to the good of all the people and the state.

The process of eliminating material incentives was accelerated, at the beginning of 1968, in the agrarian sector, as well as in the commercial and industrial sectors. By the end of 1967, the National Association of Small Farmers (ANAP) had agreed, in meetings in the provinces of Las Villas and Oriente, to end the sale of goods on the open market, in order to sell all dairy and farm products to the state, at the low prices fixed by INRA (Granma, 1967b). In January 1968, Castro announced that more than ninety percent of the small farmers of the so-called Green Belt (ring of cultivated lands around Havana) had withdrawn from commercial distribution (Granma Revista

Semanal, 1968a). Said attitude is considered a model to be extended to the entire country. Instructions for the application of the agreement of the ANAP were published a few months later (Granma Revista Semanal, 1968b). Leo Huberman and Paul Sweezy (1969: 117-121), after discussing the disadvantages of the small private farms, have supported the measures taken by the Cuban government and recommended the elimination of the private sector as soon as possible. Between 1967 and 1969, some 12,000 private farms were sold to the state (Ramírez, 1969: 33).

Against the rest of the private nonagricultural sector, the "Revolutionary Offensive" has been launched, a movement directed toward eradicating selfishness and all remaining manifestations of individualism. In March and April, 55,635 businesses, mainly trade and manufacturing enterprises of the family type, were confiscated by the government. With this step, Cuba was converted into the socialist country with the highest percentage of state property. The offensive also involved an ambitious plan of labor, political, ideological, and educational mobilization in order to reinforce the revolutionary consciousness of the masses (Castro, 1968a; Mesa-Lago, 1969b).

A small group of followers of the Soviet line of thinking (the "microfaction") that still occupied positions in government, in the Party, and in mass organizations was purged in February 1968, being accused of conspiracy against the state. Almost forty officials were condemned to prison for terms between two and fifteen years, and it was revealed that a member of the Soviet Embassy in Havana, Rudolf Shliapnikov, was connected with the activities of the conspirators. Castro labeled the microfaction as a reformist, reactionary, and right-wing tendency which propagated the idea that the government's policy of moral incentives would end in categorical failure (Mesa-Lago, 1969b; Granma Revista Semanal, 1968c; Quarterly Economic Review, 1968). A Hungarian journalist criticized the purge of the PCC and the movement against material incentives, as well as Premier Castro's excessive influence and the irregularity of meetings of the Central Committee of the PCC (Szabad

Foldmuves, 1968). But Raúl Castro responded to these and other criticisms reaffirming the radical line of thinking favoring moral incentives (Castro, R. 1968).

Fidel Castro's speech of July 26, 1969, was dedicated almost entirely to the topic of incentives and constituted the blueprint of Castro's position on the issue. The Prime Minister began by stating that the great task of the Revolution is the formation of the new man with a communist consciousness. After reiterating his right to interpret Marxist-Leninist doctrine in his own way, Castro indicated that the Cuban approach was to develop communist consciousness at the same time as productive forces. Nevertheless, he affirmed repeatedly that it was necessary to develop the material base first, in order to use this foundation to develop consciousness.

Next, Castro referred to the measures put into effect and those under study to develop the superior consciousness:

(a) The granting of hundreds of thousands of scholarships for young students who would also receive free housing, food, clothing, medical attention, recreation, and books. These young people live in a communal manner and are treated in an egalitarian way.

(b) Compulsory establishment of elementary schools (in effect) and secondary schools (planned). This program will be combined with military training and productive labor.

(c) Extension of the child day care centers, which tens of thousands of children attend free of charge, so that their parents can enter into productive labor. In the day care centers, the children live in a communal manner.

(d) Expansion of free medical attention, including prescriptions in the state hospitals (with important exceptions) as well as preventive vaccinations. Burials are also free.

(e) Development of free sports facilities and certain kinds of recreation.

(f) Eradication of private ownership of the means of production (almost completed) and interest payments on capital (in effect).

(g) Gradual lowering of taxes and rents on housing, with the hope of totally eliminating them in the future (currently house rent is equal to ten percent of wages). The public utilities–water, telephone, and electricity–will also be offered without cost (public telephones are free).

(h) Gratuitous concessions in the future (without setting the date) of food, clothing, shoes, and transportation (bus fare in Havana has been reduced by fifty percent, to $0.05). In a certain number of enterprises and in the residences of students who have scholarships, there are already free communal dining halls.

(i) Gradual elimination of money and of salaries, although both will remain for many years. In some communes, principally those of the young people (e.g., Isle of Pines, Pinares de Mayarí), but also those of a large number of families (such as the commune of San Andrés counseled by the Department of Psychology of the University of Havana), experiments with communist societies are under way in which monetary remuneration is minute and is not related to production, while the majority of consumer goods and services are granted free of charge by the state administration. Some 40,000 young workers in Camagüey province are being paid a salary worked out in each case according to needs.

(j) Gradual reduction of wage inequalities. All salareies, however, will not be equal in the near future. First, the lowest salaries and pensions will be increased (pensions until they reach the level of minimum salaries) in proportion to increases in production. The goal is for every worker to earn the same amount, whether he be a cane cutter or an engineer.

(k) Abolition of social classes. The elimination of wage differences and a more egalitarian income distribution will end class differences (most data come from Granma Revísta Semanal, 1968d; the remainder of the information was obtained from newspapers and from direct observations of visitors to Cuba).

The above information shows that a good number of these measures have been postponed to the future. Nevertheless, in his speech Castro referred to a measure that would be put into effect immediately. It deals with an ingenious mechanism to eliminate additional pay for overtime hours and to obtain greater productive effort from the workers. In all the work centers in which payment for overtime has been given up, the workers receive their entire salary in cases of disability or retirement. If said workers die because of an on-the-job accident, a pension is paid to their family, equivalent to one hundred percent of the salary which the deceased received. Since 1964-1965, the "vanguard workers" have benefited from this arrangement as well as from other privileges such as priority in receiving scarce durable consumer goods such as refrigerators and ovens (Granma Revista Semanal, 1968d; Granma, 1965b; Trabajo, 1964).

In response to the plan proposed by Castro, the official press immediately began to publish news about enterprises in which workers renounced payment for extra hours (Granma, 1968a, for an example of workers' renouncing of payment). In another move, the Minister of Labor prepared a draft for the implementation of the plan. This draft criticized the present salary scales as unjust and harmful to the development of the communist consciousness and predicted their elimination. It promised, instead, that the compensation paid in case of sickness, maternity leave, old-age retirement, and pensions for death will be equivalent to one hundred percent of the salary in the enterprises where the workers fulfill the following requirements: give up overtime pay; adopt the 44-hour work week instead of the old one of 40 hours or less; eliminate absenteeism; exceed the work quotas without collecting bonuses; and contribute unpaid labor in the enterprises or in agriculture (Granma, 1969).

The draft was approved in October, but it was not enforced until August 1969. At this time, only 1,410 enterprises having a total of 113,043 workers or a little more than five percent of the labor force fulfilled the above requirements.[5] In the fall of 1969, Zeitlin (1970: 68) discussed this plan with some mining workers, alleging that it "sounded like a material stimulus rather than a moral one." But they rejected his argument by saying that this was a collective rather than an individual incentive, and that only a small minority of the workers did not benefit from the plan. This reasoning, of course, is contradicted by the official data quoted above.

Cuba Versus Czechoslovakia

By the middle of 1968, Cuba and Czechoslovakia had become the leaders of the two opposing lines of thinking within the socialist world. Although Yugoslavia continued to be the most advanced country in the matter of economic liberalization, Czechoslovakia was realizing a notable effort to democratize the socialist system, and to develop a program of economic decentralization based on material incentives and the reintroduction of market mechanisms. At the other extreme of the socialist spectrum was Cuba, with a strictly centralized administrative regime, colored by Castro's personalism and the intense campaign to develop the "new Man."

Herbert Matthews (1969: 272) has commented on the disillusionment of Czech and Soviet technicians upon seeing that much of the help that they were giving to Cuba was being wasted, and their technical advice not being followed. Before the invasion of Czechoslovakia, the visible friction between this country and Cuba had been limited to criticisms by Czech technicians of the deficiencies in the Cuban economy. Selucky (1964) has already been mentioned. Another work published in an economic magazine in Prague by a professor and engineer, Valtr Komarek (1967a, 1967b), is more detailed and profound. This article criticized the negative attitude of Cuba with respect to material incentives as an unnecessary complication that had aggravated the economic situation and been an obstacle to development. Among the consequences of said policy, Komarek pointed out: stagnation of agricultural production and of exports, the unpopular system of rationing, the serious disequilibrium in the balance of payments, the low return on investments, the excessive and strict administrative centralization, and the exaggerated propaganda. The Czech engineer suggested that his country was ready to continue trading with Cuba, but on the basis of parity in the balance of payments, rejecting indirectly the idea that Czechoslovakia would subsidize Cuba with hundreds of millions of dollars, as the USSR does.

One point is clear in the above interpretation: Cuba could try all the economic experiments she wanted, but Czechoslavakia would not accept part of the high costs. This position is different from that maintained by the Soviets. It is logical to suppose that if the Czech reform had continued, the attitude expressed by Komarek would have been encouraged. On the other hand, if the Czech model had been extended to other countries of Eastern Europe, including the USSR, the large credits granted to Cuba would possibly have been reduced.

Another important contradiction between the two countries grew out of the political system. Castro has maintained a personalistic system of power, controlling the key posts in the government, in the party, in the planning apparatus, and in agriculture. Furthermore, the system of budgetary enterprise removes all autonomy from the administrators of the state enterprises, concentrating the decision-making power in the budget, which is managed by the government. The Czech regime, on the other hand, was moving rapidly toward political democratization and economic decentralization, characterized by the delegation of responsibility and a considerable amount of autonomy at the enterprise and municipal levels. Czechoslovakia, then, represented the political and economic antithesis of Cuba.

The above reasons, together with the fact that Czechoslovakia is a border country of the USSR, while Cuba is an island separated by thousands of miles from the USSR, explain Castro's approbation of the Soviet invasion of Czechoslovakia. Other socialist countries that sympathized with the Chinese line of thinking, including Albania, Rumania, and even China itself, criticized the invasion—Yugoslavia, strongly so.

Analysis of Castro's (1968b) speech justifying his position is important in order to indicate exactly to what extreme the

Cuban radicalization on the question of incentives had progressed. Castro assured that, "Czechoslovakia was moving toward a counter-revolutionary situation, toward capitalism only to fall into the arms of imperialism." Therefore, it was "absolutely necessary," as "an unquestionable obligation," at "whatever cost," to avoid the triumph of counterrevolution in the country. The Cuban Premier indicated that, although the Soviet invasion was a flagrant (legal) violation of the Czech sovereignty, it was justified from a political point of view. Furthermore—Castro warned—this situation would never repeat itself in Cuba, because the leaders would avoid all kinds of deviations of the type that occurred in Czechoslovakia.

The referred-to deviations, according to Castro, were not limited to Czechoslovakia, but were typical of almost all of Eastern Europe:

> There, the youth is strongly influenced by all the ideas and tastes of the countries of Western Europe; there, they only speak of stimuli, salaries, and are not really developing a communist consciousness. Voluntary labor [unpaid] does not exist, [all labor] is paid. . . . Many of our scholarship students [in Eastern Europe] have, more than once, undergone emotional stress because of this vulgarization of material stimuli.

Castro also referred to the disappearance of international consciousness in Eastern Europe. This has caused those countries to "soften" and to close their eyes to the problems of the underdeveloped countries. "The constant, foolish, and unexplainable campaign for peace" has also contributed to this problem. As a consequence of these attitudes, "many socialist countries" maintain commercial practices with the underdeveloped world "similar to those practiced by the bourgeois, capitalist world." Even more serious is the attitude concerning technical aid: "[the Czechs] sold us, at a high price, many arms that were spoils of the war with the Nazis, for which we are still paying at the present time." If this occurs in matters of defense, nothing better can be expected concerning other areas of trade. According to Castro, the agencies of foreign trade of the developed countries of the socialist bloc are eager to sell "any old junk" to the underdeveloped countries: "Many times they have sold us technologically backward factories."

Castro emphasized that he was not only against the liberal Czech reforms, but also against the moderate reforms introduced in other countries of the socialist camp, including the Soviet reforms. The speaker asked if the USSR's intervention implied that said country would put an end to the growing tendency to give greater emphasis to the use of the market mechanism. He also harshly attacked Yugoslavia and accused it of being an agent and an instrument of American imperialism within the socialist world, and the principal promoter of the Czech deviations. Castro ended his speech stating that before making a concession to imperialism, Cuba would prefer to disappear along with her Revolution.

Causes and Effects of the Application of the Sino-Guevarist Line of Thinking

In this final part of the study, an analysis is made of three variables—ideology, economics, and politics—which could have led to the use of moral incentives in Cuba. Then the impact of moral incentives on the transformation of consciousness, the development of production, and political consensus is discussed. The author does not attempt to evaluate which of the three variables has been the most significant in the process. For this, it would be necessary to have the coordinated work of specialists in the three fields, as well as more extensive and precise data.[6] The fact that the economic variable in this study receives a more sophisticated treatment than the other two is simply the result of the author's training in economics. Ideological and political variables are treated in a schematic, perhaps superficial manner, and, therefore, remain subject to revision. The author considers it opportune to incur the risk of criticism in order to present suggestions for research that could be made concerning these two variables.

CAUSES

Ideology

Evaluation of the ideological variable is extremely difficult because one cannot determine with precision the thoughts of the Cuban leaders on this particular matter. A crude content analysis of the speeches of the leaders (especially Castro and Guevara) in the years 1963-1966 shows that the thinking of Guevara was consistent, but that of Castro fluctuated notably in this period. This ideological fluctuation together with the pragmatic attitude that the Cuban Prime Minister has shown in the past could suggest that ideology has not been a crucial factor in his decision to adopt the moral-incentive model. Wondering at Castro's rashness in believing in the feasibility of this model, Matthews (1967: 249, 328-329) has quoted several Cuban leaders (e.g., President Dorticós, Minister of Armed Forces Raúl Castro, Chancellor Roa, Director of *Casa de las Américas* Haydeé Santamaría) in support of his own forecast of what would be Castro's reaction in case the Sino-Guevarist experiment would not work: "Castro is not going to stick with these ideas and go down with them. He will change as he has changed in the past. . . . It is not his idealism which has saved him through these years; it is his pragmatism."

The French planner and Marxist ideologist, Bettelheim (1969) has discussed a hidden motivation that may have played a significant role in Castro's decision in favor of moral incentives. Bettelheim indicts Paul Sweezy, as well as Castro and Guevara, for the error of "ideological obscurantism" (also see Sweezy's answer, 1969). According to the Frenchman, the decisive or dominant factor in the ideological discussion is political–i.e., the system of underlying basic social relationships or class relationships: "The practice (economic, political, ideological) of the agents [of production], and particularly of the political leaders, can be understood only in terms of the place they occupy within the system of social relationships." These agents or leaders may constitute themselves in a social class that imposes relationships of domination or exploitation upon the proletariat.

What characterizes socialism as opposed to capitalism—says Bettelheim—is not the existence or nonexistence of market relationships (the market, money, prices, incentives) but the existence of the domination by the proletariat. The idea of a direct and immediate abolition of market relationships is "utopian and dangerous" because it disregards these necessary characteristics of the period of transition.

> In given historical circumstances, the effect of ideological obscurantism mentioned earlier is increased through an effect of displacement. This occurs when the ideological positions which provoke this effect of obscurantism 'feed' a political practice. Such, I think is the case of the political practice of the Cuban leadership. If this leadership attaches so much 'importance' to problems of market relationships—to the point of making them the 'center' of its ideological conception and political practice—this cannot be the result of only a subjective 'error.' In my opinion, this is the effect of an ideology and political line which concentrate all power in the hands of a ruling group, and which therefore do not create the necessary conditions—ideological, organizational, and political—for the democratic exercise of proletarian power.

Bettelheim believes that the political practices of the Cuban leaders have a class significance: "It is related to political domination by a 'radicalized' section of the petty bourgeoisie," which identifies socialism not with the power of the laboring masses but with the disappearance of market relationships. This "disappearance" is purely mythical for it cannot occur during the transition period. Hence the fact of denying the necessity of the market and economic incentives leads—despite speeches and repression—to the opposite of the desired aim—e.g., the development of the black market.

If this is so, why is it that the Cuban leaders so greatly emphasize the elimination of market relationships? Bettelheim suggests that the presence of obsessive and mythical themes (e.g., the market, money, incentives) in the speeches of the Cuban leaders is subconscious—the fear of a threat to the highly concentrated political power that such leaders have imposed upon the masses. "These 'threats' (thought of as 'threats against socialism') present themselves in the manifest form of the 'market,' 'money,' etc., but beyond this form they 'represent' the masses, their labor, their aspirations, their always possible spontaneous movements."

If the above interpretation is accepted, one must conclude that the political variable has been decisive in Castro's adopting the Sino-Guevarist line of thinking. More will be said on this, but first, it is necessary to consider the economic variable.

Economics

Can material incentives function properly in developing, mono-crop, socialist economies where a large majority of consumer goods are not produced? In this situation, consumer goods either have to be imported or the population will be forced to endure deprivation, at least in the short run. In the case of Cuba, this problem has been particularly acute—in view of the island's isolation from the Western Hemisphere—mainly as a result of a particular phenomenon explained in detail by Andrés Vilariño (1967), an economist in the Schools for Revolutionary Instruction. According to Vilariño, the constant increase in monetary income and money in circulation on one hand, together with the decline in productivity on the other, have created a disequilibrium between the purchasing power of the population and the consumer goods available on the market. The increment in purchasing power occurred before production capacity of consumer goods increased.

Vilariño points out the factors that increased disposable income, especially during the first years of the Revolution: the expansion of employment; the increase in the minimum agricultural wage as well as in minimum pensions; the reduction of rent (and in some cases, its elimination); the decrease in the cost of certain utilities such as electricity; and the expansion of gratuitous services such as education and medical attention. Factors which had a negative effect on production were: the ignorance of the new administrators; errors in planning; the inefficiency of state investment; the underutilization of equipment, and the decrease in the labor effort. This last phenomenon requires a more detailed discussion.

Carlos Romeo (1965: 19), the Chilean planner working for the Cuban government, has explained the cause of said phenomenon: "The destruction of the capitalist mode of production implies a transformation of workers' attitudes in almost all economic sectors." The result of this—according to Romeo—was that in certain sectors, such as agriculture, "the productivity dropped due to a reduction of the work effort."

At the end of 1963, a study conducted on the state farms demonstrated that laborers were working only between 4.5 and 5 hours a day, but they were receiving their salary for 8 hours. In the same year, it was verified that labor productivity on the state farms was only fifty percent of that on the private farms (Dumont, 1964: 71). A Cuban journalist (Pascual, 1966), after reporting "an alarming apathy" among the workers on the state farms, complained: "there is no reason for this decline in effort; the rural worker should fulfill his tasks now in the same way that he always did [under private enterprise]."

As explanations for this change in attitude, an official report that the Cuban government sent to ECLA in 1966 pointed out the situation of full employment and wage stability (Cuba Socialista, 1966b: 162): "The agricultural worker has been able to reduce his work hours and still maintain the same standard of living. . . . The level of income of the rural worker exceeds his purchasing power due to the lack of manufactured products. This lack of material incentives does not stimulate the peasants to use their idle forces." The decrease in the labor effort of the rural workers induced a drop in agricultural production, and the consequent lack of food also had repercussions for the industrial workers. Thus, several Cuban economists of the Sino-Guevarist line of thinking told the Czech Selucky (1964: 22): "It is impossible to satisfy material interests when there is a blockade, rationing, and a shortage of goods. High wages can be an incentive to better work, only when more money automatically means more consumer goods. The rationing system negates most of the advantages of material incentives." Four years later, Castro (1968a: 7) himself confirmed the above idea: "Are we going to stimulate the people with money with which they can buy nothing? "

The rationing assigns to each person an equal minimum quota of scarce available consumer goods, but it does not resolve the problem of surplus money supply. This surplus could in part be spent on the purchase of consumer goods on the black market, at prices amost ten times higher than official ones. The black market, although illicit, grew rapidly between March 1962 and March 1968, when it was apparently eradicated. The surplus income also could be spent on eating in restaurants, on drinking in the bars, on trips, or on the few gambling games that were still allowed (e.g., cockfights). But these safety valves were closed or substantially reduced by the Revolutionary Offensive, rationing of gasoline, and other recent provisions.

The excess of money gave support to a unique institution that flourished in Havana until the end of 1969: the selling at high prices of turns to eat in restaurants or dance in night clubs. In order to be able to eat in a restaurant, it is necessary to stand in line for several hours to get a turn for the next day. Since meals in restaurants are fairly good (although quite expensive), lines are very long. Some 200 professional "queuers" *(coleros)* were making incredible profits in Havana by staying in these lines and then selling turns for $5 a seat. On special holidays, the turn could reach a price as high as $40. Some of these queuers had opened offices and were making as much as $80 daily. In January 1970, the Ministry of Interior conducted an investigation that resulted in the imprisonment of several of these queuers who were sanctioned by popular courts to five or six months of forced labor on state farms.[7] This action apparently liquidated the professional queuer as an absorber of surplus income.

Vilariño referred to several measures applied by the Cuban government to reestablish the equilibrium between income and available consumer goods, whether it be trying to reduce the former or increase the latter. Part of the money in circulation was withdrawn in 1961 taking advantage of the change in currency effected by the National Bank and the restrictions on withdrawing money from bank accounts. A second measure has been the strong pressure on the worker to save part of his salary with the aim of reducing his purchasing power. Donations of unpaid labor have operated, at least theoretically, as an anti-inflationary mechanism, since they produce goods and services without increasing income. Price increases (or the Soviet turnover tax—i.e., taxes on consumer goods) have not been used on a large scale (exceptions are cigarettes, liquor, and beer) for political reasons—that is to say, in order to avoid having those with lower incomes most affected by inflation. The official price of consumer goods has been slightly increased and those of luxury items and certain services such as meals in restaurants have been greatly augmented. One recent measure has been the reduction of the percentage of GNP devoted to private consumption, with the aim of accelerating the investment process in order to expand production. To this end, the percentage of unproductive investments (e.g., in hospitals and schools) has also been reduced in order to increase those of a productive nature (e.g., agriculture, cattle-raising, mining).

On the other hand, opposing factors have contributed to increasing the disequilibrium. Among them can be cited the creation of unproductive jobs or disguised subsidies to the unemployed, which have provided income to these groups without a corresponding production increase. Also, there has been an extension of certain moral incentives, such as gratuitous services granted by the state—that is to say, food, clothing and lodging to scholarship winners, as well as housing, burials, local public telephone calls, sports, and child care centers. In some cases, the granting of these services has not solved the old problems or has created new difficulties. For instance, the reduction or elimination of home rental has practically resulted in an increase in the disposable income with which nothing tangible can be achieved. Due to the housing shortage, most people still live in the same place they did before the Revolution; hence distinctions in and dissatisfactions with housing arrangements continue. Free telephone calls induced a dramatic increase in the number of calls, which in turn overloaded the lines, so the public has been asked to restrain the calls to those of absolute necessity and to talk for the least possible time.

The government does not appear to have had much success in expanding the availability of consumer goods on the market since, in spite of the increase in investment, most lines of production have continued either stagnant, falling, or growing at a low rate. This phenomenon could have been caused in part by inefficient utilization of capital and waste of resources, caused in its turn by the lack of adequate economic indices (e.g., the capital goods market, interest, and profitability). It is logical to suppose, moreover, that new restrictions on consumption, beginning in 1968, have accelerated the rate of decrease of work effort and productivity.

Politics

An internal political justification for the use of moral incentives, from the official point of view, is that the immaturity of the Revolution requires a centralized apparatus of control, mobilizations, campaigns, the emulation, and the constant pressure on the masses to avoid the possibility of a "cooling" and the risk of a counterrevolutionary coup. A liberal socialist system of the Yugoslavian or "Czech Spring" style would increase this risk.

On the other hand, the personalistic, centralized method of government applied by Castro is not conducive to a system of material incentives which supports administrative decentralization and delegation of decision-making. In the countries of Eastern Europe in which economic reform has been put in effect, a tendency in favor of political liberalization and public discussion of some national problems has been observed. In Cuba, the situation is the reverse, as is shown by the closing of magazines in which the controversy over incentives was aired and the removal of functionaries and leaders who had maintained points of view that opposed those of Castro. The question of incentives could also have been used by the Prime Minister to rid himself of the two political forces which could have presented a threat to his power—that is to say, the PSP and the Guevarists.

External political factors could also have played an important role. In 1962 and 1963, when the economic situation of Cuba was critical and aid from the USSR was badly needed, there were no serious qualms about the introduction of the Soviet method of material incentives. Later, the discrepancies between the two countries (e.g., the withdrawal of the missiles; the Soviet policy of peaceful coexistence and trade relations with Latin American nations in which Castro was supporting the guerrillas; the deterioration in Cuba's balance of payments; the Soviet pressure for Cuba to abandon her plans of industrialization) could have influenced the radicalization of Cuba. It is possible that Castro resented the deterioration of his image as an independent revolutionary in the Third World and decided to show his autonomy vis-à-vis the USSR, even at the cost of a reduction of internal consumption, in order to maintain external subversion (Jackson, 1969: 146-147).

EFFECTS

The Transformation of Consciousness

Is it possible to measure the results of moral incentives on the transformation of consciousness in Cuba? A survey in the field would be the most appropriate method to determine if any advance has been made in this matter. Serious obstacles hinder such a survey, like the apparent lack of freedom of movement and research within Cuba and the problem of dissemblance on the part of those interviewed. Between 1961 and 1962, three sociopolitical surveys were conducted in Cuba, but none of them dealt specifically with this question; nothing else has been done thereafter (Free, 1960; Cantrill, 1965; Zeitlin, 1967). The Cuban government's strict control over entry visas is another obstacle to objective academicians who have a desire to make serious investigations.[8]

Another possibility would be to conduct such a survey among those exiles who are arriving from Cuba. This method presents the serious difficulty that the sample would not be representative of the Cubans as a whole, but of only one sector. The danger of dissemblance would function in the opposite sense in this case, and it would be necessary to eliminate any distortion due to the ideological extremism which is common among the exiles.[9]

The problem could also be undertaken in the opposite manner, that is, instead of investigating whether a change has been produced, negative indices that denote either resistance to change or the existence of a behavior that is opposite to the ideal could be evaluated. Three population segments to be considered in this sense are the youth, the intellectuals, and the workers. The speeches by leaders, news transmitted over the radio, articles in the newspapers and magazines, and literary production all offer material for content analysis. For example, in 1968, Castro complained that the masses suffered from "ideological weaknesses," because "bourgeois customs still remain," and "there is no consistency in heroism." According to him, these shortcomings were the result of inadequate indoctrination of the people (Castro, 1968a: 2). Several examples follow, but the author insists that it is difficult to judge what their representativeness or significance may be.

The youth: In November 1968, the Cuban news media said that hundreds of young people were wearing American-style clothing and listening to American-style music. One of the immediate directives of the Revolutionary Offensive was to reject long hair, beards, and tight clothing on young men and miniskirts on young women, but recent reports from visitors to Cuba (e.g., Boorstein, Fagen, Zeitlin) indicate that these directives have not been implemented. The young people referred to by the Cuban news media had given way to vagrancy, promoted the prostitution of young girls between fourteen and sixteen years of age, destroyed public telephones and educational material, and burned pictures of Guevara. After the Minister of Education's efforts to dissuade the young rebels met with no success, the government conducted a raid and announced that it was going to reeducate them in state farms (Castro, 1968c). The press and radio also reported that in the second half of 1967 and in late 1968 there were various waves of robberies in Havana, and a large proportion of those guilty of these attacks on socialist property were young people (Bohemia, 1967; CMQ-TV, 1967; New York Times, 1968). A new wave of robbery and vagrancy was reported in late 1969 among teenagers from Oriente province, particularly in the cities of Guantánamo and Holguín (Radio Rebelde, 1969).

In 1969, a forum on delinquency made public the increase in crimes against property (including theft, robbery, and misuse of state funds) as well as in juvenile delinquency. Crimes against property rose in 1962 when rationing began, but decreased notably in 1963 and 1964 due to the introduction of a law which imposed punishments of up to 30 years' imprisonment or death for thieves. Nevertheless, in 1965, a new wave of this type of crime began, increasing almost three times between 1964 and 1968. The official reasons for the increase are: shortage of consumer goods, insufficient number of police and a less rigorous application of the law. It was also announced by the forum on delinquency that in 1967, in forty-one percent of the crimes (of all types), minors had participated and that this tendency was increasing (Granma Revista Semanal, 1969).

Massive desertions by young people in the labor camps have also been reported, although this may be partially due to the lack of minimum standards of living in these camps (Juventad Rebelde, 1968; Echarry, 1968). Another negative index is the large proportion of young people of military age among those who have fled from Cuba through illegal means (Clark, 1969: 15-17).

In all the described cases, groups of young people who belong to the age bracket most affected by indoctrination, demonstrated a conduct very different from that of the "ideal man." On the other side, the Cuban news media claim daily that the youth has transformed its mentality and offer examples of such change in consciousness. Typical of these examples are those groups on the Isle of Youth and in the Centennial Youth Column.

The intellectuals: In 1968-1969, there were several attacks on the intellectual liberty of Cuban literary figures. In the 1968 contest of the National Union of Writers and Artists of Cuba (UNEAC), Antón Arrufat's play "Los siete contra Tebas" (Seven Against Thebes) was awarded the National Theatre Prize. In addition, Herberto Padilla, who had worked in 1962 for "Novedades de Moscú," in the USSR, won the National Poetry Prize for his book of poems "Fuera del Juego" (Outside the Game). Both works contained concealed criticism on the strict political control, hardships, and lack of intellectual liberty in Cuba. Immediately, the magazine *Verde Olivo* of the Revolutionary Armed Forces (FAR) attacked both honored authors, labeling them as counterrevolutionaries and advocates of the "ideological softening" of the Revolution. An intense radio and press campaign followed this, in which UNEAC participated in accusing the two authors of being deviationists, defendants of a depoliticized, neutral line in literature, and liberals in the style of the "Czech Spring." Norberto Fuentes' novel on the anti-Batista struggle in the Sierra del Escambray was also condemned as counterrevolutionary by *Verde Olivo.* Fuentes had been awarded the *Casa de las Américas* Short Story Prize in 1968 for his novel "Condenados de Condado."

Other well-known authors such as the theatre writer Virgilio Piñera and the poets José Rodríguez Feo and Pablo A. Fernández also became a target of the critics. Immediately before the polemic began, a novelist, Guillermo Cabrera Infante, had deserted the Revolution, complaining about the lack of intellectual freedom. In September 1969, UNEAC expelled the writer José Lorenzo Fuentes from its ranks, accusing him of releasing information to a Mexican diplomat who was officially charged as being a CIA agent.[10]

Fausto Masó, a Cuban intellectual who worked on the revolutionary magazine *Lunes* and is presently exiled, believes that the crucial problem in the relations between literature and the construction of a socialist society in Cuba has two facets. The writers who were educated before the Revolution, those that have published valuable books, do not sufficiently criticize the prerevolutionary society, and even, at times, describe it in attractive or nostaligic tones. On the other hand, writers of the new generation, brought up under the Revolution, still have not produced a work of both literary quality and innovation from a point of view of revolutionary content and style. Cuban writers, says Masó (1969), "have been unable to implement in a creative way the ambitious project of building a new man."

The lack of revolutionary consciousness among intellectuals has been acknowledged and severely criticized by two well-known Cuban poets who have significant official posts. Roberto Fernández Retamar, the director of the journal *Casa de las Américas,* was asked in Mexico by Víctor Flores Olea why Cuban intellectuals (referring to literary men) do not participate in the discussion over incentives, the law of value, and the development of a new culture, as political leaders do. Although Fernández claimed that politicians were intellectuals too, he acknowledged that poets, novelists, and playwrights should go out of their narrow fields and approach such problems (Retamar, 1969: 232).

In late 1969, Nicolás Guillén, President of UNEAC, warned the Cuban intellectuals, by using a parable, that they could not stay away from the political problem and that they should participate in the revolutionary struggle.

> In a state of war everybody has to have a war mentality. We writers and artists can't ignore such war. Just imagine a soldier in an invaded nation who in the midst of the battle decides to use his rifle to hunt ducks. He is an excellent marksman, his weapon is in perfect condition, he has enough ammunition, but he chooses the wrong target. Hence his effectiveness is nil, and because of his improper behavior he will end before the firing squad. The Cuban writers and artists are no different than this soldier [Guillén, 1969: 5].

A harder line in cultural affairs became apparent in 1971. On March 20, the poet, Herberto Padilla, was jailed, but later released after having signed a long confession. It was personally delivered by Padilla at a meeting of the UNEAC, where he exhorted other writers to follow his example. As a result of these events, a large group of European and Latin American intellectuals, in two public letters addressed to Castro expressed their concern on the Stalinist methods being used in Cuba.[11] The resolutions from the First National Congress on Education and Culture held in April and Castro's speech closing this event further emphasized the new hard line: (a) primacy of political and ideological factors in staffing universities, mass media and artistic institutions; (b) reeducation of school-age children who show criminal or "antisocial" behavior; (c) tighter controls on literary contests to assure that judges, authors and topics are "truly revolutionary"; (d) more control on subjects of publication, giving priority to textbooks over literary works; (e) elimination of foreign influences in art and literature to wipe out "cultural imperialism"; and (f) violent attack against the "pseudoleftist bourgeois intellectuals" from abroad, warning that the doors of Cuba will be closed except for those foreigners who are "unconditionally" in favor of the Revolution (Granma Weekly Review, 1971).[12]

The workers: In March 1969, Castro said that the system of moral incentives did not motivate the manual workers sufficiently because their work lacked interest and their sense of duty was insufficient. Therefore it was necessary to eliminate routine and to introduce new motivations and organizational forms in manual jobs (Castro, 1969).

Five months later, in the National Congress of the Commissions for Administration of Labor Justice (a sort of labor arbitration body), Minister of Labor Risquet reported that wage claims had been substantially reduced to only eleven percent of the total number of claims, while claims resulting from absenteeism, negligence in work, and lack of discipline had sharply increased to reach fifty-eight percent of the total. Risquet stated that this was an indication that, besides the workers' vanguard in the matter of communist consciousness, there was an expanding rear guard, a sign of the remnants of capitalism. In trying to explain this phenomenon, Risquet (1969) pointed out two problems: the hundreds of thousands of workers coming from the private sector that have been absorbed by the state sector and who still have to undergo a long process of reeducation; and the tens of thousands of youngsters who join the labor force annually and who have also to acquire the discipline and consciousness of the vanguard workers.

Risquet's report gives a solid base for the formulation of the following hypotheses. The scarcity of consumer goods could be the main reason behind the decline in wage claims in a society in which money is becoming less and less important. This lack of incentive may have resulted in a decline of the labor effort with the consequent increase in absenteeism and labor-negligence claims. It appears also that most workers incorporated into the state sector in the collectivization waves of 1959-1961 have not transformed their labor attitudes yet, while most teenagers brought up under socialism have not developed a communist consciousness.

Some of the above hypotheses seem to be confirmed by a report on absenteeism released by the Party Commission on Revolutionary Orientation (COR) in October 1969. The report begins by stating that absenteeism is "an evil which causes great harm every day" but, in spite of it, most absentees consider themselves revolutionaries. The most significant cause of absenteeism—according to COR—is that the new socialist society has not yet fully developed methods of its own to replace the market system of checks and incentives that previously was the motivation behind production: fear of unemployment and wages. "There is more money in circulation than things on which to spend it. Every worker knows that he can live on what he is paid for working 15 or 20 days a month." Thus, he stays at home 5 or 10 days every month. Extreme measures (e.g., the transfer of the absentee from one place of work to another) do not seem to have achieved anything but the alienation of the worker. Hence, the report recommends political and ideological education and more strict managerial supervision as the only way to solve the problem. If the "appeals to the worker's sense of responsibility, his duty to society, and his consciousness as revolutionary" do not work, then less gentle techniques should be employed. The COR's report ends by saying that there is a long way to go before every worker is guided by an appreciation of the new values (Granma Weekly Review, 1969).

Four techniques recently introduced—perhaps following the COR's suggestion—tend to cut down absenteeism and to foster the labor effort by increasing control and discipline and introducing new severe sanctions. The first is a new identification card made mandatory for all workers. This card is a sort of record of labor performance (i.e., includes data on absenteeism, fulfillment of work quotas, and so on) and must be presented to state managers to get a job.[13]

A second measure, recommended by Armando Hart, former Minister of Education and now Secretary General of Organization of the Party, applies military organization to agricultural work. Comparing low productivity and absenteeism among permanent agricultural workers with the high production and discipline of the labor brigades of the armed forces, Hart pointed out the absence of a "chain of command" in the former as an explanatory reason. The examples of such labor brigades should be followed by the trade unions which—according to Hart (1969)—are still not functioning properly: "New revolutionary structures will have to be established in the future by the labor movement, more related to the needs of production, to assure greater efficiency in work and to raise productivity and technical skills."

A third step is the reinforcement in the application of work quotas (output standards) through a campaign that began in late 1970. It culminated in the first half of 1971—named "The Year of Productivity"—with the fixing of these standards in order to cut out nonessential workers in factories and exert pressure upon the remaining workers to increase their effort (Granma, 1970; Castro, 1970a).

Finally, another intensive campaign against absenteeism began early in 1971 and climaxed on March 16 with the enactment of a law against loafing. It established the obligation to work upon all men from 17 through 60 who are physically and mentally able. The law makes a distinction between the "precriminal stage of loafing" (applicable, for instance, to absentees of more than 15 days) and the "crime of loafing" (incurred by recurrent incidents). Penalties fluctuate from house arrest to imprisonment in a rehabilitation center to do forced labor for a period ranging from one to two years. As a result of the three-month campaign that preceded the enforcement of the law (in the midst of which, mass organizations such as CDR and ANAP detected and denounced men who were potential violators of the proposed law), more than 100,000 men were incorporated in the labor force, half of them in agriculture (see the draft of the law in Granma, 1971).[14]

The author is aware that evidence could be presented supporting an opposite hypothesis from that maintained by him in this paper; that is, one trying to prove that there has been a transformation of consciousness among the youth, intellectuals, and workers. In fact, this type of information is more easily available (e.g., in Cuban newspapers) and has been published and discussed in America and Europe (see as an example, Moreno, 1971). Still, the question of the reliability of this type of information persists, particularly in a country like Cuba, where all communications media are controlled by the government. It must be remembered that since 1967 all periodicals that dissented with the official line of thinking were suspended.

Recent, direct observation in Cuba by American scholars who are sympathizers of the Revolution is also contradictory. During their latest visit to Cuba in 1968, Marxist economists Leo Huberman and Paul Sweezy (1969: 152), who follow the Sino-Guevarist line of thinking, could not arrive at any conclusion about the impact of moral incentives on the transformation of consciousness: "As far as the future is concerned, it is much too early to attempt predictions. The remaking of human habits and attitudes is at best a slow process about which there is very little that could be called scientific knowledge. It is even hard to know whether or not solid progress is being made."

Sociologists like Joseph Kahl (who visited Cuba in 1968) and Maurice Zeitlin (who was back in Cuba in 1969) have, however, voiced a much more optimistic opinion of the success of the experiment (Kahl, 1970; Zeitlin, 1970). A political scientist, Richard Fagen (1969: 151-158), who has been in Cuba several times, the latest in 1969, has taken a more cautious although positive attitude. A specialist in education for development, Rolland G. Paulston, has come to the conclusion, after a visit to Cuba near the end of 1970, that, in spite of wide educational changes, the expected transformation of values has not yet materialized.[15]

The Development of Production

Comcomitant with the replacement of private property, the market system, and economic incentives by state property, central planning, and moral incentives in Cuba, the agricultural production has declined gradually. According to Table 2, the principal export and consumption crops increased slightly between the years 1957-1958 and 1960-1961, but decreased later, so that in the period 1965-1966 production levels were generally lower than were the prerevolutionary ones. The production of beef and milk has fluctuated, but in general a stagnation or decrease in production is observed between 1957 and 1966. On the other hand, the output of eggs (as well as fish) has increased in a consistent manner. It is symptomatic that the type of production that is dispersed and requires a large number of manual workers whose output is difficult to control (e.g., sugar, coffee and tobacco plantations, cattle-raising, and the like) is the one showing the poorest performance. On the other hand, certain operations that can be easily concentrated and operated with a small number of skilled, well-disciplined workers (e.g., fish and egg production) are the ones showing increase in output.

Traditionally, agriculture has been the Achilles' heel of the socialist countries and only recently, when proper economic incentives have been provided (e.g., decollectivization of land in Poland and Yugoslavia, better prices to farmers in the USSR) has this situation changed somewhat. Cuba is trying to develop its economy based in the agricultural sector, in which discipline

TABLE 2

PRODUCTION OF THE PRINCIPAL CONSUMER AND EXPORT GOODS IN CUBA: 1957-1966

(in thousands of metric tons)

	1957	*1958*	*1959*	*1960*	*1961*	*1962*	*1963*	*1964*	*1965*	*1966*
Sugar	5,672	5,782	5,964	5,862	6,767	4,815	3,821	4,590	6,082	4,867
Tobacco	42	51	36	45	58	52	48	44	43	51
Coffee	44	30	48	42	48	52	35	36	28	33
Rice	261	253	326	323	207	227	184	160	160	120
Dry beans	36	23	35	37	34	30	27	30	30	23
Beef	185	184	200	170	163	147	143	170	165	177
Fish and shellfish	22	22	28	31	30	36	36	36	40	43
Fresh milk	806	765	770	767	700	690	695	700	705	710
Eggs[a]	275	312	341	430	433	530	483	309	920	1,080
Nickel ore	20	18	18	13	15	17	20	22	27	27
Copper ore	20	18	18	12	5	6	6	6	6	5
Manganese ore	60	29	25	8	10	33	33	33	33	33
Cement	673	736	673	813	871	779	812	805	801	750
Electricity	2,357	2,589	2,806	2,981	3,030	2,998	3,057	3,250	3,355	4,100
Footwear[b]	–	20	17	14	7	12	19	19	16	16
Beer[c]	1,292	1,232	1,557	–	1,394	927	891	1,036	993	1,088
Cigars[a]	–	628	591	–	–	–	369	616	655	622
Cigarettes[a]	9,803	10,197	11,434	–	13,611	14,400	15,347	16,015	16,462	18,455

SOURCE: Based on official figures from Cuba (mainly JUCEPLAN, *Boletín Estadístico, 1966*) checked against figures of the United Nations, the FAO and ECLA. The methodology and original sources can be seen in the author's article, "Availability and Reliability of Statistics in Socialist Cuba," *Latin American Research Review* (Spring and Summer 1969), Tables 3 and 4.

a. Millions of units.

b. Millions of pairs.

c. Thousands of hectoliters.

and organization are difficult to impose. Besides, the leaders are neglecting economic stimuli. The only alternative seems to be the militarization of agricultural production, as Dumont (1970) concluded after his trip to Cuba in 1969.

Cuban performance in the mining-manufacturing sector is contradictory, but better than in agriculture. In most modern, dynamic industries which are highly concentrated and operate with a small number of skilled workers whose output can be carefully controlled, production has increased. Traditional industries which are dispersed and are labor-intensive show a poor performance. According to Table 2, the extraction of minerals declined until 1960-1961, with some recuperation thereafter, notably in nickel. This was one of the most technologically advanced industries in 1958 and suffered in 1959-1961 by the flight of technicians and skilled manpower and the lack of spare parts, but as soon as these difficulties were solved, output rapidly increased. Production in the modern cigarette and electricity industries has increased steadily, although at a slower pace than in prerevolutionary days. Production of cement and beer, which are also modern industries, declined after records achieved in 1961. Footwear and cigar output, handicraft types of operation, have fluctuated with 1966 production below the 1958 level.

It is still premature to evaluate the impact that the radicalization of the Sino-Guevarist line of thinking in the years 1967-1968 has had on production, particularly in agriculture. Nevertheless, isolated bits of news suggest a new decrease in production of milk and the extension of rationing to other consumer goods that formerly were sold on the open market, such as bread and sugar. Apparently there are also growing difficulties in the supply of meat, beans, and cooking oils (Mesa-Lago, 1969b: 29, 62). Some American scholars who visited Cuba in 1968 (e.g., Kahl) have reported that food was scarcer in that year than ever before. Table 3 shows that total agricultural output in Cuba increased fifteen percent between 1958 and 1961 but declined by twenty-three percent between 1961 and 1969. If per capita figures are used, the decline is even more dramatic—thirty-three percent between 1961 and 1969. Agricultural output per capita in 1969 was twenty-seven percent below the 1952-1956 levels.

Guevara's prediction, in 1964, that the development of consciousness does more for the development of production than material incentives, has not yet been confirmed. Either one alleges that consciousness still has not developed and, therefore, the increase in production has not been possible, or one admits that the Sino-Guevarist line of thinking has not given the expected results. One could also allege, however, that it is premature to judge the results of the application of the Sino-Guevarist line of thinking because it was not definitely established until 1966. Yet most elements of the moral incentives model have been present in Cuba since 1961-1962, (e.g., central planning, rationing, budgetary enterprise, education through unpaid labor), and the economic performance in the last ten years has been deceptive.

The economy of Cuba seems to have fallen into a vicious circle. The substantial increase of income between 1959 and

TABLE 3
INDEX NUMBERS OF FOOD AND AGRICULTURAL PRODUCTION IN CUBA: 1957-1969 (1952-1956 = 100)

	Food Production		*Agricultural Production*	
Year	*Total*	*Per Capita*	*Total*	*Per Capita*
1957	108	101	108	101
1958	108	99	107	98
1959	112	101	112	101
1960	113	100	114	100
1961	122	106	122	106
1962	98	83	100	85
1963	85	71	86	71
1964	92	75	94	76
1965	114	90	113	89
1966	93	72	94	72
1967	116	88	115	87
1968	107	80	106	79
1969	99	73	99	73

SOURCE: Based on FAO, *Monthly Bulletin of Agricultural Economics and Statistics,* XIX (July-August 1970), pp. 14-17, Tables 3A, 3B, 4A, 4B.

1960, without an adequate increase in production, brought out the scarcity of consumer goods beginning in 1962. This scarcity, in turn, was a determining factor in the decrease in the labor effort, productivity, and production between 1962 and 1966. The scarcity has been, besides, a factor influential in the establishment, in 1966, and radicalization, in 1968, of the Sino-Guevarist line of thinking favoring moral incentives. But the lack of material incentives seems to have accentuated the negative effects on labor effort and production.

THE POLITICAL CONSENSUS

The deterioration in production and the consequent scarcity of consumer goods have created problems of a political nature in Cuba. In March of 1968, Castro (1968a: 2) asserted that the deficiencies in supplies were causing dissatisfaction, discontent, confusion, uneasiness, and protests. In order to face the problem, the Prime Minister proposed a greater political control and a more intense indoctrination of the masses. Responding to the suggestion, the PCC has declared that it will guarantee control of state as well as of political and mass organizations in order to combat all kinds of opposition. The CDR has vowed to increase their vigilance and to organize meetings for the political orientation of the people. The FMC has exhorted its members to suppress rumors and criticisms that may exist against revolutionary laws and measures (Granma Revista Semanal, 1968e, 1968f).

At the end of September 1968, Castro admitted that since April (that is, in less than six months) more than eighty acts of sabotage had occurred in Cuba against: industries producing fertilizers, fodder, and automobile tires; warehouses for sugar, coffee, tobacco, wood, fertilizers, leather, and clothing; state stores, hotels, vessels, schools, other government buildings, and so on. At least one-fourth of the acts of sabotage were labeled significant, with losses of millions of dollars. It should be pointed out that the wave of sabotage began immediately after the process of collectivization of private property and emphasis on moral incentives reached its climax with the Revolutionary Offensive. Castro (1968c: 4-5) said that those who committed the acts of sabotage were not tolerant of state property and announced even more severe laws to punish these acts: "before the Revolution ceases to be, not one single counter-revolutionary will remain with his head on his shoulders in this country."

As a result of the above announcement, a decree has been enacted establishing the death penalty for those who inflict intentional damages during the sugar harvest. The FAR and CDR have also been asked to guard the cane fields and to prevent acts of sabotage. In November of 1968, the Cuban radio reported changes in military commands and inaugurated a daily radio program devoted to the political indoctrination of the members of the FAR and the Ministry of the Interior (MININ). A "Week of Homage" was also organized in honor of the army and internal police with participation of all the mass organizations.[16]

In December, it was announced that a group studying public opinion, established since the end of 1967 by members of the PCC and the Young Communists Union (UJC), was conducting surveys of public opinion in order to find out what people's attitudes were concerning measures taken by the Revolution, with special emphasis on those causing social change (Granma, 1968b). (One of these surveys reported widespread dissatisfaction with the closing of bars and night clubs, and these are now open during holidays and weekends.) In May 1969, the forum on delinquency concluded that it was necessary to reinforce the application of the law punishing crimes against state property, as well as policy and CDR vigilance.

Although it is difficult to evaluate the real significance of the above examples and cases, they tend to suggest a deterioration in political stability, apparently caused by popular dissatisfaction and increasing use of government force. Huberman and Sweezy (1969: 201-218), confronted in 1968 with the problem of a deteriorating political consensus in Cuba, indicated as alternatives an increase in the real participation of the people in decisions and responsibilities or an intensification of the repressive measures. Since his visit to Cuba in 1969, Zeitlin (1970: 20, 70, 74, 77-78) has stated that, in order to develop a new man, a decisive effort has to be made to create a new political form of democratic socialism, one such as Guevara dreamed of:

> despite their experimentalism and originality in many areas, the Cuban revolutionaries have so far done little to establish institutions to guarantee that competing points of view can be heard within the revolutionary socialist consensus; that meaningful alternatives are debated; that policies are initiated, as well as implemented, by the citizenry at large.

In practice, Zeitlin has concluded, the Party does not have real power, the trade unions seem to have "withered away" and public debate is absent. It is unquestionable, finally Zeitlin has said, that the revolutionaries must choose soon between autocratism and the establishment of socialist democratic political forms.

Both René Dumont (1970) and K. S. Karol (1970) have concluded after their visits to Cuba in 1969 that the Revolution is becoming increasingly autocratic and militarized: there is a lack of democratic discussion, production is organized along militaristic lines, army officers are being appointed to all key posts, and so on. Recent measures introduced to check labor and culture (e.g., the labor identity card, the law on loafing, the resolutions of the Congress on Education described elsewhere in this paper) point in the direction of reinforcement of the apparatus of control and discipline.

SUMMARY AND OUTLOOK TO THE FUTURE

The evidence gathered in this paper suggests that the implementation of the policy of moral incentives in Cuba has not succeeded as of this date in transforming the mass consciousness and, on the contrary, may have contributed to the decline in production, particularly in agriculture. It appears also that the deficiencies in supply, together with other factors, have caused popular discontent with resulting political disaffection. The principal measures taken by the government to confront these problems have been directed toward reducing income, increasing capital accumulation at the cost of consumption, and for investment purposes, reinforcing ideological indoctrination and political-police control, developing military-type organization in production, and stressing discipline and control among the labor force.

Although theoretically the possibility of transforming consciousness and creating a new man is accepted, the problem is presented of the costs of this experiment. Some sociologists maintain that in the long run and with adequate educational methods, change in the values of the population can be produced. Nevertheless, the experiments conducted in the USSR and China to accelerate the development of consciousness had to be interrupted because of the economic and political deterioration which these countries suffered. Although the Cuban experiment has produced similar effects, there exists an important difference; that is to say, the experiment persisted at least until 1970. The key to the problem is how long the economic and political situation, which seems to be in a deteriorating condition, will allow the continuation of the costly ideological experiment.

Three alternatives present themselves to the dilemma: (1) the continuation of the experiment of moral incentives supported by an even more strict political control (which seemed to be the line that Cuba followed until 1970); (2) a radical shift in favor of material incentives and political liberalization à la Yugoslavia (a change difficult to visualize under current conditions); and (3) a combination of pragmatism in economics (with moderate use of material incentives) and tight control in politics (that is, the Soviet model but colored by Castro's personalism, a sort of tropical Stalinism). Some signs, evident in the first half of 1971, strongly suggest that the Cuban Premier has chosen the third alternative.

In his speech of May 1, commemorating Labor Day, Castro (1970a; italics added) said:

> We must insist on the search for the development of a consciousness that will lead us to communism. However, the way to communism is not a question of consciousness alone. It also has to do with the development of both the forces of production and the material base. . . . We cannot fall into the idealism of thinking that . . . consciousness has been developed and that we already have the necessary material foundation. . . . This really is not the case [our consciousness has a long way to go in the matter of development]. *If in the pursuit of communism we idealistically go further ahead than is possible, we will have to retreat sooner or later.*

Then Castro explained that in view of the production difficulties created by the gigantic mobilization for the 1970 sugar harvest, some of the problems presented in the above quotation had been discussed. (At that time he had sadly complained: "Perhaps our major idealism has been to believe that a society which has scarcely left the shell of capitalism could enter, in one bound, into a society in which everyone would behave in an ethical and moral manner"; Castro, 1970b). As a result of such a discussion, several solutions were suggested, and a series of "realistic measures" are now under testing: "As part of this strategy we must understand that we are in a transitional [socialist] stage . . . that we cannot just act as if we were already in communism. . . ." For simplicity, the measures referred to by Castro have been summarized and grouped below into three areas by the author.[17]

First, there is the stress on wage differentials, a typical material incentive supported in Cuba in 1963-1965 by the Soviet line, but strongly opposed in 1966-1968 by egalitarianism. Now Castro warns that wages cannot be equal for all and that wage differences will have significance in the future as an incentive for those who have labor skills or bear heavy responsibilities and for those who work in hard jobs or in places deprived of minimum facilities. If these wage differentials were abolished, then those who make an extra effort to study or have physically hard jobs would be discouraged.

The second set of measures aims at the reduction of excess money in circulation, some three billion *pesos* in early 1971. If the above-explained incentives are going to work properly, the current disequilibrium between the population demand (fostered by excessive money in the market) and the scarce supply of goods and services must be solved. This excess of money—according to Castro—results in "vice, corruption and commercialism [e.g., the black market], in short, in a setback for consciousness." In order to avoid further increases in excess money, Castro has postponed indefinitely both the abolition of house rent (that was scheduled to disappear in 1970) and the raise of bottom wages in the scale (that had been announced by him in his blueprint of July 26, 1968). In order to somewhat reduce the money in circulation, Castro has announced a new increase in the price of cigarettes and beer, and a raise in the rate paid on water and electricity for those who have a high consumption of such utilities.

The third set of measures relates to the supply side of the disequilibrium—thus, the tremendous emphasis placed in 1971 in increasing productivity and output. There is now a program to refix output standards that resembles the 1963-1965 policy stressed by the Soviet line and which was played down in 1966-1968. Redundant labor released through output standard fixing is being organized into construction brigades mainly to build houses, but also schools, day care centers, and factories. As a way to stimulate the workers and reduce the severe housing shortage, the government is providing materials to workers who donate free time for home-building. Nevertheless, the houses will be owned by the enterprise in which the worker is employed (six percent of his salary will be deducted as rent) in order to "establish a link between the place of work and that of living." The possibilities open for management control of low labor productivity are obvious. Finally, a large number of former "loafers" have been incorporated into the labor force principally to help in agriculture.

If the trend continues in this direction and results are not too impressive, more stringent measures could be taken. These could be: (a) currency manipulations such as printing of new money with the concurrent obligation to change old bills for the new ones, pressures to deposit large sums at the banks and restrictions for withdrawal; (b) either a devaluation of currency or a general reform of the price system that would result in an increase in the price of consumer goods. The possibility of introducing a sales tax should not be discarded. On the other hand, the government may decide to ease off its capital accumulation rate to allow for higher consumption of both durable and nondurable goods. There is unconfirmed information to the effect that Cuba's investment coefficient, which had risen from thirty-one percent of GNP in 1968 to some thirty-three percent in 1970, declined to twenty-eight percent in 1971.[18]

Castro has stated that the place and time for making a final decision on these measures may be the Congress of the Confederation of Cuban Workers to be held by the end of 1971 or early 1972. Thus while the Twelfth Congress of the CTC in 1966 was the forum chosen by the Premier to launch the campaign in favor of moral incentives and the new man, the Thirteenth Congress could be the place to close this experiment definitely and enter into a more pragmatic, although less appealing, phase of the Cuban Revolution.

NOTES

1. Joseph A. Kahl (1970: 99) has defined the Cuban term *conciencia* as "an amalgam of consciousness, conscience, conscientiousness, and commitment." For simplicity, I am using consciousness in this paper.

2. The Minister of Labor did not maintain a consistent position in 1962-1964 and, hence, contradictions frequently occur even in a single article.

3. Richard R. Fagen (1969) has made a profound study of three institutions that have been instrumental in educating the Cubans in the new political culture: the literacy campaign, the Committees for Defense of the Revolution, and the Schools of Revolutionary Indoctrination.

4. Zeitlin (1970: 68) has reported that by the fall of 1969 there continued to be "serious differences" within the Cuban leadership on the question of incentives.

5. This information is taken from Resolution of the Ministry of Labor 260 of 1968, and Radio Rebelde of August 30, 1969.

6. A multidisciplinary research team composed of two political scientists, two sociologists, one economist, one psychologist, and one expert in education was established in 1970 at the University of Pittsburgh to evaluate the impact of moral incentives in Cuba. Unfortunately, the inability to obtain research funds has precluded the materialization of the project.

7. This information is taken from Radio Havana of February 4 and 5, 1970.

8. This control was tightened in 1971 after Castro's denunciation of René Dumont and K. S. Karol as CIA agents. These European scholars, after doing field research in 1969, published books in 1970 criticizing the Cuban Revolution.

9. In 1970-1971, John M. Clark, a Ph.D. candidate in sociology at the University of Florida, conducted a survey among Cuban exiles who had recently arrived in the United States. He included in the questionnaire both a set of questions dealing with value change and an "objectivity test" to detect potential exaggeration among respondents. Final results will be available by the end of 1971 or early 1972.

10. The official attacks from FAR were published under a pseudonym (Avila, 1968a, 1968b, 1968c, 1968d). Other information is from Radio Havana of January 17, 1969, and Zeitlin (1970: 74). Summaries of the controversy have been prepared by Adler (1969: C 1, 42), Cortázar (1969), and Primera Plana (1969).

11. Padilla's confession was released by Cuba's Prensa Latina in Paris, and excerpts of it were published in Le Monde of April 29, 1971. The texts of the intellectuals' letters to Castro appeared in Le Monde of April 9 and May 20 of 1971. For more information, see Yglesias (1971).

12. For full coverage of the events discussed briefly in this section, see Casals (1971).

13. This information is taken from Law 1225, September 1, 1969. See also Zeitlin (1970: 70, 72).

14. Law 1231 of March 16, 1971, was published in all Cuban newspapers. See the English version in Granma Weekly Review (1971b). See also Granma Weekly Review (1971c).

15. Paulston, a professor at the University of Pittsburgh, was in Cuba during three weeks in December 1970. He visited numerous schools in the four eastern provinces. The information in the text was given to me on June 10, 1971.

16. This information comes from various broadcasts of Radio Progreso, Radio Rebelde, and Radio Liberacíon in Havana, in November and December of 1968.

17. Most measures were referred to by Castro in his May 1, 1970, speech. See also Castro (1970a) and Granma Weekly Review (1971c).

18. This information was given to me by U.S. journalist James Higgins on May 14, 1971. According to Higgins, this information was passed on to him on January 29, 1971, while he was visiting Cuba, by Lt. Juan Rizzo (possibly Capt. Julio Rizzo, Secretary of the PCC in Camagüey Province) and a high official of the Economic Commission of the PCC whom Higgins could not identify.

REFERENCES

ADLER, R. (1969) "Cultural life in Cuba thriving despite government's reins." New York Times (February 10).

Asia Research Centre (1969) The Great Cultural Revolution in China. Rutland.

AVILA, L. (1968a) "Las respuestas de Cain." Verde Olivo 9 (November 3): 17-18.

--- (1968b) "Las provocaciones de Padilla." Verde Olivo 9 (November 10): 16-18.

--- (1968c) "Antón se va a la guerre." Verde Olivo 9 (November 17): 16-18.

--- (1968d) "Sobre algunas corrientes de la crítica y la literatura en Cuba." Verde Olivo 9 (November 24): 14-18.

BARROS, J. (1963) Article in Comercio Exterior 1 (June).

BELLOWS, I. (1964) "Economic aspects of the Cuban Revolution." Political Affairs 43 (February).

BETTLEHEIM, C. (1969) "On the transition between capitalism and socialism." Monthly Rev. 20 (March): 1-10.

--- (1964) "Formas y métodos de la planificación socialista y nivel de desarrollo de las fuerzas productivas." Cuba Socialista 4 (April): 51-78.

BICANIC, R. (1966) "Economics of socialism in a developing country." Foreign Affairs 44 (July): 633-650.

Bohemia (1967) April 14.

CAMPBELL, R. (1966) Soviet Economic Power: Its Organization, Growth and Challenge. Boston: Houghton-Mifflin.

CANTRILL, H. (1965) The Pattern of Human Concerns. New Brunswick, N.J.: Rutgers Univ. Press.

CASALS, L. (1971) "Literature and society," chapter 16 of C. Mesa-Lago (ed.) Revolutionary Change in Cuba. Pittsburgh, Pa.: Univ. of Pittsburgh Press.

CASTRO, F. (1971) "Speech in the rally to celebrate May Day." Granma Weekly Rev. (May 16): 7-8.

--- (1970a) "Speech at the closing session of the national plenary meeting of basic industry." Granma Weekly Rev. (December 20): 3.

--- (1970b) "Franco debate obrero sobre ausentismo y trabajo voluntario." Granma (September 8): 5.

--- (1969) "Discurso en el acto conmemorativo del 13 de marzo de 1957." Granma Revista Semanal (March 16): 2 ff.

--- (1968a) "Discurso en el onceno aniversario de la acción del 13 de marzo." Granma Revista Semanal (March 24).

--- (1968b) "Discurso analizando los eventos en Checoslavaquia." Granma Revista Semanal (August 25): 1-4.

--- (1968c) "Discurso en el acto conmemorativo del VIII aniversario do los CDR'" Granma Revista Semanal (September 29): 5.

--- (1966a) "Discurso de clausura del XII Congreso de la CTC." El Mundo (August 30): 7-9.

--- (1966b) "Discurso en la conmemoración del VI aniversario de la fundación de los Comités de Defensa de la Revolución." El Mundo (September 29): 5-6, 9.

--- (1965a) "Plan de premios a los mejores macheteros de la V zafra." El Mundo (January 22): 1-6.

--- (1965b) Article in Granma (December 29).

--- (1965c) "Discurso en el acto de entrega de diplomas a los trabajadores que más se distinguieron en la V zafra del pueblo." El Mundo (July 25): 8-9.

CASTRO, R. (1968) "Discurso en el primero de mayo." Granma Revista Semanal (May 12): 3-4.

CLARK, J. M. (1969) "Cuban exiles arrived in the United States by nonconventional means: an introductory analysis." University of Florida. (unpublished)

CMQ-TV (1967) October 6.

——— (1963) February 24.

CORTAZAR, J. (1969) "L'affaire Herberto Padilla: ni traître ni martyr." Le Nouvel Observateur 230 (April): 30-33.

Cuba Socialista (1967) "Recesa la publicación de Cuba Socialista." Volume 7 (February): 2-3.

——— (1966a) "El desarrollo industrial de Cuba." Volume 6 (May).

——— (1966b) "El desarrollo industrial de Cuba." Volume 6 (April).

DE SANTIS, S. (1965) "The economic debate in Cuba." International Socialist J. 2 (August): 518-524.

Dirección Central de Estadística (n.d.) Boletín Estadístico, 1966. JUCEPLAN.

DOBB, M. (1966) Soviet Economic Development Since 1917. New York: International.

DUMONT, M. (1970) Cuba: est-il socialiste? Paris.

——— (1964) Cuba: Socialisme et Développement. Paris.

ECHARRY, A. (1968) "Isla de Piños combate a los elementos antisociales." Juventad Rebelde (February 14).

EVENKO, I. (1962) "Le necesidad objetiva y el papel de la planificación en la construcción del socialismo." Cuba Socialista 1 (July): 71-89.

FAGEN, R. R. (1969) The Transformation of Political Culture in Cuba. Stanford: Stanford Univ. Press.

Far Eastern Economic Review (1969) Volume 66 (October 2).

FELKER, J. L. (1966) Soviet Economic Controversies: The Emerging Marketing Concept and Changes in Planning, 1960-1965. Cambridge, Mass.: MIT Press.

FERNANDEZ, M. (1964a) "Desarrollo y funciones de la banca socialista en Cuba." Cuba Socialista 4 (February): 32-50.

——— (1964b) "Planificación y control de la circulación monetaria." Cuba Socialista 4 (May): 79-97.

FREE, L. (1960) Attitudes of the Cuban People Toward the Castro Regime. Princeton.

Gaceta Oficial (1964) "Reglamento para la organización de la emulación." Resolution of the Council of Ministers, May 5.

GILLY, A. (1964) "Inside the Cuban Revolution." Monthly Rev. 16 (October).

GLEZERMAN, G. (1964) "Las relaciones economicas y los intereses personales en el socialismo." Cuba Socialista 4 (November): 93-110.

Granma (1971) January 11.

——— (1970) "Organización y normación del trabajo en 500 grandes centros industriales." (September 16): 5.

——— (1969) "Proyecto de resolución. . . ." (September 2).

——— (1968a) "Cubana de acero." (August 31).

——— (1968b) "La vida del partido." (December 11).

——— (1967a) January 16.

——— (1967b) "Asambleas regionales de la ANAP acuerdan erradicar las nentas al mercado libre." (November 1): 4.

——— (1965a) December 29.

——— (1965b) October 8: 9.

Granma Revista Semanal (1969) "El Fórum logró acercarnos aún más a nuestro pueblo." (May 11): 7-10.

--- (1968a) "Discurso en la inauguración de una nueva comunidad en el Cinturón de la Habana." (January 14): 3.

--- (1968b) April 12.

--- (1968c) "La microfacción desenmascarada." (February 4): 1-2.

--- (1968d) "Discurso en conmemoración del 15° aniversario del atque al Cuartel Moncada." (July 28): 3-5.

--- (1968e) "Los objectivos de la Ofensiva Revolucionaria." (April 7): 2.

--- (1968f) "Los comités de defensa de la revolución," and "Declaración de la FMC." (March 31): 2-4.

Granma Weekly Review (1971a) May 9. (1971b) March 28. (1971c) "Prime Minister Meets with Representatives from 487 Havana Work Centers." April 25: 2.

--- (1969) "Let's fight absenteeism and fight it competently." (November 9): 2.

GUEVARA, C. (1965a) "Fidel Castro's new phase." (A. de la Carrera). New Leader (October 25): 8-12.

--- (1965b) "El socialismo y el hombre en Cuba." Nuestra Industria Revista Económica 3 (August).

--- (1964a) "Sobre el sistema presupuestario de financiamiento." Nuestra Industria Revista Económica 2 (February): 3-23.

--- (1964b) "La banca, el crédito y el socialismo." Cuba Socialista 4 (March): 23-42.

--- (1964c) "La planificación socialista, su significado." Cuba Socialista 4 (June): 13-24.

--- (1963) "Sobre la concepción del valor: réplica a ciertas declaraciones sobre el tema." Nuestra Industria Revista Económica 1 (October): 3-9.

GUILLEN, N. (1969) "Discurso en el acta de entrega de premios a los grandores del Concurso Anual de Literatura." Granma (December 2).

HART, A. (1969) "Speech at the graduation ceremony for the 1963-1969 class of the Department of Political Science at the University of Havana." Granma Weekly Rev. (October 5): 4-6.

HOFFMAN, C. (1964) "Work incentive in Communist Cuba," pp. 92-110 in C. Li (ed.) Industrial Development in Communist Cuba. New York.

HUBERMAN, L. and P. M. SWEEZY (1969) Socialism in Cuba. New York: Monthly Review Press.

HUGHES, T. J. (1970) "China's economy–retrospect and prospect." International Affairs 46: 68-69.

INFANTE, J. (1964) "Características del funcionamiento de la empresa autofinanciada." Cuba Socialista 5 (June): 25-50.

JACKSON, D. B. (1969) Castro, the Kremlin, and Communism in Latin America. Baltimore: Johns Hopkins Press.

Joint Economic Committee [ed.] (1966) "On improving the management of industry, perfecting planning, and economic stimulation of industrial production," pp. 1041-1052 in New Directions in the Soviet Economy. Washington, D.C.

Juventad Rebelde (1968) "Entrevista con Luis Mario Isaac." (January 29): 6.

KAHL, J. A. (1970) "The moral economy of a revolutionary society," in I. L. Horowitz (ed.) Cuban Communism. Chicago: Trans-action Books.

KAROL, K. S. (1970) Les guerrilleros au pouvoir. Paris.

--- (1967) "A marathon talk with Castro." New Statesman (September 22).

KOMAREK, V. (1967a) Hospodarske Noviny (August 18): 10.

——— (1967b) Hospodarske Noviny (August 25): 11.

LATASTE, A. (1968) Cuba Hacia una Nueva Economía Política del Socialismo? Santiago de Chile.

LENIN, V. I. (1950) Collected Works. Moscow: Institute of Marxism-Leninism.

LI, C. [ed.] (1964) Industrial Development in Communist Cuba. New York.

London Times (1968) February 6.

MANDEL, E. (1967) "Le grand débat économique." Partisans (April/June).

MANDEL, M. (1964) "Las categorías mercantiles en el período de transición." Nuestra Industria Revista Económica 2 (June): 9-36.

MARTIN, M. (1966) "Informe central al XII Congreso de la CTC." El Mundo (August 26): 5.

MARX, K. (1936) "Critique of the Gotha programme," pp. 562-566 in Marx-Engels-Lenin Institute of Moscow (ed.) Selected Works. Volume II. New York.

MASO, F. (1969) "Literatura y revolución en Cuba." Mundo Nuevo (February): 50-54.

MATTHEWS, H. (1969) Fidel Castro. New York: Simon & Schuster.

——— (1967) "Fidel Castro revisited." War/Peace 7 (December): 3.

MESA-LAGO, C. (1969a) "Economic significance of unpaid labor in Socialist Cuba." Industrial and Labor Relations 22 (April): 339-357.

——— (1969b) "The revolutionary offensive." Trans-action 6 (April): 22-29, 62.

——— (1968) The Labor Sector and Socialist Distribution in Cuba. New York: Praeger.

Monthly Review (1967) Volume 18 (February): 5-16.

MORA, A. (1963) "En torno a la cuestión del funcionamiento de la ley del valor en la economía cubana en los actuales momentos." Comercio Exterior 1 (June): 2-11.

MORENO, J. (1971) "From traditional to modern values," chapter 17 in C. Mesa-Lago (ed.) Revolutionary Change in Cuba. Pittsburgh, Pa.: Univ. of Pittsburgh Press.

El Mundo (1967) November 28: 6.

——— (1966a) September 4.

——— (1966b) September 13.

——— (1965) December 9: 11.

——— (1964) "Comunicado del Primer Ministro y el Presidente de la República." (December 9): 1-2.

New York Times (1968) "Cuba reports wave of petty robberies." (December 8).

Nuestra Industria (1964a) "Renuncia el sistema presupuestario de financiamiento a la utilización de los estíulos materiales? " Volume 4 (June): 2-3.

——— (1964b) Volume 4 (July): 43-47.

——— (1964c) Volume 4 (August): 2-3.

——— (1964d) Volume 4 (November): 26-27.

PASCUAL, A. N. (1966) "Eliminar el ausentismo en las toreas agrícolas." El Mundo (July 13): 4.

Primera Plana (1969) "Cuba, el poeta fuera del juego." Volume 7 (May 20-26): 53-55.

Problems of Economics (1965a) "The Liberman discussion." Volume 8: 3-38.

——— (1965b) July: 3-51.

——— (1965c) August: 3-41.

——— (1963) Volume 5 (April): 3-28.

PURS (1963) "Los estímulos materiales y morales en el trabajo." Aclaraciones 10.

Quarterly Economic Review (1968) "Cuba. . . ." Volume 2: 2-3.

Radio Rebelde (1969) September 30.

RAMIREZ, P. (1969) "Cuba, a decade of revolutionary government." Pennsylvania State University. (unpublished)

RETAMAR, F. (1969) "Hacia una intelectualidad revolucionaria en Cuba," in R. Walsh (ed.) Crónicas de Cuba. Buenos Aires.

RISQUET, M. (1969) "En la clausura de la plenaria nacional de justicia laboral." Granma Revista Semanal (August 17): 2.

RODRIGUEZ, M. (1966) Article in Marcha (December 9).

--- (1965) Article in Hoy (January 29).

ROMEO, C. (1965) "Acerca del desarrollo económico de Cuba." Cuba Socialista 5 (December): 19.

RON, A. (1964) "Sobre el método de análises de los sistemas de financiamiento." Cuba Socialista 4 (July): 64-79.

--- (1963) "El contenido político y económico del presupuesto estatal." Trimestre de Finanzas al Día (April/June): 31-40.

SANCHEZ, M. (1963) "La implantación del sistema salarial en las industrias de Cuba." Cuba Socialista 3 (October): 8-22.

SELUCKY, R. (1964) Literarni Novini. Prague.

SHKURKO, S. (1962) "El principio del interés material y la remuneración del trabajo en la URSS." Cuba Socialista 2 (November): 38-39.

STALIN, J. (1955) Works. Volume 8. Moscow: Foreign Languages Publishing House.

Suplemento de la Revista Trabajo (1963) "Bases para la organización de los salarios. . . ." (June 10): 9-10.

SWEEZY, P. (1969) Letter in Monthly Rev. 20 (March): 10-19.

Szabad Foldmuves (1968) February 17.

Trabajo (1964) October 15: 13-15.

VALLIER, J. (1968) "L'économie cubaine: quelques probléms essentiels de son fonctionnement." Les Temps Modernes 23 (March).

VILARINO, A. (1967) "Finanzas, diñero y circulación monetaria." Teoría y Práctica (February): 29-45.

YGLESIAS, J. (1971) "A Cuban poet in trouble." New York Rev. of Books (June 3): 3-8.

ZEITLIN, M. (1970) "Inside Cuba: workers and revolution." Ramparts 8 (March).

--- (1967) Revolutionary Politics and the Cuban Working Class. Princeton: Princeton Univ. Press.

BOOK REVIEWS

Emmanuel, Isaac, S. and Suzanne A. Emmanuel, HISTORY OF THE JEWS OF THE NETHERLANDS ANTILLES. Netherlands: Royal Vangorcum Ltd., 1970. Vol. I: preface, illustrations, picture credits, abbreviations, glossary, bibliography, index (533 pp.). Vol. II: abbreviations of names (539-1165 pp.).

For many decades, Jews have bemoaned the fact that they are the objects and not the subjects of history. Contributing to this partially justified belief or fact has been the paucity of Jewish historians. The stress laid by the majority of Jewish historians and historians of Jewry upon persecutions and martyrdom has magnified the legitimacy of this belief, though some have extolled the contributions made by individual Jews to the sciences and intellectual life of Western civilization.

The former chief rabbi of the Ashkenazi English Jews (the Sephardim have their own *haham* or chief rabbi) was moved to write in his *Pentateuch* (Hertz, 1936: 936) that the primary aim of the Jewish historian should be neither

> to lament the past . . . nor to idealize it, but to understand it. He is, therefore, no longer to confine himself to the martyrdoms of the Jewish People . . . or even exclusively to the strivings of the Jewish spirit in the world of thought. . . . Both the story of the martyrdoms and the spiritual strivings, are, of course, basic. But, in addition, the historian today must seek to explain the position of the Jews in the national histories of the countries in which they dwelt. This calls . . . for a detailed study of Jewish communities . . . and a knowledge of the Jew's social, economic and political relations to the general population.

The rabbi referred to the "cross-fertilization" of Jewish and non-Jewish ideas and influences. After this, he concludes, the student of Judaism will perceive that Judaism is a *civilization* that has made distinct contributions in every sphere of life.

With rare exception, few historians have been mindful of these excellent statements. The failure of historians of Jews to observe the caveats of Rabbi Hertz and other basic tenets of historiography has resulted in the development of stereotypes of Jews. At best, these are applicable to only a small proportion of Jewry. Yet these pejorative stereotypes have been applied to all Jewish groups.

For almost 1800 years, Jews have been divided into two major segments, Ashkenazim and Sephardim, and each of these is divided into subgroups. The former inhabited northern Europe until the fifteenth century, after which their major centers of habitation were Central and Eastern Europe. The Sephardim constituted the Jewry of the Iberian Peninsula until their expulsion from Spain and Portugal in 1492 and 1497, respectively. Those who left these nations joined the existing communities of Levantine and Oriental Sephardim in North Africa, stretching from the Middle East to the Atlantic, or those in the Ottoman Empire, Italy, or southern France.

Jewish historians ascribe the "Golden Age of Spain" (circa 1000-1400) to the Iberian Sephardim. Following that period, except for the expulsions, all groups of Sephardim have been assigned to limbo in histories while the Ashkenazim, always as objects, monopolize the stage. The history of the Sephardim in the New World included roles in every facet of life in that area. This was true even during the reign of the several tribunals of the Holy Office of the Inquisition in the Spanish colonial era. Jewish journals and a few not too well known books touch upon some aspects of this history, but it is generally a neglected field.

The Sephardim wrote books, poetry, created new prayers, developed international trade and commerce and, if we accept the premises of Werner Sombart (1962), they brought modern banking and capitalism into Europe and the New World. If any credit accrues to Jews for making many of these contributions, such credit is largely due to the Sephardim. The Iberian Sephardim were among the Spanish conquistadors. They came with Cortés, Balboa, and Pizarro. They could ride horses fully armed, swing a sword, wench, march, and equal the activities of any Christian knight.

They differed from their non-Jewish colleagues in that their purpose in coming to the New World was to establish themselves, to build homes, to be enterprising inhabitants—and not for "God, gold and greed," the purposes ascribed to others. Many, undoubtedly, came to seek sanctuary from the Spanish Inquisition and its branches in Portugal between 1580 and 1640, but sanctuary was a secondary motive. Where Spanish hegemony reigned, they were compelled to observe their true faith clandestinely.

During the sixteenth and the first decades of the seventeenth century, the Spaniards and Portuguese developed their colonial empires in the New World. England and Holland, too, began to look westward for expansion of their commercial interests and to satisfy the hunger for more land to populate and rule. The area in the New World most accessible for capture or takeover was the Caribbean. Consequently, the first non-Iberian colonies were established on the Caribbean islands and in the northeast corner of South America. Among the early colonists were many Jews.

Jews in Amsterdam were straining the potential for their own development and with the influx of the Ashkenazim, beginning with 1630, there began to be a shortage of available housing. The Jewish community in Amsterdam, while possessed of an Iberian ancestry, used Portuguese as its lingua franca. The name of the community was, and still is, the Portuguese Jewish Community. Even the recently arrived Spanish Jews who came from Turkey, North Africa, or Italy adopted Portuguese for reasons not germane to this article. The use of Portuguese continued for 150 years in Curaçao (circa 1651-1800) as evidenced by their wills, contracts among the Jews, correspondence, and the epitaphs of many tombs.

The Sephardim, hardy and adventurous, found allure in the ideas of conquering the underdeveloped New World and having a share of the wealth thought to be easily attainable there. Curaçao and Surinam were the first Dutch bases in the West, and it was to these places that the Jews came. They brought with them the ability to speak Dutch, Portuguese, and Spanish; an almost inbred ability to adapt, possibly due to 1800 years of forced wanderings; their ready contacts for trade through their family relationships all over Europe and in the lands of the Sublime Porte. We mention separately their determination to practice and preserve their faith, since this was their rock. The familial devotion served to further commercial ties without the necessity of large capital, since credit was to be had for the asking. The linguistic abilities permitted contacts with the Spanish colonists who were groaning under the oppressive *alcabala* and the restraints on trade imposed under the fallacious mercantile theories of Madrid and Seville. The family contacts extended to many of the inhabitants of the viceroyalties of Nueva Granada and Peru.

Where faith was no barrier to the presence of the Jews *qua* Jews, they served in every capacity of public and private life. Holland acknowledges its debt to them for their participation in its development. Cromwell's benevolence in not opposing their reentry, after their expulsion in 1290, benefitted England. France, which had expelled them in 1309 and 1396, permitted the Sephardim to reside and conduct some businesses in the Provence area after 1500 but denied to Ashkenazim the same rights. While the French General Assembly granted full citizenship to Sephardim in January 1790, it refrained from granting this privilege to the Ashkenazim of northern France until September 1791. The Sephardim were referred to as the "Portuguese Nation." This euphemistic term was applied to the Sephardim of Hamburg, Altona, Gluckstadt, Denmark, and in the New World.

When Dr. Isaac S. Emmanuel's *Precious Stones of Curaçao* appeared in 1957, it was generally acclaimed as a monumental work. It also foreshadowed what was to come when he completed his labors. He and his wife, Suzanne Amzalak Emmanuel, authored *The History of the Jews in the Netherlands Antilles.* It is tragic that Mrs. Emmanuel did not live to see the published volumes of this magnum opus.

Although the work is primarily the history of the Jews in Curaçao from the time of their first settlements (1651-1652) until the present, concluding chapters cover their activities in *Terra Firme* and some of the Caribbean islands. The first volume limns the growth of the Sephardic community; the rifts within segments of the group; relationships with Holland as well as with the Jewry of Amsterdam; the lack of egalitarianism or tolerance of some of the Dutch governors who did not share the humanistic concepts of the directors of the Dutch West Indies Company which controlled Curaçao, Aruba, and Bonaire; the volatile nature of the Sephardim; and the factionalism that appears to be endemic among congregants vis-à-vis various spiritual leaders.

The brief period of French oppression and English rule, 1797-1816, and the role of the Jews of St. Eustatius in behalf of the Thirteen Colonies during the American Revolution and the misfortunes visited upon 101 Jews by Admiral Sir George Rodney in reprisal is included, but it is a tale that requires retelling in greater detail in a separate history. There was no Ashkenazi community until 1926, when those fleeing Europe found the doors of the United States closed under the Johnson Act. The development of this group, which has retained its individuality, is also recounted.

The Emmanuels have supplied in both volumes material of interest to the historian, the cultural anthropologist, the sociologist, and the economist. Their discussion of the economic phases, the abandonment of agriculture for commerce, the educational and cultural lives, as well as the relationships with the Christian communities are but a few of the topics that form part of what this reviewer was tempted to term the definitive history of Curaçaon Jewry. This reviewer, however, knows from personal experience that there is always another archive, other papers and documents still privately owned that can cast some light on events, personalities, and enigmas–especially of periods prior to 1800. Furthermore, "definitive" is an absolute, and there are no absolutes (written with tongue in cheek). Definitive or not, the two volumes make obsolete all previous books, monographs, and anthropological studies on Curaçaon Jews.

The communal life centered about the synagogue, Mikve Israle, still in existence may appear to the non-Jewish leader to lay too great a stress on the religious aspect of the lives of the people. It must be noted, however, that the home, synagogue, and extended family have been the sources of main interest to Sephardim and the fortresses through which their Judaism was preserved. Sephardic Jewry has integrated into the general community wherever they were permitted to reside without losing their religious and ethnic identities. When integration turns into assimilation, as sometimes happens even with Sephardim, conversion is the inevitable result.

The second volume is a collection of appendices. They include a multitude of statistics and data covering such matters as the rules and regulations of the oldest surviving Jewish institution in the New World (a claim disputed by the Jews of Surinam); records of funds sent to the Holy Land for the support of the Jewish communities of Jerusalem, Hebron, and Tiberias; ransoms paid to the English and French several times to prevent the sacking of Willemstadt; lists of plantation owners; ransoms paid to Barbary pirates for the release of Jews captured in the Mediterranean and scheduled to be sold as slaves; dowries for orphaned maidens; lists of licensed marine brokers and Jewish shipowners and ship captains. The Jew as a mariner and agriculturalist is the antithesis of the stereotype of the Jew as a moneylender and urban shopkeeper.

The Emmanuels mined the archives and records of individuals in Curaçao, Holland, and institutions, libraries, and the National Archives of the United States. The whole is augmented by an exhaustive glossary and bibliography and index. They have set a pattern of research and historiography which serves as a model for those who would emulate them in other areas. They have also demonstrated that the history of the Sephardim and their communities is a tale far from being told in its entirety and that such a history will bring about a revision of the concept of the Jews because the Sephardim have been the subjects of history as well as its objects.

–Seymour B. Liebman
Instructor in Jewish History
Miami-Dade Junior College

REFERENCES

HERTZ, M. (1936) Pentateuch. London: Oxford Univ. Press.
SOMBART, W. (1962) The Jews and Modern Capitalism. (M. Epstein, trans.) New York: Collier.

Grebler, Leo, Joan W. Moore, and Ralph C. Guzman, THE MEXICAN-AMERICAN PEOPLE. New York: Free Press, 1970. 774 pp. $14.95.

This volume represents the culmination of a massive labor covering a period of nearly five years, and an expenditure of over half a million dollars. More than twenty scholars in addition to the authors and immediate staff, plus a large but unspecified number of students, contributed to the research and writing. This final version compiles selected materials which have already been published in eleven advance reports, many or most of which are already known to scholars concerned with Mexican-American affairs.

In conception, this work is something of a parallel to Myrdal's *American Dilemma.* The authors have tried to present the Mexican-American case and cause. One of their aims seems to have been to draw together the Spanish-speaking and the Spanish-surnamed in the United States–and especially in the Southwest–into a minority group, cutting across class and regional boundaries. This study in and of itself did not do that, but the phenomenon has happened anyway, rather as a parallel development to the research. For example, when the study was in its early stages, there was much difficulty in dealing with Spanish-surnamed New Mexicans, most of whom did not appreciate being "lumped" with others. This was also true for the upper-class Spanish-surnamed person in Texas and California who frequently preferred to be "included out." In a sense, the study was ahead of its time, in that only recently has it become acceptable, even fashionable, for persons of Spanish or Mexican ancestry to recognize their similarities and to emphasize the dignity and value of maintaining their cultural differences.

The research, as represented in the advance reports, concentrated on education, employment, income, housing, immigration, intermarriage, and health. Two regional studies were also included in the early reports–one on New Mexico, which seemed to require separate treatment, not only because of the self-image of the population there, but because statistically there were many differences between the Spanish-speaking in that state and elsewhere. The other study was one of East Chicago, which similarly did not seem to fit the patterns observed elsewhere. The bulk of this book, then, concentrates upon California and Texas, especially Los Angeles and San Antonio. Although materials from Colorado, Arizona, New Mexico, and East Chicago are brought in to illuminate or contrast, the primary emphasis is on the first-named states.

The book gives a relatively brief historical background, concentrating upon the events of the twentieth century, since this is the period during which the ancestors of most of the present day Mexican-American population arrived in the United States. The socioeconomic conditions of Mexican-Americans today are then described in great detail, including statistical materials, as well as thoughtful analyses of the various causative factors involved.

A section on "the individual in the social system" presents material on social class, the family, and ethnicity, including also some attention to the various boundary-maintaining mechanisms which have been apparent in this population. A section on the role of the churches forms a particularly valuable contribution, especially since this work did not appear in any of the advance reports. Although it is rather brief, the student of Mexican-American culture will appreciate this new material and the analysis made of it.

Finally, there is a section on political interaction between Mexican-Americans and Anglos in various governmental and community agencies and institutions. A profile is given of the kinds of organization and leadership now developing, and of the probable degree of political effectiveness the population will have. Numerous appendices provide ample evidence of how the data were collected, and a bibliography containing approximately 1,500 items is an invaluable addition.

The primary value of this book will be as a standard reference for anyone concerned with Mexican-Americans today. The statistics are plentiful, the charts and tables easy to find and to read. The text itself is scholarly and massive and could well be used as a basic text in advanced courses dealing with this minority group. Because of its size and cost, it is not likely to be used extensively for actual classroom assignment, however.

Certainly it is a must for any citizen or scholar concerned with Mexican-Americans. It will be some time, if ever, before it is superseded.

–*Nancie L. Gonzalez*
Professor of Anthropology
University of Iowa

Carter, William E., NEW LANDS AND OLD TRADITIONS; KEKCHI CULTIVATORS IN THE GUATEMALAN LOWLANDS (University of Florida, Latin American Monographs, Second Series, 6). Gainesville: Univ. of Florida Press, 1969. Illustrations, references. vi + 153 pp. $3.75.

This is a detailed study of the agricultural patterns of a migrant Kekchi population in lowland northeastern Guatemala. The author undertook the research in a three-month period, primarily as a part of a broader tropical ecological study program sponsored by colleagues at the University of Florida. Its orientation is explicitly patterned on the work of Harold Conklin, but Carter clearly points out that his work was of much shorter duration, and the agricultural patterns prove to be much simpler than those Conklin described for the Hanunoo. Of the 148 pages of text, some 90% is devoted to detailed ethnographic observations on the cultivation patterns, combined from time to time with pertinent ecological data. Comparative materials are cited frequently, principally from some Yucatan studies, and from the work of Reina in the Peten. The remaining material consists of an introductory section on the Kekchi migration and tropical pioneer settlements, and a concluding section that considers some of the social, political, and ecological consequences of the nature of the patterns described. Carter mentions some broader problems, such as the future of slash-and-burn farming in tropical environments, and the presence of clearly conflicting interests between those who do the agriculture and those who own the land, but he does not discuss them. The volume is certainly a welcome addition to the still small detailed literature on primitive and peasant cultivation.

Carter is explicit that the shortness of his research time acted to make certain kinds of fairly important data unavailable to him. He could not witness an entire annual cycle and so had to depend heavily on informants' descriptions for much material, including the amount of time spent in various activities, the amount of yield, and many other matters where the lack of firsthand observation can lead to skewed results. Time limitations evidently also led him to decide not to pay even a brief visit to the nearby homeland of his migrants in order to permit a comparison at certain points with their earlier practices in the highlands. This latter point is unfortunate. The title suggests that there is to be some mention of the "old traditions" in a new setting, that is, some comparative material that will permit an understanding of the adaptive changes the migrants perform in order to work in the new locale. Also, such a visit would have allowed the author to at least obtain comparative data on estimated time use to allow him more suggestive comments on the ecological variations that were of special interest in sponsoring the study.

The ethnographic description does not permit a summary in a review. The material is treated under the following general topics: site selection, cutting, burning, cropping, dry season milpas, wet season cultivation, succession to grassland, and fallowing. In general, there is no effort at internal analysis beyond that accomplished by categorical distinctions made in the description. There is no componential or formal analysis, although it does appear that much of the data could readily have been subjected to such techniques had the original purpose included that as an intended method. Data are so extensively detailed that the reader must undertake his own analysis if he wishes to ascertain the presence of other internal patterns.

Nonanthropological or agriculturally interested readers will find the text necessarily arid; the volume really is intended for the specialist to whom the variations being described will be useful for comparative purposes. Carter does use his material to cite a number of problems concerning the Mayan area and tropical development, but for the most part they are limited to comments. He rarely "goes beyond his data"; on the contrary, his reluctance to explore further will probably limit the general interest of the volume. From the point of view of an anthropologist reviewer, Carter is to be commended on obtaining so much yield from a mere three months in the field, but chided in not thinking some of it through somewhat more thoroughly, and looking to some analytical techniques that might well have permitted him a greater crop from his own planting. For the reader drawn by the title, the "old traditions" being discussed are solely those related to agriculture, and the "new lands" are those of one small village.

–*Richard Adams*
Professor of Anthropology
University of Texas

BOOKS RECEIVED

GENERAL AND REGIONAL LATIN AMERICA

Agor, Weston H., ed., LATIN AMERICAN LEGISLATURES: THEIR ROLES AND INFLUENCE, ANALYSES FOR NINE COUNTRIES (Praeger Special Studies in International Politics and Public Affairs). New York: Praeger, 1971. Preface, tables, introduction, bibliography, xlviii + 511 pp. $22.50.

Basch, Antonín, and Milic Kybal, CAPITAL MARKETS IN LATIN AMERICA: A GENERAL SURVEY AND SIX COUNTRY STUDIES (Praeger Special Studies in International Economics and Development). New York: Praeger, 1971. Preface, tables, figures, introduction by Felipe Herrera, bibliography, xvi + 163 pp. $12.50.

Bell, Harry H., TARIFF PROFILES IN LATIN AMERICA: IMPLICATIONS FOR PRICING STRUCTURES AND ECONOMIC INTEGRATION (Praeger Special Studies in International Economics and Development). New York: Praeger, 1971. Preface, tables, charts, abbreviations, index, xvii + 168 pp. $13.50.

Cook, Shelburne F. and Woodrow Borah, ESSAYS IN POPULATION HISTORY: MEXICO AND THE CARIBBEAN, Vol. I. Berkeley: Univ. of California Press, 1971. Preface, tables, figures, abbreviations, index, xxiii + 455 pp. $15.00.

Hirschman, Albert O., A BIAS FOR HOPE: ESSAYS ON DEVELOPMENT AND LATIN AMERICA. New Haven: Yale Univ. Press, 1971. Preface, introduction, index, ix + 374 pp. $12.50.

Mutchler, David E., THE CHURCH AS A POLITICAL FACTOR IN LATIN AMERICA, WITH PARTICULAR REFERENCE TO COLOMBIA AND CHILE (Praeger Special Studies in International Politics and Public Affairs). New York: Praeger, 1971. Foreword by Irving Louis Horowitz, preface, acknowledgments, tables, charts, abbreviations and acronyms, bibliography, index, xxvii + 460 pp. $18.50.

Rabinovitz, Francine F., and Felicity M. Trueblood, eds., LATIN AMERICAN URBAN RESEARCH, Vol. I. Beverly Hills: Sage Publications, 1971. Introduction, bibliography, appendix, 313 pp. $15.00.

Sable, Martin H., LATIN AMERICAN URBANIZATION: A GUIDE TO THE LITERATURE, ORGANIZATIONS AND PERSONNEL. Metuchen, N.J.: Scarecrow Press, 1971. Foreword, preface, introduction, indexes, lxxiv + 1077 pp. $25.00.

Turner, Frederick C., CATHOLICISM AND POLITICAL DEVELOPMENT IN LATIN AMERICA. Chapel Hill: Univ. of North Carolina Press, 1971. Preface, bibliography, index, xv + 272 pp. $8.75.

Argentina

Martinez Estrada, Ezequiel, X-RAY OF THE PAMPA (Translated by Alain Swietlicki). Austin: Univ. of Texas Press, 1971. Introduction by Thomas F. McGann, index, xiii + 415 pp. $10.00.

Bolivia

Malloy, James M. and Richard S. Thorn, eds., BEYOND THE REVOLUTION: BOLIVIA SINCE 1952. Pittsburgh: Univ. of Pittsburgh Press, 1971. Illustrations, tables, preface, abbreviations, appendix tables, glossary, index, xvii + 402 pp. $11.95.

Brazil

Knight, Peter T., BRAZILIAN AGRICULTURAL TECHNOLOGY AND TRADE: A STUDY OF FIVE COMMODITIES. New York: Praeger, 1971. Acknowledgments, tables, figures, abbreviations, introduction, bibliography, index, xxii + 223 pp. $15.00.

British Honduras

Minkel, Clarence W. and Ralph H. Alderman, A BIBLIOGRAPHY OF BRITISH HONDURAS, 1900-1970 (Research Report No. 7, Latin American Studies Center, Michigan State University). East Lansing: Michigan State Univ., 1970. vii + 93 pp.

Caribbean Region

Baxter, Ivy, THE ARTS OF AN ISLAND: THE DEVELOPMENT OF THE CULTURE AND OF THE FOLK AND CREATIVE ARTS IN JAMAICA, 1494-1962. Metuchen, N.J.: Scarecrow Press, 1970. Foreword, introduction, bibliography, index, xv + 407 pp. $10.00.

Bernardo, Robert M., THE THEORY OF MORAL INCENTIVES IN CUBA. Alabama: Univ. of Alabama Press, 1971. Preface, introduction by Irving Louis Horowitz, index, xix + 159 pp. $7.50.

Fitzpatrick, Joseph P., PUERTO RICAN AMERICANS: THE MEANING OF MIGRATION TO THE MAINLAND. Englewood Cliffs, N.J.: Prentice-Hall, 1971. Tables, figures, index, xvi + 192 pp. $6.95.

Silén, Juan Angel, WE THE PUERTO RICAN PEOPLE: A STORY OF OPPRESSION AND RESISTANCE (Translated by Cedric Belfrage). New York: Monthly Review Press, 1971. Preface, introduction, notes, 134 pp. $5.00.

Walsh, B. Thomas, ECONOMIC DEVELOPMENT AND POPULATION CONTROL: A FIFTY YEAR PROJECTION FOR JAMAICA (Praeger Special Studies in International Economics and Development). New York: Praeger, 1971. Acknowledgments, tables, figures, bibliography, xiii + 134 pp. $12.50.

Chile

Agor, Weston H., THE CHILEAN SENATE: INTERNAL DISTRIBUTION OF INFLUENCE. Austin: Univ. of Texas Press, 1971. Preface, introduction, appendixes, index, xxi + 206 pp. $7.00.

Colombia

Nelson, Richard R., Paul T. Schultz, and Robert L. Slighton, STRUCTURAL CHANGE IN A DEVELOPING ECONOMY: COLOMBIA'S PROBLEMS AND PROSPECTS. Princeton, N.J.: Princeton Univ. Press, 1971. Preface, tables, figures, introduction, index, xii + 324 pp. $12.50.

El Salvador

Anderson, Thomas P., MATANZA: EL SALVADOR'S COMMUNIST REVOLT OF 1932. Lincoln: Univ. of Nebraska Press, 1971. Preface, bibliography, index, ix + 175 pp. $7.95.

Mexico

Baker, Richard D., JUDICIAL REVIEW IN MEXICO: A STUDY OF THE AMPARO SUIT (Latin American Monographs, No. 22). Austin: Univ. of Texas Press, 1971. Preface, bibliography, index, xiv + 304 pp. $8.50.

Connor, Seymour V. and Odie B. Faulk, NORTH AMERICA DIVIDED: THE MEXICAN WAR, 1846-1848. New York: Oxford Univ. Press, 1971. Preface, index, analytical bibliography, viii + 300 pp. $7.95.

Gamble, S. H., THE DESPENSA SYSTEM OF FOOD DISTRIBUTION: A CASE STUDY OF MONTERREY, MEXICO (Praeger Special Studies in International Economics and Development). New York: Praeger, 1970. Acknowledgments, tables, introduction, bibliography, xiv + 137 pp. $13.50.

Panama

Hedrick, Basil C. and Anne K. Hedrick, eds., HISTORICAL DICTIONARY OF PANAMA (Latin American Historical Dictionaries, No. 2). Metuchen, N.J.: Scarecrow Press, 1970. Editors' foreword, introduction, bibliography, vi + 105 pp. $5.00.

Paraguay

Arnold, Adlai F., FOUNDATIONS OF AN AGRICULTURAL POLICY IN PARAGUAY (Praeger Special Studies in International Economics and Development). New York: Praeger, 1971. Preface, acknowledgments, tables, figures, abbreviations, appendixes, xx + 294 pp. $17.50.

Peru

Mariátegui, José Carlos, SEVEN INTERPRETIVE ESSAYS ON PERUVIAN REALITY (Translated by Marjory Urquidi). Austin: Univ. of Texas Press, 1971. Introduction by Jorge Basadre, author's note, glossary, index, xxxvi + 301 pp. $8.50.

Quijano, Anibal, NATIONALISM AND CAPITALISM IN PERU: A STUDY IN NEO-IMPERIALISM (Translated by Helen R. Lane). New York: Monthly Review Press, 1971. Foreword, introduction, appendix, 122 pp. $6.50.

Venezuela

Arnove, Robert F., STUDENT ALIENATION: A VENEZUELAN STUDY (Praeger Special Studies in International Economics and Development). New York: Praeger, 1971. Foreword by Kalman H. Silvert, preface, tables, figures, bibliography, xxiii + 209 pp. $15.00.

Lombardi, John V., THE DECLINE AND ABOLITION OF NEGRO SLAVERY IN VENEZUELA, 1820-1854 (Contributions in Afro-American and African Studies, No. 7). Westport, Conn.: Greenwood, 1971. Preface, acknowledgments, abbreviations, introduction, appendixes, glossary, bibliography, index, xviii + 217 pp.

INTERAMERICAN RELATIONS

Glauert, Earl T. and Lester D. Langley, eds., THE UNITED STATES AND LATIN AMERICA. Reading, Mass.: Addison-Wesley, 1971. Introduction, iv + 204 pp. $2.95.

Gray, Richard B., ed., LATIN AMERICA AND THE UNITED STATES IN THE 1970's. Itasca, Ill.: F. E. Peacock, 1971. Preface, bibliography, xi + 370 pp. $5.95.

MISCELLANEOUS

Agramonte, Roberto, MARTI Y SU CONCEPCION DEL MUNDO. Puerto Rico: Editorial Universitaria, 1971. Indices (general, onomastico y analítico), 815 pp. $7.50.

Almaráz, Felíx D., Jr., TRAGIC CAVALIER: GOVERNOR MANUEL SALCEDO OF TEXAS, 1808-1813. Austin: Univ. of Texas Press, 1971. Preface, bibliography, index, xii + 206 pp. $7.00.

Earle, Peter G., PROPHET IN THE WILDERNESS: THE WORKS OF EZEQUIEL MARTINEZ ESTRADA. Austin: Univ. of Texas Press, 1971. Preface, introduction, bibliography, index, xii + 254 pp. $7.50.

Esquenazi-Mayo, Roberto and Michael E. Meyer, eds., LATIN AMERICAN SCHOLARSHIP SINCE WORLD WAR II. Lincoln: Univ. of Nebraska Press, 1971. Introduction, contributors, xi + 335 pp. $10.00.

Franck, Thomas M. and Edward Weisband, WORD POLITICS: VERBAL STRATEGY AMONG THE SUPERPOWERS. New York: Oxford Univ. Press, 1971. Preface, index, xiii + 176 pp. $5.95.

Gropp, Arthur A., compiler, A BIBLIOGRAPHY OF LATIN AMERICAN BIBLIOGRAPHIES. Metuchen, N.J.: Scarecrow Press, 1968. Introduction, index, ix + 515 pp. $30.00.

Hayter, Teresa, AID AS IMPERIALISM. Baltimore: Penguin Books, 1971. Foreword, preface, abbreviations, appendix, glossary, index, 222 pp. $1.45.

Rendon, Armando B., CHICANO MANIFESTO: THE HISTORY AND ASPIRATIONS OF THE SECOND LARGEST MINORITY IN AMERICA. New York: Macmillan, 1971. Introduction, appendix, vii + 337 pp. $7.95.

Sauer, Carl Ortwin, SIXTEENTH CENTURY NORTH AMERICA. Berkeley: Univ. of California Press, 1971. Figures, maps, glossary, index, xii + 319 pp. $10.95.

Vol. 14 No. 2

May 1972

JOURNAL OF INTERAMERICAN STUDIES

and WORLD AFFAIRS

A Publication of the Center for Advanced International Studies,

The University of Miami

Journal of
INTERAMERICAN
STUDIES
and WORLD AFFAIRS

Vol. 14
No. 2
May
1972

CONTENTS

Editorial Note IONE S. WRIGHT 131

Social Anarchism: An Atavistic Ideology of the Peasant
PETER E. B. COY 133

Ancestor, Emperor, and Immigrant: Religion and Group Identification of the Japanese in Rural Brazil (1908-1950)
TAKASHI MAEYAMA 151

The Brazilian Novel: Some Paradoxes of Popularity
JON S. VINCENT 183

Political Attitudes of Mexican Women: Support for the Political System Among a Newly Enfranchised Group
WILLIAM J. BLOUGH 201

The Andean Common Market: A New Thrust at Economic Integration in Latin America
KEVIN C. KEARNS 225

Book Reviews

Landsberger, Latin American Peasant Movements
WILLIAM GLADE 251

Mercier Vega, Guerrillas in Latin America
WILLIAM F. BARBER 255

Rout, Politics of the Chaco Peace Conference, 1935-1939
CHARLES J. KOLINSKI 257

Ealy, Yanqui Politics and the Isthmian Canal
THOMAS M. LEONARD 259

Colby & van den Berghe, Ixil Country, a Plural Society
ALAIN Y. DESSAINT 260

Alexander, The Communist Party of Venezuela
M. F. HASSAN 262

Books Received 265

Beverly Hills *SAGE PUBLICATIONS* *London*

JOURNAL OF INTERAMERICAN STUDIES AND WORLD AFFAIRS is published four times annually–in February, May, August, and November.

Journal of INTERAMERICAN STUDIES and WORLD AFFAIRS

Editor: Ione S. Wright

Associate Editor: Julian I. Weinkle

Editor-Designate: John P. Harrison

Book Editor: Harry W. Hutchinson

Published quarterly by SAGE PUBLICATIONS
Sara Miller McCune, *Publisher*
Connie Greaser, *Editorial Director–Journals*
Rhoda Blecker, *Production Editor*

POLICY: *The Journal of Interamerican Studies and World Affairs* reflects the interests of the scholarly community and interested public concerned with the social, economic, political, and cultural aspects of life in Latin America (including the Caribbean); particularly in those instances where the subject is of concern to more than one of the traditional disciplines. As these concerns change, so will the content of the journal. ¶ Articles which have special relevance for interrelationships between American nations and of those nations with the rest of the world will be given special consideration. An effort will be made to include occasional articles that state an unusual or even discordant position on a subject of broad interest to be supplemented by critical comments of authorities representing differing positions on the topic. The editors continue to welcome articles by scholars from all parts of the world.

MANUSCRIPTS: Manuscripts should be submitted in duplicate to: Editor, *Journal of Interamerican Studies and World Affairs,* Box 8134, University of Miami, Coral Gables, Florida 33124. ¶ Correspondence regarding book reviews should be sent directly to: Book Review Editor, *Journal of Interamerican Studies and World Affairs,* Box 8123, University of Miami, Coral Gables, Florida 33124.

Subscriptions: Regular institutional rate $15.00 per year. Professionals and teachers may deduct one-third from the regular institutional rate (one-year rate $10.00); full-time college and university students may subscribe at $8.00. Add $1.50 for subscriptions outside the U.S., Canada and Latin America. No student discounts outside the U.S., Canada and Latin America. Orders from U.K., Europe, the Middle East, and Africa may be placed at £7.00 annually, and should be sent to the London office (address below).

Inquiries: Address all correspondence and permissions requests to SAGE PUBLICATIONS, INC., 275 South Beverly Drive, Beverly Hills, California 90212. Inquiries and subscriptions from U.K., Europe, the Middle East, and Africa should be sent to SAGE PUBLICATIONS, Ltd, St George's House, 44 Hatton Garden, London E C 1. Other orders should be sent to the Beverly Hills office. ¶ **Exclusive Advertising Representatives:** R. K. Armstrong & Associates, Inc., 11661 San Vicente Boulevard, Suite 210, Los Angeles, California 90049.

Back Issues: Single copies of issues are available at $5.00 each. Orders for 10 or more copies of a single issue for course adoption will be billed at $2.50 per copy. Prior to Volume 10, back issues published are available through Swets & Zeitlinger N.V., Keizersgracht 471 and 487, Amsterdam, Holland. ¶ **Claims for undelivered copies** must be made no later than three months following month of publication. The publisher will supply missing copies when losses have been sustained in transit and where the reserve stock will permit. ¶ **Change of Address:** Six weeks' advance notice must be given when notifying of change of address. Please send old address label along with the new address to insure proper identification. Please specify name of journal.

EDITORIAL NOTE

With this issue, I conclude an eight-year editorship of the *Journal of Interamerican Studies and World Affairs,* as I plan to retire from academic life at the University of Miami on June 1, 1972.

I shall miss the *Journal:* the daily excitement of the mailbox surprises–sometimes a treasure chest, sometimes a Pandora's box–and the many, many interesting, rewarding, challenging, frustrating, exciting professional and personal contacts with my colleague Latin Americanists.

The problems–unexpected, critical, time-consuming, exacerbating, and frustrating–I can do without. They are, in fact, already forgotten in the satisfying realization that the *Journal* has now passed through its hectic, strenuous period of adolescent growth to a quieter, but hopefully even more impressive, maturity under the continuing sponsorship of the Center for Advanced International Studies, University of Miami, and with a new editorial staff.

Speaking for myself, the associated editor, Julian I. Weinkle, and the book review editor, Harry W. Hutchinson, together we say "Thank you so much" to all those who have made this possible.

It's been fun! My congratulations and best wishes to the incoming editors: John P. Harrison and Jan Peter Wogart.

–*Ione S. Wright*
Editor

Latin American Urban Policies and the Social Sciences

Edited by JOHN MILLER *and* RALPH A. GAKENHEIMER

Accelerated urbanization and rapid population growth have drawn particular attention to Latin American in recent years. Current statistics on the growth rate of the nations of South America indicate the highest continental growth rate in the world, and there is no evidence that it may decelerate significantly.

Editors Miller and Gakenheimer have addressed various policy issues related to urban development in Latin America at international, national, and local levels from the points of view of different social sciences. The problems and potentials generated by rapid urbanization and the use of the social sciences for understanding and guiding urbanization and the process of national growth are treated extensively.

This volume is based on the Jahuel, Chile, Conference sponsored by the Ford Foundation—at which eminent scholars from both North and South America met to discuss Latin American Urban Policies.

Table of Contents

I. The New Urban Era in Latin America: A Challenge—The Urban Phase: Raison d'étre for Policy, **John Miller**

II. Integrating Urban-Regional Policies Among Nations—The Rapprochement of Nations with Contiguous Regions, **John Miller** / Economic Integration and the Spatial Development of South America, **Paul Ove Pederson** and **Walter Stohr**

III. Urban Growth Policies for the Nation—Channeling National Urban Growth in Latin America, **John Miller** / The Role of Cities in National Development, **John Friedmann** / Planning, History, Politics: Reflections on John Friedmann's 'The Role of Cities in National Development,' **Richard M. Morse** / Rejoinder to Richard M. Morse, **John Friedmann**

IV. Political Development Vis-a-vis Urban Growth—The Distribution of Political and Governmental Power in the Context of Urbanization, **John Miller** / Urbanization Policy and Political Development in Latin America, **Robert T. Daland**

V. Metropolitan Policy for the Squatter Settlements—Three Proposals Regarding Accelerated Urbanization Problems in Metropolitan Areas: The Lima Case, **Carlos Delgado**

VI. A Future Role for the Social Sciences: Policy and Action—The Contribution of the Social Sciences to Urban Policy Formulation in Latin America, **John Miller**

Appendix: Jahuel Seminar Summary, **Kalman H. Silvert**

ISBN 0-8039-0056-2 **1971** **384 pages** **$12.50**
L.C. 70-103481 **Market: World**

SAGE PUBLICATIONS, INC.
275 S. Beverly Dr. / Beverly Hills, CA. 90212

SAGE PUBLICATIONS LTD
44 Hatton Garden, London E C 1

PETER E. B. COY
Department of Sociology
University of Stirling
Stirling, Scotland

SOCIAL ANARCHISM
An Atavistic Ideology of the Peasant

In 1874, a group of Frenchmen in revolt against the academic rules of their profession was dubbed "Impressionist"; this attempt at destruction by ridicule failed when the painters turned the intended insult into an honored label. The inflated value put upon their work since has not diminished the honor of the title. Another type of blowing up has had the opposite effect: Anarchism, whose modern emergence was contemporary with Impressionism, has pejorative connotations today. Too often, it is used as a synonym for "anarchy," and we have been encouraged to think of it as merely a revolutionary creed like communism with, if anything, more nihilistic and destructive overtones. In the empty dialogue of political denunciation, the epithet "anarchist" has become the countercharge to the accusation "fascist," without the protagonists having much idea what either term means. The height of absurdity was reached when long-suffering Polish workmen were described as "anarchists" by their socialist masters after the economic crisis of Christmas 1970.

More piquant still is the use of the term "anarchy" by some political figures to describe the activities of university students. The notion that the violence of the latter anywhere approaches the deliberately homicidal behavior of a few psychopaths, who supported and tried to further acratic aims at the end of nineteenth century, is, of course, laughable. The idealism, optimism, and libertarianism of most of the student demands, however, do indeed relate to anarchist doctrine, but this is not what their opponents are implying. The piquancy stems from the students' reluctance to call themselves anarchists. Despite their anti-authoritarianism, some students apparently believe "Marxism" to be a more respectable label; one can only point out, in this context, that Bakunin described Marx as "authoritarian from head to foot" (Joll, 1969: 108). Most students, one imagines, would prefer not to be labeled at all.

The rise of European Anarchism as a formal theory is usually associated with William Godwin and Pierre Joseph Proudhon. The context in which their writings gained attention was, on the one hand, the Industrial Revolution and, on the other, the failure of the contingent aims of the French Revolution: the old rural economic systems and the former provincial political systems gave way to factories and to central administrations whose control was taken even further out of the hands of the agricultural masses. The irksome yoke of accumulators of property or of power began to make itself increasingly felt. The institutions of the state—archives, magistrates, police—all came to be seen as perpetuating this accumulation, so that an equitable redistribution of the fruits of labor seemed to nineteenth-century socialists to need the removal of those currently in power.

By 1871, however, a breach arose between the Russian Michael Bakunin and the German Karl Marx over the meaning of "removal": for Marx, it meant a transfer of governmental power out of the hands of the bourgeoisie; for Bakunin, it meant the abolition of state government altogether. Abolition of state government implied abolition of statewide political action. Hence, Bakunin's further disagreement with Marx on the means of achieving the emancipation of the lower classes: Marx wanted the proletariat to capture and exercise political power for themselves; Bakunin saw power as evil, whoever might wield it and wanted its exercise abolished altogether.

Whereas Marx was more realistic in seeing the possibility of success in a centralized, disciplined political party, Bakunin was more idealistic in anticipating the voluntary association of autonomous groups of free men. Bakunin recognized the impossibility of the total exercise of free will by every individual, but he wanted to restrict arbitrary government of man by man, especially when governor and governed were out of face-to-face contact with each other.

Liberty, meaning the isolated freedom of the romantics or the limiting dyadic contracts of the liberals, formed no part of his thinking. True individual liberty, for Bakunin, was the knowledge that all those around him were free. A memorable phrase to be found in Brenan (1950: 134) affirms: "The liberty of my neighbour, far from being a curb or a denial of my liberty, is, on the contrary, necessary for it and its confirmation." According to Joll, Bakunin was aware that there is a strong and inevitable relationship between means and ends in the making of a revolution: as you begin, so you will go on; the organizational forms of the group effecting so total a social change will be perpetuated in the subsequent society. Coercion into action of subordinate groups by a central committee or General Council of the International was therefore anathema to Bakunin and may account for his rejection of Marx's view of the right road to an egalitarian future. Policy should not be passed down from above but proposed by the delegates of loosely associated groups to be discussed at such consultative levels as the proposers' constituents as required.

This was too much for Marx, and he organized the expulsion of the Bakuninists from the International at The Hague in 1872. International socialism was henceforth predominantly Marxian in the industrialized countries of northern Europe, but Bakunin retained the support of the peasants of Italy and Spain, and of the small watchmakers of the Swiss Jura, where a purely Bakuninist International was set up. The split was now complete.

Bakunin, however, while he was throwing off the yoke of authoritarianism, was in the process of saddling himself, and anarchism, with a fatal reputation for violence. A follower, Sergei Nechaev, published a manual of active terrorism called *Catechism of Revolution* in 1869, with Bakunin's collaboration. It introduced a new concept: that of "propaganda by the deed." Bakunin repudiated Nechaev, but he died, in 1876, before the full consequences of Nechaev's invitation to violence were manifested. The last two decades of the nineteenth century were spattered with assassinations and attempted assassinations of kings, presidents, and prime ministers.

Apart from the image of cloak, whiskers, and smoking bomb thus fixed upon Anarchism during Bakunin's declining years and the following quarter-century, the method itself was self-defeating and counterproductive. The other half of the spiral of violence has been termed by Sartre "the moment of the boomerang" (Fanon, 1965: 17)–i.e., the moment when the violence of colonialist exploiters returns upon their heads. But, of course, a reaction to violence occurs whoever perpetrates it: the violence of "propagandists by the deed" releases upon their own heads the latent aggressiveness of the opposite wing of the political spectrum, drumming up its cudgel-parties and *agents provocateurs.* It may also alienate the very people it is intended to hearten or benefit, especially if it is carelessly or indiscriminately applied.

In his earlier and more productive period, Bakunin had recognized that revolution was only successfully made by the propagation of basic ideas and by exploiting massive unrest, not by precipitating disturbances prematurely. In his last years, his impatience for success betrayed him into lending his great reputation to a perversion of his libertarian vision. As Kropotkin was to point out after him, terrorism is a form of government and the abolition of government is what Anarchism is all about. Moreover, even Lenin recognized that pamphlets were more effective agents of social change than were firearms. If Anarchism is ever to conquer the mind of Western man, it will be by the idea rather than by the deed.

American Interpretations of Anarchism

Individual Anarchism as a destructive expression of personal desperation has merely been a technique which has failed when it has been applied inappropriately. The result which the method attempted to produce was *social* Anarchism, and this is demonstrably a very ancient tradition. As Brenan has pointed out, Anarchism has a strong element of nostalgia within it; this has led to the suggestion that Anarchists like Bakunin and Tolstoy were inspired by utopian memories of the Russian villages of their childhood. Certainly, when the socialist International had to choose between Marx and Bakunin, it was the cantonal Swiss and the Italian and Spanish villagers who were attracted to Bakunin's preference for a decentralized and autonomous social organization, so reminiscent of their own regions and villages. Long before the Parisian Communard experiment of 1870, which so excited Bakunin, the Spanish *comuneros* had extracted a measure of autonomy for their villages from the Holy Roman Emperor in 1520. Independence and self-sufficiency, born of necessity as border communities between Christendom and Islam, were the key notes of such villages as Fuenteovejuna, whose collective punishment of a corrupt royal governor was celebrated and justified by the royal dramatist Lope de Vega.

Spanish history for the last hundred fifty years has reflected the desire to escape the centralist control initially imposed by Napoleonic France: at levels where the desire for freedom and autonomy were more difficult to obtain, Spaniards had to be content with the next best thing, federalism. The theoretical orientation for this step in the nineteenth century was derived from the same source as the Anarchists had used: the writings of Proudhon. The federal prime minister of 1873, Pi y Margall, if not a thorough-going anarchist, followed and translated Proudhon. His projected eleven self-governing Spanish provinces, held together loosely and containing independent municipalities, were to carry out a program containing much of the dogma dear to acratic thought: the separation of church and state; the abolition of conscription; free, compulsory education; expropriation of unexploited land; the provision of agricultural credit; plus some purely socialist reforms, such as introduction of the eight-hour day. Despite the enthusiasm expressed, the whole scheme collapsed almost before it had begun, mainly due to a political rebellion which prevented the announced intention to abolish conscription.

For the rest of the nineteenth century, while the rest of Europe and the United States were being propagandized by "the deed" and the upper echelons of Spanish society were considering federalism, the peasants of the south were being proselytized by "the idea." The "apostles of the idea" formed the nucleus of dedicated and informed anarchists organized, after the split between Marx and Bakunin, at the Congress of Córdoba in 1872. They travelled about Andalusia without pay and were housed and fed by the peasants. They organized their hosts against their employers, imparting the doctrines of Bakunin and, through him, Proudhon. The ideas they taught and the reforms they drove into the heads of their absorbed listeners included the social and economic equality of all men, and therefore the abolition of classes, property, and inheritance; the corrupting influence of all power, so that the activity of the state should be withered away to a mere administrative function; the equality of opportunity, so that children of both sexes should enjoy full education; and the notion that religion is a form of slavery, so that cults should be abolished and scientific and human justice substituted.

There was a strongly puritanical flavor in the doctrine which persuaded the peasants to give up drink, meat, tobacco, and even coffee and remain faithful to their wives. Brenan (1950: 191) uses this evidence of puritanism to give an ingenious explanation for the undoubtedly severe anticlericalism which pervaded the actions of Spanish anarchists thereafter: their anger toward the churches and the priesthood, he says, was "the anger of an intensely religious people who feel that they have been deserted and deceived." The rich, too, had to be separated from their luxuries, not because the anarchists wanted to have them but because they were deemed bad in themselves. The anarchists did not want the leisure which a share of the landowners' wealth might give; they wanted the rich to share in the ennobling experience of manual labor.

These groups of anarchists readily took to syndicalism when it penetrated Spain at the turn of the century. The significance of these localized unions, as opposed to national craft unions, was that they included all the local men, so that not only was strike action effective in the rural situation, but also that the syndicate proved to be a ready-organized body capable of taking over the functions of local government. In Andalusian villages, "participatory democracy" was an accomplished fact with total involvement in the discussion of local affairs, with voting and enforcement of resolutions under the control of the village's own leading men.

More recently, at the start of the Civil War in 1936, the traditional desire for self-government and local independence, which is always lying close to the surface in rural Spain, was observed to break through as soon as the political apparatus began to wither away. The first step was usually the abolition or destruction of all the tools, symbols, and agents of higher government—for example, money—which represented the power and the resources of the outside world. The archives, proof of the status quo ante in so many legal and economic affairs, especially relating to land ownership, had to be burned, removing the temptation for some future central power to come back and start all over again. The police, it goes without saying, were locked up, chased out, or killed.

The next step was to continue to till the land, but now for the collective good, rewarding each family head, not with money, but with coupons appropriate to the size of his family. The village committee would perform the marriages, judge transgressors, and so on and suppress the use of luxuries, such as liquor, tobacco, and coffee, as already noted.

The last formal elaboration of the charter for the Spanish anarchists' dream was promulgated in the early days of the Civil War at their Congress in Zaragoza. The resolution reiterated the determination to abolish private property, state authority, and classes. Anarchist economy required that the necessities of life be exchanged between free associations of workers' syndicates. Social control was to be achieved by each commune electing committees to deal with agriculture, hygiene, culture, discipline, and production. Production was to be subject to daily discussions and policies to be approved by communal assemblies. Intercommunal problems were to be taken to regional federations. There was to be a mass campaign against illiteracy. But the Spanish anarchists were never to find out if they could sustain their ideas over a long period, for within a year they had to conform to Communist control and within three they had both suffered military defeat at the hands of Franco.

Joll (1969: 223) saw 1937 as marking "the end of anarchism as a serious political force." But insofar as the coherent complex of particular ideas, contained in what came to be known on an intellectual level as Anarchism, was already an ancient tradition, it continued and is practiced to this day. The complex is not a mirror image of any individual's version of what is meant by Anarchism, but then each explicit version was flavored with its particular owner's idiosyncracies and prejudices: Proudhon's concerned property and religion; Bakunin's were the state and conspiratorial cadres against it; the American Emma Goldman's prize concern was with the equality of women. When the idea came from Bakunin, through his emissary Malatesta, to the apostles who were to carry it to the villagers of Andalusia, it may have contained such notions of free love and abortion as might have been suited to a northern European urban proletariat. If it did, it fell on deaf ears as not conforming to the local, contemporary system of values: Andalusian men were exhorted to love their wives and were firmly married to them. In another environment, such practices might well be accepted naturally as indivisible features of the libertarian creed.

As we know from cultural studies, the diffusion of cultural traits and social systems does not guarantee the acceptance of every part of these items: the environment and the preexisting system of values of the lost society will accept and perhaps magnify out of all recognition this or that aspect and ignore some other. Usually, however, the essence and the more important integrating features remain. Each community that was exposed to the acratic creed needed to resolve for itself what it understood by each of the crucial aspects. What was liberty? How much of it was to be extended to each individual? What was government, and who was to exercise it locally? How far should the collective ownership of all resources be taken? When was religion slavery to some external entity, and when was it part of local experience? What was a luxury and what a necessity? Beneath the overarching belief in libertarian collectivism, each community was to pick its own path.

One part of the world in which social Anarchism is practiced in a manner that recalls its ancient past is Mexico. Before the conquest of the Aztec confederation by the Spaniards each rural community in the valley of Mexico had a local system of social control nurtured by the individual exploitation of collectively owned land. Even before the Spanish conquest, the pristine liberty of Indian villagers had been eroded by the division of labor in an emerging, oriental-type civilization, in which a military hierarchy and the great institutions of the state were forcibly supported by the tribute of the free villages and the labor of serflike workers bound to their overlords' lands. With the introduction of draft animals and therefore more efficient ploughing methods, hitherto unused land was put to use to enrich the conquerors; a process of cornering land into large, privately owned estates thus gathered speed into the twentieth century. The process did not stop when all land was in use; no means were ignored to acquire title to government land, church land, and land of the remaining free villages.

At saturation point in 1913, the Indian peasants of Mexico overtook a political rebellion, which had already overthrown the long-term dictatorship of Porfirio Díaz, and turned it into a social revolution with the specifically anarchist war-cry of "Land and Liberty." The peasant leader in Mexico, Emiliano

Zapata, can be linked tenuously through Flores Magón (Horowitz, 1964: 484) and through the International Workers of the World movement in the United States back to Bakunin; but Zapata's principal inspiration was the traditional self-supporting and self-regulating village of the Indian past. Although urban progressives have not entirely carried out the reforms as he might have wished, the peasants for whom he won them act as if they had; today many Mexican villages enjoy a measure of autonomy and economic independence which they may not have experienced since before the reign of Moctezuma.

Postrevolutionary Anarchism

There are three topics within which one may seek the consequences of a hypothesis which suggests that Mexican villages can be understood as practising de facto, if not de jure, Anarchism: the first and basic topic is authority within the village; the second is the economic system which is characteristic of the village; and the third is the system of beliefs which governs the interpersonal relationships within the community. Within and without the Mexican highland village, there is on the one hand a stubborn sense of independence about absolute autonomy concerning its own lifeway which resides in the village, and on the other a recognition by functionaries of the very real existence of that autonomy. To start with, urban institutions and semi-urban officials who need to negotiate with the villages do not as a rule order compliance with regulations or admittance of visitors: they suggest, point out, and request. Occasionally some event of national importance needs attention, such as a census: the village authorities carry it out themselves, having been persuaded of its usefulness and innocuous character. National functionaries, however, who lean too hard or fail to prepare the ground for other well-meaning official measures may find that their enthusiasm is self-defeating. For example, plans by health departments to vaccinate village dogs against rabies may end in frustration, unless they can be carried out at no cost to the villagers. Measures to counteract soil erosion may end in violence if the mountain woodcutters concerned have no other work to turn to. The suppression of unhygienic open-air foodstalls by progessive state authorities needs to be preceded by the provision of alternative facilities and employment if it is not to lead to civil unrest. It is not that Mexican villagers are particularly reactionary or unable to appreciate the benefits of modernization; there is a right and a wrong way of approaching and convincing autonomous groups with long memories of exploitation in the past. Some Mexican functionaries have a talent for it and some do not.

Administrative control of Mexican highland villages is exercised by elected committees whose tenure of office varies from one to three years. The committees are comprised of the usual offices of president, secretary, and treasurer, and those who fill them are chosen from the leading families; not everyone gets an equal number of turns, despite the sometimes arduous nature of the tasks. Since there are other controls that rectify material advantages which may be gained from possession of an office, formal election is sometimes a formality: the acceptable and willing candidates are not often exposed to the risks of a vote. This does not vitiate the essentially democratic nature of the system: it merely underscores the emphasis laid upon cooperation and communal service *(cargo)* as a prestigious duty rather than as a prize to be gained or as the outcome of a conflict of interests. The act of giving money toward some communal enterprise is actually called *"co-operación,"* so the cooperation afforded in the service of the community is recognized as entailing more giving than getting. Service on a village committee certainly affords opportunities to indicate one's prestige in an environment that provides few material means for doing so.

The village committee which first comes to mind in the post-Revolutionary context is the commission for collectively owned land *(Comisariado Ejidal).* It allocates usufruct of parcels of land to members of the village entitled to it; it administers communally owned implements such as the *ejido* tractor; it exploits any resource which may exist within the confines of the ejido, such as a sand-mine; it regulates the nonarable use of the ejido, such as housing extensions or grazing upon the stubble in the fallow season; finally it cooperates with another committee over an archaic institution called the "school parcel of land." The provision of a parcel of land for the agricultural education of the village children and for the financial support of the school is redolent of both pre-Conquest practice and modern anarchist dogma. The Aztec federation's economic system not only used private and communal land, but it also applied "public" land to the support of such institutions as temples, palaces, and the army. The training of youth was partly carried out by the priests in the temples; it would not be unreasonable to suppose that the specialist military instructor *(teachcauh)* and his "song house" *(cuicalli),* where the remainder of the training took place, were similarly supported.

On the other hand, great emphasis was laid upon the provision of universal education by the European anarchists, and a measure of self-help in education was a feature of the Andalusian villages that came under their influence. In Mexico, not only is there a genuine recognition of the benefits of education among the villagers but a real concern for the welfare of the primary schools which are invariably built by the collective labor of the able-bodied men. In one respect, the Comisariado Ejidal does not follow through the peculiarly acratic optimism and faith in the perfectibility of man of the anarchists: a "shadow" commission is required by national agrarian law to be chosen by the minority vote of the *ejidatarios.* This vigilance commission is intended to ensure that the executive commission carried out its duties properly. The practice possibly arises from the curious nineteenth-century habit of some North American republics of electing to the vice presidency the losing candidate for the presidency. The virtues and vices of such a system lose much of their dynamic potential in the fact-to-face situation of small rural communities, but this does not seem to disturb unduly the villages' economic effectiveness.

To finance the primary school, there is a Parent/Teacher Association *(Sociedad de Padres de Familia);* this also co-operates with the Ejido Commission over the school parcel. Their control over the village teacher, who may be the only outsider residing in the village, will depend upon the character and idiosyncracies of the latter. He or she is a person of great prestige, meriting the universal title of Master. The teacher may feel himself in competition with the visiting priest for the hearts and minds of not only the children but also their parents; often he may be of extreme left-wing views and an unbeliever. Nevertheless, the most extreme teacher is unlikely to prejudice his chance at influence in the village by manifesting such views: when the image of the patron saint passes by, the schoolteacher will be found on his knees with the ethnographer and everyone else. While this discloses the coercive character of the village culture, it also shows the independence of the village from the national authority, for, in Mexico, religious processions are prohibited by law. As Brenan has pointed out so engagingly, libertarianism is concerned only with freedom from external authority, not internal authority. What if one of the Andalusian villagers had not wanted to conform to some part of anarchist practice? The anarchist was likely to have commented: "Why then he is one of *los malos, los perversos. . . .* A bullet in the head for this *compañero*—without hate, of course, without hate. He can smoke a last cigarette before dying. After all, *compañero,* death is nothing" (Brenan, 1950: 194).

Mexican Rural Officials

The Chapel Council *(Comité del Patronato)* organizes feast-days, the soliciting of contributions, and the arrangements for collective visits and other pilgrimages. Any religious activity, of course, contravenes one of the most cherished tenets of formal nineteenth-century Anarchism. There are grounds, however, for regarding the "folk Catholicism," which is generally agreed to be a characteristic of Mexican villages, as not being related to an external religious hierarchy and system, but as being a localized complex of beliefs and practices for which a visiting priest is *sometimes* necessary. Certainly no Mexican priest who is kept scurrying between six or seven mountain villages is in any position to enforce strict compliance with dogma or to attend every occasion for ritual; each house has its domestic altar and its religious idiosyncracies, and the village chapel has perhaps several shrines in constant use by suppliants. Villagers are permitted by their fellows to vary in the quantity and quality of their piety according to their needs and means. There is only one minimal standard: that no one within the community publicly demonstrate his disbelief; he who does so, whatever his power and position, is likely to find himself thrown into the village lockup; and he will be put there by the voluntary security patrol, comprised of three male adult villagers, different ones for every night of the month. With which we return to the solid purity of anarchist doctrine.

Mexican rural religion, however, is not merely a matter of individual communion with a favorite deity: there are collective responsibilities toward the perhaps several superhuman patrons of any small village. These take the form of the celebration of the anniversary of each particular saint, which will also be the anniversary of the birth, on and around that date, of a number of the members of the village. But saints' feast-days also serve a more purely social and egalitarian function. The provision of a banquet, to which the whole village is nominally invited, is a very expensive affair, for which a Mexican peasant may take up to eight years to save. Success in marketing, or the equally observable good fortune in the accretion to a small domestic herd, will attract an invitation to act as a collective feast-day host *(mayordomo, -a)* next year. Thus is the socialist prophecy fulfilled in rural Mexico: "from each according to his ability." It is an occasion, moreover, when economic equality of the sexes can be celebrated in a divided way: men and women both market their products, but women act as mayordomas for female saints and men for male ones.

The most ancient committee, perhaps, of those villages which have inherited pre-Conquest irrigation systems, is that of the Society of (water-) Users *(Sociedad de Usuarios).* Although there are federal laws governing all waters belonging to the nation, users of small traditional systems are permitted to frame their own regulations and apply their own minor sanctions to infractions of these. In practice, the whole and the parts of a society of water-users are usually both greater and smaller than the community of a single village: i.e., two, three, or more villages may share the use of a main channel, which may be more than 15 kilometers long; and within one village only one distribution channel and its dependent clan will get water at any one time. So that the Water-board committee *(Junta de Aguas)* elected by the several villages appoints from among its own members distributor-judges *(Jueces)* for each village and together they resolve conflicts, ration the water *(tanda),* supervise the repairs and upkeep, and withhold water from transgressors.

The village committee which perhaps conforms most closely to the ideals of formal nineteenth-century anarchists is one that all of them have: this is the Moral, Civic and Material Improvements Junta, better known by its key-word, Improvements *(Mejoras).* Its province is intervillage cooperation on such projects as roads, markets, and communications and the building, within its own village, of school, bathhouse, walls, paths, and so on. The work for all these committees, when required, is carred out in turn by the able-bodied men. There has been a suggestion that collective labor, reported for Mexican peasants in 1926, was a fading institution by 1943. I observed it in full working order in 1965 and 1970, and it seems to me to be the basic expression of the ethos of the highland Mexican. The description of the organizational features of a Mexican village derives from more general studies of peasant life in the state of Mexico carried out by me during these two years under the auspices of the Wenner-Gren Foundation for Anthropological Research and the Australian Research Grants Committee respectively. Apart from rural social organization, other aspects of contemporary social structure and the manner in which the present lifeway of the peasant had developed were studied for a total of seventeen months in the field. The second period of fieldwork included a tally of the frequency and of the specific years in which individual members of a particular village had participated in the various committees.

The last and perhaps most prestigious group of officials is that of the three delegates. In the matters of good order, representation both administrative and ceremonial, census-taking and other paperwork, and permission to enter the village, the delegates are responsible to their people. The delegates also interpose themselves between their people and an unsafe and puzzling world outside. A delegate's principal dilemma is that, whereas his people consider him their delegate to the world outside the village, the officials of the world outside may regard him as responsible to the national power for the good behavior of the people he represents. If he manages to maintain local independence without attracting intervention, he will be asked to be a delegate again.

Conclusion

It has been well noted that the problem of Anarchism is that it is a system difficult to operate above the level of a small, self-sufficient community; even such an enclosed society as a factory run on anarchistic lines must compromise its economic principles unless it has control of its sources of raw materials. On the other hand, some see "a free association of free communities" as eventually needing some external arbiter. Others believe that man's problems are not to be solved by an introspective return to past forms but by a positive and scientific process of manipulated change and improvement. The Mexican Revolution was largely a clash between a concern for ancient values on the part of the vast Indian majority and a trust in modern solutions which tended to forget the cost of those solutions to human beings. This was not far removed from the revulsion against the tyranny of machines and the inhumanity of the state apparatus that inspired the European anarchists.

Whereas Europe has generally opted for an "either/or" solution to the clash between nostalgia and modernity, Mexico seems to have accepted a compromise: in the countryside where it can be a viable system, a form of social Anarchism suited to the Mexican cultural heritage has remained entrenched, protected by statute against the assaults of individualistic ambition. In the urban context, where Anarchism would in any case have been difficult to maintain, the complexity of an industrial national life has been controlled and guided by a monolithic central authority. The two parts of Mexican society live in an uneasy but respectful symbiosis; on the face of it, the urban sectors appear to have the better part of the arrangement. One might imagine, however, that the peasant is more free: he has the freedom to change his environment to that of the city; the city-dweller has to remain in thrall to his machines, who are his masters.

REFERENCES

BRENAN, G. (1950) The Spanish Labrynith. Cambridge, Eng.: Cambridge Univ. Press.

FANON, F. (1965) The Wretched of the Earth. London: McKinnon & Kee.

HOROWITZ, I. L. [ed.] (1964) The Anarchists. New York: Dell.

JOLL, J. (1969) The Anarchists. London: Methuen.

SCOTT, R. E. (1964) Mexican Government in Transition. Urbana: Univ. of Illinois Press.

"This is an intellectually stimulating book. Its systematic treatment of problems in international organization politics is refreshing. It is well written and clearly argued."

—Annals of the American Academy of Political and Social Science

THE MAJORITY OF ONE

Towards a Theory of Regional Compatibility

by MINERVA M. ETZIONI, *with a Preface by* RICHARD A. FALK

This book is a study of relations established over the last twenty years in the handling of political and security matters between a universal and a regional international organization——the United Nations and the Organization of American States. The unusual quality of this particular regional organization is expressed in the Latin American quotation that the OAS is governed by "the majority of one . . . the minority of twenty"—a reflection of the strength of United States influence.

"The Majority of One is an illuminating study in the use of regional institutions as a comtemporary vehicle of great-power diplomacy. The book reveals, in its analysis of principal incidents of peaceful settlement and enforcement, the extent to which American foreign-policy-makers have succeeded in using the OAS to legitimate more or less unilateral uses of force in the Western Hemisphere in such a fashion as to contradict UN purposes and to defeat the indended jurisdiction of the world organization." ——from the Preface by RICHARD A. FALK

Table of Contents

Preface by RICHARD A. FALK
I. Towards a New Theory of International Organization
II. Regional and Universal Forces at the Founding of the United Nations
III. The United Nations Charter: *Regional and Universal Clauses*
IV. The Cold War and the Rise of Incompatible Regionalism: *Tendencies After San Francisco*
V. Incompatibility in the Peaceful Settlement of Disputes at the Regional Level
VI. Incompatibility in the Adoption of Enforcement Action at the Regional Level

ISBN 0-8039-0042-2 **1969** **238 pages** **$7.50**
L.C. 78-84220 **Market: World**

SAGE PUBLICATIONS, INC.
275 S. Beverly Dr. / Beverly Hills, CA. 90212

SAGE PUBLICATIONS LTD
44 Hatton Garden, London E C 1

TAKASHI MAEYAMA
Department of Anthropology
Cornell University
Ithaca, New York

ANCESTOR, EMPEROR, AND IMMIGRANT

Religion and Group Identification of the Japanese in Rural Brazil (1908-1950)

"The oldest," said the ancient Aryas, "was begotten for the accomplishment of the duty due the ancestors: the others are the fruit of love."
–Fustel de Coulanges (1901: 108)

The early 1950s mark a turning-point in the history of religious movements among the Japanese minority in Brazil. Various religious groups, particularly certain Buddhist sects and the so-called "new religions" of Japan for the first time undertook active proselytization through organized propaganda and missionary activities. The following are representative types of these religious groups:

(1) those which had been transplanted from Japan to Brazil by Japanese immigrants in the period before World War II and immediately after: *Honmon Butsuryū Shū* (a Buddhist sect), *Tenri-kyō, Ōmoto,* and *Seichō-no-Ie* (all three new religions), and the like;

(2) Buddhist sects which began to try to organize their "potential adherents" among the Japanese on the basis of household religious affiliation, regardless of how tenuous or how thoroughly lapsed;

(3) those which had grown rapidly in postwar Japan and extended their propagation activities overseas: new religions like *Sekai Kyūsei Kyō, P.L. Kyōdan,* and so on;

(4) those which originated with the Japanese minority in Brazil on the basis of traditional Japanese folk beliefs: Nossa Senhora de Kannon (Our Lady of Kannon, or *Sei Kannon Shū Hakkoku Kannon Dō), Kaminoya Yaoyorozu-kyō, Fudō Myōō, Shinrei-kyō,* and the like;

(5) *Umbanda,* a syncretic fusion of African cults, Catholicism, and spiritism.

Throughout the 1960s, all these religious movements became increasingly active and gained more and more followers. The pace of development is especially remarkable among the new religions such as *Seichō-no-Ie, Sōka Gakkai,*[1] *P.L. Kyōdan,* and *Sekai Kyūsei Kyō.*[2]

Japanese immigration to Brazil started officially in 1908, and the total number of immigrants came to 188,615 by the time it ceased with the outbreak of World War II (IBGE, 1954: 59). Nevertheless, it is not too much to say that in spite of this very large number, there was hardly any organized religious activity among the immigrants until around 1950, with the exception of Catholicism, the quasi-national religion of Brazil.

What explains the activation of religious movements at this particular period after forty years' stagnation? What does this forty years' stagnation mean? Why are these "Japanese religions" apparently becoming increasingly popular among Japanese immigrants and their descendants, who are usually considered to have been "successful" in their rapid acculturation and assimilation to the Brazilian sociocultural context?

The meaning of the period around 1950 for the Japanese minority in Brazil may be sketched briefly as follows: the defeat of Japan in World War II precipitated an immediate and intense psychological and social crisis in the immigrant community, which consequently split into two major factions. One was the *make-gumi* (defeat group) which openly acknowledged Japan's loss of the war, and the other the *kachi-gumi* (victory group) which denied that Japan had been defeated and even insisted that it had won a glorious victory *(dai shōri).* There were a few marginal groups which maintained a position somewhere between these two. The conflict among these groups often was openly manifested in physical violence, typified by the fanatic terrorism of the secret society *Shindō Remmei* (League of the Way of the Subjects) which achieved worldwide notoriety at the time. It was only in the 1950s that this open conflict gradually subsided into latent psychological hostility.

It was also not until this period that normal communications between the two countries were resumed, with the result that the real conditions in postwar Japan came to be understood by the majority of Japanese in Brazil. Furthermore, it was in this period that a growing number of Japanese immigrants became fully aware of the fact that they had in reality put down roots in Brazil, notwithstanding their firm expression of intention to "return home." As a result, they slowly came to abandon the notion completely. In other words, the series of "Back to Japan" movements, of which the terrorism of the Shindō Remmei is an example, may be seen as the last direct manifestation of "anti-acculturationism" against the growing trend of assimilation and accommodation to Brazilian society.

With respect to wider socioeconomic conditions, Brazil and other Latin American countries had greatly increased their economic and political autonomy during World War II while the United States and European powers had been devoting all their energies to the conflict. Brazil enjoyed economic prosperity due to the war. In particular, agricultural products commanded high prices in world markets for a long period, which greatly enhanced the prospects for upward mobility of the Japanese immigrants, about 90 percent of whom were then living in rural areas. At the same time, industrialization and urbanization were proceeding rapidly in the São Paulo metropolitan region, and, as a consequence, a considerable part of the Japanese population was taking up urban residence, especially in the city of São Paulo. In short, the great majority of the Japanese had risen or were rising into the middle classes in both the rural and urban areas of southern Brazil.

With respect to acculturation, there is a study conducted by Willems and Saito (1947) concerning the problem of in-group conflict after the defeat of Japan. It attempts to interpret the subject in terms of cultural shock of the immigrants at the sociopsychological level, particularly with regard to the assimilationist policy toward foreign immigrants adopted by the Vargas regime during the period of the *Estado Novo* (the New State) after 1937. Later, the present author studied how these direct manifestations of the reaction against assimilation had been transformed into latent, internalized behavior, particularly at the moral and religious levels which lead to the formation of several exclusive religious organizations. His concern was with the normalization of the psychological situation of the immigrants and mobility within the class stratification (Maeyama, 1967: 260-280).

Although there are some studies of the Japanese minority in Brazil from the acculturation point of view, very few deal with the topic in the context of Brazilian social stratification. There is no study which approaches the topic with reference to urban social class structure, in part because research on Brazilian society itself in this respect has been initiated only in recent years.

The main concern of the author lies in the relationship between religious behavior and class differentiation. To be more specific, he is concerned with correlation of the rise of the religious movements of the early 1950s with the fact that the Japanese had risen into the middle classes during the preceding decade. It must be asked if the phenomenon is the result of the fact that the Japanese began to show the pattern of behavior and ideology typically associated with the middle classes.

In this short essay, it is not possible fully to analyze class differentiation and its relationship to religious movements. We shall be concerned chiefly with the religious attitudes of the Japanese before their rise into the middle classes, in particular with the period of religious stagnation and its causes. Needless to say, a thorough consideration of this period provides an indispensable background to the study of the religious movements themselves. The paper deals with the historical background of the Japanese in Brazil in terms of religion, and the period in question is that before 1950, especially the early 1930s.

Social Background of the Immigrants

For the three decades from the beginning of Japanese immigration until World War II, about 90 percent of the Japanese in Brazil lived in the state of São Paulo (Comissão de Recenseamento da Colônia Japonêsa, 1964: 259). The 1934 census of the state of São Paulo shows that 91.7 percent of the Japanese residents of the state lived in the rural areas and 8.3 percent in urban centers. In consequence, the main object of the following discussion is the rural population in the state of São Paulo (Govêrno de Estado de São Paulo, 1939: 181). Let us first consider their status in agricultural activities during the period in question.[3] In 1932, 27.2 percent of the rural Japanese (including the very few who had been born in Brazil) were landowners, 19.9 percent tenant farmers, 15.3 percent sharecroppers *(parceiros)* and 37.1 percent rural wage laborers *(colonos)* (Comissão de Recenseamento de Colônia Japonêsa, 1964: 314). In this period, many of the tenant farmers and sharecroppers were characterized by their extreme dependency on landowners and consequently share some of the attributes of wage laborers. Moreover, most of the Japanese landed farmers had acquired their lands only recently in the remote virgin forests of the pioneer regions, land which they were still struggling to bring under productive cultivation. Because most of them had bought land of the cheapest category, they were generally located at some distance from markets. A careful check of the advertisements for lotted lands carried in the *Burajiru Jihō* (Notícias do Brasil), a Japanese newspaper in São Paulo in the early 1930s, shows that the standard price for one *alqueire* (2.5 hectares) was 300 to 800 *mil reis* (U.S. $36 to 96 in 1930), and furthermore that it was possible to make only a small down payment (or none at all, in which case payments were started only after the first harvest) followed by three- to five-year installment payments. It may be said, therefore, that this was the period in which the great majority of the Japanese were essentially rural laborers, and a considerable number of them were in the transitional stage to the middle classes.

Considerably more attention will be paid to the social structure of rural Japan, which is the "home" of the immigrants, the pattern of emigration, and Japanese religious beliefs, than to the social structure and religion of the host country for the following reasons: (1) the majority of the immigrants had only recently arrived by the period in question–that is, about 75 percent of the prewar immigrants came to Brazil during the decade after 1925; and (2) those who were living on the big coffee plantations *(fazendas)* as *colonos* were new immigrants, and those who were sharecroppers, tenant and landed farmers usually had settled in groups in the pioneering fringes, where Brazilian communities, representing the host society, were only vaguely formed, with the result that the ethnic Japanese communities were relatively isolated, permitting their inhabitants to preserve Japanese institutions.

How may the immigrant be characterized sociologically? To become an emigrant, an individual means to separate himself from the network of the social structure of his home society. The English term "the uprooted" is a particularly apt one to describe the emigrant. To be an immigrant, on the other hand, means that the uprooted, holding the value system of the home society acquired through socialization, is put within the social network of a different society. As an immigrant, he comes into contact with a different value system, to which he is expected to adapt himself.

As we have shown above, the prewar Japanese immigrants in rural São Paulo experienced relatively limited contacts with the Brazilian value system, at least until the early 1930s. As for the uprootedness and severance of sociocultural roots at emigration, it was not thoroughgoing, at least on the level of their consciousness, as we shall see below.

Although immigrants leave home with their "cultural baggage," they do not necessarily intend to reconstruct everything based on their original value system even if the host society permits them to do so. They will display behavior patterns somewhat different from those of the home society and of their statuses there, even with minimal contact with different value systems, since they are definitely conditioned, through migration (either temporary or permanent), by factors which are structurally and environmentally different from those they would have experienced had they remained in their home society. In order to account for this, we have to examine how an individual or a group of individuals is transformed from a normal component of home society into an emigrant.

Sociologically speaking, from what institutions do the Japanese emigrants separate themselves when they leave their home society? For most, the home society is a rural community. The Japanese rural community is made up of hamlets (*mura* or *buraku*), the primary group whose basic constituent unit is the household *(ie)*.[4] The individual is not an independent unit in the hamlet setting as far as the ideal type in traditional Japan is concerned. He is significant only as a member of his ie.

There are three major types of inter-ie groupings–*dōzoku, shinrui kankei,* and *kumi*–which are not necessarily subsystems of a community. The dōzoku is a local group formed on the basis of the relationship between the *honke* (the main ie) and its *bunke* (the branch ie), the core of which is the patrilineal kinship tie. The shinrui kankei is a bilateral relationship of kinsmen and affines, not a localized group. A kumi is a local corporate group of neighboring ie which are not tied by main and branch ie relationships. A kumi is by nature an egalitarian organization; a dōzoku, on the other hand, is an inegalitarian one. These relationships overlap greatly in most of the cases, forming a complex network (Ariga, 1954). It is from these rural institutions that Japanese emigrants separate themselves. Above all, both ie and dōzoku are of particular importance with respect to their religious attitudes.

The separation of immigrants from these institutions may be more clearly understood when it is considered with respect to the pattern of urbanization of the Japanese rural population, since they are two facets of the same phenomenon. (No specific study on emigration in this respect is known to the author, but the studies of urbanization sometimes deal with this topic.) Urbanization and emigration of the rural population have shown a peculiar pattern due to the unique characteristics of Japanese capitalism and the above-mentioned rural social structure.

Japanese rural society has been characterized by small-scale farming (Ouchi, 1952: 167-169), parallel to which the dōzoku system has developed, especially in the industrially underdeveloped areas of Japan during the Tokugawa and Meiji periods (Nakane, 1967: 119-122). The branch ie were socioeconomically dependent on the landowners, who were the main ie in the context of the dōzoku system, in which a paternalistic relationship of superordination and subordination was dominant. Under the impact of the growth of a cash economy and industrialization, nonsuccessors, especially of the small-farmer ie, were liable to migrate to urban centers. The demand for an industrial labor force, however, was not constant enough to create a true proletariat living permanently in the cities, because of the character of Japanese capitalism. The limited size of domestic and foreign markets and the suddenness of the transition into the stage of monopolistic capitalism on the basis of the importation of highly developed technology are the chief causes of the "backwardness" of Japanese capitalism in the international context (Ouchi, 1952: 172-174). Consequently, urban laborers ordinarily did not cut their roots in the rural institutions for any considerable period of time. Wage laborers in the cities were by and large *dekasegi* (seasonal or sojourner labor force) and *kengyō* (side employment) who, to use Okōchi's expression, kept "one foot in agriculture" (Okōchi, 1952: 216).

Okōchi and his followers, analyzing the pattern of dekasegi, which is essentially by-employment and a secondary source of cash income, and the depressed wage-scale and labor unionism of Japanese industries, showed that the relationship between urban-dwelling laborers and their "home" ie in the rural area was never completely severed. These people were expected to return eventually to their agricultural roles, or to return "home." Urban laborers psychologically were always prepared to return home whenever faced with some difficulty such as unemployment, illness, or economic depression. Thus, the social security of both the urban laborers and the rural surplus population inhered in the mechanism of rural institutions. Concerning this aspect of social security, the paternalistic relationships dominant in ie and dōzoku organizations had important functions. (Of course, the author cannot deny the fact that the paternalistic relationship in somewhat different form obtains between urban employer and employee as well. This issue is not discussed here simply because the focus is on the rural areas.)

As for the patterns and motivations of migration, there appears to be no basic difference between internal urbanization and overseas emigration. To some extent the pattern of belongingness of the uprooted to their home society was similar at least in their perceptions, although the factors of geographic distance, political barriers, and cultural contacts came to differentiate them in the course of time. (This statement is the result of observations by the author in Brazil.) It is regrettable that we have no good data on the immigrants who returned from Brazil to Japan. A single clue is found in the continuing records kept by an immigrant named Kumaki Nakao over a period of 50 years respecting a group of immigrants composed initially of 40 families (139 individuals) from their arrival to Brazil in 1914. During the first 20 years, 23 individuals returned to Japan, 14 of them because of "success," and 9 because of "failure" (Saito, 1961: 209). This high proportion of "failed" *(rakugo)* returned immigrants offers, even if indirectly, good evidence of the nature of the relationship between the immigrants and their "home."[5] It should be noted also that a considerable number of immigrants had left their children in the care of their relatives in Japan. This must have seemed a natural course of conduct for those who never doubted that they would return home after saving a certain sum of money.

In modern rural Japan, further subdivision of lands has become almost impossible. The customary practice of establishing branch ie with a portion of land within the same territory as the main ie has therefore become less and less likely. Thus primogeniture and single-heir inheritance has been further emphasized. The ie complex, including property, business, and the ritual of ancestor worship, is inherited exclusively by a single successor, usually the eldest son. The nonsuccessors are spun off from their ie as a surplus labor force, usually leaving the community without taking any share of the property. (Educational costs, for example, came to replace a share of the property itself.) Sharing no property, they are instead potential claimants of support on occasions when they encounter some difficulty. Furthermore, they are potential legal successors should the eldest brother die or defect. (Their home may in turn make the same claim to some extent whenever in some difficulty.)

They continue to maintain some relationshp with, and a sense of belonging to their home, even if they do not actually return there. Being simply "the fruit of love," they do not inherit any ritual objects connected with ancestor worship. They are expected to participate in the religious observance at the eldest brother's ie, having neither object nor place for worship until someone of their own ie dies. The strong attachment of the immigrants to Japan, their obstinate desire to return home, and their continuing effort to send money home may be accounted for, in part, in this way. Large advertisements of the Rio de Janeiro branch of the Yokohama Specie Bank respecting *"kyōri sōkin"* (literally "sending money home"; i.e., remittances) appeared daily in the Japanese newspapers in the prewar period. Returning home with one's fortune in "glory" *(nishiki o kazaru)* and returning home failed and exhausted *(rakugo suru),* seeking refuge, are two different manifestations of the same behavior pattern.

According to research conducted by Shungorō Wako in 1938 respecting 12,000 Japanese families living in the states of São Paulo and Mato Grosso (virtually all in the former), the family heads, including some born in Brazil, replied as follows to the questions about their hopes and plans: 85 percent of them wanted to return home, 10 percent planned to stay permanently in Brazil, and 5 percent were still undecided (Wako, 1939: 1). There were some nisei (born in Brazil) who wanted to "return home," that is, to a Japan they had never seen. In this respect, we should not overlook the obvious influences of the atmosphere of rising nationalism among the Japanese in Brazil which was attributable to the political situation of fascist Japan. Even disregarding this point, however, there is no doubt that they sincerely wanted to return eventually. There is another piece of research on the same topic conducted by Seiichi Izumi (1954: 12) in 1952. He reports that the initial ideas of the immigrants upon their arrival in Brazil were the following: 70 percent wanted to return home; 11.1 percent to stay in Brazil; and the rest (18.9 percent) unknown (or better, inapplicable, because most were those who had arrived too young to have any opinion and those who had been born in Brazil).

In short, the immigrants felt that they were resident in Brazil only provisionally, considering themselves to be absentee members of their home communities, but not part of Brazilian society. They felt themselves only temporarily away from the rights and duties in their original communities. They considered themselves "sojourners" *(zairyū-min)* or "wayfarers" *(tabi-bito)* in Brazil with a specific aim, the fulfillment of which would naturally end in their leaving the country. They did not psychologically belong to the host society, and consequently they were willing to some extent to "respect the rules" in the "host house," because they were "under the care of" *(sewa ni natte iru)* the Brazilians. This means that they perceived their situation in terms of the ie principle.

The Japanese immigrants used to say: "We left our home in someone's care during our absence. We came here leaving everything behind: ie, relatives, ancestors *(hotoke)* and gods *(kami)*".

Religious Attitudes

From 1918 until the end of World War II, the Japanese Ministry of Foreign Affairs prohibited missionaries, with the exception of Catholic priests, to go to Brazil. It is reported that some of the emigrants were forced to leave on record their written promise not to proselytize in Brazil (Tenri-kyō Burajiru Dendōchō, 1958: 47). It was the Japanese consul in Brazil who was ultimately responsible for this policy (Noda, 1930: 476-477), which was a reaction to anti-Japanese activities on the part of Brazilians. More basically, it reflects the visible and invisible pressure from the masses of the dominant society over the minority. The major reason, however, that such a policy remained in force for decades, without protest on anyone's part, must lie in the fact that very few immigrants were interested in religious activities while resident in foreign lands.

For example, in 1932, when four Japanese were jailed by the Brazilian officials as protection from being lynched at Triângulo Mineiro, Minas Gerais, because of their active proselytization to Omoto-kyō among Catholic Brazilians, the following editorial appeared in one of the most influential Japanese-language newspapers in São Paulo:

> Since Catholicism is the de facto official religion of Brazil, any propagation of other religions should be restrained. We have kept warning repeatedly, both in writing and in speech, that we the Japanese, who are to emigrate more and more to Brazil and who consequently have to promote goodwill between the two countries, Japan and Brazil, must definitely refrain from propagating any religion other than Catholicism or from any similar activities, and must be all the more careful not to make the Brazilians suspicious and anxious about religious matters [Burajiru Jihō, 1932a].

Here we can see the typical attitude of a minority group under social pressure by a dominant group. Also expressed is the religious attitude of the Japanese, who had not brought their ie and its correlative ancestor worship to their temporary residences.

For Japanese, the most common religious practices are those connected with ancestor worship. Ancestors are inseparable from ie, and ancestor worship cannot be considered apart from ie organization. According to Kunio Yanagida, in traditional Japanese folk belief "no matter what else they may be, ancestors are something to be worshipped, and moreover they are souls who are worshipped only in their *ie,* that is to say, ancestors are something necessarily bound up inextricably in the *ie*" (Yanagida, 1962: 7). Thus, ancestors are bound exclusively to members of the same ie, serving an integrative function for the group. A new ie is established by ie branching *(bunke),* which tends to divide ancestors into two categories. Any individual is likely to have two types of ancestors according to the most common view: (a) those who belong to ego's ie and are the object of the cult of dead there—that is, the founder and the deceased members of the ie; and (b) those of his main ie *(honke).* Ancestors remain in the main ie, and are inherited there through primogeniture. The newly established ie does not have ancestors of type a until some of its own members die.

As Yanagida (1962) says, "Performing rituals for ancestors is not only an obligation of descendants, but originally was a right belonging to the legal successor [of the ie] and his wife." Ancestors are inherited exclusively by a single successor, accompanying the ie and its property, of which they are exclusive guardians. Furthermore the ancestor is a symbol of authority as well, and rituals for them are a *right* rather than an *obligation.* This is why nonsuccessors do not share their ancestors by bringing them into their own ie even when they obtain a portion of land at the time of ie branching. Traditionally, the nonsuccessors, establishing their own ie in the same territory, lived in socioeconomic and religious dependency on their main ie. They were obliged to participate in ancestral rites held at the main ie and regarded the ancestors of the main ie as their own. In this way, the ancestors of the main ie were viewed as those of the dōzoku itself.

In the course of time the new ie comes to have its own ancestor of type a, besides those of type b. It depends upon the degree of the socioeconomic dependency on their main ie whether they attach more importance to the ancestors of their own ie or those worshipped in the main ie (Nakane, 1967: 106). The more dependent they are socioeconomically on the main ie, the more important are the ancestors at the main ie. Thus, ancestors are symbols of authority and superiority of main ie over their branch ie in the dōzoku context, and of ie head over the members in the ie context, serving functionally to maintain the continuity of the patriarchal and paternalistic familism of ie and dōzoku organizations and further of the order of the class system where landlords (main ie) dominated the tenants and laborers (branch ie). In other words, ancestor worship had an important integrative function for the group, particularly at the ie and dōzoku levels.

Since most of the Japanese immigrants were "the fruit of love," that is, nonsuccessors of their ie, they did not inherit ancestors to be worshipped in their own house. Since they usually emigrated when very young (the average age of all the immigrants to Brazil has always been twenty; Comissão de Recenseamento de Colônia Japonêsa, 1964: 399), they did not have any religious obligation at the time of their arrival. They tended to say, "We have left our religion behind in Japan," "I have nothing to do with religion, because my brothers in Japan take care of our ancestors," and, in the cases of successors or eldest sons,[6] "I have left both house and ancestors in the charge of my parents (or brothers) during my absence." There is a group of immigrants from Okinawa who for some decades have continued to send cash contributions to the yearly festival of the tutelary deity in their home community.

The crucial point is that it was not until the immigrants had finally managed to build a fixed foundation for their productive activities, stabilize their livelihood, and consequently create a solid attachment to their real property in Brazil, that they came to realize that they were firmly fixed to the soil of Brazil. Only then did they establish their own ie there. Before that, the center of religious rites had remained in Japan, and they had not been interested in observing ancestral rites in Brazil. The immigrants commonly understood the situation in the following ways: "It is quite unnecessary for us to have any religion *(shinkō),* because we are in a foreign land" (Tenri-kyō Burajiru Dendōchō, 1958: 51), or "How can we justify bringing *our* religions into the *foreigners' ie,* which we are now dependent upon?" Being the mere "fruit of love," born into the world without any objective "reason," and having become proletarian immigrants, they had no reason to have any religion in the Japanese sense—that is, in the form of ancestor worship. Very few Buddhist temples, and almost no tutelary deity or dōzoku shrines were built in Brazil before 1950.

People do die, however, and something has to be done.

Emílio Willems (1948: 93) reported the following in this study of the acculturation of the Japanese in Brazil: "They say that when a Japanese dies, his soul goes back to Japan." Such expressions are seldom heard today, yet it can be inferred that such a view probably was not rare among the Japanese in the prewar period. Death in Brazil was to them a mere accident or misfortune, quite outside their expectations. It was called "alien death" *(kyaku shi),* which is essentially accidental and does not have any defined position in the regular cycle of life, as when a Japanese traveler dies abroad. The soul of any Japanese dying while temporarily abroad is expected to return home and join the ancestral community. A similar view seems to have been common among the immigrants.

The crucial difference between immigrants on the one hand and tourists and soldiers on the other is that the former have their families with them. If the departing soul goes "home" alone leaving his family behind on "alien soil," it must be with self-reproach and regret, because protecting one's descendants is an important duty of any ancestor. If he had established his own ie in Brazil, his soul would have remained with his bereaved family to be their guardian. Yet, as far as the departing soul is concerned, he probably had been confident that his family also would eventually return to the "homeland," and thus may have been said to have chosen to depart "a step in advance" to join their common ancestral spirits. A serious dilemma for the immigrants was that of the souls. The bereaved family prepared a homemade "provisional" ancestral tablet *(ihai)* of unpainted wood for the deceased, and performed some ancestral rites before it. However, Japanese belief does not necessarily imply that the soul ought to stay with his tablet. The soul might reside with his ancestors somewhere close to heaven, visiting his home village in Japan at the time of the Buddhist Festival of the Dead *(bon)*[7] in August, returning to the Brazilian "colony" at the time of "Brazilian bon" held on November 2, the Day of the Dead *(Os Finados)* in Catholicism. (The Buddhist bon has long been associated with this Catholic ritual in Brazil.)

Of course, it would not be strictly contradictory for the souls to go back to Japan and simultaneously to serve as guardians for, and receive memorial services from, their bereaved family in Brazil. Many of the souls would probably have chosen not to return to Japan. Although there is no good evidence, some people claim that this idea of the souls going back to Japan was never commonly discussed among them. The author thinks, however, on the basis of indirect evidence, that it is likely that the participants in funeral ceremonies speculated and talked in whispers about the fate of the soul at the wake in this way, because, traditionally, it is the time to discuss such a topic. It seems to have been the case particularly when the dead had lived without family in Brazil. (This paragraph is largely deductive and not valid as ethnographic data.)

"Brazil is five times farther from the home country than Hawaii, and the wages paid there are less than one-fifth of those in Hawaii" (Izumi, 1957: 18). The wages paid to the colonos on coffee fazendas (plantations) were usually not enough for them to save any substantial amount of money. Realizing this situation, and taking advantage of cheap land and labor, the immigrants gradually shifted their original plan of short-term gain through selling labor into the long-term one of using cheap land and laborers. Thus, they became sharecroppers, tenants, and eventually landed farmers, small producers of cash crops, such as cotton, rice, and coffee. In so doing, they gradually extended their stay in Brazil.

They commonly rented or purchased lands as a group, forming "colonies" *(shokuminchi),* a localized ethnic community. As they did not have social solidarity in terms of ie, dōzoku, and other kinship ties, they tended instead to create fictive kinship relations with other Japanese on the basis of having emigrated from the same prefecture (easily distinguishable by dialects), sailed on the same emigrants' ship, or worked on the same coffee fazenda during their first years in the alien land. These three factors tended to overlap, operating very effectively for group formation. They commonly said, "People from the same prefecture *(dōken-jin)* are one another's kinsmen," "People from the same boat *(dōsensha)* are brothers," or "We are brothers-in-arms *(senyū),* because we worked on the same fazenda, eating at the same mess *(onaji kama no meshi o kuu).*" They thus came to form groups of *shinrui zukiai* (literally "kinship relations," but usually applied only fictively), substituting these for kinship ties broken through migration.

These fictive kinship relationships were, like *kumi* and shinrui kankei in Japan, of an egalitarian nature in most of the cases. Although we lack detailed data, some evidence suggests that there were also many cases of unequal relationship between economically successful "old immigrants" *(kyū imin)* and newly arrived and uninformed "new immigrants" *(shin imin).* This is in some respects similar to the dōzoku institution's characteristic patron-client relationship. On a more formal level, kumi organizations came to be reconstructed in such forms as agricultural cooperatives, youth associations *(seinen dan* or *seinen kai),* girls' associations *(shojo kai),* and the like. Above all, the "Japanese associations" *(nihonjin kai)* were formed on the level of the local community. The organization of these localized ethnic communities was in many respects strikingly similar to that of rural communities in Japan. This relatively successful reconstruction of Japanese social organization was favored largely by the absence of any well-established Brazilian institutions in the frontier regions.

On the other hand, religious activities were put off and tended to be forgotten. Burial practices and the cult of the dead did not develop beyond a kind of "emergency treatment measure." When a person died, someone who remembered even fragments of the Buddhist sutras was brought in to offer an amateur requiem. On the anniversary of death, these men would chant some vaguely remembered verses of the sutras.[8] These nonprofessional, ready-made priests used to be found in any *shokuminchi* (colony), being called "priest-substitutes" *(bōzu gawari),* or "sutra readers" *(o-kyō yomi)*–terms possibly coined locally (for further details, see Maeyama, 1967: 93-96). Thus, these services may be seen as an extension of secular reciprocal relationships within the community, although some of the "priest-substitutes" later actually became Buddhist priests. The bereaved family would make an ancestral tablet of coarse unpainted wood, bearing in clumsy Japanese characters the secular name of the decased, the date of death, and his age. The tablet was simply placed on a table or in any small wooden box in the bedroom of the family head, creating a ready-made *butsudan* (domestic Buddhist altar) before which memorial rites were practiced. Very simple painted boxes to serve for butsudan, which later came to be manufactured for sale, are still in use in many Japanese houses.

Compared with those found in Japan, they are extremely small and simple without any decoration, reminding newcomers and visitors from Japan of toys. Keeping in mind the immigrants' attitudes toward "temporary residence," we might say that the size of the immigrants' butsudan corresponded initially to the degree of their attachment to "the alien soil," as today it does to the size of the Japanese minority group in the Brazilian population.

Immigrants in Ethnic Communities

Although they were strongly attached to their home communities on the conscious level, the immigrants were actually forming living and working groups in Brazil. Although they neglected many religious practices, they had to arrive at some consensus in forming groups. Because they came to form a community different in kind from the one they had known in Japan, they came to have a different kind of group identification.

There are different religious practices and deities (basically ancestral ones, whether fictive or latent) on each level of ie, dōzoku, local community, and to some extent the state in Japan, functioning to maintain group identification, integration, and in-group control. In Brazil, however, the ie tended to be neglected, dōzoku and kinship ties were fictive in character, and the local community was formed in terms of ethnicity. Principles of ethnic group and community soon surpassed fictive kinship relations in importance. In this way, "Japaneseness" came to be emphasized as a major principle of group identification, at least on the levels of the localized community and the Japanese minority in general. Arriving in Brazil, they became "Japanese"–that is, they came to be called "Japanese" in their daily life for the first time in their lives. They had never identified themselves as Japanese within the purely Japanese setting. Only by living among racially and culturally different peoples did they come to be "Japanese," identifying themselves as such. As the Emperor was the essential symbol of "Japaneseness" until the end of World War II, emperor worship came to replace ancestor worship in terms of group identification among the Japanese in prewar Brazil.

Emperor worship itself may be understood as a variety of ancestor worship in the broadest sense. Japan as a nation tended to be considered a patriarchal "family" with the Emperor as its head. The Emperor was said to be the "father" and the Empress the "mother" of the Japanese people by the fascist government in Japan. In this sense, Japan was to be regarded as a single ie.

This application of the ie principle to the wider society is intrinsic to the Japanese way of life and thinking which is called the "familial constitution of Japanese society" (see e.g., Kawashima, 1950: 3-25). On the basis of this Japanese behavior pattern, it is hardly surprising that the replacement of ancestor worship by emperor worship among the Japanese in Brazil took place smoothly.

In this connection, we cannot neglect the enormous influence of the Japanese fascism of the time. The bulk of the prewar immigrants came during the decade of 1926 to 1936. The immigrants of this new current, who had been to some extent "brainwashed" under the new state in Japan, tended to be called "the newcomers" *(shin imin),* as distinguished from *macaco velho* (old monkey) the old immigrants.[9] Under the fascist regime, Japan developed a pseudotheocracy emphasizing unconditional loyalty to the Emperor. This naturally affected the nature of emperor worship among the Japanese in Brazil.

The center of emperor worship in any Japanese community in Brazil was invariably the "Japanese school." Today it is called the "Japanese language school" *(nichigo gakkō),* yet it used to be called the "Japanese school" *(nippon gakkō)* in the prewar period. This change corresponds to that of the difference in meanings attached to the institution in the two periods. It was not regarded as a language training school at all, as it is gradually becoming defined today, but as a place to make their children, youth, and even adults into "Japanese"–that is, to be "real human beings." Those Japanese living in the same territory who did not participate in these activities were regarded as somehow not "Japanese," and consequently were not treated as members of the community. Much evidence suggests that such a person was literally nonexistent socially at the time in question.

The Japanese schools were managed and administered by local Japanese associations.[10] Invariably, they displayed the *go-shinei* (the Emperor's Portrait) to be venerated and the *kyôiku chokugo* (Imperial Rescript on Education). This last was considered to embody the most important principles and virtues of Japaneseness. It was read exactly as any sutra is read or chanted. The Imperial Rescript on Education was in effect the sacred sutra of emperor worship of the Japanese communities in Brazil. It was in the Japanese school that general education as well as Japanese education and values in particular were given to children; community policy was discussed; meetings were held; most of the youth activities took place; and ceremonies of all kinds were carried out. People gathered there on any occasion of importance, such as the New Year's celebration *(shihō hai),* Empire Day *(kigen setsu)* the Emperor's Birthday *(tenchō setsu),* anniversary festivals of the community *(nyūshoku kinen sai),* graduation ceremonies, weddings, and so on.

Many formal rituals necessarily preceded other activities at the school: the worship of the Imperial Palace while facing to the East which uniquely in Brazil was frequently called *tōhō yōhai* (the worship of the East); the veneration *(sai keirei)* of the Emperor's portrait; the solemn ritual of reading the Imperial Rescript on Education; and the singing of the Japanese national anthem *kimi ga yo* (Imperial Reign). Particularly important is the fact that all the members (at least all the family heads) of the community were expected to, and actually did, participate in these ceremonies, as well as their children. This is the crucial difference from the practice in Japan where only schoolchildren were obliged to participate. The Japanese school in Brazil served as the spiritual center of the community, lent some religious atmosphere with its practices of emperor worship, and consequently became in a sense a community shrine of the *uji gami* (tutelary deity) type. It was sacred. The shrine was the Japanese school, the deity was the Emperor, and the sutra was the Imperial Rescript on Education. Thus, emperor worship in Brazil resembled closely community ancestor worship in Japan. As late as 1959, there were many Japanese schools in which these same practices were still being observed (Kōya no Hoshi, 1959, 1957; and many other sources in publication and interviews).

The defeat of Japan, which put an end to deification of the Emperor, resulted in the breakdown of the logical and symbolic foundation of group integration and identification. This fact must be taken into account in analyzing the conflicts which emerged among the Japanese in Brazil immediately after the war. As seen above, there is a structural reason for the Emperor's having assumed much more importance among the Japanese in Brazil than in Japan, thus making for far more serious disturbances among them after the defeat in war and the collapse of the mystique of the Emperor. Many of the Japanese who talked openly of the defeat of Japan died in the name of *tenchū* (divine punishment) at the hands of Shindō Remmei terrorists.

Sports activities, which had a somewhat similar function among the younger generation, also centered around the Japanese school. As we cannot go into this matter in detail, only one bit of evidence will be offered here. The following is the declaration of foundation issued by the "Pan Sorocabana Sports Federation" in 1932:

Declaration

> We are the youth, the embodiment of spirit, justice, and innocence. Our ancestors possessed *bushidō* (the way of the samurai). We will attain the same realm by means of sports as they did by *bushidō.* There exists no *yamato minzoku* (Japanese race or nation) without *bushidō.* Youth is nothing without sports. And without them, how can we take pride in ourselves as citizens of growing Brazil glorified by high ideals? And without them, how can we unify these 150 thousand brothers scattered across this vast land? Aiming at the future foundation of a wider Sports Federation as well, we will promote the national policy of "Order and Progress" through sportsmanship.[11]
>
> March 20, 1932 [Burajiru Jihō, 1932b].

We should not forget that this extraordinary declaration was made in the context of growing Brazilian nationalism under the Vargas regime. This was an official declaration published in a Japanese newspaper. Doubtless there were some young people who wanted to be good "Brazilians." Even they, however, in most of the cases, aimed to be "good Brazilians" by means of the cultivation of *yamato damashii* (Japanese spirit) and bushidō. The "brothers" to be unified were the 150 thousand Japanese in Brazil, not the 40 million Brazilians.

The somewhat contradictory sentiments expressed in this statement reflect the internal conflict experienced in trying to be Brazilian and Japanese simultaneously. One of its important implications is that "sportsmanship" came to replace bushidō, at least in name, and the first is interpreted in terms of the second. In other words, they played baseball with the spirit of bushidō. Athletic meetings *(undō kai),* a typical annual festival of Japanese communities involving all members, young and old, and also the baseball matches and *sumō* (Japanese wrestling) tournaments were almost everywhere held on the Emperor's Birthday, which for them was the most important holiday in the year.

They played and competed in the playground of the "sacred" Japanese school, as if in the presence of the Emperor himself, who was presumably expected to superintend the newly reinterpreted "sportsmanship." In this way, playing at sports meant doing something sacred. It seems to the author that it must have been inevitable and obligatory for any young man to join in at least one of the sports. There is a short story published in São Paulo in 1938 in which a young *nisei,* who failed accidentally to participate in a communal activity of the youth association, was accused publicly of being *koku zoku* (a traitor to Japan; Sugi, 1938). In this way, this "sportsmanship," sanctified by bushidō and yamato damashii (Japanese spirit), played a role similar to religion in terms of group identification and integration.[12]

The nationalistic policy of the Estado Novo (the New State) of President Vargas, which started at the end of 1937, especially its accelerated program for the assimilation of foreign immigrants—including restrictive regulations concerning foreign language schools—came as a great shock to the Japanese minority (Willems and Saito, 1947: 132-152). The forced closing of the

Japanese schools meant not only an end to Japanese-oriented education for the immigrants' children, but also symbolically and, in many cases, actually the end of activities in general around the "spiritual center" described above. However, the effect upon emperor worship was basically different from that which later followed Japan's defeat in the war. In the latter case, the change came in a sense from within, but in the former the prohibition came from without, so that it did not mean internal breakdown at all. The Japanese schools simply went underground or sought refuge in private homes, and education in the home was publicly advocated. Emperor worship as public ritual was rarely practiced and finally stopped completely with the outbreak of the war. It survived, however, at the individual and familial levels, and also informally on the level of the community.

Chibata Miyakoshi, one of the most influential immigrant leaders and the general representative of the Brazilian branch of Kaigai Kōgyō Kabushiki Gaisha (Overseas Development Company, the quasi-official emigration agency, commonly referred to as K.K.K.K.), published an interesting essay concerning the situation of the Japanese under the restrictions cited above. This essay serves to illuminate the religious attitudes in question:

> In the Japanese family, it is quite common to see father and mother, grandfather and grandmother, living under the same roof, and children consequently receiving affection from the grandparents as well as from the parents. And within the *ie* are kept the domestic shrine *(kami dana)* where gods are deified and the domestic Buddhist altar *(butsudan)* where the ancestral tablets are worshipped. The *ie* is inherited from the ancestors. Granting that people die and the house changes, the residents still think that they are actually living together with their ancestors. Thus *ie* is handed down from father to son, and from sons to their descendants.
>
> Revere and deify with all your heart
> Your father and mother
> As the gods of your *ie,* as your gods,
> You man, child of man.

This is a verse of Norinaga Motoori, concerning the idea that parents regard their children as the treasures of the *ie,* and the children in turn look upon their parents as the gods of the *ie.* This has been the time-honored thought of Japan, handed down by our ancestors over the centuries.[13]

This pious ancestor worship, which seems to be unique to Japan, tends to decline in the minds of the immigrants, who change their residence frequently, moving from *fazenda* to *shokuminchi* (colony) and from *shokuminchi* to cities. Particularly those who grow cotton move annually from here to there and have their relatives' graves scattered around in many places and consequently are not able to pay homage to the ancestral tombs on the anniversaries of the dead. In this way, they will automatically come to lose the idea of worship, and frequently tend to be given to dissipation, self-destruction or self-abandonment. This tendency makes a harmonious family life difficult to achieve and creating familial warmth is impossible for them. Although we cannot, of course, expect to practice exactly the same religious rites as we did in Japan because we live on alien soil, we should preserve this noble idea of ancestor worship. It is, of course, financially impossible in most of the cases to hold only one stable unified tomb or to establish a permanent residence. It seems to me, however, that it must be the indispensable duty of all Japanese to live in a peaceful environment under the affectionate care of the ancestors through the establishment of the domestic shrine and Buddhist altar in every *ie.* This beautiful idea of ancestor worship, a unique attribute of the Japanese people, must be transmitted to our descendants despite the fact that we are living on alien soil.

Now that Japanese schools are prohibited, the future development of *zaihaku hōjin* (the Japanese in Brazil) through education in the Japanese language is now primarily the responsibility of the parents in the context of family life [Miyakoshi, 1941: 9-10].

In these passages, we can see that the rituals of ancestor worship were being urged upon the immigrants as a replacement for emperor worship in this time of crisis as a means of maintaining integration of the group, confronted by the prohibition of the "sacred" Japanese schools. As emperor worship was threatened, and public meetings largely suppressed, ancestor worship and education at the familial level came to substitute for and complement the integrative function of emperor worship on the community level. This shift was natural enough because in their home society social integration on the levels of local community and to some extent the whole Japanese nation functioned in relation to ancestor worship.

Permanent Residence

We have dealt with the social background of the immigrants, stressed the religious attitudes of the rural laborers and of those who were socioeconomically unstable, and described those who, forming localized ethnic communities, were in the process of rising into rural middle class. People of the last category, who had very recently passed through an earlier stage, were in the minority in the 1930s. The latter was in an essentially transitional stage from the lower to the middle classes, carrying many of the socioeconomic and religious features attributed to the former. It was not until the 1950s that the great majority of the Japanese could be characterized as members of the middle classes.

Although they participated in localized ethnic community and emperor worship, they did not necessarily practice ancestor worship in their domestic life. In fact, domestic ancestor worship was not commonly practiced and remained latent in their consciousness. Naturally there were those who did not conform to this pattern of behavior, especially among those who had decided definitely to stay in Brazil. Gaining social and economic stability, some Japanese gradually developed an attachment to their achieved means of production, land, status, and property in general, and simultaneously their ties with and sense of belonging to the home country weakened. As a consequence, the consciousness of ie, the issues of inheritance and succession, and the cult of the ancestors began to revive.

Before they had attained economic stability, they were potential claimants of social security in their home communities on the occasion of encountering any difficulty. Risen now to the middle classes, they no longer tried to seek such support in Japan, which had revealed its incapacities finally by the defeat in war. Immediately after the end of the war, in a complete reversal of the earlier relationship, the immigrants formed the Nihon Sensai Dōhō Kyūen-kai (Comitê de Socôrro de Vítima de Guerra do Japão, or, Committee for the Relief of the War Victims in Japan) and systematically sent money and subsistence items to Japan to help *bokoku* (the mother country) for three years. In so doing, they came at last to abandon their identification with their home society.

The idea of permanent residence emerged first among those who had acquired coffee farms of high productivity, officials of Japanese government and emigration agencies, those who were directly connected with enterprises in Brazil, such as K.K.K.K., Burajiru Takushoku Kumiai (Brazilian Colonization Cooperative, or simply Bura Taku), Japanese newspapers, industrial and commercial entrepreneurs, and the like. Generally speaking, the elite, the rich, the officials, and the leaders tended to advocate permanent residence in Brazil to the ordinary Japanese immigrants. There was a movement called *Gatto Undō* (written *GAT Undō*), started in 1934 and especially promoted by Bura Taku. "GAT" is an abbreviation of *gozar a terra,* which was a direct Portuguese translation of their motto *aido eijū* (literally "loving the land, settle down permanently"). This movement was especially active in some typical Japanese communities such as Bastos, Aliança (Mirandópolis), Tietê (Pereira Barreto) in 1934 and 1935.

This gradual turn to permanent residence resulted in discrediting and denigrating the "return home" idea as *dekasegi konjō* (the mean disposition of sojourner laborers). Today those who have decided definitely to reside permanently in Brazil sometimes say, "We are ancestors," or "We, the immigrants, will be the ancestors in Brazil." Here ancestor means a man who provides a foundation for something, prototypically ie, and in a wider sense the Japanese community in Brazil as a whole by analogy with the ie institution. Yanagida (1962) writes that there are nowadays few persons in Japan who profess themselves to be ancestors. There are many in Brazil who say it. This means that the ie institution has revived.

They commonly call Brazil *yōkoku* (adoptive country), a term coined locally. The implication is that now they see themselves as having emigrated as *yōshi* (adopted son) to their "adoptive country," which is Brazil, by analogy with "adoptive ie" *(yōka),* or "adoptive father" *(yōfu),* and "adoptive mother" *(yōbo).* These are all common terms concerning the adoptive practices of ie organization in Japan. But the word yōkoku (adoptive country), which is more frequently used in Brazil, does not exist in Japan. Immigration is interpreted in terms of kinship and familial principles and consequently the Brazilian nation is here understood in terms of ie. Brazil, which used to be the "host house," now is their adoptive country." They are no longer "sojourners" or "wayfarers." According to the Japanese folk morality, "adopted sons" should never return home except to visit there. Referring to going to Japan, today they no longer say to "return" but say to "visit Japan" *(hō nichi)* or to "visit the mother country" *(bokoku hōmon).* Also important is the display of piety on the part of the "adopted sons" to the "adoptive country."

There are some individuals, known personally to the author, who have visited Japan recently and brought back such religious objects as a butsudan (domestic Buddhist altar), ashes of their ancestors, or a time-honored censer to Brazil, in effect moving their center of religious practice to the "adoptive country." They say, "Now we've really immigrated." There were some who said this only after forty or fifty years of actual residence in Brazil. Finally, "The ie has come to immigrate."

An adherent of a new sect (Kaminoya Yaoyorozu-kyō) with a Shinto background said to the author in an interview: "I thought we had left politics and the gods behind in Japan, but now the gods are recovered."

There was a Japanese, the president of a Japanese newspaper in São Paulo, who had twice been deported from Brazil because of his acrimonious pen. He eventually died in Japan. His friends in São Paulo spoke of his death as *kyaku shi* (alien death). Today this term is applied only to cases in which an immigrant dies while he is visiting Japan or any other country, but it will not be applied to those who die in Brazil.

Favored by the prosperity of Brazilian economy during the war, the economic conditions of the Japanese improved greatly during the 1940s (Izumi, 1957: 18-38), and they moved up socially into the middle classes in both rural and urban settings. The bulk of them became members of the rural and urban old middle classes. Later as the native-born Japanese have grown up, those who have come to be members of the new middle class, especially in the city of São Paulo, are increasing in number. These two Japanese groups of the middle classes are distinctive in terms of group formation by voluntary associations and religious affiliation. The movements of the "Japanese religions" in the 1950s were particularly successful among the Japanese of the old middle classes in both rural and urban areas, but not among those of the new middle class in the cities, who are interested in Christianity if in any religion at all. It seems to the author that religions, as well as ethnicity and other factors, are today important in group identification. Ancestor worship is being revived among the Japanese of the old middle class, although it is rapidly being transformed, and it is doubtful that it will survive for many more generations.

Summary

(1) The Japanese emigrants to Brazil were those who did not inherit ie, which included property and the cult of ancestor worship. They were proletarian immigrants, although most of them had been born into middle-class families. They sought social security and feelings of belonging in their home community in Japan rather than in the host society of Brazil, at least before 1950. Thus they did not establish ie in Brazil, and consequently tended to neglect ancestor worship on the "alien soil."

(2) As they formed a kind of localized ethnic community which was basically different from the community in Japan, they had a different kind of group identification. As ancestor worship was neglected, some alternative had to be found. Thus emperor worship replaced ancestor worship, because they identified themselves in terms of "Japaneseness," which was symbolized by the Emperor.

(3) Achieving relative economic security, entering the middle classes, and no longer expecting to have to take refuge in the home community on the occasion of difficulty, they came to identify with the Brazilian soil, tending to revive ie consciousness and, consequently, ancestor worship.

(4) When emperor worship was to all intents and purposes destroyed by defeat in World War II, ancestor worship, which had been about to revive again on the basis of ie consciousness, replaced it.

(5) The religious movements activated after 1950 may be accounted for by the fact that the immigrants had risen into the middle classes, and, as a result, they came to revive the ie institution, although ie and ancestor worship are likely to have been signficantly transformed by acculturation, urbanization, and so forth.

(6) Today, emperor worship has only a secondary meaning in terms of group identification. In this respect, religions, besides other factors such as ethnicity and social class, play a crucial role.

NOTES

1. The use of the name Sōka Gakkai was discontinued after the visit of President Daisaku Ikeda to Brazil in 1966 because of strongly negative reactions overseas against their intensive methods of proselytizing. Today only the Nichiren Shōshū, the legal name of the sect, is used by the group in any place outside Japan, although it continues to be called Sōka Gakkai by nonmembers.

2. Although it is extremely difficult to calculate the numbers of the adherents of these groups, a tentative calculation was made by the author on the basis of surveys conducted in 1967: Sōka Gakkai, 15,000-20,000; Seichō-no-Ie, 15,000; P.L. Kyōdan, 8,000-10,000 (non-Japanese origin, 10-20 percent); Sekai Kyūsei-kyō,

5,000-7,000 (non-Japanese origin about 60 percent); Tenry-Kyō, 4,000; Omoto, 600 (non-Japanese origin, 50 percent); Kaminoya Yaoyorozu-kyō, 140. These are estimated numbers of the adherents, not including floating and occasional visitors and supplicants. Detailed descriptions of each of these groups are found in Maeyama (1967: 72-125).

3. In the author's view, ownership of land and ambiguous status in agriculture are not sufficient indicators of class position. The data used here are, however, the best available for the period in question.

4. The following definition of ie is useful for our understanding. "As distinguished from 'family,' *'ie'* is an organizational body (or an organizational core), whose business is managed on the basis of its property, the members share the livelihood, and a common ancestor is worshipped, and which is a housekeeping entity, being a constituent part of inter-*ie* groupings" (Nakano and Matsushima, 1958: 51).

5. As a whole, the returned immigrants were very few in number. The official records at the port of Santos show that 176,775 Japanese entered and 12,615 went out during 1908-1936. The number of those who went out constitutes only 7.1 percent of those who entered, and most of these reimmigrated to Argentina (D.T.C.I., 1937: 54).

6. There are no good data on the immigrants in terms of birth order of the distinction of successor and nonsuccessor. We have evidence that a considerable number of immigrants were eldest sons. According to the research on the process of urbanization in Japan, it is common that the eldest sons, as well as the others, go to work out of their home, coming back only after the death of their father in order to succeed to their ie, in the cases of smaller farmers (Namiki, 1959: 74). Similar cases may be found, if in lesser degree, among the emigrants to Brazil, because they were sure they would be able to return home.

7. This religious practice is a fusion of the indigenous Japanese folk belief in *marebito* (literally "visitor") and Buddhism, the idea being that the ancestral spirits visit their native villages and descendents regularly on certain days of the year and then return to the world of the spirits.

8. The Buddhist sutras are chanted in Sanskrit in Japan so that only professional priests and a few secular people know them.

9. *Macaco velho* is a Portuguese term with no equivalent in Japanese and is used, among the Japanese in Brazil, to describe men who are experienced, old-fashioned, amiable, staunch, and Brazilianized. On May 26, 1967, the Centro de Estudos Nipo-Brazileiros in São Paulo held a seminar on macaco velho, from which some information is drawn here.

10. Because there were few Brazilian schools in the frontier regions, the settlers had either to establish their own schools or let their children remain illiterate.

11. "Order and progress" is the Brazilian national motto.

12. Today, athletic meetings, which used to be held on April 29, the Emperor's birthday, are usually scheduled for May Day, the Brazilian official holiday closest to April 29. Although social and psychological conditions have greatly changed in recent years, the athletic meetings still have something of the old atmosphere. May Day is, in effect, for the Japanese nothing more than the Emperor's birthday.

13. Norinaga Motoori (1730-1801) is one of the first Japanese scholars to seek to explicate the indigenous and unique life style and mind of the Japanese people, as a counter to what he regarded as the insidious influences of Buddhism and Chinese culture.

REFERENCES

ARIGA, K. (1959) "Nihon ni okeru senzo no kannen," pp. 3-23 in S. Kitano and Y. Okada (eds.) Ie: Sono Kozō Bunseki. Tokyo: Sōbunsha.

––– (1954) "Sonraku," pp. 857-859 in Japanese Society of Ethnology (ed.) Nihon Shokai Minzoku Jiten. Tokyo: Sei-bundō Shinkōsha.

Burajiru Jiho (1932a) May 25.

––– (1932b) April 14.

Comissão de Recenseamento da Colônia Japanêsa (1964) The Japanese Immigrant in Brazil. Tokyo: Univ. of Tokyo Press.

DE COULANGES, F. (1901) The Ancient City. Boston: Lee & Shepard.

D.T.C.I. (1937) Boletim da Directoria de Terras, Colonização e Immigração 1. São Paulo.

Govêrno do Estado de São Paulo (1939) Boletim do Departamento Estadual de Estatística 5. São Paulo.

IBGE (1954) Anuário Estatístico do Brasil. Rio de Janeiro: Conselho Nacional de Estadística.

IZUMI, S. (1957) "Burajiru no Nikkei colônia," in Imin. Tokyo: Kokon Shoin.

––– (1954) Burajiru ni Okeru Nikkei Colônia no Keizai Seikatsu. Tokyo: Gaimushō Obei-kyoku Imin-ka.

KAWASHIMA, T. (1950) Nihon Shakai no Kazakuteki Kōsei. Tokyo: Nihon Hyōron Sha.

Kōya no Hoshi (1959) Volume 55 (August).

––– (1957) Volume 42 (June).

MAEYAMA, T. (1967) "O imigrante e a rēligião: estudo de uma seita religiosa Japonêsa em São Paulo." M. A. thesis. Escola de Sociologia e Política de São Paulo.

MIYAKOSHI, C. (1941) "Katei kyōiku ni kansuru kōsatsu," in Pa Enchōsen Kyōiku-shi Kankō Kai (eds.) Pa Enchōsen Kyōiku-shi. São Paulo.

NAKANE, C. (1967) Kinship and Economic Organization in Rural Japan. London: University of London's Athlone Press.

NAKANO, T. and S. MATSUSHIMA (1958) Introduction to Japanese Society. Tokyo: Univ. of Tokyo Press.

NODA, R. (1930) Jissa 18 Nen Burajiru Jinkokuki. Tokyo: Hakubun Kan.

OKOCHI, K. (1952) Shakai Seisaku no Keizai Riron. Tokyo.

OUCHI, T. (1952) Nihon Shihonshugi no Nōgyō Mondai. Tokyo: Univ. of Tokyo Press.

SAITO, H. (1961) O Japônes no Brasil: Estudo de Mobilidade e Fixação. São Paulo: Editôra Sociologia e Política.

SUGI, T. (1938) "Fukushu." Chiheisen 8.

Tenri-kyō Burajiru Dendōchō (1958) Tenri-kyō Burajiru Dendō Shi. Baru, Brazil.

WAKO, S. (1939) Baurú Kannai no Hōjin. São Paulo: private printing.

WILLEMS, E. (1948) "Aspectos da aculturação de Japonêses no estado de São Paulo." F.F.C.L. Boletim 82. Universidade de São Paulo.

––– and H. SAITO (1947) "Shindō-remmei: um problema de aculturação." Sociologia 9, 2: 132-152.

YANAGIDA, K. (1962) "Senzo no hanashi," in Teihon Yanagida Kunio Shū. Tokyo: Chikuma Shohō.

JON S. VINCENT
Department of Spanish & Portuguese
University of Kansas
Lawrence, Kansas

THE BRAZILIAN NOVEL
Some Paradoxes of Popularity

"Popular literature" is a term that appears in serious literary context most often as a means of disparaging the unremitting yokelism of the larger reading public and the cynical but uninspired writers who prey on the pocketbooks of yokeldom. The term may also appear in contexts in which its meaning is altogether different, as in the sober studies carried out by anthropologists and folklorists in which the literary manifestations of folk culture are studied. In the latter instance, the term loses its burden of vague antagonism and assumes a scholarly respectability based on the tested relevance and importance of primitive, preliterate, or peasant societies. In literate societies such as ours, the large area between this popular literature and the real literature of the truly cultured minority is dealt with gingerly, if at all. It is tacitly taken to represent the same kind of mindless consumerism that makes such an innovation as the electric canopener an overnight commercial success.

In the case of a relatively sophisticated form such as the novel, the antipathies are subtly conceived. Dwight MacDonald

AUTHOR'S NOTE: This paper is based on a talk given at the colloquium series "Conversations in the Disciplines," sponsored by the State University College at Buffalo, November 13, 1970.

(1962) distinguishes true high culture from two lower orders which he labels "midcult" and "masscult." For the sake of symmetry, we might supply the catchy epithet MacDonald neglects to provide and call the real culture level "upcult."[1]

An application of MacDonald's scheme to American fiction would, I think, lead to the conclusion that the bulk of our fiction is midcult. The principal criterion for classification appears to be commercial success, and thus best-sellers would by definition be labeled midcult phenomena. The intimation is that most people who read novels are no more than a bunch of churls, and consequently any novel able to sustain sales over a long period is inevitably an inferior work. I would suggest, nevertheless, that sales alone are a misleading indicator of consumption. There is in the United States a literary market composed of the literary jet-set and the academic profession which guarantees that some novels are read by several thousand professors, graduate students, and literary insiders even though the masses of midcult never buy a single copy. In addition, there is no guarantee that a novel's commercial success has any proven relationship to its being widely read. As in the case of electric canopeners, purchase, possession, and display may often supplant utilization. Such writers as Bernard Malamud, John Barth, and William Burroughs are probably the best representatives of this class of surreptitious upcult writers. We all know dozens of people with copies of *The Sot-Weed Factor* prominently displayed next to their Great Books. We probably know very few people who have read it.

But real midcult novels are not only sold, but are read. Joseph Heller and Philip Roth are among the more respectable of these writers. Harold Robbins is among the less respectable, since reviews of his books are infrequent in *The New York Review of Books,* and he is not considered by literary professionals to be any more a novelist than Al Capp is regarded as a towering intellect.

A very similar attitude about commercially successful literature obtains in Brazil. If anything, Brazilian literati are even less forgiving of continued success than their American colleagues, and it is tacitly understood that if midcult writers are to be mentioned, they are not being taken very seriously. But adjustments are necessary if we attempt to transfer this construct of levels of culture to Brazil. The most obvious alteration would have to account for the enormously different social structures of Brazil and the United States. I will mention this so that it may be kept in mind but leave the adjusting to the sociologists and anthropologists. A less apparent modification would have to compensate for the extraordinary social and intellectual prestige that Brazilian writers enjoy outside academic and literary circles. Americans may attribute minor magical powers to writers, but in Brazil there is an aura of sorcery about the profession that Americans are unlikely to ascribe, perhaps because of our puritanical preference for deeds over words.

The paradox here results from the dual nature of literary prestige in Brazil. Writers are held to possess powers of reason denied to the mass of the populace, and consequently readers tend to expect information and enlightenment, even from fiction. But Brazilian culture is also a verbal one, in which oratory is still considered an art and conversation is still more important than television. The importance of the rhetorical tradition has tended to blur the distinction between different kinds of writing, so that not only literature but also criticism, history, sociology, and anthropology are appreciated for their style as much as for their content. One result of this has been the production of a considerable amount of lyrical sociology, poetic history, and epic anthropology. It has also affected the novel.

On the one hand, successful Brazilian novels have often been rather florid affairs by our dry standards, and even in translation may appear almost impossibly verbose. On the other hand, Brazilian fiction shows a marked didactic tendency which emphasizes the writer's role as prophet and teacher. The two antagonistic elements only infrequently appear in perfect balance, but the interplay between rhetoric and information can provide basic insights into the character of the popular fiction of Brazil during the last four decades.

In the recent history of the Brazilian novel, no period made the choice between style and content more difficult than the decade of the thirties. Writers were faced with the dilemma of responding to new and very complex political and social phenomena which were rapidly polarizing national opinion, and at the same time taking advantage of the artistic freedoms so recently made possible by the Modernist movement. A reawakened sense of nationalism and a sharpened awareness of the immediacy of the problems of Brazilian society stimulated an unprecedented interest on the part of the reading public in novels of social and political content—ranging from the vague problem novel to the novel of social protest, including those with an openly Marxist bias.

The Brazilian situation thus has obvious parallels with the American tendencies of the same decade, when some of the best-known writers in this country, and a great many new writers, attempted to make of the American novel a sounding-board for political opinion and a vehicle of protest. The difference is that American radical fiction of the doctrinaire variety was practically an overnight failure, while one kind or another of neo-Marxist bias is a characteristic of much Brazilian fiction until well into the forties. The more obstreperous brands of social protest fiction did not sell at all well in the United States, and thus party writers such as Michael Gold and Edward Newhouse receded into a generally deserved obscurity (Rideout, 1956: 197-198, 239-244). Social protest literature in this country was made popular and respectable by independent radicals like Steinbeck and Dos Passos. In Brazil, however, even the most orthodox leftist writers were part of the radical group that wrote the novels that became the dominant literary medium and the best-selling variety of fiction.

The two most successful writers of this period were Jorge Amado and José Lins do Rêgo, who alternated writing best-sellers for over a decade. Both had the proper credentials for political writing. Amado was for many years a member of the Brazilian Communist Party, a fact at times made overwhelmingly evident in his novels. José Lins do Rêgo was widely held to belong to the same party, although a few original souls suspected that he was a reactionary at heart. To my knowledge the only thing he was not accused of being was a liberal. The novels of both Amado and Lins do Rêgo were, at any rate, characterized by an emphasis on the sociological and political and a deemphasis on style. Amado's early novels were rendered in a kind of lumpenproletarian realism, complete with political jargon and solidarity of the masses, with all the literary elegance of a strike placard. In the late thirties and early forties, Amado gave more attention to style, perfecting a unique kind of subversive lyricism which nevertheless allowed message to take precedence over medium. Lins do Rêgo's greatest commercial success was his series of novels referred to as the sugar cane cycle, in which he traced the decay and fall of the rural sugar aristocracy in a correct but nonetheless doughy prose which leads the reader to concentrate more on content than on form.

From the early forties to the mid-fifties, popular taste in fiction appears to have moved gradually in the direction of style. The upcult literature of this period was composed principally of literary criticism and poetry, two forms which also reflected an increasing concern with form and technique. One of the most popular writers of fiction of this period was Erico Veríssimo. Veríssimo's early novels, published in the thirties, were relatively successful, but it was with the publication of the first volume of his trilogy (1949-1962) *Time and the Wind (O Tempo e o Vento)* in the late forties that he ensured a place for himself as one of Brazil's consistently successful novelists. A political moderate, Veríssimo articulates perhaps the closest thing to liberalism that can be found in popular Brazilian fiction. His works are neither technically adventurous nor as slipshod as some of the fiction of the thirties; the trilogy is restrained and comparatively well wrought. He is unabashedly a midcult writer. But the sociological element remains important. The trilogy is a fictionalized account of the history of the author's native state of Rio Grande do Sul.

In the same period there was a considerable increase in the availability and popularity of foreign fiction in translation, especially after World War II, and nonfiction became more important in the domestic book market as Brazil's stake in the technology of the Western world increased. One of the notable successes in the field of nonfiction was a biography of the durable leader of the Brazilian Communist Party, Luiz Carlos Prestes. First published in Argentina, this romanticized biography circulated illegally in Brazil until 1945, when a first highly successful Brazilian edition was released. The author of this work, aptly entitled *The Cavalier of Hope (O Cavaleiro da Esperança),* was Jorge Amado (1956). But this appears to have been the crest of the wave of political literature. In the early fifties, Amado published a trilogy entitled *The Freedom Underground (Os Subterrâneos da Liberdade),* a fictionalized account of life under the Vargas dictatorship. Generally considered Amado's (1961-1964) most politically sectarian work, the trilogy was largely ignored by readers and critics alike.

Since the mid-1950s, the midcult has grown both in absolute numbers and in proportion to the society as a whole. Because of some of the same economic and political factors that have brought about this growth, the midcult has become more omnivorous and more cosmopolitan in its literary tastes, and therefore is more demanding of its national writers. Brazilian fiction today is in many respects very different from the kind of fiction being sought by large numbers of readers in the thirties and forties. The surprising constant is that it is still being written by the same man.

The landmark of the popular fiction of the fifties and sixties—one of those books that will still require a footnote in any study of the literature of the period fifty years hence—was Amado's *Gabriela, Clove and Cinnamon (Gabriela, Cravo e Canela),* published in 1958. *Gabriela* has become one of the best known and most widely read novels ever written in the Portuguese language. It won no less than five national awards in 1959 alone and had reached a sixteenth printing within two years of publication, having sold over 100,000 copies. It was the best-selling book of any kind in Brazil in the late fifties. Within a little over a year, it had sold so well in Brazil that it had become the holder of the record for sales of a fictional work for a period of twenty years (Perez, 1960; Villaça, 1960).

Dozens of other novelists have had their moment of glory in popular Brazilian fiction, and periodically a new writer or a single novel will occupy national attention for several months and sell like some new kind of canopener. But it is apparent that the inventor of this marvelous device was Jorge Amado, and he still appears to hold the patent. Not even José Lins do Rêgo, who continued writing until his death in 1957, managed to live by the pen. In fact, the only novelists who have ever managed to do so in Brazil have been Jorge Amado, Erico Veríssimo, and a relative newcomer, José Mauro de Vasconcelos.

Amado has published four other novels since 1958; each is an automatic best-seller. His publisher is so certain of this that the first press runs of a new Amado novel are ordinarily 75,000 copies, a truly gargantuan figure in the Brazilian market. Veríssimo's novels also continue to sell well, and his earlier works are periodically reprinted for his loyal readers. His more recent works, such as *Mr. Ambassador (O Senhor Embaixador),* tend to hit the top of the lists shortly after publication and then recede into respectable—and profitable—second or third place. The only writer who has posed a serious threat to Amado and Veríssimo in recent years is José Mauro de Vasconcelos. At the moment, Vasconcelos has thirteen novels in print, some of them in an eleventh or twelfth printing. I confess that I would have preferred not to mention Vasconcelos, but such success demands at least token recognition.

Vasconcelos is a midcult writer of the lower fringes, and I suspect that his commercial success is largely due to the increase in the size of the reading public in Brazil rather than to any identifiable trend in the preferences of midcult readers. He is the only one of the writers I have mentioned who cultivates a purely escapist variety of fiction; his novels are models of the kind of popular melodrama that literary critics point to as vindication of their snobbery—proof positive that the novel is dead, that the public thrives on vulgarity, and that the world is being taken over by boors. But since Vasconcelos is a newcomer to the ranks of the perennial best-selling authors in Brazil, perhaps only time will tell if the kind of detergent drama he churns out will constitute proof that things have really come to such a pass.

It is unjust to dispense so summarily with a writer whose commercial success merits him a place in this essay. But it should be apparent that whatever paradoxes can be discovered in Brazilian popular fiction will be most likely to emerge from a discussion of Brazil's most persistent purveyor of best-selling fiction, and I now propose to discuss in more detail some of the features that critics consider to have been at the root of Jorge Amado's inordinately protracted success.

As has already been suggested, the first major paradox confronting the writer desirous of writing successful fiction in Brazil, that of somehow enclosing message in the proper decorative wrapper, was resolved by the public's sudden awakening to the chaotic political situation of the thirties. This response was to make the political novel the most profitable kind of fiction in the county. This fact in itself contains another paradox, since the political novel by its very nature tends to have a somewhat restricted audience. Political fiction of this variety is designed to irritate, not to please, since it attempts to pinpoint the excesses of society and inspire action against the established order.

I would submit that a careful comparison of radical fiction in the United States and Brazil in this period would resolve this dilemma. Brazil's very anemic liberal tradition was all but destroyed in the political upheavals of the 1930s, while that in the United States not only flourished in the mind of midcult, it was made the guiding philosophy of the national government. Labor agitation in the United States resulted in the concessions of industry and in legislation protecting the disadvantaged. In Brazil, the same agitation resulted in the imposition of the right of protest. In the face of such a situation, it is obvious that the Vargas government contributed substantially to the success of social protest fiction by holding periodic book-burnings and by tossing the authors of this fiction in jail. Jail sentences were at this time, and still are, a mark of intellectual integrity in Brazil, even more so than in the United States. In addition, the fear of the Red Menace has tended to be comparatively weak in Brazil, excepting of course the official stance of the national government. A large part of the reading public in Brazil is not at all disturbed by the fact that writers are one variety or another of Marxist,[2] and in intellectual circles militant conservatism has always been considered a mark of vague dowdiness.

It has also been mentioned, however, that Amado's most successful novels of the period represent a kind of neo-proletarian realism, written in simple and even vulgar language, and supposedly addressed to "the people." Amado's inference here is clearly made in the Marxist mold, leading us to believe that the Brazilian proletariat constituted the mass of his audience. This is a paradox based on self-deception. In 1935, only about 40 percent of the Brazilian population was literate (Cândido, 1965: 164). Appending to this the rather erratic methods and slippery criteria employed for determining literacy in Brazil, it would be necessary to subtract a substantial functional illiterate segment from that figure, leaving perhaps 30 percent of the population even technically qualified to read a book. Amado also depended on economic return and became a minor capitalist in the process of attacking capitalism. He still claims that he writes for "the people," and though the size of the reading public and their access to money have grown since 1935, the cost of books remains exorbitant to all but the bourgeoisie. In 1967, a worker earning the minimum wage in Amado's home city of Salvador would have had to shell out almost 10 percent of his monthly salary to buy a single copy of Amado's latest novel. The Brazilian proletariat is necessarily more concerned with rice and beans than with the electric canopener.

Another paradox in the success of political fiction in Brazil is that political novels, especially those of the radical variety, are characteristically puritanical. American radical fiction of the thirties is again a case in point. This feature is even more clearly demonstrated in Soviet socialist realism (a term incidentally used by Amado in reference to his own work), in which the protagonist's most passionate love interest is likely to be his tractor. This is paradoxical, because both Amado and Lins do Rêgo have been accused of becoming successful on the basis of the "erotic delirium" contained in their works (dos Reis e Mello, 1960: 18). Amado, in fact, is widely held to be one of Brazil's leading pornographers, both for his frequent descriptions of sexual activity and for his liberties with the dirty word.

Brazilians are no less committed to the traditions of the lusty Latin than any other nationality in Latin America, and it would therefore be no surprise to find sexiness a characteristic of the Brazilian novel. But Brazilians have had an oddly puritanical attitude about writing down the things that most of them do. Such erotic delights as *Playboy* magazine are sold under the counter in Rio for about eight times their original price, presumably because of their scabrous content. At the same time, there is a real pornography market in Brazil, of both the graphic and fictional varieties. In the novel, a practitioner of the art uses the obvious penname "Brigite Bijou," probably to disguise the fact that he is a man. In works with such titles as *Thirst* and *Nights of Love (A Sêde, Noites de Amor),* Miss Bijou (1968, 1969) recounts the time-honored episodes of erotic literature with one, two, three, and sometimes more participants of any of the various sexes. The scenes could be from *Fanny Hill* or *The Pearl.* But the descriptions, including the terminology for the equipment involved, are clinical. In addition, neither *Thirst* nor *Nights of Love* has begun to compete with Jorge Amado's novels in sales.

It is odd that sexiness became a standard part of Brazilian fiction in the social and political novel, but the presumed dirtiness of these works is obviously exaggerated. One wonders if those who accuse Amado of being a pornographer are indulging in wishful thinking, his novels being for them without standard of comparison. Julio Cortázar, one of Argentina's most famous novelists, claims in his latest work *Last Round (Ultimo Round)* that inability to write really good pornography is endemic in Latin America. He asserts that Latins tend to be extreme about sexual matters, and either veil their intentions in euphemism or else lavish epithets uncontrollably, as when they simultaneously impugn the chastity of the Virgin Mary and then go on to elaborate on her unconventional sexual preferences (Cortázar, 1969: 149-154). At any rate, writers of the ilk of Henry Miller, whose books are incidentally selling very well in Brazil in translation, are few and far between. I think Jorge Amado produces the closest approximation to this artful pornography.

Amado's early novels used sex practice and dirty words both for shock effect and as a means of characterizing heroes and villains. In the proletarian novels, the unavailability of sex was merely another indication of the destitution of the poor. When it was available, it was given free by prostitutes, in an admirable display of class solidarity. In the more complex later novels, which deal increasingly with the bourgeoisie, Amado takes the opportunity further to reveal the villainies of bourgeois characters through insights into their sexual preferences. Sex becomes a means of alleviating boredom, and since most of his characters have a certain inherent depravity, there are suggestions of the gaudier perversions. The third manner of presenting sexual material is one which appears in every novel since *Gabriela.* It was merely suggested in earlier novels, particularly when lower-class heroes and heroines were involved.

Sex in these later novels is treated with warmth and a kind of ribald delight which tends to reduce the erotic effect and emphasize the comic. The sexy scene has become part of the social satire which characterizes Amado's later novels, and this presentation is both more elaborate and more satisfying literarily than the previous methods. Amado's later heroes are all amoral, and the ethical terminus of his novels rests on an appreciation of the peculiar crude morality of the lower class. The bourgeois reader cannot help but be impressed that this is both slightly immoral and probably a lot more fun than he is having. The satisfaction provided here is not the kind of literal titillation offered by the orgasmic odysseys of *Nights of Love,* but is part of an experience that is both sensorial and intellectual, since social satire and an appreciation of the absurd are both part of the response.

Amado has increasingly employed sensorial imagery in his novels, so that colors, odors, food, music, and sex are a constant point of reference. They may appear as theme or merely as elaboration, but it is unquestionable that Amado's lyrical appreciations of the delights of table, glass, and bed are a major contribution to the pleasure of reading his works–and thus, of course, to sales.

As a corollary to this colorful concupiscence, it must be noted that Amado is one of the few accomplished humorists of modern Brazilian fiction. Even in the more erotic passages, Amado consistently humors his reader. His earlier tendency to use the dirty word as a means of baring the crude realities of episodes was a recognition of the shock value of words. In more recent novels, such crudities are generally found in contexts which emphasize the tension-relieving effect of the same words–that is, their comic effect. As for the more graphic terminology used for the sex scenes, Amado avoids altogether the clinical approach favored by Brigite Bijou and employs any of the dozens of synonyms commonly used in Brazilian slang for such activities and for the paraphernalia involved. Even here, a very careful selective process is evident, and Amado invariably chooses not the most graphic term but the funniest. The range of comic effect in these later works is so great as to preclude a full discussion. His recent novels have comic plots, comic characters, comic situations. There is satire, parody, a keen sense of the absurd, irony, hyperbole, epigram, and pun.

Again, this is paradoxical, at least in theory, since the political novel is generally a sober affair. I refer you again to the Soviet tractor romance for corroboration. But the final paradox of Brazilian popular fiction lies in its regionalistic character. Amado and Lins do Rêgo are considered two of the major figures in the regionalist generation of the thirties, and in both cases their most successful fiction has been the most regional. Amado's early works about the conquest of the cacao zone in southern Bahia, written in the forties, were still best-sellers in the sixties, and Lins do Rêgo's sugar cane cycle continues to sell in successive editions. Even Erico Veríssimo has enjoyed his greatest success with a semi-regionalist form of fiction. And Amado's later works, his most successful, have all dealt with the local color and picturesque characters of the exotic and erotic city of Salvador.

This is paradoxical first in that regionalist fiction generally has appeal only to part of the larger public, and generally only for short periods of time. But beyond this, it almost never sells in translation, if in fact it gets translated. Amado's (1965: 455-462) works have nevertheless been translated into at least 31 different languages (see also Jornal do Brasil, 1967: 6). In some cases, his novels have sold better in translation than in Portuguese. His most frequently translated novel is the first of the epic cacao cycle, which has been translated into 22 languages. Amado's largest foreign market has been Poland, where by 1956 he had sold over 860,000 copies of this works (Perez, 1960: 209). In Czechoslovakia, the first press run of the translation of *Gabriela* was twice the size of the Brazilian edition, in a country with a population about 15 percent that of Brazil (Costa, 1961: 2). This could, of course, be explained away by the sectarian bias of his fiction. But *Gabriela* is not one of Amado's most propagandistic works. Also, Amado's novels have recently become successful in nonsocialist countries, including Portugal and the United States. Within fifteen months of the appearance of the English translation of *Gabriela,* 60,000 hardcover copies and over 100,000 paperbacks of the novel had been sold (Grossman, 1967: 8). It is conceivable that the extramural success of Amado's regionalist fiction is dependent on a feature of his work only marginally responsible for his success at home: the exotic tropics-cum-dark-and-sensuous-ladies ambience, probably of similar appeal to a culture consumer in New Jersey and to a bureaucrat in Warsaw. In addition, there is no doubt that a portion of Amado's foreign audience is able to find in his novels the comforting confirmation of Latin inferiority, a response most Brazilian readers would find inconceivable.

I think that the paradoxes of Brazilian popular fiction can be resolved by a realistic approach to the labels so graciously lavished by critics and by the public. The fundamental paradox of the predominance of information or experience was resolved by a simple matter of responding to the principal concerns of the reading public. In the thirties, a general discontent with the ways the government was going about not solving the nation's problems made political fiction successful. The end of the dictatorship and Brazil's emergence as a regional power after World War II prompted a more reasoned and less simplistic examination of society. This political content is at the moment somewhat more veiled but no less important.

All the works I have mentioned contain as a conspicuous terminus ethical appreciations of the society depicted. But in no case is it orthodox political fiction. Amado no longer attempts to provoke his audience to action—like Swift, he now attempts to enlist popular support for his viewpoint rather than polarizing opinion. This relatively reasoned approach has been that of Veríssimo all along. In Amado's case, the approach is more perverse, and generally more entertaining, but nonetheless the similarity is apparent. But Amado convinced himself and his critics that he was really writing for the masses. The masses, of course, were neither able to buy a book nor particularly interested. What has been forgotten in all this theorizing is that the novel is in itself basically a bourgeois medium. In fact, literature about the poor is best digested by the rich. The poor themselves prefer the romance of chivalry and Donald Duck. At the same time, the reading public in Brazil is not easily broken into three exclusive categories. If Amado's readership has been, as I suspect, a midcult readership all along, it is necessary to add that the Brazilian reading public, being small and construed along lines different from those of American society, must by necessity also include a large portion of the upcult. The cultural elite of Brazil constitutes a disproportionately important segment of the reading public, and it might even be said that very popular books, even those by Vasconcelos, must be read by at least a part of the upcult to attain best-seller status.

As for sex, it has proven itself inadequate as a means of selling books in Brazil. It is merely an option. In Amado's works, after all, the plot is of primary concern, and Miss Bijou will, I think, concede the difficulty of writing 200 pages of prose with a plot nucleus of the vicissitudes of orgasm. The sexiness of the novels of Amado, Veríssimo, and Lins do Rêgo is neither pornographic nor decadent. The popularity of these three writers has, in fact, contributed to the general respectability of sex as a theme in Brazilian fiction. But some novels with a lot of it sell badly. Others, such as Vasconcelos' (1968) *My Lime Tree (O Meu Pé de Laranja Lima)* ignore it altogether and still become best-sellers. Also, the fact that a number of popular Brazilian novels have sold well in translation might indicate that their presumed regionalism is less esoteric than it appears. I do not deny that they are regional, sociological, or political, but I would suggest that in many cases these authors have transcended the picturesque sufficiently to appeal to an international midcult-upcult audience.

What, then, accounts for the success of this handful of novelists? First, it is obvious that they are in the literary sense rather traditionalistic. Little of the experimentation thought to characterize the modern novel appears in their works. The preeminence of plot and the tendency to dramatize plot elements are, from the vantage point of the upcult, atavistic traits. But only one of these writers, Vasconcelos, consistently construes plot as a substitute for experience. The hedonism involved in reading the works of the other three authors is obviously more complex than simple escapism.

I would submit that Amado, Lins do Rêgo, and Veríssimo appeal to a large audience in part because of their concern with national self-awareness. Nationalism of one kind or another has been conspicuous in all kinds of Brazilian literature since the colonial period. Veríssimo offers the point of view of the enlightened bourgeoisie. Lins do Rêgo traces the decay of the rural sugar aristocracy, a highly appealing subject—not of course to the aristocracy, but to the middle class. But what about Amado? It would seem to me that upcult and midcult have become progressively more cosmopolitan in Brazil, in the sense that they are increasingly like European and other American groups of the same levels—increasingly blander, if you will. The only group in Brazil that retains a vigorous cultural complex significantly different from that of other countries is the lower class. And Amado makes a great deal of the difference, emphasizing and even exaggerating that which is more different, particularly the Africanness of the lower class in Bahia. For Amado, the disinherited are the source of theme, language, and attitude, which I think also appeals to a Brazilian self-image. Whether or not the image is accurate is irrelevant. But his portraits in later works of the anarchistic rascal of immense charm, insatiable appetite for sex and drink, and no responsibilities is the kind of self-image I think the Brazilian midcult—and upcult—like to cultivate, if only secretly.

The paradoxes of popular Brazilian fiction are thus largely only apparent. The electric canopener comes in four sizes and several decorator colors, and the people who buy it are almost all middle-class. As in the case of the canopener, the upcult disapproves and buys it only because it is handy, easy to operate, and entertaining.

NOTES

1. MacDonald's (1962: 14, 34, 12-13, 48) term for the patrician level of culture is simply "High Culture." I have supplied a substitute for this term not in the name of the democratic principle but for the sake of lexical balance. I have also abandoned the ornamental capital letters for each term, which I think lead us to believe that this division is more precise than it actually is. MacDonald's view of culture levels in the United States recognizes the upcult's influence on folk art, but not the reverse. He feels that folk art and upcult art have come to be separated into "fairly watertight compartments," and that midcult is characterized by its "homogenization" of mass and upcult tastes. He nevertheless claims that the midcult writer always worries about the intellectuals "however he pretends to despise them."

2. Discussions of the scope and importance of Marxism as part of the common background of Latin American intellectuals can be found in Poppino (1964: 40); Ellison (1964: 89).

REFERENCES

AMADO, J. (1965) Gabriela, Cravo e Canela. São Paulo: Livraria Martins Editôra.

--- (1961-1964) Os Subterrâneos da Liberdade. Volume I: Os Asperos Tempos; Volume II: Agonia da Noite; Volume III: A Luz no Túnel. São Paulo: Livraria Martins Editôra.

--- (1956) O Cavaleiro da Esperança: Vida de Luiz Carlos Prestes. Rio de Janeiro: Editorial Vitóra.

BIJOU, B. (1969) Noites de Amor. São Paulo: Editôra Terra.

--- (1968) A Sêde. São Paulo: Editôra Terra.

CANDIDO, A. (1965) Literatura e Sociedade. São Paulo: Companhia Editôra Nacional.

CORTAZAR, J. (1969) Ultimo Round. Mexico City: Siglo Veintiuno Editores.

COSTA, F. (1961) "Jorge Amado para o Nobel." Jornal da Bahia 1 (February 11).

ELLISON, F. P. (1964) "The writer in Latin America," in J. J. Johnson (ed.) Continuity and Change in Latin America. Stanford, Calif.: Stanford Univ. Press.

GROSSMAN, W. L. (1967) "O moralista." Jornal de Letras 207 (July).

Jornal do Brasil (1967) "A defesa dos fracos." 1 (September 15).

MacDONALD, D. (1962) "Masscult and midcult," in Against the American Grain. New York: Random House.

PEREZ, R. (1960) Escritores Brasileiros Contemporâneos. Rio de Janeiro: Editôra Civilização Brasileira.

POPPINO, E. (1964) International Communism in Latin America: A History of the Movement, 1917-1963. London: Free Press.

DOS REIS E MELLO, C. (1960) "As duas racheis." Leitura 42 (December).

RIDEOUT, W. B. (1956) The Radical Novel in the United States, 1900-1954. Cambridge, Mass.: Harvard Univ. Press.

DE VASCONCELOS, J. M. (1968) O Meu Pé Laranja Lima. São Paulo: Edições Melhoramentos.

VERISSIMO, E. (1965) O Senhor Embaixador. Pôrto Alegre: Editôra Globa.

--- (1949-1962) O Tempo e o Vento. Volume I: O Continente; Volume II: O Retrato; Volume III: O Arquipélago. Pôrto Alegre: Editôra Globo.

VILLACA, A. C. (1960) "Gabriela." Jornal da Bahia 1 (December 8).

Peasants, Power, and Applied Social Change

Vicos as a Model

Edited by HENRY F. DOBYNS, Prescott College
PAUL L. DOUGHTY, Indiana University
HAROLD D. LASSWELL, Yale University

Analyzes one of the most exciting instances of planned social intervention in the history of modern social science—the fifteen years during which the Cornell Peru Project (under the leadership of the late Allan R. Holmberg) undertook to assist in the self-transformation of a group of peasants in the village of Vicos, from what was essentially a fifteenty-century condition of serfdom to a late-nineteenth-century stage of economic, political and social development. The theoretical framework of this report is based upon a value-institutional system developed in large measure by one of the volume's co-editors (Harold Lasswell) and lays heavy emphasis upon the power variable . . . which is seen as the key to obtaining positive change effects. The relevance of this study to contemporary trends in anthropology is also underscored.

Based on the March 1965 issue of the American Behavioral Scientist.

Table of Contents

Introduction—Henry F. Dobyns, Paul L. Doughty, Harold D. Lasswell
A Note to Anthropologists—Henry F. Dobyns and Paul L. Doughty
I. Experimental Intervention in the Field—**Allan R. Holmberg**
II. The Role of Power in Changing Values and Institutions—**Allan R. Holmberg**
III. The Interplay between Power and Wealth—**Mario C. Vazquez**
IV. Human Relations: Affection, Rectitude, and Respect—**Paul L. Doughty**
V. Well Being—**J. Oscar Alers**
VI. Enlightenment and Skill Foundations of Power—**Henry F. Dobyns**
VII. The Transferability of Vicos Strategy—**Harold D. Lasswell**
VIII. The Significance of Vicos for the Emerging Policy Sciences—**Harold D. Lasswell**
Appendix A: Vicos Area and Population Growth—**J. Oscar Alers**
Appendix B: Local and National Power Structure in Relation to Vicos—**Paul L. Doughty**
Select Bibliography of Cornell Peru Project Publications
General Bibliography / Index

ISBN 0-8039-0049-x **1971** **224 pages** **$10.00**
Market: World

SAGE PUBLICATIONS, INC.
275 S. Beverly Dr. / Beverly Hills, CA. 90212

SAGE PUBLICATIONS LTD
44 Hatton Garden, London E C 1

WILLIAM J. BLOUGH
Department of Political Science
Winthrop College
Rock Hill, South Carolina

POLITICAL ATTITUDES OF MEXICAN WOMEN

Support for the Political System Among a Newly Enfranchised Group

Any time a political system has to induct a formerly excluded group into the political process, there is apt to be some uncertainty about what the consequences will be. This has been true in the United States on several occasions. When the Nineteenth Amendment was under discussion, there was considerable interest in what effect the feminine vote would have. When Southern blacks began to vote in large numbers in the 1960s, politicians and scholars wondered what the consequences would be. In 1971, with the ratification of the Twenty-Sixth Amendment, the impact of the youth vote is being debated, even though we have twenty years of sophisticated behavioral research to guide our speculation.

In the United States, the political process is basically stable and institutionalized. But many countries are not so fortunate, particularly those that are moving rapidly from a traditional to a modern style. These countries are faced with the problem of

AUTHOR'S NOTE: The data used in this study were made available by the Inter-University Consortium for Political Research. The data were originally collected by Almond and Verba (1963). Neither Professors Almond and Verba nor the Consortium bears any responsibility for the analysis or interpretations presented here.

developing stable political institutions at the same time that the populations are being socialized rapidly into political activity (Lerner, 1958: ch. 2, deals with the transformation from traditional to modern life styles; Huntington, 1965, discusses the problem of too-rapid social change). In such circumstances, any large group entering the political arena for the first time can produce increased instability. If the political impact of Southern blacks and eighteen-year-olds in our own country is a phenomenon worth investigating, it is even more desirable to inquire into the effect of new political groups on the political process of countries with less predictable and less thoroughly studied political processes.

The purpose of this study is to explore the political attitudes of Mexican women at the time they were admitted to full political rights. Their attitudes are of interest because for nearly forty years after the Constitution of 1917 Mexican women were unable to vote. The constitution did not specifically deny women the vote, but from the beginning it was so interpreted. During the 1920s, a small woman suffrage movement began to claim for women a political equality commensurate with the democratic goals of the constitution (the following discussion of woman suffrage is based on Morton, 1962). This was, however, a period of instability, during which Mexican leaders were engaged in the delicate process of constructing new political institutions out of the chaos of the Revolution, and they were fearful that the entry of women into politics would threaten the stability of the political order they were building. The Roman Catholic Church at the time was a particular obstacle, though by no means the only one, and the demand for votes for women was seen as posing a counterrevolutionary threat. This feeling was expressed by a member of the Chamber of Deputies reacting to a feminist demonstration in the late 1920s: "Twenty-five thousand Mexican women coming before the Chamber to ask the vote for women! How horrible! It means that, if they obtain their object, we shall have a Bishop for President" (see Morton, 1962: 13).

The church-state controversy in Mexico, the lesson of the

1933 elections in Spain where the votes of women influenced by a hostile church set back the parties supporting the Republic (Morton, 1962: 23), and the feeling that Mexican women had not developed a "revolutionary conscience" (Luna Arroyo, 1936) all worked against the enfranchisement of women in the 1930s. In 1939, with a strong, conservative, church-supported challenge shaping up for the following year's elections, the Mexican congress failed to take final action on a suffrage amendment (Morton, 1962: 39-41). In 1946, women finally received the vote in municipal elections, and in 1953 an amendment giving them the right to vote in national elections as well was approved. Women voted nationally for the first time in 1955 in elections for the Chamber of Deputies, and a few even ran for office. But the only really important election in Mexico is for president, and it was not until 1958 that they had an opportunity to vote in a presidential election.

As the 1958 election approached, there was some feeling that the women's vote would be "a real menace to the PRI" (the governing *Partido Revolucionario Institucional*).[1] President Adolfo Ruiz Cortines assured the uneasy politicians that "the Mexican women citizens merit the absolute confidence of the whole nation," but in almost the same breath he implied that women should not assume too active a role.

> They will continue to be the principal guardians of their homes as mothers, wives, and daughters; they will not be misled by mistaken assumptions; they understand well what are their obligations in order that they may dignify themselves as women and as citizens, for the autonomy of the family and for the sovereignty of the nation [see Morton, 1962: 91].

Official candidate Adolfo López Mateos made a definite appeal for the votes of women, but he too sounded a cautionary note (see Morton, 1962: 94):

> The right to vote does not uproot women from family and home to lure them into politics. Rather, women's suffrage brings into the home a deeper understanding of great national issues, a daily inquiry

> on matters that are of concern to us all. This will prove once again that neither contentious preaching nor deceptive enticement can change women's most intimate sentiments or wean them away from their home and family.

The 1958 election returns clearly indicated that the conservative, pro-clerical opposition PAN *(Partido de Acción Nacional)* had received no notable advantage from the female vote, since López Mateos received 90 percent of the vote. But the opposition candidate was inexperienced and inept, clericalism was not an issue, and there remained the fear that at some future time of crisis a counterrevolutionary demagogue backed by the church could pose a serious challenge with the help of women's votes (Morton, 1962: 133-134).

How did Mexican women really feel about the political order at the time they cast their first presidential votes? Had they come to hold essentially the same attitudes as men? Or was this formerly excluded group hostile, as the revolutionary leaders feared, with this hostility masked by abstention from the polls and by the fact that there really was no contest in 1958? The remainder of this paper is devoted to providing some answers to these questions. The best way to find out about the attitudes of a large population is to conduct a sample survey. Fortunately, a comprehensive inquiry into the attitudes of urban Mexicans was conducted in 1959, the year after that first presidential vote. The following comparison of Mexican women and men is based on data collected in that survey (see Lerner, 1958; Huntington, 1965).[2]

The Approach

What the Mexican leaders were concerned about, basically, was support for the Mexican political community. "Support" is partly a matter of overt behavior, like willingly obeying laws, paying taxes, and voting in elections, but it also consists of generally positive feelings. In the last analysis, the survival of any political system, but especially one that is modern and democratic or aspires to be, depends upon how favorable the populace feels toward it. If a system commands pride, loyalty, and affection, it may weather severe crises, but if the feelings of the population are at best only acquiescent, the system will be vulnerable in times of stress.

David Easton (1957) distinguishes three levels at which supports are fed into a political system. These are the political community, the regime, and the government. The political community is the most comprehensive object of support and involves a feeling of mutual interest in settling conflicts peacefully in order to preserve the community—for example, a feeling of national "one-ness" binding people together and transcending partisan feelings or local loyalties. The second object of support, the regime, consists of "all those arrangements that regulate the way in which the demands put into the system are settled and the way in which decisions are put into effect. They are the so-called rules of the game" (Easton, 1957: 392). This may be thought of as agreement on the constitutional order. The third object of support is the government, as it makes decisions resolving conflicts for the society. Easton's approach suggests that an inquiry into sex differences in attitudes toward the Mexican political system might best move from the most generalized objects of affect to the more specific. Consequently, we will examine first attitudes toward Mexico as a country and the Mexican Revolution, and then deal with attitudes toward the Mexican government and the governing party.

In pursuing this inquiry, three variables in addition to sex are examined. One is education, for there is a great difference in the amount of education received by the men and women in the sample. Three educational groupings were used: those who reported no schooling at all, those who received only some primary schooling, and those who had some education beyond the six primary grades.[3]

A second variable is intensity of religious feeling, since one of the bases for opposition to woman suffrage was the belief that women were more apt to be swayed by the church and would be inclined to favor political movements that wanted the church restored to a position of great influence. Intensity could only be measured crudely with these data, using one question which asked how often the respondent attended church. Seventy-five percent of women and 62 percent of men claimed to attend church at least once a week; only 1 percent of each sex said they never went to church.[4] Those who attended church at least once a week were assumed to have a stronger attachment to the church than those who went to church less regularly.

The third variable is level of actual participation. The remarks of López Mateos and Ruiz Cortines indicated that they hoped women would participate in moderation. Since only those citizens who act have an impact on political life, it is especially useful to see how the active women resemble men; but the attitudes of the inactive also are important in that inactivity may conceal alienation which could be disruptive if these citizens should at some time be stimulated to action. Experience in other countries has shown that when women first get the vote they are considerably less likely than men to use it, and that they tend to be less active than men even after generations of legal political equality.

Thus, it is not surprising to find Mexican women much less participant than men in all the forms of activity which the survey questions explored. Whereas 82 percent of the men said that they had voted in the 1958 presidential election, only 48 percent of the women did so. While 55 percent of the men said that they talked about politics and public affairs with other people at least occasionally, only 25 percent of women did so. About 23 percent of the men and 8 percent of the women said that they were or had been at one time members of a political party. Sixteen percent of the men and only 4 percent of the women reported ever having tried to influence a law or decision of the national or local government. Even among the best-educated, the gap between men and women was marked in all of these activities.

Altogether, nearly three-fifths of the men and one-fourth of the women said they had participated in two or more ways, 30 percent of men and 38 percent of women in only one way, and 12 percent of men and 39 percent of women in none of these modes of political activity. Therefore a three-part division into "high," "medium," and "low" participants, corresponding to these three groupings, has been used to make comparisons based on participation.[5]

The following analysis is based on percentage comparisons presented in tabular form. No tests of statistical significance have been used because, due to the nature of the sample and the degree to which it has been subdivided, they are of doubtful value. In a study such as this, consistent patterns of difference or similarity may lead to important and valid conclusions even if individual tables do not meet tests of significance (for a fuller discussion of the problems of statistical tests and sampling error, see Almond and Verba, 1963: appdx. A, 523-525).

The Analysis

We turn now to the examination of attitudes toward elements of the political system, moving from the more general to the more particular objects of affect.

ATTITUDES TOWARD THE COUNTRY

Any citizen who has become even partially modernized can be expected to have some feeling for his country, regardless of what he thinks of the government of the day or even the constitutional order. This was true of the Mexican respondents. All were asked an open-ended question, "In general, what are some of the things about our country that we as Mexicans ought to be proud of? " As Table 1 shows, the great majority of both women and men named at least one object of pride, even though about twice as many poorly educated women as men were unable to answer the question. Women were more likely than men to say there was nothing to be proud of, but less than one woman in twenty did so.

TABLE 1
Objects of Pride as a Mexican, by Sex and Education (in percentages)

	Men			
Objects of Pride	*None*	*Primary*	*Higher*	*Total*
Political objects	36	45	45	43
Social legislation	0	2	2	2
International position	7	3	15	6
Economic system	20	34	33	32
Characteristics of people	5	12	27	15
Spiritual values and religion	9	4	4	4
Contributions to arts and education	12	10	14	11
Contributions to science	0	1	2	1
Physical attributes of country	21	21	18	20
Nothing	5	1	0	1
Other[a]	20	16	19	17
Total[b]	136	147	178	153
n giving responses	56	278	96	433[c]
Percentage saying "don't know"	15	5	4	7
Total n	66	294	100	464[c]
	Women			
Political objects	29	27	40	29
Social legislation	1	2	3	2
International position	1	1	0	1
Economic system	22	27	26	26
Characteristics of people	15	18	19	18
Spiritual values and religion	17	12	3	12
Contributions to arts and education	9	8	26	11
Contributions to science	0	1	0	–
Physical attributes of country	24	28	32	28
Nothing	6	4	4	4
Other[a]	8	15	27	15
Total[b]	132	142	181	145
n giving responses	128	476	93	698[c]
Percentage saying "don't know"	33	12	2	16
Total n	191	544	95	831[c]

a. "Other" responses consisted mainly of miscellaneous patriotic sentiments such as pride in the heroes and events of Mexican history, pride in the flag, and the like.

b. Column totals are of unrounded percentages and may not agree exactly with the sums of the rounded percentages used in the table. Totals reflect multiple responses.

c. Level of education not ascertained for four men and one woman, hence the difference between the total n and the sum of the educational groups.

Responses to this question also indicate a rather strong sense of pride in what Easton termed the "regime." Forty-three percent of the men and 29 percent of the women answering the question cited specific political qualities as objects of pride. If indications of feelings toward the general political order may be thought to include not only strictly political objects of pride but also pride in things which probably can be credited to the satisfactory operation of the political system—that is, social legislation, Mexico's international position, and the operation of the economic system—55 percent of the responses given by men and 39 percent of those of women indicate favorable feelings. However, even though the best-educated women were about as likely as well-educated men to express pride in Mexico, they were less likely to name political and politically related objects.

One might expect that the more politically active citizens would be more likely to name political objects of pride, but there is no clear relationship. Of those answering, 42 percent of men scoring low in participation name political objects, compared with 47 percent of the medium group and 46 percent of the high. The figures for women are 29 percent, 25 percent, and 35 percent, respectively. Likewise, we would expect the more devout to be less apt, if anything to name political objects, but the reverse seems to be true: of men, 46 percent of regular churchgoers and 39 percent of the less regular named political objects, while with women the proportions are 30 percent and 25 percent, respectively.

ATTITUDES TOWARD THE MEXICAN REVOLUTION

The Revolution of 1910 was such a crucial event in Mexican history that it still plays a vital role in political life. As Robert Scott (1959: 96) wrote:

> Today, after the passing of a generation . . . the Revolution remains a vital force in Mexican life. Everything and everyone Mexican . . . exists in an atmosphere permeated with its spirit. Every major public topic is approached, considered, accepted, or rejected in terms of what the Revolution is supposed to stand for, and no serious

> proponent of just about anything would dream of forgetting to claim legitimacy for his particular point of view by labeling it the authentic voice, perhaps the only authentic voice, of the Revolution.

Because of its importance as a legitimizing myth and because Mexican politicians were concerned that women had not developed a "revolutionary conscience," attitudes toward the Revolution must be explored. In addition, answers to questions about the Revolution may imply some evaluation of the political group which rules the country and preaches the myth, since pursuit of Revolutionary goals has been monopolized by the PRI.

Despite its importance, 17 percent of the men and fully 45 percent of the women in the sample were unable to volunteer a single goal of the Mexican Revolution when asked to do so. The difference between the sexes is most pronounced among those with the least likelihood of having been formally exposed to the myth: about four-tenths of uneducated men and seven-tenths of the uneducated women were unable to volunteer any objectives of the Revolution. Among the best-educated, however, nearly nineteen respondents out of twenty of both sexes were able to name some goal. Of those naming goals, almost no one named evil or undesirable objectives.

Those respondents who named goals were asked if they thought these goals had been achieved, if they had been forgotten, or if they were still in the process of being realized. Overall, men and women were very similar in their responses: 23 percent of each sex thought the goals had been realized; 61 percent of men and 55 percent of women thought that people were still working to achieve them, while only 12 percent of men and 13 percent of women thought that they had been forgotten. As Table 2 shows, there was some tendency with increased education to regard the Revolution as an ongoing process (which is the official view). Women were about equally inclined to feel that the goals had been forgotten regardless of their education, while the pattern for men is very irregular. The more politically active respondents of both sexes also seemed

TABLE 2
Achievement of the Goals of the Mexican Revolution, by Sex and Education[a] (in percentages)

	Men			*Women*		
Achievement of Goals	*None*	*Primary*	*Higher*	*None*	*Primary*	*Higher*
Goals have been realized	28	23	20	29	24	16
Still working toward them	56	57	71	47	53	70
Goals have been forgotten	5	16	6	12	14	11
Don't know and other	10	4	2	12	9	2
Total	99	100	99	100	100	99
n	39	249	94	58	311	88

a. Includes only those who were able to name some goal of the Revolution.

more inclined than the less active to accept the Revolution as an ongoing process and to reject the proposition that its goals had been abandoned, but among the women the differences between the three levels of participation are generally quite small. At all levels, but especially among the most active, men and women differed little in their responses (Table 3).

Since the Revolution involved such bitter conflict with the church, the more devout Mexicans might be expected to have more negative feelings about the Revolution than the less religious. The data offer little confirmation of this. The more

TABLE 3
Achievement of the Goals of the Mexican Revolution, by Sex and Political Participation[a] (in percentages)

	Men			*Women*		
Achievement of Goals	*Low*	*Medium*	*High*	*Low*	*Medium*	*High*
Goals have been realized	23	33	19	21	26	20
Still working toward them	46	51	66	53	52	62
Goals have been forgotten	19	15	11	15	15	11
Don't know and other	12	1	5	11	8	7
Total	100	100	101	100	101	100
n	26	99	244	129	186	133

a. Includes only those who were able to name some goal of the Revolution.

regular churchgoers of both sexes were at most only slightly less able to name goals of the Revolution. There may have been some tendency among regular churchgoers to think that the goals of the Revolution had been forgotten, but the difference is small: 14 percent of the regular churchgoers of both sexes thought so, compared with 11 percent of the less regular.

ATTITUDES TOWARD THE NATIONAL GOVERNMENT

Potentially, one of the most useful questions to tap the feelings of urban Mexican men and women toward their government asked whether, all things considered, the laws and decrees of the national government tended to improve the life of the respondent or whether he would be better off without them. Unfortunately, this question was asked only of those respondents who previously had said that the national government's activities had some effect on their daily lives, and about two respondents out of three of both sexes said that they did not. Of those who did perceive some effect, about one man in seven and one woman in five thought they would be better off without its activities, while about one-fifth volunteered that its effects were mixed. As Table 4 shows, the definitely negative feelings were most pronounced among the uneducated and minimal among those with schooling above the primary level, but women seem more negatively disposed than men, at least among those respondents with some education.

Among men, the small number of respondents in the low and medium groups makes it impossible to say whether level of political activity was related to feelings about the impact of government policies. Among women, the more participant women were, the less likely they were to regard government policies as definitely harmful, with 34 percent of the low participants, 20 percent of the medium, and 15 percent of the high holding this view. Among the most active participants, men and women differed little: 67 percent of men and 60 percent of women thought government actions tended to improve life, 18 percent of men and 20 percent of women thought they were sometimes beneficial and sometimes not, and 14 percent of men

TABLE 4
Feelings About the Effects of the Laws and Decrees of the Mexican Government, by Sex and Education[a] (in percentages)

Feeling	*None*	*Primary*	*Higher*	*Total*
Men				
They tend to improve life	(48)	59	85	66
Sometimes improve; sometimes not	(24)	19	13	18
Would be better off without them	(24)	19	2	14
Other and don't know	(5)	2	0	2
Total	(101)	100	100	100
n	(21)[b]	73	47	141
Women				
They tend to improve life	55	50	73	54
Sometimes improve; sometimes not	9	22	18	19
Would be better off without them	32	22	6	21
Other and don't know	5	7	3	6
Total	101	101	100	100
n	44	181	33	258

a. Includes only those who said that the government's activities affected their daily lives.

b. Parentheses indicate that the base number is less than two percent of the total sample.

and 15 percent of women thought the country would be better off without them.

Frequency of church attendance appears to have a mixed relationship to attitudes about the national government, but one that is similar for both men and women. Church attendance was unrelated to the respondents' perceptions of whether they were affected by the government. Table 5 shows that of those who were affected, the more regular churchgoers of both sexes may have been a little less likely than the less regular to give unqualified approval or disapproval of the government's policies and more likely to have mixed feelings about them.

Another indication of how citizens feel toward government is whether they expect to be treated fairly by government officials. Almond and Verba (1963: 108-109) found in their five-nation study that Mexicans were less likely than citizens of the other countries to expect to be treated the same way as anyone else if they had to go to a government office about

TABLE 5
Feelings About the Effects of the Laws and Decrees of the Mexican Government, by Sex and Church Attendance[a] (in percentages)

	Men		*Women*	
Feeling	*Regular*	*Less Regular*	*Regular*	*Less Regular*
They tend to improve life	62	70	54	56
Sometimes improve; sometimes not	21	11	21	10
Would be better off without them	14	18	20	26
Other and don't know	3	0	5	8
Total	100	99	100	100
n	87	44	190	62

a. Includes only those who said that the government's activities affected their daily lives.

TABLE 6
Expectation of Equal Treatment at a Government Office, by Sex and Education (in percentages)

Expect Equal Treatment?	*None*	*Primary*	*Higher*	*Total*
Men				
Yes	26	49	63	48
Depends and other[a]	12	7	2	7
No	53	43	35	43
Don't know	9	1	0	2
Total	100	100	100	100
n	66	294	100	464[b]
Women				
Yes	17	42	56	38
Depends and other[a]	5	5	4	5
No	70	51	40	54
Don't know	7	2	0	3
Total	99	100	100	100
n	191	544	95	831[b]

a. Almost all of the "depends and other" responses implied unequal treatment.

b. Level of education not ascertained for four men and one woman, hence the difference between total n and the sum of the educational groups.

some matter. Nearly all the Mexican respondents of both sexes had an opinion on this matter and, as Table 6 shows, women were even more pessimistic than men. This was true even among the best-educated respondents. Among the least politically active, men appeared to be even more negative than women: only 19 percent of men and 31 percent of women in this group expected equal treatment without qualification. But among the medium and high participants, men were the more optimistic sex. In the highest group, 54 percent of men and 46 percent of women expected equal treatment. Men who attended church weekly were about as likely to anticipate no discrimination as those who were less regular (47 percent and 49 percent, respectively), while the regular women may have been a little less likely than the less devout to expect equal treatment (36 percent and 43 percent, respectively). What we can infer is that women as a group are more pessimistic than men, that a sex difference seems to exist even among the best-educated and most politically active respondents, and religion is probably related to this pessimism only among women, if at all.

ATTITUDES TOWARD THE OFFICIAL PARTY

Mexico has been governed for so many years through the instrumentality of a "Revolutionary party" that for most Mexicans the government and the PRI are for all practical purposes indistinguishable. Attitudes toward the PRI, then, are not merely directed toward a political party, as might be the case in the United States, but are a further indication of how Mexicans feel about their government. In the present discussion, three indicators are used: whether respondents believed that the policies of the PRI might endanger the national well-being, the respondents' identification with the official party and with the only viable opposition group, and how respondents actually voted in the 1958 election.

All respondents were asked whether they thought the activities of the PRI were very likely, moderately likely, or unlikely ever to endanger the well-being of the country. Ten percent of the men and 24 percent of the women were unable to venture an opinion on this question, but beyond this the sexes differed little in their estimates. Of those with an opinion, 14 percent of the men and 12 percent of the women thought it very likely that the PRI's actions would be harmful, while 57 percent of men and 51 percent of women thought this was unlikely. The rest thought there was some likelihood of harm. Responses did not seem to be related in any regular way to the other variables, nor did these variables seem to make any difference between men and women. There is no regular relationship between education and attitudes toward the PRI's policies (Table 7), although the uneducated of both sexes seem to be the least apprehensive. Controlling for political activity also reveals no regular relationship (Table 8). Women gave almost identical responses regardless of church attendance, although the less regular men may have been a little more likely than the more regular churchgoers (61 percent to 54 percent) to expect no harm.[6]

A second indication of how Mexicans felt about the official party and its performance is party identification. Party identification is essentially a feeling of attachment to a political party and, in countries where it has been studied, far more people identify with political parties than hold formal membership. Although studies have emphasized the strong influence party

TABLE 7
Likelihood that the Policies of the PRI Might Endanger the Welfare of the Country, by Sex and Education (in percentages)

	Men			*Women*		
Likelihood	*None*	*Primary*	*Higher*	*None*	*Primary*	*Higher*
Very likely	11	14	14	12	11	15
Moderately likely	30	28	33	29	41	32
Unlikely	59	58	53	60	48	53
Total	100	100	100	101	100	100
n giving responses	46	273	100	112	437	81
Percentage saying "don't know"	30	7	0	41	20	15
Total n	66	294	100	191	544	95

TABLE 8
Likelihood that the Policies of the PRI Might Endanger the Welfare of the Country, by Sex and Political Participation (in percentages)

	Men			*Women*		
Likelihood	*Low*	*Medium*	*High*	*Low*	*Medium*	*High*
Very likely	15	11	15	12	14	8
Moderately unlikely	12	37	27	35	39	37
Unlikely	73	52	58	53	46	55
Total	100	100	100	100	99	100
n giving responses	33	118	252	198	246	176
Percentage saying "don't know"	37	11	4	38	20	9
Total n	52	132	262	318	308	194

identification has on political attitudes and behavior, this emotional attachment to a party is also the result of experiences and attitudes. Thus, while we would expect persons identifying with the PRI to have more positive attitudes toward what it has done, we would also expect that persons who were generally satisfied with the operation of the political system would tend to identify with the PRI, while those who were less contented might identify with the opposition PAN, which has been a vigorous critic of the PRI's performance.[7]

Sixty percent of the men and 34 percent of the women in the sample identified with a political party.[8] Of these, 80 percent of women and 84 percent of men chose the PRI, while 16 percent of women and 13 percent of men preferred the PAN, the remainder naming minor political groups. At all educational levels, women apparently were a little more likely than men to prefer some party other than the PRI, and among the best-educated, more than one-fifth of both sexes identified with the PAN. As Table 9 shows, the sex differences were small. Despite the lower preference for the PRI among the better-educated, it appears from Table 10 that the more politically active respondents were more likely to prefer the PRI, with men and women virtually identical at the highest level of activity.

Since the PAN has a reputation as a pro-clerical party, one

TABLE 9

Party Identification, by Sex and Education (in percentages)

	Men			*Women*		
Identifies With	*None*	*Primary*	*Higher*	*None*	*Primary*	*Higher*
PRI	88	85	76	(80)	83	71
PAN	12	10	24	(12)	15	22
Other party	0	5	0	(8)	2	7
Total identifiers	100	100	100	(100)	100	100
n	26	196	55	(25)a	205	55

a. Parentheses indicate that the base number is less than two percent of the total sample.

would expect the more devout respondents to tend to prefer it, and apparently this was the case. Here again, however, the differences between the sexes were small. Of the regular churchgoing men, 79 percent preferred the PRI, 17 percent the PAN, and the remainder, other parties; the proportions for regular churchgoing women were 77 percent, 18 percent, and 5 percent. Among those attending church less frequently, 91 percent of the men chose the PRI, 8 percent the PAN, and 1 percent other parties, while the proportions for less regularly attending women were 88 percent, 10 percent and 2 percent respectively.

TABLE 10

Party Identification, by Sex and Political Participation[a]

(in percentages)

	Men			*Women*		
Identifies With	*Low*	*Medium*	*High*	*Low*	*Medium*	*High*
PRI	(b)	76	86	68	78	86
PAN	–	21	11	29	17	11
Other party	–	3	3	2	4	4
Total identifiers	(b)	100	100	99	99	101
n	(6)	68	188	41	115	104

a. Because current party membership was a factor in both party identification and political participation, nine men and nineteen women whose level of participation was affected by current party membership have been omitted from this calculation.

b. Too few cases; base number is less than one percent of the total sample.

Altogether, apart from the fact that far fewer women identified with any party, women were at most only slightly more likely than men to prefer the PAN, regardless of what variables were held constant.

Party identification is probably a better indicator of basic feelings than the 1958 presidential vote. In that year, the PRI nominated an extremely attractive candidate, Adolfo López Mateos, while the PAN fielded an inexperienced and unknown businessman who conducted a rather inept campaign. To top it off, the clerical question only came up in a negative way, for the church did not object to the candidacy of López, while his opponent took such an embarrassingly pro-clerical stand that the church felt obliged to disavow any ties with the PAN (Cline, 1962: 169). Nevertheless, it would be inappropriate to ignore an election, for it is one obvious way of expressing dissatisfaction with the government.

The official count in 1958 gave López Mateos 90.4 percent of the vote, against 9.4 percent for the PAN candidate. The sample gave a slightly larger share to the PAN, which is not surprising considering the sample's urban nature and the PAN's greater strength in urban areas: 11 percent of the men and 14 percent of the women voted PAN. As with the party identifiers, women were more likely to vote PAN if they were better educated: 5 percent of the uneducated, 14 percent with some primary schooling, and 18 percent of those with some higher schooling did so. Among men, there was no association, for PAN received one vote in every eight or nine regardless of educational level. On the other hand, the only evidence of association between church attendance and voting was among the men, with 13 percent of the regular churchgoers and 8 percent of the less regular voting PAN, while 14 percent of both groups of women did so.

Those who voted in 1958 had participated politically at least at the medium level by definition. What about those who were active in other ways as well? With men, the more active were more likely to vote PRI: only 9 percent of those who acted in other ways voted for the opposition candidate, compared with 17 percent of those who did nothing but vote. This pattern, similar to that seen in the discussion of party identification, did not hold for women, for 14 percent of women of both groups voted PAN. Looked at a different way, those who were sufficiently discontented with the ruling party to vote for the oppostion in 1958 were no more likely (women) or less likely (men) to engage in other kinds of political activity.

The relationship of education, church attendance, and political activity to the 1958 vote is less clear than their relationship to party identification. As far as sex differences are concerned, however, the same overall conclusion emerges: Mexican women were only slightly more likely than men to prefer the PAN.

Before leaving this analytical section, a word should be said about the three questions on which a large number of respondents, especially women, responded with "don't know." These asked for objects of pride as a Mexican, estimates of the danger of the PRI's policies, and goals of the Mexican Revolution. Since large numbers of women (ranging from 16 percent on the first of these to 45 percent on the last) did not give an answer, it might be that they were concealing hostility by feigning ignorance. If so, this hostiliity should have been reflected in their responses to the questions they did answer. However, a check against other questions indicates that the "don't knows" of both sexes differed from those giving answers primarily in being somewhat less likely to answer other questions, too. Otherwise, their responses overall were little if any more negative than those of respondents who did answer the three questions.

Summary

The foregoing discussion has considered the attitudes of urban Mexican men and women toward important elements of the political system, proceeding from the most general aspects (attitudes toward Mexico as a country and toward the Mexican Revolution) to the more specific (attitudes toward the national government and the governing party). The purpose has been to see whether at the time they entered into full political equality the attitudes of women differed from those of men to any marked degree. In the process, sex differences in education, frequency of attendance at church, and degree of political activity also were considered because it was felt that such things might contribute to any differences in attitudes that might be revealed. Our interest has been in discovering whether there are any consistent patterns of sex differences, since differences on individual questions would probably not be significant by themselves.

Let us first review overall sex differences and then look briefly at the impact of each of the other variables. Women were markedly less able to answer some of the questions, a fact that can probably be attributed to their lack of political experience rather than to any latent hostility toward the political system. There were only three questions on which men and women seem to differ clearly in their actual responses. Women were less likely than men to name something political as an object of pride. Women seem to have been about half again as likely as men to feel that the national government's activities were harmful. Women apparently were less hopeful of receiving equal treatment at the hands of government officials.

On the other questions, sex differences were small or nonexistent. Although much less likely than men to be able to name an objective of the Mexican Revolution, women were very close to men in their estimate of the achievement of these goals. Although less able to voice an opinion, women appeared to be only a little more likely than men to expect harm to come from the PRI's policies. Women seemed to be a little more inclined to identify with and vote for the opposition PAN, but sex differences were small. However, on no question did women respond more favorably than men. Taking all of the questions together, it appears that Mexican women probably were a little less favorably disposed toward the political system than were men, but what is most striking is the basic similarity between the two sexes.

Since even the largest differences between the sexes were relatively small, it is not surprising that there was no consistent relationship between the other variables and sex differences.

The impact of education was clearest in that the more educated respondents, especially women, were more likely to answer the questions. More favorable attitudes toward the activities of the national government and greater expectation of fair treatment at the hands of government officials seemed to accompany increased education, but in neither case did education erase the differences between women and men. On the other hand, the better-educated were more likely to identify with the opposition party, and respondents with some education may have been more apprehensive than the uneducated about the effects of the PRI's policies; again, however, education did not seem to affect the sexes differently. On other questions, education did not seem to be consistently related to either the attitudes of the respondents or the differences between the sexes.

Even less can be said about the other two variables. Women were somewhat more likely than men to attend church regularly, but there was no consistent relationship between devoutness and attitudes toward the system. While the more devout men and women in two cases (achievement of Revolutionary goals and party identification) may have been somewhat more negative than the less devout, on at least one quetsion (naming objects of pride) the more devout appeared a little more favorable. On the other questions, there was no consistent relationship between devoutness and attitudes. In sum, there was no indication that the somewhat greater devoutness of the women was related materially to any sex differences in attitudes.

Increased political activity seems to have little relationship with attitudes toward the system or with sex differences. On some questions, the more participant respondents tended to be more favorable (in expecting fair treatment at a government office and in identifying with the PRI), but this was not always the case. On most questions the relationship between activity and attitudes was irregular, small, or different for men and women. In the absence of any consistent pattern, we must conclude that the lower political activity of women was essentially unrelated to their slightly more negative feelings toward the political system.

Conclusion

No brief discussion like this can satisfactorily answer all the possible questions about the attitudes held by Mexican women as they embarked on a new role as the political equals of men. The evidence presented here has allowed us to come to some tentative conclusions. Of these, the most important is that, despite slightly more negative attitudes held by women, the two sexes were essentially similar in the way they felt about the political order. This basic similarity appears to have existed regardless of level of education, religious feeling, or political activity.

The leaders of the PRI waited until the tumultuous period of the Revolution was well past and the "Institutional Revolution" was securely established before they granted women the right to vote. From the data presented here, it appears that these leaders judged correctly in calculating that by the 1950s women were no longer—if indeed they ever had been—a potentially disruptive political force.

NOTES

1. See the statement by Eduardo J. Correa of the newspaper *Excelsior,* in Morton (1962: 112).

2. A complete discussion of the sampling procedures may be found in Appendix A of Almond and Verba (1963), but several things need to be mentioned here. First, for practical reasons, the universe sampled was limited to adults residing in cities of ten thousand or more. Although this means that more than half the adult population was excluded from the universe, the omission is probably not of much consequence for the purposes of this study. Second, because Mexico City made up such a large proportion of the total population in the universe, it was undersampled to permit adequate coverage of other cities. When tabulated, the interviews from Mexico City were upweighted to bring them into proper proportion with the rest. This upweighting means that an actual sample size of 1,008 individuals was enlarged to 1,295 for purposes of analysis. The number of respondents (n) given in the tables is based on the expanded sample and thus overstates the actual number of respondents, a fact which must be kept in mind when interpreting the figures. This procedure did not affect the distribution between men and women. Third, women were unintentionally oversampled (831 women to 464 men in the enlarged sample), but

this was an advantage when subdividing the two groups in the analysis, for women were more likely than men to say "don't know," to be inactive politically, and so on.

3. Fourteen percent of men and 23 percent of women reported that they had not attended school at all, while 22 percent of men and 11 percent of women had some schooling beyond the primary level. Level of education was not reported by four men and one woman.

4. All but two respondents claimed to be Roman Catholic. These and the seven percent of men and four percent of women who gave unclear answers about frequency of church attendance have been excluded from the analysis.

5. Where level of participation is discussed, the men and women who were too young to vote in 1958 or who refused to answer the question on voting have been excluded. These totaled eighteen men and eleven women.

6. While some lack of confidence in the PRI's policies seemed to be shared by all groups, it is worth noting that there was more fear of the policies of the opposition PAN. This was true even among the regular churchgoers of both sexes.

7. Identification with the PAN does not signify rejection of the political system as a whole, however. Another study using these data has shown that PAN identifiers tended to have somewhat more negative feelings than followers of the PRI about some aspects of the Mexican political system, but the differences between the two groups were too small to support a conclusion that rank-and-file PAN identifiers were alienated from the political order (see Blough, 1969).

8. Party identification here was based on respondents' answers to a series of questions. They were first asked if they were current members of any political party. If not—and most were not—they were asked if they considered themselves supporters *(partidarios)* of any party, and if they did not, they were then asked with which party they sympathized the most. If they named a party in answer to any of these questions, they were considered to identify with it.

REFERENCES

ALMOND, G. and S. VERBA (1963) The Civic Culture. Princeton, N.J.: Princeton Univ. Press.

ARROYO, A. L. (1936) La Mujer Mexicana en la Lucha Social. Mexico City.

BLOUGH, W. L. (1969) "Party identification and political attitudes in Mexico," pp. 9-17 in H. L. Johnson (ed.) Contemporary Latin America. Houston, Tex.: University of Houston Office of International Affairs.

CLINE, H. F. (1962) Mexico: Revolution to Evolution: 1940-1960. New York: Oxford Univ. Press.

EASTON, D. (1957) "An approach to the analysis of political systems." World Politics 9 (April): 391-393.

HUNTINGTON, S. P. (1965) "Political development and political decay." World Politics 17 (April): 386-430.

LERNER, D. (1958) The Passing of Traditional Society. Glencoe, Ill.: Free Press.

MORTON, W. M. (1962) Woman Suffrage in Mexico. Gainesville: Univ. of Florida Press.

SCOTT, R. E. (1959) Mexican Government in Transition. Urbana: Univ. of Illinois Press.

KEVIN C. KEARNS
Department of Geography
University of Northern Colorado
Greeley, Colorado

THE ANDEAN COMMON MARKET
A New Thrust at Economic Integration in Latin America

The decade of the 1960s could well be termed the First Economic Integration Decade in Latin America. During this period the republics of Latin America experienced a "collective awakening," inspiring an environment in which superficial and exclusivist values gave way to pragmatic and cooperative attitudes. Economic alliances were formed among neighbors, predicated on the rationale that, by joining forces in the spirit of cooperation and applying an ecumenical approach to common problems, each of the participating countries would be better off than pursuing a strictly autarkic course (see Figure 1).

The initial effort at integration was the Central American Common Market (CACM), formed in late 1960 and including all the countries of Central America except Panama.[1] That same year, the Latin American Free Trade Association (LAFTA) was created and, measured in terms of territory and population, represented the most significant economic cooperative. A third grouping was the Caribbean Free Trade Association (CARIFTA), established in 1968 as an agreement among eleven British Commonwealth nations and territories. The compelling logic of integration as the only sensible means of overcoming certain structural obstacles to economic development became an accepted principle in Latin America.

In May of 1969, a new economic association emerged, referred to originally as the Andean Group but now better known as the Andean Common Market (ANCOM). Forged in many respects from the failures of LAFTA, this bloc manifests an even more plausible raison d'étre than its predecessors.

ECONOMIC INTEGRATION PACTS IN LATIN AMERICA

Figure 1.

Failures of LAFTA

An insight to the weaknesses and failures of LAFTA provides an understanding for the justification and objectives of ANCOM. The Treaty of Montevideo, the agreement providing for the creation of LAFTA, stated in its preamble that the objectives of the pact were "the expansion of national markets through the gradual elimination of barriers to intraregional trade . . . and the pooling of efforts to achieve the progressive complementarity and integration of national economies on the basis of an effective reciprocity of benefits" (Cale, 1969: 2). The original signatories were Argentina, Brazil, Mexico, Peru, Chile, and Uruguay. Later, the countries of Paraguay, Colombia, Ecuador, Venezuela, and Bolivia joined, thus giving LAFTA representation among 90 percent of Latin America's population and over 94 percent of its area (Inter-American Development Bank, 1970: 45). The organizational structure for the administration of the treaty was less elaborate than that of CACM, and the intent was essentially the achievement of free trade within the region rather than the creation of a true common market. Still, it was with much optimism that the foundation of LAFTA was laid. Member countries expected at least a palliative, if not a panacea, to their problems of intraregional trade and small, limited markets.

From inception, LAFTA had to contend with problems inherent in its system. Regional infrastructural deficiencies in transportation and telecommunications almost immediately retarded progress, bringing to light more clearly than ever before the immensity of the geographical area which needed to be united. Equally impeding were the problems posed by characteristically unstable governments notorious for their lack of manageability of domestic economies and often wholly devoid of the resolve to carry out long-range and consistent international policy. To be sure, any multinational integration scheme encounters structural and functional difficulties, as evidenced by the history of the European Common Market, but it was quickly realized that LAFTA's problems were more formidable than most. The major weakness was the member nations' extremely diverse representation of levels of development, ranging from countries with a relatively strong economic base and sizeable markets, such as Brazil, Argentina and Mexico, to countries like Ecuador and Bolivia still striving to establish foundations in light industry. It was the fervent hope of the poorer members that these disparities could be reduced, with some tangible proof seen by the end of their first decade of cooperation.

Quite to the contrary, Latin Americans, who had hoped that their Free Trade Association, like that of the CACM and European Common Market, would provide dynamic and equitable stimulus to all participating members, became sadly disillusioned. While substantial increases in intra-LAFTA trade had, in fact, been realized (Table 1), some fears of the lesser member countries appeared as harsh realities. Foremost among these apprehensions was that the ABRAMEX (Andean Air Mail and Peruvian Times, 1968a: 8) countries (Argentina, Brazil, and Mexico) would continue to dominate, especially with respect to the production and trade of manufactured and semi-finished goods. During the period from 1962 to 1967, Argentina accounted for 39.7 percent of the total in this category; Brazil, 23.7 percent; Mexico, 9.1 percent (Bank of London and South America Review, 1970: 194). These figures were cause for much resentment. Other countries of LAFTA also became concerned that, should this trend continue, they could become mere economic vassals to the stronger powers. The overall pattern of intra-LAFTA trade, 1965-1969 (Table 1), supports the contention that most of the ANCOM countries have fared poorly within the LAFTA framework when compared with Argentina and Brazil.

A further source of irritation was that the early enthusiasm of the ABRAMEX countries steadily waned as they turned again toward their non-LAFTA markets which still account for nearly 90 percent of their exports (Cale, 1969: 3). The prestige of LAFTA's image clearly reached its nadir when, at the end of 1967, negotiators could not agree on the second stage of the common list of products to be freed from tariffs and duties by 1973 (Sanders, 1968: 2). At this point, many felt that the organization had collapsed into a state of virtual stagnation. It was also at this time that the countries of Andean South America, feeling that they were not receiving the benefits they had been promised from LAFTA, began to consider seriously the alternatives to the predicament.

TABLE 1
The Status of ANCOM Countries in Intra-LAFTA Trade, 1965-1969
(in millions of dollars)

	1965	*1966*	*1967*	*1968*	*1969*
EXPORTS (f.o.b.)					
Argentina	246.6	254.5	283.7	338.1	364.3
Bolivia[c]	3.5	7.7	9.9	13.9	14.0[a]
Brazil	201.7	187.7	161.2	193.1	241.4[a]
Colombia[c]	20.0	31.9	23.1	34.2	54.7
Chile[c]	56.4	60.0	84.3	91.8	94.4[a]
Ecuador[c]	13.4	13.0	14.5	16.4	16.1[a]
Mexico	44.0	64.3	57.2	62.2	86.7
Paraguay	17.6	19.9	15.6	,16.2	18.9
Peru[c]	62.2	60.4	40.0	50.5	57.5
Uruguay	16.0	26.9	17.1	18.9	30.6
Venezuela	160.8	149.5	145.1	165.1	168.3
Total	842.2	875.8	851.7	1,000.4	1,146.9
IMPORTS (c.i.f.)					
Argentina	289.4	352.3	253.6	275.3	365.9
Bolivia[c]	14.0	15.2	17.6	18.9	24.5[a]
Brazil	273.0	238.0	226.5	276.7	296.0[a]
Colombia[c]	39.3	57.9	37.9	48.0	75.3
Chile[c]	137.5	166.5	185.6	178.1	207.3[a]
Ecuador[c]	19.5	14.9	28.9	20.6	20.6[b]
Mexico	30.0	34.9	38.6	42.9	51.9
Paraguay	13.9	15.1	17.2	16.9	17.1
Peru[c]	88.0	100.2	104.1	107.8	106.3
Uruguay	45.1	57.3	46.9	42.0	58.2
Venezuela	36.2	35.0	38.7	47.1	61.5
Total	985.9	987.3	995.6	1,074.3	1,284.6

SOURCE: LAFTA *Newsletter*, no. 3, 1970.

a. Estimates.

b. 1968 figures repeated due to incomplete 1969 data.

c. ANCOM countries.

The Andean Subregional Pact

The concept of a way out of the LAFTA impasse through subregional integration originated in Colombia and Chile. In 1967, President Carlos Lleras of Colombia and Eduardo Frei of Chile became increasingly integration-minded, a fact in no small way attributable to LAFTA's lethargy. They presented to other Andean presidents their conviction that the west coast countries of South America should form a new economic power bloc that would constitute a potent counterforce (Sanders, 1968: 3-4) to the preponderant role of ABRAMEX. It was suggested that these countries already possessed attributes essential to a successful common market endeavor—namely, a degree of physical contiguity, a limited but connecting system of transportation, similarity in low income level, crucial need for increased market size, and even a history of common experiences and problems.[2]

During the next three years, the presidents of the Andean countries met frequently as a group, seeking to formulate policy for subregional solidarity. Integration of the Andean states was emphasized as a stimulus to LAFTA, not to be perceived as a rival to the parent organization. An Andean Development Corporation was created to conduct economic studies concerning opportunities for investment, acquisition of internal and external credits, and the feasibility of complementation projects. Finally, on May 26, 1969, Bolivia, Chile, Colombia, Peru, and Ecuador signed a treaty known as the Cartagena Agreement and formed the Andean Common Market.

Venezuela, one of the most ardent advocates of integration during the preliminary conferences, abruptly withdrew its application for membership at the last moment. This action resulted from pressures brought to bear on the administration of President Leoni by private industry (Latin American Newsletters, 1969: 1). The most direct threat, in the mind of the private sector, was the invasion of the Venezuelan market by goods produced in neighboring Colombia with cheaper labor (Andean Air Mail and Peruvian Times, 1968b: 4). The Colombian Government made little effort to hide the fact that it was disappointed over Venezuela's change of heart—especially at a time when the two countries were gaining momentum toward a closer social and economic relationship.[3]

In enumerating the goals of ANCOM, the Cartagena Agreement, which is really a blueprint for regional economic development rather than just a roadmap for integration, specifically cites the following as having the highest degree of priority (Republica de Chile, 1969):

(1) Harmonization of economic and social policies.

(2) Joint planning and execution of industrial projects predicated on multinational resources and markets, through sectorial development programs.

(3) Gradual and automatic elimination of all barriers to the free movement of goods among members at a faster pace than that followed within LAFTA.

(4) Establishment of a common external tariff to create a margin of preference for regional producers.

(5) Coordination of programs to speed development of the agricultural sector.

(6) Improvement of transportation and other facets of the region's infrastructure.

(7) Preferential treatment to be granted to the less-developed member countries of Bolivia and Ecuador.

Profile on Andean Bloc

In area, the ANCOM region, with 1,761,858 square miles, lies between Argentina (1,072,067 square miles) and Brazil (3,286,470 square miles)—or is about half the size of the United States. With a combined population of 53.6 million, the Andean Bloc includes in its membership Colombia, with 20.5 million people, as well as Bolivia, with a more modest 4.6 million (Table 2). And if Venezuela decides to join, a move that many

TABLE 2
National Population and Production Profiles in the Andean Group and Venezuela

Country	*Population* 1969 (millions)	*Population* Growth Rate[a] (%)	*Population* Urban Portion (%)	*Gross National Product* Per Person[b] (U.S. $)	*Gross National Product* Growth Rate (%)
Andean Group					
Colombia	20.5	3.2	52	301	+2.7
Ecuador	5.9	3.4	36	258	+0.2
Peru	13.2	3.1	47	371	–1.4
Bolivia	4.6	2.4	35	182	+3.0
Chile	9.4	1.9	68	616	+1.4
Total	53.6	2.9	50	341	+0.9
Venezuela	10.0	3.5	72	949	+1.5
Grand total	64.6	3.0	54	434	+1.2

SOURCE: *Foreign Agriculture,* Vol. VIII, no. 49, U.S. Department of Agriculture, 1970, p. 7.

a. Average of rate between 1967 and 1968 and of rate between 1968 and 1969.

b. In terms of 1968 prices.

observers anticipate will occur sometime within the next few years,[4] another 10 million potential producers and consumers can be added to this total. The average rate of population growth is slightly less than 3 percent, with Chile representing the only marked departure from this norm at a rate of 1.9 percent. ANCOM's combined gross national product of $20 billion is equal to that of Argentina, 70 percent of Mexico's or 60 percent of Brazil's. With respect to GNP per person, some disparities do appear, especially between Chile with $616 and Bolivia at $182. These differences do not, however, approach those which would be evident by comparing Argentina to one of the poorer Andean countries. Likewise, it is encouraging to note that Bolivia has been increasing its GNP at a faster rate than the other group members.

Combined resources provide the bloc with perhaps its greatest single asset. Countries of the Andes lead Latin America in the production of many minerals, accounting for between 70 and 100 percent of the copper, tin, molybdenum, tungsten, and bismuth (ECLA, 1970: 3). And nearly 50 percent of the coal and 65 percent of Latin America's iron is produced in the countries bordering the Pacific.[5] Regional hydroelectric power potential, especially in Peru and Colombia, is tremendous. Even in the agricultural sector, the Andean Bloc shows strength, ranking as a major producer of bananas, sugar, cacao, cotton, and coffee.

It is judicious, however, to remember that the shaping of five countries into a single bloc far transcends the simple addition of people and resources. It will require amiable relations not traditionally considered a characteristic of the Andean neighbors. A cursory glance at the region's history reveals more strife than cooperation and clashes between old rivals have left a residue of grievances and distrust not easily forgotten, even in the spirit of mutual betterment. For example, since the War of the Pacific in the 1880s both Peru and Bolivia have been politically at odds with the Chilean nation. Resentment persists with the remembrance that Chile expanded at the expense of their territories. The fact that Bolivia, to this day, finds itself landlocked causes considerable economic frustration. And the occurrence of new political disputes, such as that between Chile and Bolivia over the Lauca River (see Glassner, 1970), depicts more graphically than ever the need for new understanding and alternatives. In the titanic task of integrating national economies, political rifts seem an unaffordable luxury.

Trade, Tariffs, and Complementation

Historically, the Andean countries have traded very little with one another, a fact at least partially explained by two things. First, while they have attained a degree of industrial development since the end of World War II with enterprises ranging from food-processing, textiles, clothing, cement, glass, chemicals, and iron and steel to some kinds of machinery and equipment, the national economies of the countries are still at an early stage of development, and so there are few manufactured commodities for export. Second, the agricultural and mineral products, which comprise the bulk of Andean exports (Table 3), are often items (tin, copper, bananas, sugar, coffee) which are common to several or all of the members. Consequently, until ANCOM generates industrial and manufactured products for exchange, there are really relatively few complementary (noncompetitive) articles for intraregional trade.

Despite the fact that most of the countries are heavily reliant upon the agricultural sector of their economy (Table 6), they are by no means self-sufficient in foodstuffs. Since agriculture is primarily geared toward products for export rather than domestic consumption, most require additional amounts of meat, feedgrains, wheat, and vegetable oils—deficiencies generally alleviated by importation from the United States. In 1969 alone, the Andean group provided a $91 million market for U.S. farm products (Hutchinson, 1970: 4). Trade with the United States has long been one of the salient features of their economy. Between 1963 and 1967, total sales by the Andean members to each other averaged $59.1 million annually, while during the same period total sales to the United States averaged $843.3 million a year (Hutchinson, 1970: 5), or in excess of fourteen times as great. In reciprocation, the United States is a major provider for Andean markets. A synopsis of U.S.

TABLE 3

ANCOM Countries Total Exports–1968 (in U.S. millions of dollars)

Copper	918
Coffee	385
Fish meal	162
Bananas	143
Iron ore	129
Tin	91
Sugar	75
Oil	61
Cacao	28
Others	525
Total	2,517

SOURCE: International Finance Statistics.

TABLE 4
ANCOM Countries Imports from U.S. 1968 (in U.S. millions of dollars)

Machinery and equipment	443
Manufactured goods	156
Chemicals	98
Food and live animals	93
Crude materials	23
Mineral fuels	17
Beverages and tobacco	13
Fats and oils	13
Others	23
Total	879

SOURCE: U.S. Department of Commerce.

exportation to ANCOM countries (Table 4) shows machinery, equipment, and manufactured goods accounting for over half the trade. The Andean governments hope that, through their alliance, they can soon modulate this unfavorable import-export pattern and the attendant dependency upon the United States for their manufactured goods.

ANCOM could have a massive effect in increasing trade among its members, if only because there is so little intra-ANCOM trade now (Table 5). Of the five countries, Ecuador is

TABLE 5
Intra-ANCOM Trade, 1968 ($ millions, f.o.b.)

	Importer						
Exporter	*Bolivia*	*Chile*	*Colombia*	*Ecuador*	*Peru*	*Total ANCOM*	*% Total Trade*
Bolivia	–	1.4	–	–	2.3	3.7	2.2
Chile	0.8	–	3.2	1.7	4.4	10.1	1.1
Colombia	0.3	4.7	–	6.4	6.3	17.7	3.2
Ecuador	0.1	4.8	5.9	–	0.3	11.0	6.2
Peru	1.7	8.0	5.3	2.1	–	17.1	2.0
Total ANCOM[a]	4.5	20.4	17.5	10.8	18.3	71.5	–
% total trade[b]	2.9	2.8	,2.7	4.4	2.9	3.0	2.2[c]

SOURCE: Latin American Free Trade Association.

a. Imports c.i.f.

b. ANCOM c.i.f. imports from ANCOM divided by total c.i.f. imports.

c. ANCOM f.o.b. exports to ANCOM divided by total f.o.b. exports.

the most dependent on its partners as a market (6.2 percent of its total exports in 1968) and as a source of goods (4.4 percent of imports). Colombia follows with 3.2 percent of total exports going to ANCOM and 2.7 percent of imports originating in the four other countries. The higher-than-average figures registered by these two is explained by their trade with each other. Peru, Chile, and Bolivia buy about 2.9 percent of their imports from ANCOM and sell between 1.1 percent and 2.2 percent of their total exports to the bloc (Business International Corporation, 1970: 33). Even LAFTA as a whole is not an overly important market or source for ANCOM traders. In 1968, none of the Andean countries exported more than 10 percent of its total foreign sales to LAFTA countries (including ANCOM).

To achieve the objectives of a balanced and harmonic industrial development, as well as equitable distribution of the benefits from integration, ANCOM proposes sectorial industrial programming. In accordance with this strategy, members will obligate themselves to pursue a course of industrial development for the *subregion* rather than just for their own country. This can mean expansion, specialization, and diversification of production, maximum utilization of regional resources, and the advantages of industries and economies of scale. Through the concerted efforts of sectorial programming, determination is made as to which industries should be promoted in each country, as well as the most expedient locations for particular manufacturing plants. Such decisions are made after taking into account such factors as accessibility to raw materials, transportation, and markets. An integral part of linking up industrial production targets is the bilateral and multilateral complementation agreement, a device used for furthering specialization and diversification in industry while ensuring against needless and costly competition or duplication of regional products. This is accomplished by an ANCOM Commission which, after careful study, assigns countries the responsibility for specializing in the manufacture of particular products. Members not responsible for these commodities then pledge to prohibit, discourage, or refrain from promoting production within their country.

The Andean Petrochemical Agreement was the first multilateral agreement to be enacted and is illustrative of the complementation concept. All Andean countries are producers of petroleum, so a scheme was developed for regional exploitation of petroleum industries in which duplications could be avoided. By unanimous approval, 39 petrochemical products, many of which are primary products used in making synthetic fibers, plastics, rubber, paints, adhesives, and pesticides, were apportioned among the countries of Colombia, Peru, Chile, and Bolivia (Colombia Today, 1969: 4). All are to be tariff-free by 1973, and no more than two countries will produce any one article. Bolivia, for example, under its preferential status was allotted 22 products, including styrene and DDT (Business International Corporation, 1970: 33). Further complementation is planned for production of pharmaceuticals, plastics, data processing equipment, glass, electrical goods, domestic appliances, office equipment, and automotive parts.

In encouraging complementation of manufacturing within the subregion, ANCOM will also place heavy emphasis upon the saving to be accrued from industries of scale. One of the traditional evils of Latin American economies is the prevalence of small and inefficient industrial plants. Under the auspices of the Common Market, this will be vigorously discouraged in the future. Instead, one large steel rolling mill will be built to serve an area in which perhaps three smaller and less economical ones might be installed if each country were acting on its own. The economy of this measure is considerable when one realizes that, in a steel rolling mill with a 100,000-ton capacity per annum, the average amount of investment per ton of installed capacity is $700, while in a plant of 1.5 million tons' capacity this unit investment figure drops to about $300, or a savings of 57 percent. With new steel mills dotting the Andean landscape each year, member countries can hardly afford to ignore such statistics—especially when the savings can be passed on to another facet of regional development. The pulp and paper industry offers still another example. In 1964, there was only a single Latin American plant with an output capacity of 150,000 tons per year (a figure generally considered optimal), while there were in excess of 180 pulp mills and paper factories with a capacity less than 5,000 tons annually (Business International Corporation, 1970: 37-38). ANCOM plans new mills with a minimum yearly capacity of 60,000 tons. The principles for production of scale can be applied to a wide array of processing and manufacturing plants in the region. As in all countries, the small- and medium-sized industry will always have a place, but often in a complementary role to large-scale industry by the system of subcontracting.[6]

As complementary manufacturing accelerates, new products and their markets appear, thereby laying the foundation for additional intrazonal trade. The goal is to remove all tariffs and other restrictions from these trade items by 1980, and herein lies one of the strengths of the Andean group over its parent organization. LAFTA continually became imbedded in a series of frustrating micronegotiations on literally thousands of individual articles to be listed for free exchange (LAFTA Newsletter, 1970). Conversely, ANCOM's methodology for dismantling barriers to internal trade calls for dividing all products into general categories, bypassing the interminable haggling over each item. Many major categories (automobile parts, pulp and paper, nonmetallic minerals) have already been designated.

A number of goods are now freely crossing borders. Fifty items–manufactures, raw materials, and intermediate consumer goods–produced by Ecuador are being admitted duty-free by Chile, Colombia, and Peru (Embajada del Ecuador, 1971: 1). And Colombia is receiving typewriters, radios, sewing machines, and printing machinery from Peru and Chile (OAS, n.d.: 3). To ensure the continued successful flow of this trade, a common external tariff will be fixed around the region, thus converting it from a mere free-trade zone into the true common market. While this will not be consummated for nine years, the initial stage, a minimum common tariff, is already in effect offering adequate protection for local production by creating a margin of preference against external competition. Also, several preferential benefits have already been accorded Bolivia and Ecuador, not the least of which is the privilege to maintain their import restriction regulations for several more years while enjoying the right to export their products to Peru, Chile, and Colombia without restriction.

Potentials for Transport Integration

In theory, the integration of industry and free flow of trade work well, but in practice it is somewhat more difficult—and especially so in the Andean region. Nowhere can the resistance to subregional cohesion be seen more lucidly than in the physical realm. The utterly discordant physiography of western South America is among the most astringent and restrictive on earth. The land is fraught with barriers. The high ranges of the Andean cordillera, heavily forested selva plains, and broad and treacherous rivers work at keeping people and resources apart rather than joined. Yet these divisive obstacles must be overcome if a regional transportation network is to be established—as indeed it must, since the most fundamental requisite to any viable common market is a reliable system for transferring goods and materials throughout the region.

Because of the terrain, maritime transport is still the principal means of transdisposition of commodities between Andean countries, but highway and air travel are becoming increasingly important. Highway transportation, especially, is more commonly evolving as the major mode of travel and shipment in countries such as Colombia and Peru. The network of major South American highways (see Figure 2) does provide linkage of the ANCOM countries but, once removed from these main arteries, decent all-weather roads become scarce. And, to varying degrees, the Andean states are all plagued by problems endemic to most developing countries—namely, their economy tends to be closely tied to those of the United States and Western Europe, fostering a concentration of production for export rather than intraregional trade. Therefore, transportation systems are all too frequently directed toward foreign markets with the roads linking inland regions and cities to ports, but not to one another. There is an urgent need for drastic reorientation of this existing road pattern. Under ANCOM, a transport system must be devised in which there is freedom to connect markets with production centers without regard to either foreign markets or national frontiers, and therefore in the most economic fashion.

NETWORK OF MAJOR SOUTH AMERICAN HIGHWAYS

Figure 2.

Since the end of World War II, several new highway projects have been funded by international loans, but generally the Andean countries have themselves done too little in promoting this part of the infrastructure. Chile is the only one of the five countries to show an appreciable increase in the percentage of its labor force engaged in the transportation and communication sector of the economy (Table 6). Bolivia and Ecuador, in 1968, actually had a smaller proportion of their national work force in this occupation than in 1960. And these are precisely the two countries that suffer most from transport deficiencies. In Ecuador, the lack of roads and communication has played such a serious role in national development that the people are inclined to ascribe to it all the material and spiritual ills from which the country is suffering (Linke, 1964: 112). In Bolivia, the situation is even worse. Roads are uniformily bad and outside the urban areas are rarely surfaced or repaired. This so severely restricts the transfer and exchange of goods within the country that Argentine meat is often cheaper in La Paz than meat from the nearby Beni Province (Osborne, 1965: 36).

ANCOM planners are studying numerous proposals for providing direct overland transportation between geo-economic regions, completely disregarding the superficiality of national borders. The most grandiose effort at planned transport integration is the Carretera Marginal de la Selva, the proposed highway which, upon completion, will extend 3,000 miles along the eastern slope of the Andes from western Venezuela to southern Bolivia (see Figure 2). When finished, this project is expected to open vast tracts of fertile land (estimated at 7.4 million hectares; see Business International Corporation, 1970: 59) which so far have been untapped because of their inaccessibility. The highway should generate at least $134 million annually in additional agricultural production alone for the adjacent countries.

Oceanic transportation could benefit greatly from integration. All the countries have shipping lines, the major ones being Gran-Colombiana (owned jointly by Colombia and Ecuador), Corporación Peruana de Vapores, and Chile's Linea Subameri-

TABLE 6

Internal Production Structure for the Economic Sector of the ANCOM Countries 1960 and 1968 (in percentages total labor force engaged in activity)

	Bolivia		*Colombia*		*Chile*		*Ecuador*		*Peru*	
	1960	*1968*	*1960*	*1968*	*1960*	*1968*	*1960*	*1968*	*1960*	*1968*
Agriculture, forestry and fishing	30.6	23.3	34.6	31.4	12.2	10.5	36.8	32.5	24.1	18.9
Mining and quarrying	10.5	14.8	4.0	3.0	10.3	9.8	2.4	1.8	8.1	6.8
Industrial manufacturing	11.8	14.1	17.0	18.5	23.6	26.5	15.6	16.9	17.9	21.8
Construction	3.9	6.4	3.7	3.9	4.8	4.1	3.9	4.0	4.0	3.9
Electricity, gas and water	1.1	1.2	0.9	1.2	1.2	1.5	1.2	1.5	0.8	1.1
Transportation and communication	9.1	8.7	6.4	6.5	7.8	10.8	4.3	4.2	4.6	5.1
Commerce and finance	10.9	10.0	15.3	16.1	18.3	17.9	14.2	16.5	14.3	16.0
Other services	22.1	21.5	18.1	19.4	21.8	18.9	21.6	22.6	26.2	26.4
Total	100.0	100.0	100.0	100.0	100.0	100.0	100.0	100.0	100.0	100.0

SOURCE: United Nations Economic Commission for Latin America.

cana. Of lesser importance is the newly formed Transmaritima Boliviana, a Bolivian-owned freight line operated with chartered vessels. Landlocked Bolivia manages this feat via the Chilean port of Arica. ANCOM has suggested the feasibility of pooling merchant fleets to form a single Andean Line serving west coast ports. This could make possible improved shipping schedules designed to meet the needs of the region rather than to fit the requirements of foreign shippers, as is now largely the practice. The most imposing obstruction to consolidation of shipping and melioration in intracoastal trade is the dilapidated condition of many of the ports. Latin American ports are noted for their lack of modernization and inefficient operation (OAS, 1962: 2-9).[7] Before the full effects of coordinated shipping could be felt, there would need to be a general improvement in port facilities as well as loading and unloading techniques.

Colombia, perhaps because it is the only nation in South America with two seacoasts, is more alert to potentials of international shipping and the need for better port facilities. A $37.6 million development program, which could serve as a model for other Andean countries, is under way directed toward the overhaul and augmentation of Colombia's principal ocean terminals of Barranquilla, Cartagena, and Santa Marta in the Atlantic, and Buenaventura and Tumaco along the Pacific. The result will be a 65 percent increase in dock space for oceanic vessels, augmentation in warehouse space at these ports of 75 percent and a doubling of cargo-handling capacity (Colombia Today, 1968: 2). A move by ANCOM to the wider use of containerization shipping would lend even further justification to the idea of pooling fleets, since the Andean Line with standardized equipment would make this process easier. Colombia has been shipping cargo in containers since 1963 and strongly favors this type of shipping for the future.

Air freight service, which assumes the role as the long-range mobile arm of industry and commerce (Sealy, 1966: 159), is well suited to the Andean region where land travel is slow and costly. But despite the relatively well-developed air cargo service within some of the countries and between these and the United

States, there is still little air cargo traffic between one Andean country and another. Like the founding of a combined shipping fleet, an Andean airline would offer advantages. For several years, the existing national carriers have discussed financing jointly the purchase of new jet freighters, the cost of which is beyond the resources of any one airline. A unified air transport operation would ensure the region of obtaining maximum use from its aircraft, while a system of common schedules, equipment, and staff would enhance the acceleration of intraregional trading. Indeed, the possibilities for the integrated regional development of land, sea, and air transport are impressive.

Other Proposals for Cooperation

Multinational exploitation of natural resources provides still another avenue for cooperation. The joint extraction of minerals in border areas is both logical and practicable. Ecuador and Colombia are actively seeking to develop together the Putumayo Basin and its attendant oil prospects straddling both countries. Peru and Chile could follow suit with regard to the copper deposits of the Atacama.

The question of mutual development of water resources is one which has received much attention, even prior to the formation of ANCOM. Many water bodies in South America center on geo-economic zones which encompass areas of more than one country. The precedent for this sort of enterprise was set when Brazil, Argentina, Paraguay, and Uruguay agreed to unite in developing the potentials of their common watershed, the River Plate System (for coverages of these proposals, see Fifer, 1970; Inter-American Development Bank, 1969). Three areas in the Andean region have been selected for possible dual development: the Catatumbo Basin shared by Colombia and Venezuela, Lake Titicaca between Peru and Bolivia, and the Tumbes Basin along the border of Ecuador and Peru (see Figure 3). In each case, the countries concerned stand to make considerable gains in irrigation and power generation from the cooperative tapping of water resources. Then, with the availability of this irrigation and power, additional programs could be studied for the contiguous border zones.

The Role of Foreign Investment in ANCOM

Many of the industrial and infrastructural development schemes proposed by ANCOM will require capital which the

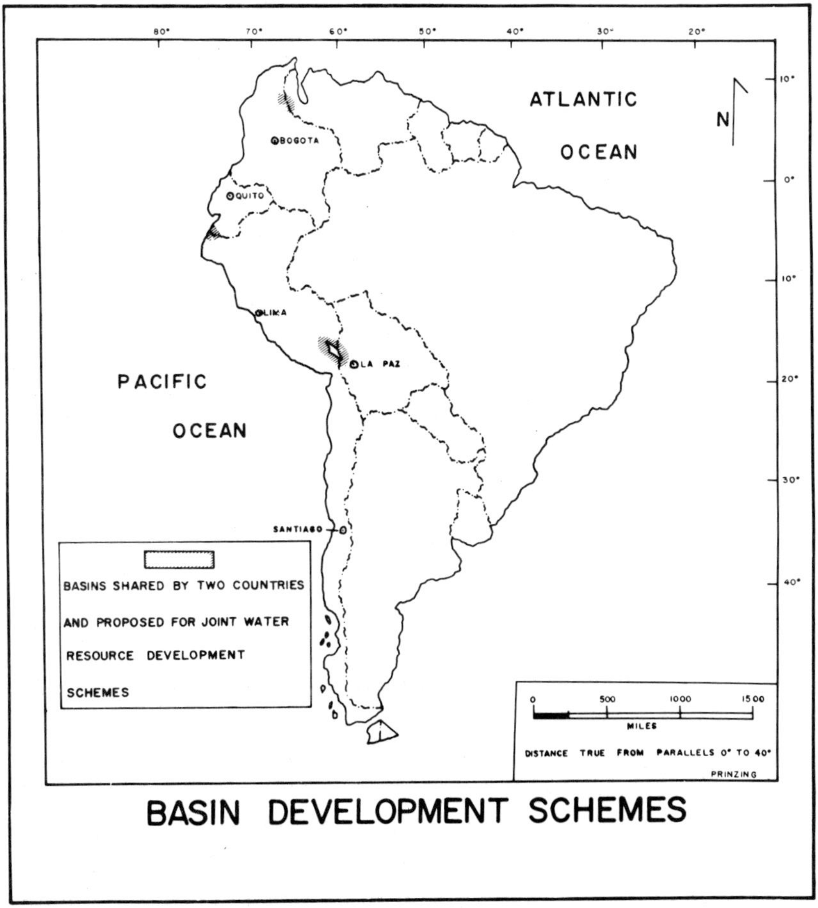

Figure 3.

member countries do not now possess—even collectively. This poses the question of the role of foreign investment in the Common Market. It also brings to the surface one of the sharpest dichotomies within the Andean family of nations—namely, the ideological gap between the soft-liners and the hard-liners. Each country is in possession of a strong sense of nationalism, but some are more protectionist than others. Considerable compromise can be expected in fabricating a functional code for foreign investment. Peru, Bolivia, and Chile are characteristically more nationalistic (as they have proved in recent years by the expropriation of numerous foreign holdings) than Colombia and Ecuador and can be expected to champion a stiff code for alien interests. They propose, among other things, that all foreign companies be coerced into selling a majority (at least 51%) of their interest to local nationals. Naturally, the United States, because of its well-documented history of exploitation in Latin America, is a prime target of the protectionists. But even these countries realize that it would be suicidal to take any rash steps toward severing economic ties with either the United States or Western Europe.

Perhaps a harbinger of commerical reorientation is the recent warming trend of the Andean countries toward Soviet investment and trade relations. In 1968, Quito and Moscow signed an agreement for reciprocal import-export trade. Under a recent commercial accord, Colombo-Soviet trade exchanges may reach $25 million a year. And both Peru and Chile have agreed to the exchange of commercial representatives with the Soviets (OAS, 1970: 3).

As is the case with the Central American Common Market, foreign investment in ANCOM should prove to be a strong generative force in making the system of economic integration work. Since ANCOM cannot itself possibly come up with the funds needed to promote its many schemes, it would seem judicious to encourage wealthy prospective clients—be they Soviet, European, or American.

Concluding Remarks

The road to successful economic integration in the Andean region is a long and arduous one, strewn with obstacles that would beleaguer even countries sophisticated in the ways of commerce and industrialization. But the emergence of the Andean Common Market is an unmistakable manifestation of the member states' evolution beyond the stage of deliberation and into an era of commitment. Their alliance offers a far more rational subject for integration than does that of the Latin American Free Trade Association.

Peru's Minister of Economic Affairs and Finance, Francisco Bermúdez (1970: 103-104), voiced the sentiments of all ANCOM countries when he stated:

> Peru's participation in the Andean Subregional Group is both a challenge to the industrial sector and an incentive based on competition in an expanded market. We believe that integration is a historic requirement in a realistic policy of survival that seeks joint action as an external mechanism for achieving development, respects the sovereign will of the states, decreases the heavy dependence on industrialized countries, and encourages the formation of a new style of international community, implementing new, more equitable and more humanistic formulas of cooperation that define a true "development strategy" for reducing today's growing imbalances and correcting the injustices it entails.

The references to "survival," "international community," and "humanistic formulas" reveal the scope and spirit of the pact. The Andean countries have learned a pragmatic lesson from the experience of LAFTA—that integration, if it is to be successful, must provide tangible and measurable benefits to all participant nations, and no government can be expected to sacrifice its own national interests on the regional altar. Although the Andean Common Market will be for some time a fledgling organization, there is much to support its becoming a highly viable economic entity, and a stance of cautious optimism seems warranted.

NOTES

1. In January of 1971, the government of Honduras announced withdrawal from the Central American Common Market. Reasons given for this action were rather obscure, but apparently the prime motivation was the deterioration of relations with neighboring El Salvador.

2. Peru, Ecuador, and Bolivia each faces the problem of integrating the sizable Indian culture group into the mainstream of national life; they also share a common historical heritage strengthened through the career and achievements of the great liberator, Simón Bolívar.

3. The two countries were even in the planning stage for an integrated military system to strengthen internal security and mutual national defense.

4. The new government of Venezuela under President Rafael Caldera has reversed the view of the previous administration with regard to participation in the Andean Common Market. President Caldera is convinced that economic integration is not only desirable but absolutely essential. If Venezuela's private industry can be coaxed from behind its high protective tariff walls, it is expected that the country will move quickly toward ANCOM membership.

5. One of the significant assets of the ANCOM policy to share resources is that of Colombian coal. The other four countries have a deficit in coal supplies and have to rely upon importation. These imports are mostly choking coals for the steel industry. But luckily their new ally of Colombia possesses the largest Latin American reserves of bituminous and anthracite coals (about 64 percent) and leads in production with 29 percent of total output. With water and rail transportation available to transfer the coal to ports, it is reasonable to assume that steel-producing coastal cities of Peru, Chile, and Ecuador will become the major recipients.

6. Small-scale industries are already performing this function in countries such as Brazil and Mexico, especially in the motor vehicle industry. For a report on the role of small-scale industry in Latin America, refer to ECLA (1967).

7. One of the findings of this conference was that there is a tendency in many Latin American countries to seek solutions to port problems by creating new ports instead of directing efforts at improving and modernizing existing ones.

REFERENCES

Andean Air Mail and Peruvian Times (1968a) "Six-nation Andean group emerging as economic force." (April 5): 8.

--- (1968b) "Andean group nations suspend common market talks." (August 23): 4.

Bank of London and South America Review (1970) "Latin America: diminishing expectations of integration." Volume 4, 40.

BERMUDEZ, F. (1970) Proceedings of the Eleventh Meeting of the Board of Governors, Interamerican Development Bank, Runte Del Este, April.

Business International Corporation (1970) Andean Common Market. New York.

CALE, E. G. (1969) Latin American Free Trade Association: Progress, Problems, and Prospects. Washington, D.C.: U.S. Department of State Office of External Research.

Chile, República de (1969) "Antecedentes, objetivos y mecanismos del Acuerdo de Cartagena." Ministerio de Relaciones Exteriores, Santiago.

Colombia Today (1969) "The Andean group: a step toward Latin American economic integration." Volume 4, 9.

--- (1965) "Major expansion of Colombian ocean port facilities a vital component of trade expansion program." Volume 3, 5.

ECLA (1970) Algunas Características y Problemas de la Economía de los Paises del Pacto Andina. United Nations.

--- (1967) "Small-scale industry in the development of Latin America." Economic Bull. for Latin America: 63-103.

Ecuador, Embajada del (1971) Boletin 3091 (January).

FIFER, J. V. (1970) "The Plate basin project: new proposals for South American economic co-operation." Geography 55, 247.

GLASSNER, M. I. (1970) "The Rio Lauca: dispute over an international river." Geographical Rev. 60, 2: 192-207.

HUTCHINSON, J. E. (1970) "The Andean group: a bigger market for U.S. farmers? " Foreign Agriculture 8, 49.

Inter-American Development Bank (1970) "Socio-economic Progress in Latin America." Ninth Annual Report. Washington, D.C.

--- (1969) The River Plate System: A Summary Report. Washington, D.C.

LAFTA Newsletter (1970) "Expanded intra-regional trade drive." Latin American Free Trade Association, no. 3 (September): 1-2.

Latin American Newsletters (1969) "Andean integration: a treaty at last? " Latin America. Inter-Press Service, London, April.

LINKE, L. (1964) Ecuador: Country of Contrasts. London: Oxford Univ. Press.

OAS (1970) "Soviet trade drive in Latin America." Alliance for Progress.

--- (1962) "Second inter-American port and harbor conference." Document 5.

--- (n.d.) "Columbia frees 39 classes of goods for import." Alliance for Progress Weekly Newsletter 8, 44.

OSBORNE, H. (1965) Bolivia: A Land Divided. London: Oxford Univ. Press.

SANDERS, T. G. (1968) "Andean economic integration: a new stage in Chile's industrial growth." Amer. Universities Field Staff Report-West Coast South America Series 15, 2.

SEALY, K. R. (1966) The Geography of Air Transport. Chicago: Aldine.

BOOK REVIEWS

Landsberger, Henry A., ed. LATIN AMERICAN PEASANT MOVEMENTS. Ithaca, N.Y.: Cornell University Press, 1969. Preface, index of persons, index of subjects. xi + 476 pp. $12.50.

Just as the bitter episode at Cananea, Mexico, served years ago to symbolize the early stirrings of fledgling industrial labor organizations in Latin America, so also the conflicts of 1955 at Galiléia in northeastern Brazil may be taken as a signpost calling attention to equivalent organizing efforts among rural workers. Between these two modern-day echoes of the biblical passion for justice, however, the social sciences had come into their own. The Cananea episode provoked a rash of comment in the press of that time, but systematic analysis of the rise of industrial-urban trade unions in Latin America was not to appear for decades. Today, thanks to a population explosion of social scientists and to the availability of funding for itinerant scholars, the analytical supply response is far quicker—and the quantity of analysis supplied far greater.

Neglected though they may have been for centuries, the rural workers of Latin America were finally discovered during the late 1950s and the 1960s, at least as far as concerns the priestly ministrations of the guardians of the contemporary cult: the academicians. Whatever else may have happened to them of late, the peasants and their problems have been subjected to nearly all the legitimizing rituals that our secular civilization has to offer. Conferences have been called to consider their plight, committees have been formed, and government programs devised, and all the while scholarly articles and monographs have poured forth to bear witness to their significance. (Zapata never had it so good, except posthumously, but today's rural leaders can even have their musings recorded on tape.) An exceedingly helpful bibliography of much of this literature is included in the distinguished volume under review. Without doubt, Henry Landsberger's book will stand as the definitive treatment of the subject for years to come, a standard reference work for all who are interested in Latin American social change.

Actually, of course, rural collective action in Latin America did not begin with the especially well-published efforts of Francisco Julião, just as the Cananea mine workers were neither the first to organize nor the first to strike. Legal action by indigenous communities to recover stolen village lands was a fairly common feature of the colonial era, and, as in the Tupac Amaru uprising, more direct means of redressing wrongs were occasionally resorted to. Peasant discontent was also an element in the ill-fated rebellions led by Hidalgo and Morelos just before Mexico gained its independence. By and large, however, such episodes were doomed to failure, and perhaps the most notable characteristic of peasant movements was, in organizational terms at least, their ephemerality.

In the present century, though, it became gradually but increasingly difficult to ignore the oppressive conditions of life under which most of Latin America's people live. The first major agrarian protest movement to surface was that associated with the Mexican Revolution. In an admirably incisive essay, Robert A. White, S.J., of St. Louis University, traces the origins of this dramatic upheaval in the structural changes which occurred under the Porfiriato. While the leadership ability of Zapata was important, Fr. White indicates—convincingly, I believe—the vital role of structural factors in laying down the preconditions for a vigorous peasant response. Also taken into account is the work of nonpeasant political and intellectual activists who did much to transform the regional uprising into a generalized, societywide, value-oriented movement. Indeed, the crucial contribution made by outside (nonpeasant) allies in mobilizing resources on behalf of peasant aims is repeatedly noted in the essays and appears to be one of the key variables bearing on the success or failure of such movements.

Fr. White's analysis of the Zapata movement posits the weakening of the system of social control as another explanatory variable. This, too, appears to have been operative in the case of the Bolivian peasant movement which, like its earlier Mexican counterpart, contributed significantly to a revolutionary movement that produced far-reaching social change. Dwight Heath, of Brown University, finds the Chaco War as the event which did much to discredit and undermine the old order in Bolivia (as well as to provide peasants with the new reference groups) thereby clearing the way for peasant leaders and their MNR allies to undertake a massive organizing campaign. In contrast to Richard Patch, who assigns primary credit for this effort to the peasants themselves, Heath tends to agree with those who consider the role of the MNR activists decisive. In any case, peasant syndicates sprang up in many communities, and Heath's essay provides much constructive insight into the structure and operations of these groups in the postreform situation. In terms of evolutionary process, Heath's emphasis is mainly on a later stage of organizational development than the study of the Mexican case.

Roughly contemporaneous with many of the events described by Heath are the 1944-1954 Guatemalan developments dealt with by Neale Pearson of Texas Technological University. Here, however, the fragility of peasant organizations stands out with clarity. Although a movement of some size emerged after the inception of the post-Ubico regimes, largely, one gathers, at the initiative of nonpeasants (but with substantial involvement of peasant leaders at the local level), its search for stable relationships with important external allies was repeatedly frustrated by the maneuverings of communists and noncommunists for control of the left-of-center government. With the overthrow of the Arbenz government, this shaky effort at peasant mobilization headed quickly for extinction.

With the foregoing summary remarks providing some idea of the range of experiences reported in the book, it should suffice to indicate only briefly the coverage of the other studies. Peru is the object of two exceptionally interesting chapters: one by Wesley Craig of Brigham Young University, dealing with the peasant organization in a particular valley, and the other by Julio Cotler and Felipe Portocarrero of the Instituto de Estudios Peruanos, of a more general focus. Landsberger himself discusses a Chilean attempt at peasant unionization in an uncommonly masterful (and gripping) manner, extracting from this single case an abundance of rich analytical insights. The contribution by Cynthia Hewitt, of the University of Leiden, on the Brazilian movement in Pernambuco is also particularly informative. Considering the factionalism present within the organized peasant sector and the complicated political situation which impinged on the peasant activities at several points, she handles her materials well and sorts out the tangled elements of the case in a way that is both admirable and meaningful. The other case study included in the book deals with Venezuela; its author is John Powell, who is on the faculty at Tufts.

Two chapters which deal with comprehensive aspects of the subject complete the book. One (the concluding chapter), by Ernest Feder of the ECLA staff, examines the nature and variety of the opposition to peasant movements. In part, this consists of identifying the vested interests which oppose any substantial improvement in the lot of rural people, but of even greater value is Feder's explanation of how it is that the whole socioeconomic and political structure tends to function in a manner antithetical to peasant aims. Feder writes with an authority based on extensive involvement in the analysis of Latin American agriculture, so that his pessimistic conclusions must be taken seriously, however uncomfortable they may be for those who retain some residue of belief in the possibilities of incremental reform.

The other general focus chapter is Landsberger's introductory one, in which he sets forth a comprehensive analytical framework distilled from a wide-ranging review of the history of peasant movements and from an intimate familiarity with the literature on social organization. This is a virtuoso performance which, instructive as it is in its own right, also deserves to be widely assigned to students simply as a model of how to prepare a research design. Indeed, this chapter alone would justify the volume as a whole even if the other contributions were not of such generally high quality. Some of the chapters, it must be said, are not as profoundly analytical as this introduction, but this shortcoming is largely remedied by the fact that Landsberger's framework also draws upon the findings of his collaborators, "putting it all together," to use the current expression.

When so much has been achieved, it seems captious to ask for more. Yet, one wishes that there had been included a follow-up essay on the Mexican case, dealing with the later institutionalization—and taming—of the peasant mobilization launched with such vigor under Zapata. Perhaps the omission of this most mature of the Latin American rural sector organizations means that the editor no longer considers it to be a peasant movement, and certainly a case can be made to that effect. Nevertheless, what has happened there may shed some light on the range of possibilities which lie ahead of such groupings as the sindicatos of, say, Bolivia, Venezuela, or Chile. Whatever this follow-up might reveal, it would probably demonstrate that recourse to outside allies not only carries benefits but also entails certain costs, among the chief of which is goal displacement.

Finally, it is unfortunate that no direct examination is made of the Colombian case, although Craig does allude to it by way of noting certain similarities between the Colombian peasant situation of the twenties and thirties and the conditions which later precipitated collective action in the La Convención Valley of Peru. The breakdown of social controls during the violencia period, the presence of talented rural-sector leaders such as Eugenio Colorado, the potential availability of allies (from the church, the UTC, or political parties seeking to expand their voting base) all suggest a possible readiness of conditions for concerted action by rural workers, yet FANAL has amounted to naught, and other peasant organizations there seem to have fared no better. One hopes that in time this curious instance will be taken up for consideration to round out the picture.

–*William Glade*

Luis Mercier Vega, GUERRILLAS IN LATIN AMERICA. THE TECHNIQUES OF THE COUNTER-STATE. Translated by Daniel Weissbort. New York: Praeger, 1970. 246 pp. $6.50.

Fidel Castro's speaking tour of Chile in December 1971, during which he urged the support of President Allende's administration, renewed the speculation in anti- and pro-communist circles alike as to the tactics likely to be followed during the remainder of the 1970s by leftist revolutionary forces. For much has been said, and even more has been written about the alternatives: whether to attempt a seizure of power by violent means at the earliest propitious moment or to forge a coalition among moderates, liberals, and radical leftists in order to advance by legal–but not necessarily democratic–means. Luis Mercier Vega, of Chilean nationality, is Director of the Latin American Institute for International Relations in Paris. His career as participant, advocate, and commentator on liberation and revolutionary activities spans the time from the 1930s, when he fought in the Spanish Civil War, through the 1940s, when he fought with the Free French in Africa and the Middle East against the Nazis, to recent years as observer and analyst of guerrilla movements in Latin America.

In an earlier book, *Roads to Power in Latin America,* the author surveyed the efforts of student and military groups to achieve power, and came to the unorthodox conclusion that some of the contemporary revolutionaries merely reflect the strong and weak traits common to existing establishment leaders. In the present volume, Mercier Vega is more precise in identifying and evaluating numerous revolutionary parties operating in different countries and in characterizing the militants and activists involved. Originally published in French, the volume's translation into English loses some of its zest. As with many other treatments of the techniques of the counter-state, Mercier Vega all but ignores the cities, favoring the countryside. (The contemporary Uruguayan insurgents form one group of the many who do not make that error.)

Ernesto (Ché) Guevara, as might be expected, receives considerable attention. Here, as in the bountiful literature celebrating the redoubtable Ché, he is more revered since his death in Bolivia than he was influential in furthering the cause of revolution in that country. The chapter devoted to Bolivia is essentially a recital of the background of Guevara's efforts and the mobility of the small guerrilla group he led, culminating in the author's judgment that the movement "did not have the slightest chance for victory" (p. 138). In the portrayal of partisan intrigues and power ploys among the leaders of revolutionaries in other countries, Mercier Vega again and again demonstrates the divisiveness caused by the Russian-oriented Communist parties in Chile, in Venezuela, in Peru, and elsewhere. The Bolivian Communist leadership, apparently unwilling to share its primacy with Guevara, refused to assist him. But at Guevara's death,

> there was at once an impassioned message from the Communist Party of the Soviet Union, tears from the Chilean Communist Party, and condolences from the Italian Communist Party. As the Communist party secretaries put it so well, Ernesto Guevara became a legend. One can be certain that Fidel Castro, on the one hand, and the old pre- and post Stalinist apparatuses, on the other, will make sure that he remains so, because for Fidel, Ché is less of a nuisance dead than alive, and for the Communist parties, the significance of wreaths is that the deceased had to be buried. (p. 139).

Harsh though this appraisal may be, it is probably less cynical than it is realistic.

The internecine contest between Peking and Moscow for domination and guidance of insurgency in Latin America is not neglected by Mercier Vega. He believes that there are not sufficient grounds for concluding that a pro-Chinese apparatus on a continental scale exists. Rather, there was "a temporary amalgamation, under Peking's banner, of Communist cells and groups that already existed." The Russian purpose is to prevent the development of rival factions and to get the backing and control of popular movements. The Soviet Union is trying to expand trade contacts with South America, and thus it follows a double standard, on the one hand maintaining good relations with Latin governments and, on the other, exploiting the negative feelings between the United States and the southern countries. For fear of leaving a political vacuum in the left, the Kremlin Communists feel that they are forced to maintain their connections with indigenous parties.

It is in Part III of the book that the nitty-gritty of guerrilla warfare is documented. Full and sometimes repetitious details on all aspects of guerrilla life are recounted by the publication of a dozen documents emanating from diarists, party councils, and governmental investigations in Argentina, Russia, Peru, Venezuela, and Colombia. Revealing of individual sacrifices in jungle conflicts, couched at times in the jargon of ideologues, these basic reports afford ample proof of the ambivalent motivations of guerrilla caciques. Their followers move from the exhilaration of idealism to the torments of despair. As Mercier Vega aptly puts it: "it is a case more of despair or adventurism than of the application of the theories of the counter-state."

–*Willard F. Barber*
University of Maryland
Lecturer in International Affairs

Rout, Leslie B., Jr., POLITICS OF THE CHACO PEACE CONFERENCE, 1935-1939. (Latin American Mongraphs, No. 19). Austin, Texas: Univ. of Texas Press, 1970. Preface, acknowledgments, bibliography, index. xviii + 268 pp. $7.50.

To most North Americans of today, a reference to the Chaco elicits either blank responses or vague suggestions involving most other continents except that of South America. Few are those who will pinpoint the last frontier of the Americas, the western two-thirds of Paraguay located at the geographic center of South America and bordered by Argentina, Bolivia, and Brazil. Peace in the area and near isolation have all but completely blotted out memory of the early 1930s when the great Chaco War made headlines as yet another bloody forerunner to World War II.

The Chaco War of 1932-1935 is recorded as twentieth-century Latin America's longest and grimmest conflict. It also follows the War of the Triple Alliance of the 1860s as the second greatest in Latin America's history. Yet because of such other concurrent events of the 1930s, including the rise of Hitler, the collapse of the League of Nations, Sino-Japanese problems, and the Spanish Civil War, it aroused but passing international interest except in those nations neighboring Paraguay and Bolivia, the two contestants.

Some 80,000 Bolivians and Paraguayans died fighting in an area which was alternately both a "green hell" and a parched scrub desert–the most unlikely of forbidding regions in which to stage a full-scale war. Paraguay ultimately won, and the major portion of the Chaco now forms Paraguay's western two-thirds west of the Paraguay River. To the vanquished Bolivia, the war added the last blow to a series of misfortunes that transformed it into an Andean republic minus a seacoast or an outlet to the sea.

The story of the 1930 military operations in the Chaco is competently told in several modern scholarly works, particularly in *The Conduct of the Chaco War* by David H. Zook, Jr., and in *The Epic of the Chaco: Marshal Estigarribia's Memoirs of the Chaco War* by Pablo Max Ynsfran. Though these accounts thoroughly describe the Chaco struggle, they remain primarily military histories. The dense labyrinth of prewar haggling over ownership of the Chaco, the almost incredible diplomatic efforts to halt the struggle once it began, and the prolonged postwar negotiations to secure an acceptable frontier settlement and a lasting peace were matters which remained largely unevaluated. This task is now accomplished in a concise and well-organized study by Dr. Leslie B. Rout, Jr., Associate Professor of History at Michigan State University.

Employing a thorough and methodical search of archival materials in the United States and in South America, as well as field investigation including interviews with surviving participants of Chaco War diplomacy, Dr. Rout skillfully draws an outline of the deadly game of power and pride which led to the war. He also explores the underworld of early Interamerican diplomacy which ultimately produced a successful formula for an enduring peace between Bolivia and Paraguay. The work reaches several perceptive conclusions. For example, the author points out the difficulties of achieving mutual agreement among nations all of which have special interests to safeguard, and the ultimate worth of even the most protracted and delicate negotiations, as against recrudescence of a war as terrible as that of the Chaco.

Dr. Rout selects 1853 as the beginning of the events which finally led to the war—the year in which Argentina recognized Paraguayan independence and sovereignty over the west bank of the Paraguay River north of its confluence with the Paraná River. In succession, he then traces the growth of Paraguayan-Bolivian rivalry in the Chaco after the Paraguayan War of the 1860s and especially after the 1879-1883 War of the Pacific, in which Bolivia lost its Pacific coast. Of particular note are his studies of the effects of the Kellogg Plan of 1929, which confirmed Bolivia's loss and stimulated the Andean nation's search eastward for a river port, the impact of the subsequent discovery of "black gold" in Bolivia's Oriente Chaco region, and his analysis of Standard Oil's Bolivian operations, which suggests that still-prevalent suspicions of the company's responsibility for the Chaco War are largely groundless. Equally of interest are his treatment of the growth of "Doctores en Chaco" in Paraguay—experts specializing in championing Paraguay's claims—and the rise of Bolivian *reivindicacionismo*—the developing need among Bolivia's upper and governing classes to revindicate at Paraguay's expense the losses suffered in the War of the

Pacific. Such feelings superseded diplomatic efforts and led to a war which only subsided when both sides were totally exhausted.

In subsequent chapters, Dr. Rout ably treats the excruciatingly long and often secret negotiations that finally, in 1939, brought peace and a lasting frontier agreement. In his opinion, the key figure in this last and most important phase was that of Paraguay's Chaco War hero José Félix Estigarribia. Returning from a U.S. mission and soon to become president, Paraguay's second national hero correctly estimated the need for sensible comprehension of boundary demands and thus stimulated the final settlement of the Chaco question. The survey of this latter phase also casts much light on efforts by the State Department to accommodate itself to Argentina's policy of seeking primary hegemony over the entire La Plata region. Likewise, Dr. Rout emphasizes the immediate goal of the United States in seeking an amicable Chaco solution which might negate possible intrustion and establishment of Fascist-inspired ideologies and leanings in a sensitive area of the New World.

Dr. Rout's study is a well-documented and convincing appraisal that satisfies a previous need in available materials on modern Latin America. Perhaps only two suggestions are appropriate to align its otherwise admirable historical approach: one, it was Brazil rather than Paraguay which intervened in Uruguay's pre-Triple Alliance War political chaos; and two, Paraguay's marshal president and national hero Francisco Solano López was killed in battle in March 1870, not in the Chaco as Dr. Rout reports, but rather at Cerro Corá, a famed historic site and modern-day national shrine located in northeastern Paraguay.

–*Charles J. Kolinski*
Professor of History
Florida Atlantic University

Ealy, Lawrence O., YANQUI POLITICS AND THE ISTHMIAN CANAL. University Park, Pa.: Pennsylvania State Univ. Press, 1971. Notes, index. vi + 192 pp. $8.50.

The author claims to venture a fresh approach to the study of the Panama Canal by attempting to relate the canal project to U.S. domestic politics. Approximately one-half of his essay has been spent chronicling the history of international interests in the construction of a trans-isthmian canal, indicating the various time periods when American politicians expressed concern. On each occasion the administration in power demonstrated an interest in a canal, the opposition party, for political reasons only, challenged the president's judment. For example, the efforts of John Quincy Adams, after his election in 1824, were doomed to failure because the Jacksonians in Congress deliberately set out to embarrass the new chief executive. The surge of "Manifest Destiny" in the 1840s was opposed by the Whig Party, and with the election of one of their own, Zachery Taylor, in 1848, a willingness to compromise the issue resulted in the Clayton-Bulwer Treaty. The trend continued into the twentieth century. Democrat Henry T. Rainey chaired a committee whose sole purpose was to reveal the misdeeds of former Republican President Theodore Roosevelt in Panama. Politics contributed to the pigeonholing of the 1968 treaties.

After the canal opened to world traffic in 1914, it came to stand as a symbol of U.S. dominance, not only in Panama but in all of Latin America. The Panamanians came to feel that their economy, social values, and political system had been flagrantly corrupted by the North Americans. Efforts to adjust the situation resulted in the treaties of 1936 and 1955. However, Panama will not be satisfied until it gains full sovereignty over the canal zone and the greatest possible income from the canal's operation. Evidently, the three treaties signed by the two countries in 1968 failed to satisfy Panamanian demands.

As one faces the future, two points clearly emerge from this work. First, the United States has come to support the Panamanian military dictatorship of Omar Torrijos because of its anti-communist stand. Second, by this decade's end, the canal will be obsolete to a good portion of the world's maritime fleet, and technology may bring a speedier and cheaper means of trans-isthmian transportation than a new sea-level waterway. Thus Panama's insistent nationalism may augur ill for the tiny republic.

One may disagree that Ealy has presented a "fresh approach" to his study. For what he says here is implicit in several earlier works dealing with United States–Panamanian relations. Other criticisms can also be leveled. The scanty attention given to the years 1920-1955 leaves a gaping hole in the author's thesis. The bibliography fails to include many of the sources used in the footnotes. Finally, at $8.50, the book is overpriced.

–*Thomas M. Leonard*
Associate Professor of History
St. Joseph College

Colby, Benjamin N. and van den Berghe, Pierre L., IXIL COUNTRY, A PLURAL SOCIETY. Berkeley, Ca.: Univ. of California Press, 1969. Bibliography, index, glossary, photographs. xviii + 218 pp.

The title of this work conceals its broader relevance. Rather than an ethnography, it is a study of the relations between Ixil Indians and non-Indians in the northwest highlands of Guatemala. It is an important contribution to the study of ethnic relations and plural societies, not limited to middle America.

Most of the book is based upon field research carried out on and off in 1966-1967 by both authors and a host of assistants. Fortunately, the town of Nebaj, their main base, has a population of 5,000, large enough so that their presence does not seem to have disrupted the local scene too much. A good deal of reliance seems to have been placed upon a 50-item interview schedule given to 90 Ixil and a 64-item questionnaire returned by 40 ladinos (non-Indians). It would have been interesting to know the age, sex, and class characteristics of the Ixil respondants. In place of this pseudostatistical approach, I should have preferred consideration of individual case studies in greater depth; however, this is largely a matter of individual approach.

The book is well organized and to the point. A geographical and historical introduction is followed by a discussion of groups in terms of ethnicity, religion, and class differences; the institutions in which they participate together; and the ways in which group differences and institutional structures manifest themselves in individual behavior. Finally, there is a stimulating discussion of the dynamics of plural societies in middle America and elsewhere. A few typographical errors and mistakes in the bibliography and index should be corrected in the next edition. The photographs are interesting, although it is surprising that there are none of the colorful Ixil dance dramas or of the Ixil ritual specialists.

The strongest section of this work is the analysis of political, economic, and religious institutions which serve to integrate ladinos and Ixil, yet at the same time are sources of conflict. The interplay between these institutions was particularly evident when the conservative political party joined forces with local ladinos and progressive Ixil Catholics to defeat the progressive political party which had allied itself with supporters of traditional Ixil religion.

Colby and van den Berghe write that Guatemalan Indians have "preserved a more complete, internally differentiated and autonomous version of their pre-Columbian culture than was the case in most of Mexico" (p. 175). Based on their analysis, as well as my own work with the Ixil and in the highlands of northern Thailand, a major reason for this cultural conservatism seems to be the contiguity of Ixil settlements. While social scientists commonly lump all highland Maya communities together, in the same manner as ladinos do, Indians themselves find they have as little rapport with other Indian groups as they do with non-Indians. In fact, the economic and political links are frequently much more important with the latter. The highlander-lowlander dichotomy in southeast Asia has also been greatly overstressed. Pan-highlander alliances are likely to form only in response to clear and immediate threats (as occurred in Vietnam shortly after independence from France). However, in northern Thailand, where ethnic groups have not maintained contiguous tribal territories, there is a great deal of intermarriage, adoption across ethnic lines, cultural borrowings, mixed ethnic communities and changes in ethnic identity. This is not the case with the Ixil. The amount of intermarriage between Ixil and other Indian groups or between Ixil and ladino is negligible. Change in ethnic identity, either temporary or permanent, seems relatively uncommon and is largely associated with Ixil emigration to haciendas and plantations. There is little incentive to pass as a ladino, since material goods can be acquired through social mobility within the Indian society (the same applies for a ladino passing as Indian).

A related reason for the cultural conservatism of the Ixil (and some other Guatemalan groups) is that significant ladino settlement of their area is recent and remains proportionately small (the area is over 90 percent Ixil). While the ladinos control land and labor resources in Guatemala as a whole, the Ixil have been able to retain most of their land (and thus continue a subsistence agriculture basic to their life way) and have managed to adapt the temporary wage labor that they accept on lowland plantations so as to support rather than erode their way of life—at least until the present.

—*Alain Y. Dessaint*
Lecturer in Anthropology
University of Hawaii

Alexander, Robert, THE COMMUNIST PARTY OF VENEZUELA (Hoover Institution Studies; 24). Stanford, Ca.: Hoover Institution Press, 1969.

The Communist parties in Latin America, and in developing countries in general, feed the aspirations and ambitions of the masses who are frustrated by a weak economy which cannot satisfy even their essential needs. They claim that any real improvement in the lot of the masses must be accomplished by the masses themselves, working through and in support of their Communist parties, whose primary objective is to awaken the political consciousness of the proletariat, and lead it to political power. Alexander's book analyzes the positions of the Partido Comunista de

Venezuela (PCV) as it sought power in a period of changing national regimes. It is one of a series of monographs (sponsored by the Hoover Institution, Stanford University), which together study the comparative politics of nonruling Communist parties.

Alexander, who on several previous occasions showed his imaginative engagement in the analysis of Communism in Latin America, has provided, in this book, a firsthand insight and a useful account of the history, organization, and role of the Partido Comunista de Venezuela, as well as the attributes of the Venezuelan environment which made it difficult for PCV to achieve power.

The book sketches the history of PCV from its foundation in 1931, to the period of its unsuccessful experiment with violence and its eventual withdrawal from guerrilla activity in 1966. The history is divided into two parts. The first part covers the period from 1931 to January 1958, when Pérez Jiménez' dictatorship was overthrown. This is the period during which the Communist movement in Venezuela was divided.

The second period covers 1958-1967. The early years of that period witness the rise of PCV and the substantial strength it gains. The latter years of that period brought the decline of PCV.

The rise and fall, or the success and failure, of a Communist party depends on its operational environment. The Communists succeed where they adjust to the operational environment (as in Italy and France), or where the environment favors their means or goals (as in Asia). They decline where their operational environment is hostile (as in Canada and the United States). An important section of this book analyzes the Venezuelan environment and examines its effect on the performance of PCV. It shows that the Venezuelan environment was favorable to the Communists for a very short period after the downfall of the Pérez Jiménez regime. During that period, the Communists gained an unprecedented degree of power, influence, and respectability. This gain was due to several factors among which are their participation in the efforts that brought down a hated regime, the key positions in periodicals that they gained and used to their advantage, and the attitude of other political parties which emphasized the unity of all civilian political figures to form a solid front vis-à-vis the military.

The Venezuelan environment, however, soon developed problems which the PCV was not able to solve successfully. Perhaps the strongest factor in the environment which constituted a formidable block in PVC's path to power consisted of government programs that included advanced social reform, a nationalistic program for the key oil industry, advocacy of rapid economic development, and support of political democracy. Unable to compete with such programs, the PCV decided to follow the violent road to power, first by launching a campaign of urban terrorism to discredit the government, and by later emphasizing guerrilla war in the rural sector to overthrow the government.

The monstrous way in which these activities were carried out precipitated the disapproval of the masses, as well as all democratic political organizations, of the Communists' means to achieve their goals. As a result, PCV suffered a severe decline in its influence in the labor movement, in its infiltration into the various levels of power, and in its contacts with the masses, particularly the workers and the peasants. The Communist party of Venezuela also became isolated in the political field, where it was quarantined by all democratic political groups, even the most radical. This disastrous experience forced the Communists to withdraw their campaign of terrorism and guerrilla activity in an attempt to return to the mainstream of Venezuelan political life.

The authoı analyzes PCV's experience with violence and explains how it contributed to the growing breach between the Communist parties of Latin America and the party and regime of Fidel Castro. PCV's decision to withdraw from guerrilla warfare created a bitter polemic within the Communist party of Cuba, which encouraged the use of violence in Venezuela. It also contributed to a realignment of forces of the Latin American Soviet Union-aligned extreme left, which supported PCV's decision and backed its declaration of independence from Fidel Castro's domination.

The book concludes that the "Partido Comunista de Venezuela seems to be effectively prevented from making any dramatic headway in the foreseeable future." This conclusion, which was made in 1968 when the book was completed, is still relevant. The reviewer spent the latter part of the 1971 summer in Venezuela, during which time he heard comments about the current and expected performance of the Communist party similar to those presented in the book. It is hoped, however, that this conclusion does not reduce the interest of the United States in Venezuela's economic, social, and political development, for there seems to be a high positive correlation between U.S. interest in a country and the strength of Communist activities in that country.

The book should be very useful to students in Latin American history, political science, sociology, and economics. It should also be an enjoyable reading for the general reader who is interested in Latin American affairs.

–M. F. Hassan
Associate Professor of Economics
Illinois State University

BOOKS RECEIVED

GENERAL AND REGIONAL LATIN AMERICA

Feder, Ernest, THE RAPE OF THE PEASANTRY: LATIN AMERICA'S LANDHOLDING SYSTEM. Garden City, N.Y.: Doubleday, 1971. Foreword, glossary, index. xv + 304 pp. $2.50.

LATIN AMERICAN RESEARCH AND PUBLICATIONS AT THE UNIVERSITY OF TEXAS AT AUSTIN, 1893-1969 (Guides and Bibliographies Series:3). Austin, Texas: Institute of Latin American Studies, Univ. of Texas at Austin, 1971. Foreword. viii + 187 pp. $7.50.

Ranis, Peter, FIVE LATIN AMERICAN NATIONS: A COMPARATIVE POLITICAL STUDY. New York: Macmillan, 1971. Preface, introduction, index. x + 337 pp.

COUNTRIES OF LATIN AMERICA

Brazil

Roett, Riordan, THE POLITICS OF FOREIGN AID IN THE BRAZILIAN NORTHEAST. Nashville, Tenn.: Vanderbilt Univ. Press, 1972. Preface, glossary, bibliography, index. xii + 202 pp. $8.95.

Saunders, John, ed., MODERN BRAZIL: NEW PATTERNS AND DEVELOPMENT. Gainesville, Florida: Univ. of Florida Press, 1971. Introduction, biographical sketches, index. x + 350 pp. $12.50.

Caribbean Region

Mesa-Lago, Carmelo, ed., REVOLUTIONARY CHANGE IN CUBA. Pittsburgh, Pa.: Univ. of Pittsburgh Press, 1971. Preface, illustrations, tables, abbreviations, bibliographical notes, index. xv + 544 pp. $14.95.

Mexico

Alisky, Marvin, GOVERNMENT OF THE MEXICAN STATE OF NUEVO LEON. Tempe, Arizona: Center for Latin American Studies, Arizona State Univ., 1971. Preface. 50 pp. $1.00.

Cancian, Frank, CHANGE AND UNCERTAINTY IN A PEASANT ECONOMY: THE MAYA CORN FARMERS OF ZINACANTAN. Stanford, Ca.: Stanford Univ. Press, 1972. Acknowledgements, introduction, appendixes, bibliography, index. xiii + 208 pp. $7.95.

Meyer, Michael C., HUERTA: A POLITICAL PORTRAIT. Lincoln, Nebraska: Univ. of Nebraska Press, 1972. Preface, abbreviations, appendixes, bibliographical essay, index. xvi + 272 pp. $9.50.

Gonzalez Casanova, Pablo, DEMOCRACY IN MEXICO. New York: Oxford Univ. Press, 1970. Preface, foreword, introduction. xii + 244 pp.

Peru

Paulston, Rolland G., SOCIETY, SCHOOLS AND PROGRESS IN PERU. Oxford, England: Pergamon Press, 1971. Preface, tables, comparative studies, acknowledgements, appendix, index. xxiv + 312 pp. $4.50.

Ferguson, Yale H., CONTEMPORARY INTER-AMERICAN RELATIONS: A READER IN THEORY AND ISSUES. Englewood Cliffs, N.J.: Prentice-Hall, 1972. Preface, introduction. xi + 543 pp.

Gray, Richard B., ed., LATIN AMERICA AND THE UNITED STATES IN THE 1970's. Itasca, Illinois: F. E. Peacock, 1971. Preface, bibliography, index. xi + 370 pp.

MISCELLANEOUS

Bakke, E. Wight and Bakke, Mary S., CAMPUS CHALLENGE: STUDENT ACTIVISM IN PERSPECTIVE. Hamden, Connecticut: Archon Books, 1971. Preface, appendix, bibliography, index. x + 573 pp. $14.50.

Carballido, Emilio, MEDUSA: OBRA EN CINCO ACTOS (edited by Jeanine Gaucher-Shyltz and Alfredo Morales). Englewood Cliffs, N.J.: Prentice-Hall, 1972. Preface, vocabulary. viii + 183 pp.

Castillo, Homero, ed., ANTOLOGIA DE POETAS MODERNISTAS HISPANO-AMERICANOS. Englewood Cliffs, N.J.: Prentice-Hall, 1972. Palabras preliminares, índice, introducción al estudio del modernismo, glosario, vocabulario. xix + 505 pp.

Guerra, Francisco, THE PRE-COLUMBIAN MIND. New York and London: Seminar Press, 1971. Preface, map of pre-Columbian civilizations, illustrations, bibliography, indexes. xiv + 335 pp. $13.50.

Montagu, Ashley, STATEMENT ON RACE: AN ANNOTATED ELABORATION AND EXPOSITION OF THE FOUR STATEMENTS ON RACE ISSUED BY THE UNITED NATIONS EDUCATIONAL, SCIENTIFIC, AND CULTURAL ORGANIZATION (3rd ed.). New York: Oxford Univ. Press, 1972. Preface, appendix, references, bibliography, index. xiii + 278 pp. $7.95.

Pike, Fredrick B., HISPANISMO, 1898-1936: SPANISH CONSERVATIVES AND LIBERALS AND THEIR RELATIONS WITH SPANISH AMERICA. Notre Dame, Indiana: Univ. of Notre Dame Press, 1971. Preface, notes, name index. xx + 486 pp. $15.00.

S&G | SIMULATION AND GAMES

. . . an international journal of theory, design, and research intended to provide a forum for theoretical and empirical papers related to man, man-machine, and machine simulations of social processes. The journal publishes theoretical papers about simulations in research and teaching, empirical studies, and technical papers about new gaming techniques.

Co-editors: James S. Coleman and Keith J. Edwards, Johns Hopkins University

Published quarterly in March, June, September, and December.

Yearly rate: $18.00; $12.00 with professional discount; $9.00 to full-time students.

EUS | EDUCATION AND URBAN SOCIETY

. . . a new independent quarterly journal of social research with implications for public policy.

Editor: JAY D. SCRIBNER, Graduate School of Education, University of California at Los Angeles

During recent years an increasing number of social scientists have been conducting research on education as a social institution, and have also begun to explore educational institutions and processes as agents of social change. Much of this work, of course, centers on the problems and needs resulting from the national concern with improving the urban environment, but also involved is the role of education in a society which is urban. *Education and Urban Society* exists to foster such research and to provide a *multidisciplinary* forum for its communication.

Published quarterly in November, February, May and August.

Yearly rate: $15.00; $10.00 to professional individuals; $8.00 to full-time students.

UE | URBAN EDUCATION

Published quarterly in April, July, October, and January.

. . . exists to improve the quality of education in the city by making the results of relevant empirical and scholarly inquiry more generally available. *Urban Education* invites contributions not only from within education, but from other relevant fields as well—including jurisprudence, the behavioral sciences, medicine, philosophy, history, and administration.

Editor: WARREN BUTTON, *Dept. of Social Foundations of Education, SUNY, Buffalo*

Yearly rate: $15.00; $10.00 to professional individuals; $8.00 to full-time students.

■ ORDER FORM ■

☐ **Please enter my subscription to:** OR ☐ **Please send more information about:**

- ☐ American Behavioral Scientist
- ☐ American Politics Quarterly
- ☐ Comparative Group Studies
- ☐ Comparative Political Studies
- ☐ Criminology
- ☐ Education and Urban Society
- ☐ Environment and Behavior
- ☐ International Studies Quarterly
- ☐ Journal of Black Studies
- ☐ Journal of Comparative Administration
- ☐ Journal of Interamerican Studies and World Affairs
- ☐ Pacific Sociological Review
- ☐ Poverty and Human Resources Abstracts
- ☐ Public Finance Quarterly
- ☐ Professional Papers in Comparative Politics
- ☐ Professional Papers in Int'l Studies
- ☐ Simulation and Games
- ☐ Sociological Methods and Research
- ☐ The New Atlantis
- ☐ Urban Affairs Quarterly
- ☐ Urban Education
- ☐ Urban Life and Culture
- ☐ Urban Research News
- ☐ Youth and Society

☐ Bill me at: ☐ Institutional ☐ Professional ☐ Student rates

☐ Check enclosed

Prices valid until 9/30/72

NAME ____________________

ADDRESS ____________________

CITY ____________ STATE ____________ ZIP ________

Students indicate institution and status ____________________

Vol. 14 No. 3

August 1972

JOURNAL OF INTERAMERICAN STUDIES

and WORLD AFFAIRS

A Publication of the Center for Advanced International Studies,

The University of Miami

GREAT CITIES OF THE WORLD

Their Government, Politics, and Planning

Edited by WILLIAM A. ROBSON and D. E. REGAN

A new edition of this remarkable book has long been awaited. Now, after nearly five years' intensive preparation, the third edition is being published. The new edition is produced under the joint editorship of Professor William A. Robson and Dr. D. E. Regan.

The purpose of the book is to describe in depth the local government of a selected group of the world's great cities; to consider the problems these vast communities are confronting and what steps they are taken to overcome them.

Twenty-seven cities are described by contributors who have lived and worked in them, often for most of their lives. Nine cities appear for the first time (Belgrade, Birmingham, Cairo, Delhi, Ibadan, Manila, Mexico City, Pretoria and Warsaw). Thirteen of the eighteen cities previously included are dealt with by new authors in entirely new contributions. (They are Amsterdam, Buenos Aires, Calcutta, Chicago, Johannesburg, London, Montreal, New York, Paris, Rome, Stockholm, Sydney, and Toronto.) The chapters on the remaining five cities (Copenhagen, Los Angeles, Osaka, Rio de Janeiro and Tokyo) have been thoroughly revised by their original authors.

In Part One of the book, entitled 'The Great City of Today,' Professor Robson contributes a masterly synthesis of the material contained in the separate studies. This has been rewritten and is substantially enlarged. Among the items he deals with are: the metropolitan community, special constitutional features, the elected council, the alternative varieties of dealing with executive functions (i.e., city councils, council-appointed executives, elected mayors, elected committees and executives appointed by the central government); also considered are municipal services, the need for integration, expansion attempts, the ad hoc authority for special purposes, politics in great cities, divided civic and political interest, relations with higher authorities, municipal finance, planning the great city, and the metropolitan region of tomorrow.

GREAT CITIES OF THE WORLD was a pioneer work which stimulated the production of a considerable amount of research and writing on metropolitan cities. It remains, however, not only a standard reference work, but the only one which contains studies by experts of more than two dozen metropolitan areas scattered throughout the world.

Political scientists, urban geographers, planners, political leaders, governmental officials (at all levels of government), and public administration specialists will find the new edition of this classic reference tool an important addition to their professional libraries.

ISBN 0-8039-0155-0 (Volume I)
0-8039-0156-9 (Volume II)
Market: U.S.A.

Third Edition
L.C. 75-167875

1,170 pages (both volumes) Illustrated Clothbound
$50.00 (complete set--volumes will not be sold separately)

1972

SAGE Publications, Inc. / 275 South Beverly Drive / Beverly Hills, California 90212

Journal of
INTERAMERICAN
STUDIES
and WORLD AFFAIRS

Vol. 14
No. 3
August
1972

CONTENTS

Elections and Political Campaigns in a Racially Bifurcated State: The Case of Guyana
RALPH R. PREMDAS 271

Colombia, the United States, and Interamerican Aviation Rivalry, 1927-1940
STEPHEN JAMES RANDALL 297

Governing the City-State: Notes on the Politics of the Small Latin American Countries
ROLAND H. EBEL 325

The Mercantile Potpourri Called Panama
THOMAS V. GREER 347

Books Received 361

Beverly Hills *SAGE PUBLICATIONS* *London*

JOURNAL OF INTERAMERICAN STUDIES AND WORLD AFFAIRS is published four times annually–in February, May, August, and November.

Journal of INTERAMERICAN STUDIES and WORLD AFFAIRS

Published quarterly by SAGE PUBLICATIONS
Sara Miller McCune, *Publisher*
Constance U. Greaser, *Editorial Director–Journals*
Rhoda Blecker, *Production Editor*

POLICY: *The Journal of Interamerican Studies and World Affairs* reflects the interests of the scholarly community and interested public concerned with the social, economic, political, and cultural aspects of life in Latin America (including the Caribbean); particularly in those instances where the subject is of concern to more than one of the traditional disciplines. As these concerns change, so will the content of the journal. ¶ Articles which have special relevance for interrelationships between American nations and of those nations with the rest of the world will be given special consideration. An effort will be made to include occasional articles that state an unusual or even discordant position on a subject of broad interest to be supplemented by critical comments of authorities representing differing positions on the topic. The editors continue to welcome articles by scholars from all parts of the world.

MANUSCRIPTS: Manuscripts should be submitted in duplicate to: Editor, *Journal of Interamerican Studies and World Affairs,* Box 8134, University of Miami, Coral Gables, Florida 33124. ¶ Correspondence regarding book reviews should be sent directly to: Book Review Editor, *Journal of Interamerican Studies and World Affairs,* Box 8123, University of Miami, Coral Gables, Florida 33124.

Subscriptions: Regular institutional rate $15.00 per year. Professionals and teachers may deduct one-third from the regular institutional rate (one-year rate $10.00); full-time college and university students may subscribe at $8.00. Add $1.50 for subscriptions outside the U.S., Canada and Latin America. No student discounts outside the U.S., Canada and Latin America. Orders from U.K., Europe, the Middle East, and Africa may be placed at £7.00 annually (£4.70 to individuals), and should be sent to the London office (address below). Non-institutional orders **must** be paid by personal check.

Inquiries: Address all correspondence and permissions requests to SAGE PUBLICATIONS, INC., 275 South Beverly Drive, Beverly Hills, California 90212. Inquiries and subscriptions from U.K., Europe, the Middle East, and Africa should be sent to SAGE PUBLICATIONS LTD, St George's House, 44 Hatton Garden, London EC1N 8ER. Other orders should be sent to the Beverly Hills office. ¶ **Exclusive Advertising Representatives:** R. K. Armstrong & Associates, Inc., 11661 San Vicente Boulevard, Suite 210, Los Angeles, California 90049.

Back Issues: Single copies of issues are available at $5.00 each. Orders for 10 or more copies of a single issue for course adoption will be billed at $2.50 per copy. Sterling prices available upon request from the London office. Prior to Volume 10, back issues published are available through Swets & Zeitlinger N.V., Keizersgracht 471 and 487, Amsterdam, Holland. ¶ **Claims for undelivered copies** must be made no later than three months following month of publication. The publisher will supply missing copies when losses have been sustained in transit and where the reserve stock will permit. ¶ **Change of Address:** Six weeks' advance notice must be given when notifying of change of address. Please send old address label along with the new address to insure proper identification. Please specify name of journal.

RALPH R. PREMDAS
University of Guyana
Box 841
Georgetown, Guyana

ELECTIONS AND POLITICAL CAMPAIGNS IN A RACIALLY BIFURCATED STATE

The Case of Guyana

In democratic, integrated political systems characterized by a sharing of fundamental social values and "primitive beliefs" among the population, elections serve a salutary purpose. They not only reaffirm the commitment and involvement of the citizen to the prevailing political system by the ritual act of voting participation, but simultaneously legitimize the means and processes by which political values are authoritatively allocated (Milnor, 1969: 1-2). Elections and voting "draw attention to common social ties and to the importance and apparent reasonableness of accepting the public policies that are adopted (Edelman, 1964: 3). For these reasons, elections serve to integrate the citizen into the polity.

Typically in integrated political systems (for example, the United States and Great Britain), political parties compete to mobilize voters so that citizen preferences are registered

AUTHOR'S NOTE: I wish to thank the Ford Foundation Center for International Comparative Studies for the grant given me to conduct field research for this article in 1968-1969. I also wish to thank Professor Robert E. Scott of the Department of Political Science at the University of Illinois and Anne Premdas of the University of California at Berkeley, for their invaluable editorial advice in putting this article together.

collectively and political decision-makers are selected. The political parties serve therefore as mechanisms through which citizens relate electorally to the political process. The parties are not interested in the psychological political satisfaction that citizens obtain from voting participation in elections, however, or in the role of elections in integrating citizens into the polity, but in the immediate outcome of the electoral contest. Parties aspire to control of the government via elections; their actions and behavior can be explained largely from this perspective.

Because of the body of shared values that underlies an integrated political system, competition among parties tends to be limited as regards issues, so the electoral contest tends to be relatively low-key in intensity. The losers in the party competition at elections do not seek to sabotage the government, but "when the campaign is over . . . the intensity of emotion on the part of the losers tends to evaporate and they salve their wounds with various psychologically soothing devices. The losers find that they didn't care as much, or see aspects of the situation they did not see before" (Lane, 1965: 178).

Results of party competition are accepted without the loss of face partly because of the pluralistic social infrastructure in most integrated polities. Voter preferences are not determined rigidly by a single and compelling particularistic value such as race or religion, but are the function of multiple group interests and identification. The inherent social institutional pluralism of integrated political systems results not only in citizen membership and identification with several diverse organizations and interests but, most importantly, dictates that political parties seriously interested in governing the state be broadly based in their appeals (Lipset, 1960: 12-13). In these circumstances, parties tend to be nonideological and to campaign for votes on issues that do not advocate a radical restructuring of the social and political order. Consequently, the major parties tend to be relatively similar and the stakes involved in the competitive struggle are not high. In other words, each of the major parties is acceptable essentially to most citizens. Consequently, political campaigns tend to be subdued.

In an integrated political system, therefore, competing parties serve several constructive functions simultaneously. Legitimate decision makers are elected; a sense of citizen participation is imparted; the citizen reaffirms his commitment to the political system; and the ultimate stability of the political system is assured. It does not necessarily follow that competitive parties and periodic elections are always useful to a polity, however. Indeed, the above discussion was careful to delineate those conditions under which competitive parties and periodic elections can be of value to a specific type of social and political system. As a corollary, the commentary raises implicit questions about the limitations of competitive parties and elections in promoting political integration and stability in states that are not (a) socially pluralistic, and (b) bounded by "primitive beliefs" and values. La Palombara and Weiner (1969: 28) raised this question when they noted that "where the central values concerning the political process are not adequately shared, we often find unstable political systems in which the continuation of competitive parties is somewhat problematical."

More particularly, in terms of the present study, the hypothesis is advanced that, in a cleavage-ridden state such as Guyana, political parties formed around a nucleus of members from one or another subsystem, such as a tribe or an ethnic group, and which are engaged in competitive elections tend to accentuate sectional differences. In Guyana, the country's political parties do not operate in an integrated political system with a pluralistic social infrastructure, and do not possess a racially overlapping membership.[1] In Guyanese elections, the political campaign for votes is fought bitterly, and its outcome is not accepted as the legitimate decision of all the people. Party competition evokes the most hostile intercommunity sentiments during elections. Campaign tactics are inordinately "dirty" and covertly appeal to racial instincts.

Contrast this to the general pattern in integrated political systems where, when elections are over, the tendency is for the participants in the contest to minimize whatever ill will may have been evoked during the campaign so that life can return to normal during interelection periods. In countries with unintegrated political systems, class, regional, ethnic, or religious predispositions which have been stimulated during heated political campaigns are not so readily suppressed or forgotten. Each succeeding election campaign raises the level of intergroup distrust and fear to a new high point until, after several elections, intercommunity differences become so intolerable that continued mutual coexistence among the subgroups in the society is close to impossible. Figure 1 illustrates the point graphically.

For Guyana, 2, 4, and 6 would represent the elections of 1957, 1961, and 1964. The number 7 represents the general intolerable situation that has existed since 1964, a situation requiring an unprecedented number of police and army regulars to prevent the disparate sections in the population from resorting to full-scale civil war.[2]

The contention of this article is that, in Guyana, competitive parties in quest of electoral votes deepen the divisions in the social system. Election periods are particular movements when the greatest harm is done. The following discussion describes the activities of the two major parties in Guyana during a typical election campaign. It seeks to demonstrate how and why

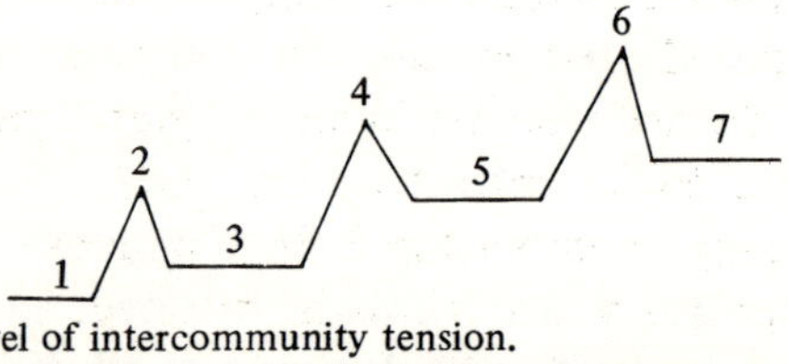

1: Pre-election level of intercommunity tension.

2: Unprecedented level of tension created by election campaign.

3: New level of intercommunity tension created in the wake of last election campaign.

4: Unprecedented level of tension created by new election campaign.

5: New level of intercommunity tension.

6: Unprecedented level of tension created by new election campaign.

7: Intolerable new level of intercommunity tension.

Figure 1: LEVELS OF RACIAL TENSION GENERATED BY THREE SUCCESSIVE ELECTION CAMPAIGNS party competition during the electoral contest accentuates intersectional suspicion and hostility, weakening the integrity and stability of the political system.[3]

This paper is divided into two parts. The first part is very brief; it provides a description of the Guyanese party system and a record of voting participation since 1957. Specifically, the variable race is correlated to voter preferences, to show the increasing intensity of racial voting patterns since the 1957 general elections. The second part of the paper provides a detailed analysis of campaign tactics, to show how they deepen racial cleavages between Indians and Africans in Guyana.

The Party System in Guyana

Guyana has two main political parties, the People's National Congress (PNC) and the People's Progressive Party (PPP), which together generally garner up to ninety percent of all votes cast at general elections. One smaller party, the United Force (UF), which is capable of picking up about eight to ten percent of votes in general elections, has operated discontinuously and sporadically in recent Guyanese political history and may very well be on its way out of the political scene permanently. For these reasons, the UF would be omitted from the following analysis of party activities. The two major parties, the PNC and PPP, have dominated modern Guyanese political history since the mid-1950s. From 1957 to 1964, the PPP led by Dr. Cheddi Jagan ruled Guyana; from 1964 to 1968, a PNC-UF coalition led by Mr. L.F.S. Burnham governed the country; and finally, after the controversial elections of 1968, the PNC alone ran the government.

The two principal political parties receive their support from solid racial voting blocs in the Guyanese population. The PNC, which presently controls the government, depends overwhelmingly upon the African segment of the population for its support, electoral and otherwise, while the PPP, which is the opposition party in the unicameral House of Assembly, draws its support almost exclusively from the Indian part of the population. In the general elections of 1961 and 1964,[4] Africans and Indians almost unswervingly supported the PNC and PPP, respectively. If there is one indisputable fact of Guyanese political life, it is that ethnic identification is the determinant of party preference.

Prior to the emergence of the PPP and PNC as ethnic parties in the mid-1950s, the two party leaders, Mr. L.F.S. Burnham and Dr. Cheddi Jagan, were friends and comrades in a single, ethnically united People's Progressive Party, a post-World-War-II independence movement that was formed in 1950 to expel colonialism from British Guiana. Under the dual leadership of Dr. Jagan and Mr. Burnham (the former was the leader of the party, while the latter was the chairman), the original PPP, projecting itself as a socialist equalitarian liberating force of all the Guyanese people, won the momentous general elections of 1953—the first elections ever held under universal adult suffrage in Guyana. This was also the first time a majority of seats was ever won by a party in the colonial parliament. Following victory and an initial period of less than nine months of "governing" Guyana under a restrictive colonial constitution, the ruling PPP was abruptly evicted from office by British troops to prevent what was thought of then by a wholly misguided British colonial office as an imminent takeover of British Guiana by "international communism." The PPP leaders, who throughout their brief administration uninhibitedly extolled the virtues of socialism and communism, were either jailed or confined to restricted quarters while a newly appointed interim government, composed of members of the old reactionary colonial elite and plantocracy, ran Guyana until 1957, when new general elections were held.

Between the suspension of the constitution in 1953, when the PPP was ousted from power, and 1957, when new general elections were held, the two leaders of the People's Progressive Party quarrelled, parted company over differences regarding tactics and strategy of the independence movement, and constituted their own separate parties. The faction led by Dr.

Jagan has continued to call itself the People's Progressive Party, and the faction led by Mr. Burnham, although initially also claiming the name People's Progressive Party, subsequently altered its name in 1958 to the People's National Congress. The two new party configurations, each headed by a separate leader who was very popular among members of his own ethnic group, formally organized the lives of their respective ethnic constituents for electoral ends, thereby deepening and further structuring the racial cleavages in the polity. From the 1957 general elections, when the two parties first confronted each other, to the 1964 general elections, competition between the two racial parties for votes was accompanied by increasingly bitter physical and social struggles between Indians and Africans. Talk of partitioning Guyana was widespread, for virtual civil war had broken out between Africans and Indians by 1964. Using the 1957, 1961, and 1964 general election results, the immediately following discussion attempts to show the increasing intensification of racial voting preferences by Indians and Africans for the PPP and PNC respectively.

Voting Participation and Race

The 1957 elections occurred during the transitional period when the political system was moving from an aggregating political party mechanism toward racially polarized parties. Following the PPP split in February 1955, the Jaganite and Burnhamite factions scrambled for supporters, mainly in the Indian and African sectors, respectively. The Jaganite PPP and Burnhamite PPP have become de facto racial parties; those voters who had been attracted to the older, more inclusive version of the PPP in the 1953 general elections chiefly because of the party's ideological program were left without any meaningful partisan choice in the 1957 elections. Most of these persons stayed home on election day, which resulted in the lowest voting participation in Guyanese history from the time when universal adult suffrage was introduced in 1953 to the 1964 general elections.[5]

TABLE 1
VOTING TURNOUT

Electoral District	*Number of Electors*	*Ballots Cast*	*%*
1. Eastern Berbice	31,794	18,877	59.4
2. New Amsterdam	5,879	3,192	52.8
3. Berbice River	5,429	3,015	55.5
4. Western Berbice	8,324	6,041	72.6
5. Eastern Demerara	18,295	11,151	60.95
6. Central Demerara	25,137	14,427	57.4
7. Georgetown North	10,444	5,960	50.5
8. Georgetown Central	12,473	6,800	54.6
9. Georgetown South	24,244	12,299	50.7
10. Demerara River	26,972	12,461	46.2
11. Demerara/Essequibo	15,182	9,041	59.55
12. Essequibo River	13,649	7,026	51.5
13. Western Essequibo	11,215	6,799	60.6
14. Northwestern District	3,481	1,619	46.5
Total	212,518	118,708	55.8 (average)

SOURCE: Report on the General Election (1957: Appendix II, Table 1).

For the 1957 general elections, the country was divided into fourteen constituencies. The results are shown in Tables 1 and 2.

In this interpretation, the 55.8% turnout of electors essentially represents votes cast for racially oriented parties. The parties which contested these elections, the Jaganite PPP (Indian), the Burnhamite PPP (African), the National Labour Front (Indian middle class), and the United Democratic Party (African middle

TABLE 2
PARTIES AND RESULTS

Party	*Number of Candidates*	*Ballots*	*%*	*Seats Won*
1. PPP (Jaganite)	13	55,552	47.50	9
2. PPP (Burnhamite)	13	29,802	25.48	3
3. National Labour Front	14	13,465	11.51	1
4. United Democratic Party	8	9,564	8.18	1
5. Guiana National Party	1	199	.17	0

SOURCE: Report on the General Election (1957: Appendix I, Table 1).

class) all pitched their appeals in racial terms.[6] The two PPPs did this covertly, but the practice became so widespread that the racial appeals of these parties soon became an open secret. The National Labour Front, an offspring of the local middle-class East Indian Association, and the United Democratic Party, a product of the local middle-class League of Coloured People, did not provide an acceptable nonracial alternative program to the two PPPs for those voters who sought ideologically or nonracially oriented parties. In other words, voting choice was among racial parties in the 1957 general elections.

Many voters responded to their limited range of choice in the 1957 elections by staying home. To be sure, other reasons might have contributed to the low voting turnout. After the suspension of the constitution in 1953, British troops paraded the coastal plains frequently, a factor that may have deterred voters from going to the polls in 1957. The main drawback to this explanation is that virtually all the British troops who landed in 1953 had left the colony at least two years before the general elections. This was known by nearly everyone in the country. Another reason advanced is that voters were so confused by the presence of two PPPs in the 1957 elections that many did not vote. This argument could be considered seriously if the ballots (prototype copies of which were circulated widely long before the elections occurred) simply indicated as follows:

PPP Jaganite	☐
PPP Burnhamite	☐

But this was not the case. Appearing beside each PPP's name on the ballot was a large copy of the party's symbol. The PPP (Jaganite) used the cup, and the PPP (Burnhamite) used the broom, so that the nonliterate person only needed to identify the symbol of his choice to indicate his voting preference. The small size of the Guyanese population (approximately half a million in 1957) and its solid concentration along the coast allowed each PPP group to communicate easily to its supporters how to mark the ballot.

Therefore, to account for the low voting turnout in the 1957 general elections some reason other than British troops or the presence of two PPPs must be found. The thesis advanced here is that the low voting participation can be traced to the limited range of political choices offered the Guyanese voting public. This reasoning is based primarily on information gathered through direct interviewing.[7] In the five villages studied (two predominantly African, two predominantly Indian, and one mixed), both persons who voted in 1957 and individuals who were eligible to vote but did not cast their ballots were interviewed. Both voters and nonvoters expressed sentiments deploring the infighting between Dr. Jagan and Mr. Burnham for the PPP's leadership. Nearly all voiced the hope that the two leaders would be reconciled. For their part, the nonvoters were emphatic in stating that in 1957 they were unable psychologically to bring themselves to vote for either Dr. Jagan or Mr. Burnham, since this would necessarily entail disrupting the relatively peaceful racial harmony that existed between Indian and African communities at that time.

This point cannot be overstressed. Not only 1957 nonvoters but also voters stressed that at the time of the election they feared that the interracial modus vivendi that had existed between Africans and Indians was threatened by the racial nature of the choice presented by the two PPPs. For this reason, many persons simply decided to stay home rather than vote for racially oriented parties.[8]

By the 1961 general elections, the nonvoters of the 1957 elections were eliminated by the intensification of *Apanjaat* politics. The PPP and PNC (the Burnhamite PPP altered its name to PNC in 1958) continued and completed their efforts to organize nearly the entire Guyanese electorate into racial political blocs. Each party wanted to ensure that *all* members identified with it ethnically would in fact vote for it. Neither the PPP nor the PNC expected that this would result in the formation of inflexible racial voting blocs. Rather, they counted on persuading persons not identified with them ethnically to join them, but only after they each had corralled their respective ethnic sectors behind them.

In the four years after 1957, then, the reluctant nonvoter of that year's election practically disappeared. Because of the growing pervasiveness of Apanjaat politics, he was forced to seek personal and family security by conforming to the predominant political norms of this ethnic section. The local party organization, mainly at the grass-root level, isolated nonconformists for special persuasion. By 1961, the process of total ethnic commitment of Indians and Africans to the PPP and PNC respectively was almost complete. We shall utilize results of the 1961 elections to demonstrate this.

In the 1961 general elections, the colony of British Guiana was divided into 35 constituencies. The candidate who received the highest number of votes among the contenders won a constituency, regardless of whether this number was a majority or a plurality. Considering the new kinds of party allegiance, this "first-past-the-post" system meant that a party could predict the outcome of an election by ascertaining the racial distribution in any constituency. The PPP and PNC both possessed this information.

The election law required each candidate who contested a constituency to make an initial deposit (in 1961, $240 B.W.I. currency) and, win or lose, to obtain a certain minimum percentage of the votes cast in order to have his deposit returned. By using its constituency racial distribution data, a party could decide whether or not running a candidate in a particular constituency was a practical investment. This the PPP did; it placed candidates in only 29 of the 35 constituencies. On the other hand, in order to avoid charges of racism, the PNC competed in all 35 constituencies. The United Force, which had come into existence in 1960, entered the 1961 elections and competed in 34 of the 35 constituencies.

For statistical analytic purposes, the main consequence of selective constituency competition is the great difficulty this poses for comparing electoral gains of the parties against the percentage distribution of Indians and Africans in the population. Since the PPP competed in only 29 constituencies, the overall number of votes amassed by that party cannot be used

TABLE 3
VOTES RECEIVED BY THE TWO MAJOR PARTIES IN THE 1961 ELECTIONS

Party	*Number of Candidates*	*Ballots*	*%*
PPP	29	93,085	42.6
PNC	35	89,501	41.0

to represent the total it might have received by competing in all 35 constituencies. On the other hand, because the PNC competed in all 35 constituencies, the conclusion that the total votes cast for that party represented approximately the size of its ethnic voting bloc seems justified. The results are shown in Table 3.

These figures clearly do not reflect the Indian-African racial distribution which is shown, according to the 1960 census, in Table 4. The "mixed" category is included because at least half this group tends to identify with the PNC sector. In 1961, with racial feelings rising high, ambivalence regarding sectoral identity was not the safest personal policy for "mixed" individuals to follow, except for those who obviously could claim color affinity to the Portuguese or European group by virtue of very light skin texture. Hence, in electoral terms the Negro sector was at least:

$$32.83\% + 1/2\,(11.99\%) = 38.72\% \text{ (approximately, 39\%)}.$$

Conceivably, the two percent differential between the votes obtained by the PNC (41%) and the electoral strength of the

TABLE 4
INDIANS, AFRICANS, AND MIXED AS A PERCENTAGE OF THE TOTAL POPULATION

Race	*Percentage of Population (1960)*
Indian	47.79
Negro	32.83
Mixed	11.99

TABLE 5
VOTES RECEIVED BY THE TWO MAJOR PARTIES IN THE 1964 ELECTIONS

Party	*Percentage of Ballots Obtained*
People's Progressive Party	45.84
People's National Congress	40.52

African section (39%) could be accounted for by one or both of two reasons: (a) the percentage of "mixed" who voted for the PNC was higher than 50%; (b) African voting turnout was higher than Indian voting turnout. In any event, a comparison between the population of the African sector and the votes gained by the PNC in 1961 shows a very close correlation.[9]

In the 1964 elections, when the PPP and PNC both competed in all 35 electoral districts, and racial animosities had reached their highest peak in Guyanese history, the results displayed more faithfully an even closer correlation between the size of an ethnic group and partisan voting preferences. Unlike 1961, when the election was relatively peaceful, during 1964 violence was common and intersectional hostilities had reached their highest peak in Guyanese history. The 1964 results are shown in Table 5. Voting turnout was a phenomenal 96.98%, despite the fact that voting was not compulsory. Comparing these results with the census data in Guyana reveals the very close correlation between race and voting preference. The 45.84% performance of the PPP, instead of the 47% which was estimated as the size of the Indian population in 1964, is accounted for mainly by the fact that a substantial part of the Indian population was below 21 during the 1960s. The 40.52% of the PNC comes closer than the 1961 figure in reflecting the size of the African voting bloc.[10]

Political Campaigns and Racial Cleavages

Let us now describe and analyze a typical election campaign[11] to show how racial differences and sectional consciousness between Indians and Africans were evoked by the parties between 1955 and 1964. As pointed out at the beginning of the article, racial hostilities provoked during the six-month period immediately preceding each election are not forgotten after the elections are over. Even though they definitely fall off in intensity, the attitudes engendered carry over to leave a significantly higher level of racial antagonism between the Indian and African sections in interelection periods. Over a period of three elections, the consciousness of Africans and Indians has been so saturated with mutual hate that my interviews showed that interethnic violence became common and talk of partitioning Guyana gained widespread currency.

In Guyana, the intensification of racial animosities is substantially traceable to political campaigns waged by the parties during election years. From 1957 to 1964, three general elections have been held; each election drew more voters than the previous election (55.8% in 1957; 89.4% in 1961; and 96.9% in 1964). The increase in voting participation attests not to growing political sophistication of the Guyanese electorate so much as to the intensity and pervasiveness of racial intersectional hostilities and, concomitantly, to the grave importance Indians and Africans attached to electoral outcomes.

Political campaigns primarily between the two major competing parties (the PPP and the PNC) have evoked acute consciousness of the ethnic cleavages in Guyanese society. To assure its continued existence, each party wanted a sizeable segment of votes in the electorate, at a minimum. Ideally, each party wanted a majority, in order to win control over the government. In the Guyanese context, the two objectives were inconsistent, considering the 1964 population distribution, which gave neither Indians nor Africans an electoral majority at the polls. Indeed, as pointed out earlier, the two objectives were inconsistent, given the manner in which the two parties vied for votes. Each party first sought to organize under its own umbrella the ethnic group identified with it, then proceeded to attempt cross-sectional conversions. This resulted in a stalemate, with each racial unit standing as a cohesive voting bloc behind its respective party. To understand why this occurred, the manner in which a typical campaign is conducted must be understood.

THE CAMPAIGN: TWO FACES AND TWO STRATEGIES

Dualism pervades Guyanese politics. Just as each party tries to camouflage its uni-ethnic predominance by displaying in its offices African and Indian personnel, so during elections each party projects a public image of waging a clean, issue-oriented campaign. In fact, each party allocates most of its grass-roots campaign resources to making racial appeals for votes. The two faces of each campaign are accompanied by two campaign strategies. The campaign organization of both the PPP and PNC approximate the structure shown in Figure 2.

THE CLEAN CAMPAIGN: FACE I

The "formal" aspect of each campaign is directed mainly by the party's overall campaign coordinator and his staff. The clean campaign typically (a) utilizes the best party speakers at public meetings, (b) defines its appeals in terms of well-reasoned arguments over various issues, (c) reports party speeches at length in the party news organ, and (d) vehemently denounces racism. The party distributes thousands of pamphlets elucidating its positions, buys advertising space in newspapers, and

Overall Campaign Coordinator
("advised" by party leader and
assisted by a staff)

↓

Regional Coordinators

↓

Sub-Region (a set of villages) Activist or
"Precinct" Captain Responsible to Regional Coordinator

↓

Local Auxiliaries Mobilized to Assist in Campaign
(pandits, school teachers, civil servants, YSM,
PYO, women's section groups)

Figure 2: CAMPAIGN ORGANIZATIONAL CHART OF THE PPP AND PNC

uses the free radio time allocated to it by the government to disseminate its views. All these activities, elaborated upon below, point to the clean face of a Guyanese political campaign.

The best speakers: Among its leadership, each party has notables who are highly regarded by the Guyanese population. Most frequently, these persons hold academic degrees from overseas universities, a fact which in the Guyanese context endows them to speak authoritatively on literally any issue, regardless of whether the person holds a degree in mechanical engineering or in law. The leader of the party himself is such a notable. Dr. Jagan holds a D.D.S. (Doctor of Dental Surgery) from Northwestern University and Mr. Burnham a law degree from London University. In the PPP's leadership hierarchy are several lawyers (one, Fenton Ramsahoye, holds a Ph.D. from London University), a medical doctor (Subhan Ali Ramjohn), an eye specialist (Charles Jacob, Jr.), an educator (Cedric Nunes), and a Harvard liberal arts graduate (Randi Chandisingh). Similarly in the PNC are several lawyers, a veterinary surgeon (Ptolemy Reid), several educators and other college graduates with liberal arts degrees. Generally, these persons speak for the party at huge public meetings where the press is likely to be in attendance. The fact that most of these notables have been educated overseas means that they are likely to receive keen attention from the audience.

Issues: Before an election, each party decides what issues are to be discussed at public meetings. The issues selected are researched by the campaign coordinator's staff, which also determines the general strategy in presenting the issues. Each notable member of the party's hierarchy is allocated one general issue area in which he specializes at public meetings. For example, Dr. Ramjohn is the medical health and welfare specialist speaker for the PPP; Mr. L. John, a lawyer with a keen interest in local government, is the local government specialist speaker of the PNC.

Although the PPP and the PNC are supported by preponderantly different occupational groups (Indians as rice farmers and sugar workers; Africans as civil servants), neither party concentrates on economic and occupational issues which affect their respective sectors. Instead, generally, the PPP makes a big issue of supporting demands of civil servants, while the PNC, in a similar vein, deplores the "plight" of the rice farmers. Publicly, each party insists on championing the rights of the section not ethnically identified with it, if only to convince itself of its fictional multiracial character and outlook.

Newspaper reports and pamphlets: The PPP and PNC publicize their positions on issues through the various media. The party news organ faithfully cites the "great" speeches of their principal speakers on various issues. Pamphlets and handbills carrying the main points of these speeches are distributed to the population and posted on billboards, telegraph poles, and public buildings for display. Rarely is anything racially offensive printed by the PPP or PNC for public distribution during political campaigns.

Racism: One of the most common themes in the public meetings of the PNC and PPP is the denunciation of racism. In an obsessive ritual act, regardless of the topic of his discussion, each speaker finds an opportunity to denounce Apanjaat politics. In all the available public media—pamphlets, radio broadcasts, newspaper advertisements—racism is denounced by both parties.

If Guyanese national elections were contested solely by the application of the various clean campaign tactics described above, the probability that racism would be the determining basis of party preference would be very small. Not that racism or sectionalism would not be a main variable accounting for party preference in such a circumstance, but that the incentives for doing so would be limited and minimized. Unfortunately, in Guyana, political campaigns are not conducted only on a clean level. In fact, the clean campaign methods are relatively unimportant in the overall repertoire of activities carried out by the PNC and PPP to win votes. In Guyana, the major parties depend on a different set of tactics to mobilize support for themselves.

THE UNCLEAN CAMPAIGN: FACE II

While the clean campaign strategy is directed and executed solely by the overall campaign coordinator's staff, the "informal" campaign is left to the regional managers, assisted by grass-roots party activists and volunteer personnel, including teachers and civil servants. Analysis of the "unclean" campaign follows under the following topics: (a) planning and tactics, (b) appeals, (c) registration and canvassing, and (d) small meetings.

Planning and tactics: Planning and tactics of political campaigns at the grass-roots level involve the participation of the regional campaign managers, who are paid party activists normally assigned to the region permanently; these are assisted by representatives of the auxiliaries and the youth sections of the parties, and other influential persons such as local teachers or civil servants who normally are not affiliated openly with a party during off-election years. A region may cover as many as fifty to sixty villages and small towns; the regional manager functions to direct and coordinate the activities of the party campaign in a specific region. Each of the regularly paid party activists is subordinate to the regional manager; as such, he is given responsibility over a number of villages and towns contiguous to each other in a particular region. The activities of the volunteer party workers in villages and towns—the group leaders, teachers, civil servants and so on—are supervised in turn by the paid party activist. The hierarchical chain of command can be diagrammed as shown in Figure 3.

The paid party activist responsible for a number of villages is

Regional Manager

↓

Paid Party Activists Assigned to Specific Parts of the Region Including Several Contiguous Villages

↓

Group Leaders; Auxiliary and Section Leaders; and Other Personnel in Specific Villages

Figure 3: GRASSROOTS CAMPAIGN ORGANIZATIONAL CHART OF PPP AND PNC the workhorse in this "informal" campaign strategy. He communicates to the regional manager the problems and needs of local activists and supplies funds and general campaign paraphernalia (e.g., jeeps, microphones, campaign buttons, and the like) to the local activists. Because he is on the spot, the field commander is answerable for negligence in a campaign. Above all, the paid party activist is responsible ultimately to get the voters to the polls. He does so by enlisting the help of the volunteer local activists who are at his disposal in the villages and towns in his subregion.

One of the consequences of the regional campaign strategy is the intense political pressure upon most parts of the Guyanese electorate by the parties during the political campaigns. From 1957 to 1963, the intense campaign coverage of the electorate was concentrated mainly in certain constituencies; from 1964 to the present, all areas in Guyana were subjected equally to intense racial political campaigning tactics and methods. This shift in tactics occurred because of the change in 1964 from the "first-past-the-post" system to proportional representation. Under the "first-past-the-post" method used from 1953 to 1961, a party could decide not to contest a constituency because the racial distribution of the population in the constituency did not indicate an outcome favorable to it. Consequently, most of the competitive party battles were concentrated in constituencies with large numbers of Indians and Africans. Under the "proportional representation system" introduced in 1964, however, the entire country became a single constituency, so every vote became important to the party, regardless of where it was located.[12] In the 1964 elections, therefore, intense grass-roots campaign strategy was extended to the entire country by all parties. While the electoral evidence shows no significant change in voting patterns between 1961 and 1964, racial feelings grew more intense in 1964, if only because the competitive campaign battles were extended over a greater area of the coast. To be sure, by 1961, racial voting preferences had solidified, but proportional representation intensified campaigning by exposing the entire electorate equally to intense Apanjaat politics. With nearly all the small Guyanese population concentrated in villages and towns on the coast, and with roads providing easy access to any coastal area, the grass-roots campaign strategy of the parties was carried out easily and thoroughly, literally leaving no area unmapped or untended.

Appeals: The appeals employed by grass-roots party workers are of two varieties. The first involves invoking old negative stereotyped views held by Indians of Africans, and by Africans of Indians, to reinforce community solidarity of a particular ethnic section. The second variety concerns making economic promises which say that if the party wins, the resources of the government will be channeled for the improvement of Africans or Indians. Both appeals are discussed in detail below.

Over the years of their common existence in Guyana, Indians and Africans have developed certain stereotyped views of each other. Not all the stereotypes are negative; indeed, some are very complimentary to an ethnic group.

Typically, an Indian conceives of an African as: (1) physically strong and powerful. (Most Indians are relatively small in stature as compared with most Africans.) While this appears to be a positive stereotype with regard to the African's physical endowment, most Indians view the physical power of the African as a threat to their security. (2) The Indian sees the African as economically undisciplined. Indians view the high consumptive habits of the African as irresponsible behavior. Instead of saving some of the high earnings which come from good civil service and teaching jobs, as well as from cane-cutting on the sugar estates, the African, as seen by the Indian, spends all his money on liquor, dances, and good clothes. For the Indian, the "economic extravagence" of the African accounts for the shabby houses in which Africans live, and the paucity of African businesses. In holding this economic stereotype of the Africans, Indians have failed to consider the numerous cases in their own villages and towns which attest to the economically conservative behavior of many Africans. For Indians, the "economic irresponsibility" stereotype is not peculiar to a segment of the African population, but is true of all Africans generally. (3) Indians view Africans as culturally inferior. Most Indians regard the wholesale adoption of "British" ways by Africans as a mark of the African's inferiority. Although partly as bastardized as Africans by British norms, Indians consider the African inferior for not retaining any traits of his cultural heritage. (Some cultural traits which obviously have been retained are either not recognized by Indians or are condemned as "juju" culture.)

On the other hand, typically, Africans conceive of Indians as (1) physically weak and inferior. African disrespect of Indians substantially stems from the rather frail physical features of the Indian. Indians are "dholl and rice coolies," a slur phrase which points to the dietary habits of Indians, who generally eat split peas, rice, vegetables and fish, but little meat. (Most Hindu Indians do not consume beef, and Muslim Indians similarly do not consume pork; the African eats both.) (2) The African considers the Indian economically miserly. Africans view the Indian as a miserly person who sacrifices his dietary well-being and clothing habits for saving a few cents from every pay package. While this appears as a positive stereotype, most Africans view this (exaggerated) behavior trait as a threat in the long run to the superior status of the African in the colonial social hierarchy which has accorded the lowest rung to the Indian. (3) The African holds the Indian culturally inferior quite as much as the Indian holds the African culturally inferior. Most Africans pride themselves on having acquired the English language and English norms (which in colonial British Guiana were the criteria for status and jobs), and regard the "retarded" acquisition of English ways by Indians as a mark of the Indian's inferiority. Hence, Indians are frequently called derogatorily "coolie babu," and Indian ways are called "coolie culture."

These stereotypes rarely are expressed openly by Indians to Africans or vice versa, but party activists do exploit them for political ends. On the part of the PPP activists, Indians are told that the PNC government run by "Africans" would transfer their sectional stereotyped traits to the government. That is, the PNC government will be (a) economically irresponsible and extravagant, spending public tax money for dances and other such activities; (b) favor persons who are Christians and have adopted British values in the allocation of government jobs and privileges; and (c) allow Africans to beat Indians and take their property.

On the part of the PNC activists, Africans are told that a PPP government will (a) recognize Indian values and consequently eliminate the old English criteria for government jobs, allowing Indians to take over the civil service and teaching profession; (b) enable Indians to use their savings to buy land and property at low prices, resulting in the economic preeminence of Indians in Guyana; and (c) allow Indians to become more powerful (economically), notwithstanding the obvious physical weakness of Indians generally.[13]

The second variety of appeals employed by the party activists pertains to the economic interests of the Indian and African sectors. In the clean campaign, both the PPP and PNC display concern for the economic welfare of all citizens, regardless of sectional affiliation. However, at the grass roots, these cross-sectional appeals are forgotten. Indians are told flatly by PPP activists that when the PPP wins, the government will be "ah'we government" (our government). Indians are promised more land, high prices for rice, and more government jobs. On the other hand, Africans are told just as brazenly that a PNC government will concentrate on urban needs such as housing and will expand the government to provide more jobs for Africans.

Both the "stereotyped" and "economic" appeals of the two parties tend to emphasize and exploit the cultural and occupational differences between Africans and Indians. A campaign waged intensely along these lines at the grass roots for six months before elections and for three consecutive elections over a decade inevitably has deepened the differences between Africans and Indians. The parties have succeeded in assuring themselves of a minimum number of votes by invoking the differences between Africans and Indians. In the end, this has resulted in the expression of unprecedented, intense racial hostilities and violence.[14] Most importantly, each party has discovered, to its "amazement," that once in power its grass-roots appeals have succeeded in intensifying sectional divisions in the polity, rendering effective and legitimate government literally impossible without the use of force.

Small meetings and canvassing: The appeals of the parties at the grass roots are conveyed through small, semi-private meetings and by door-to-door canvassing. Small meetings are held in back or front yards in an area where, tacitly, only individuals of one ethnic group can attend. At the small meetings, issues are hardly discussed; instead, the stereotypes are invoked to secure votes.

Door-to-door canvassing is carried out not only to make appeals for votes, but also to inquire into (a) party preference, and (b) difficulties a family may have in getting to the polls on time. A canvasser typically enters a house where he or she generally urges that "ah'we people must stay together or else the (coolies) or (black people) go take over." Then the entire stereotyped syndrome gradually is expressed, to remind the voter to vote for his own kind (Apanjaat).

Summary

More than any other single party activity, the "informal" political campaign evokes the historical and social differences between Indians and Africans to intense and even violent pitches. As demonstrated earlier in this article, these social differences were reflected politically in the development of rigid racial voting preferences from 1957 to 1964. In a competitive game, the "vote-getting motive" of the PPP and PNC compelled these parties to utilize unclean campaign methods to obtain a minimum of votes. Consequently, after the elections were over, the few intersectional community norms and understandings that might have existed between Africans and Indians before each election period were put to a severe test and not restored to the status quo ante.[15] As of 1964, after several elections, nearly all interethnic norms were destroyed, for all practical purposes. More than ever before the sectional bifurcation in Guyana was unmediated by any reliable cushion of understanding to keep Africans and Indians from violent warfare.[16] The integrity and stability of the state had been impaired severely by party competition for votes.

NOTES

1. For a description of the settlement of various ethnic groups in Guyana, see Smith (1962). The most recent reliable data on Guyana's ethnic distribution is as follows:

Race	*Total*	*% of Total*
Indians	320,000	50.2
Africans	199,830	31.3
Mixed Races	75,990	11.9
Portuguese	6,380	1.0
Chinese	3,910	0.6
Europeans	2,420	0.4
Amerindians	29,430	4.6
	637,990	100.0

(Data extracted from the British Guiana Commission of Inquiry, 1965: 33).

2. In recent years, open racial conflict between Indians and Africans has subsided and has practically disappeared. However, latent intersectional animosities are not far below the surface; elections carried on in the manner of 1961 and 1964 in particular are likely to provide the occasion for open racial confrontation. Fortunately or unfortunately, depending upon how much importance one puts on the electoral process, since the 1968 controversial elections, most Guyanese have come to regard elections under the present government as rigged. Both Indians and Africans express this view. The significance of this development has been that elections are not regarded as "competition" or as an intercommunal confrontation anymore.

3. In this article, integration refers to the development of a common set of values and orientations of citizens to the political system.

4. Until reliable data are available, no analysis would be done in this study of the 1968 general elections.

5. Voting participation for the years 1953, 1957, 1961, and 1964 was 74.8% 55.8%, 89.4%, and 96.9%, respectively.

6. For a detailed discussion of the racist campaign waged by the National Labour Front and the United Democratic Party, see Premdas (n.d.: ch. 2).

7. Interviewing in the villages studied was conducted mainly by way of discussions. Fear that the use of a pencil and paper to record responses would evoke distorted answers, to say nothing of making it difficult to find a relatively willing representative sample, prompted the use of informal discussions as a means of obtaining the data for this part of the study. The interview-discussion approach necessarily limited the number of persons who were selected for the sample. However, the consistency in the answers to similar questions suggested a large number of observations would not have made any significant difference in the final outcome.

8. From the sample, one of every three and one-half persons eligible did not vote; that is, at least 25% of the eligible voters stayed home mainly because of the nature of the choices in 1957.

9. In Premdas (n.d.), I have provided a poll-by-poll breakdown of voting patterns in a number of constituencies to further confirm the close correlation between race and party. Since Indians and Africans live in predominantly uni-ethnic areas in the country, a poll-by-poll analysis of aggregate voter performance proved very revealing regarding racial voting behavior.

10. For a detailed constituency-by-constituency comparison of the 1961 and 1964 results showing the persistence and intensification of the racial voting patterns in Guyana, see Premdas (n.d.: 157, Table 15).

11. Of the four elections held since the split of the old pre-1955 PPP, this researcher has observed those of 1957, 1961, and 1968. The 1964 election campaign was studied through documentary sources in 1968 when research for this project was conducted. On the basis of directly and indirectly "observing" those election campaigns, a set pattern of party tactics was discovered and is described here as "typical."

12. In the 1964 general elections, although the entire country was considered a single constituency, the 35 electoral districts used in the 1961 general elections were used as fathering stations for votes. This procedure allowed for comparison of constituency-by-constituency party performance in the 1961 and 1964 elections.

13. Occupationally, Africans who are mainly urban dwellers, are found in the public services and factories. Indians are preponderantly rural dwellers are rice cultivators and sugar estate workers (see Smith, 1962, for a description of these occupational patterns and their history).

14. One expression of the bitter intercommunal conflicts between Indians and Africans was the widespread exchange of houses between Indians who lived in predominantly African communities and Africans who lived in predominantly Indian communities. Today, fewer multiracial residential areas exist in Guyana than before 1960.

15. For an excellent discussion of the tranquil state of African-Indian interelations in the mid-1950s, see Skinner (1960).

16. Since the controversial 1968 elections, an uneasy tranquility bordering on lethargic helplessness has charactized the behavior of Indians in relation to the present government. No open racial animosities have been expressed between the two main sections of the population, but continued mutual hate and premeditated wide social distance mark the nature of the relationships between Africans and Indians. Because of the firm control of the electoral machinery by the PNC and the belief by Indians that elections are now fraudulently conducted, it is doubtful whether future

elections in Guyana would evoke the same intensity of intersectional emotions that the 1961 and 1964 elections generated. The possibility even exists that future electons supervised by the present PNC regime would be boycotted by the Indian voting population. This occurred in 1970 when the countrywide local government elections were boycotted by Indians and the PPP.

REFERENCES

British Guiana Commission of Inquiry (1965) Report on Racial Problems in the Public Service. Geneva: The International Commission of Jurists.

EDELMAN, M. (1964) The Symbolic Uses of Politics. Urbana: Univ. of Illinois Press.

LANE, R. E. (1965) Political Life. New York: Free Press.

LA PALOMBARA, J. and WEINER, M. (1969) "The Origin and Development of Political Parties," p. 28 in J. LaPalombara and M. Weiner (eds.) Political Parties and Political Development. New Jersey: Princeton University Press.

LIPSET, S. M. (1960) Political Man. Garden City, N.Y.: Doubleday.

MILNOR, A. J. (1969) Elections and Political Stability. Boston: Little, Brown.

PREMDAS, R. R. (n.d.) "Political parties in a bifurcated state: the case of Guyana." Ph.D. dissertation. University of Illinois.

Report on the General Election, 1957.

SKINNER, E. P. (1960) "Group dynamics and social stratification in British Guiana 904-912 in V. Rubin (ed.) Social and Cultural Pluralism in the Caribbean. New York: Annals of New York Academy of Sciences.

SMITH, R. T. (1962) British Guiana. London: Oxford Univ. Press.

STEPHEN JAMES RANDALL
Department of History
University of Toronto
Toronto, 181, Canada

COLOMBIA, THE UNITED STATES, AND INTERAMERICAN AVIATION RIVALRY, 1927-1940

Recent research on U.S. diplomacy in Latin America has indicated the prominent role of the State Department in gaining for American airlines a major share of interamerican aviation in the mid-1920s. The department's campaign to "de-Germanize" commercial aviation in the western hemisphere immediately prior to and during World War II has also drawn the attention of historians (McCann, 1968; Newton, 1965; Conn, 1960; Burden, 1943). Yet little analysis has been directed to U.S. policy in the late 1920s and early 1930s, crucial years for the shift of power away from European-supported commercial airlines in Latin America to Pan American Airways.[1]

One of the results of interamerican aviation is that the wartime program of de-Germanification has been viewed as a diplomatic response peculiar to the exigencies of war rather than as a logical extension of traditional aviation policy in the Americas. Certainly, strategic considerations—the defense of the Panama Canal and of the petroleum refineries in Aruba and Curaçao—were predominant after 1940; but the record suggests that such strategic factors cannot be presented out of the commerical context in which they originated. Government support for Pan American Airways in the 1927-1938 period established the pattern for the subsequent decade. The Americanization of commercial aviation in Latin America after 1938 was little more than the intensified implementation of an earlier policy.

Phases of this Policy

One of the most revealing and important phases of this policy was the relationship between Pan American Airways and the Colombian line Scadta (Sociedad Colombo-Alemana de Transportes Aéreos),[2] which operated in Colombia from its establishment in 1919 until its absorption into the Colombian national airlines, Avianca, in 1940. The efforts of Scadta to resist the southward expansion of the Pan American system in the 1927 to 1931 period was a catalyst in the formation of U.S. policy in these years. Because of Colombia's proximity to the Panama Canal and its command of both Pacific and Caribbean coasts in northwestern South America, Colombian adoption of a pro-American aviation policy had become an important objective of State Department officials by late 1927. Following Pan American's maiden flight to Havana on October 19, 1927, the State Department viewed its presence in Latin America as vital to the economic and strategic interests of the United States and actively worked to reduce Scadta's ability to compete with the American company.

The timing of Pan American's flight to Havana in late 1927 itself reflected the American preoccupation with the activities of Scadta in the Caribbean. In the mid-1920's Scadta's president, Peter Paul von Bauer, an Austrian national, made several unsuccessful attempts to obtain permanent landing rights for the company in Panama, but he met with opposition from the U.S. government until Colombian officials intervened. In possession of temporary permission to land in the Canal Zone, in 1925 von Bauer sent two planes through Central America to Havana, and, at the conclusion of this survey flight, he suggested to Washington that the service might be extended to Key West, Florida (El Porvenir, 1927; Newton, 1965: 354).

The American government remained strongly reluctant, however, to facilitate Scadta's operations; yet the Scadta initiative served as an impetus in the formulation of American aviation diplomacy. On August 14, 1925, Secretary of War Dwight Davis expressed to the Secretary of State his concern that Scadta represented a potential threat to American interests in the Caribbean. "It would appear to be highly desirable to formulate a national policy in regard to American dominance of aerial commercial and postal activities in Central America, and to determine ways and means by which this policy may be made effective." The State Department concurred in Davis' assessment of the situation and instructed its representatives in Latin America to report on the operations of the German-Colombian company (DS 821.796 Sca 2/35, August 28, 1925).

Scadta continued to press for a consolidation of its lines in Central America despite the overt hostility of the U.S. government. A year after von Bauer approached Washington officials with plans for a service from Havana to Key West, his brother Victor discussed Scadta's plans with officials of the State Department and with William P. MacCracken, the assistant Secretary of Commerce for aviation. The von Bauers both expressed their willingness to cooperate with American capital and assured the Americans that the company had no "political or other aims inimical to the United States." On the other hand, they were equally emphatic that they were not prepared to lose control of their operations.[3]

By mid-1927, Scadta's determination to develop a Central American line had led to the formation of the Compañía Aeromarítima de Colombia designed to operate from Barranquilla to the Canal Zone, as an extension of Scadta's Girardot-Barranquilla service; Scadta itself controlled 48% of the new company's stock and individual Colombians, the balance. Of the eight directors, six were Colombian, and the preseident, Alberto Osorio of Barranquilla, was also Colombian. The operations manager, however, was Hermann Kuehl, prominent in the

Scadta organization see (White and Olya Herrera memoranda of September 26, 1927).

In late November, the persistent procrastination of the U.S. government over Scadta's requests for landing rights in Colón precipitated a resurgence of popular anti-Americanism in Colombia. While an interdepartmental committee, composed of the Departments of State, Treasury, Navy, War, and Post Office, met in Washington to discuss air mail routes, rumors of American hostility to Scadta's expansion received considerable attention in the Colombian press. Scadta itself and business interests in Colombia and Panama, equally anxious to profit from the increased commercial activity, were the source of much of the agitation.[4]

The Bogotá press vehemently supported Scadta's petition for an extension of its service to the Canal Zone. On November 22, *El Tiempo* headlined its front page story: "Yankees will deny . . . permission . . . because Scadta would compete with North American lines." The following day, all Bogotá papers carried a full-page Aeromarítima advertisement appealing to Colombian nationalism. It read in part:

> Colombians:
>
> The extension of our commercial air lines from Barranquilla to Cristóbal, C.Z. (Colón) . . . is on the verge of aborting.
>
> It is, therefore, the patriotic duty of each citizen to . . . assert the Sacred Right of the Colombian nation to extend its air line network to neighbouring countries, based on the outstanding achievements of Colombian commercial aviation (El Tiempo, 1927b).

The same morning, *El Tiempo* commented in its regular column "Cosas del Día":

> Colombia should defend as its own cause the right of the hydroplane company to land in Colón. This proposal presents a threat to no one, but on the other hand represents a major advance in our external communications. The reasons which the United States Government has given . . . for denying the request do not stand up under even casual scrutiny.

> American hegemony over the Canal Zone would not be challenged by allowing Colombian planes to land in the Bay of Colón. As for competition with American lines—that problem too is non-existent since there are as yet no American companies in the area and little prospect of one in the immediate future.
>
> On the contrary, the commerce between the United States and Colombia stands to profit from the closing of distances which the new line would accomplish.

El Diario Nacional, a leading liberal organ of Bogotá, echoed the sentiments of *El Tiempo* in an article on November 23 entitled "The Yankee Attitude to Our Aviation." The paper argued that the dominant financial interests of Colombians in the company negated American objections to its operation and raised a very delicate question of sovereignty. The following day it suggested:

> The Compañía Aeromarítima de Colombia is a purely commercial venture. . . . If such an action is taken in the United States, it can be explained only as a veto inspired by sordid commercial rivalry, since the North Americans are planning to establish a company similar to ours—although no doubt with greater capital backing.

El Diario Nacional concluded with an expression of support for Peter von Bauer's suggestion that Colombia instruct its delegates to raise the issue at the forthcoming Sixth International Conference of American States, in Havana. Unless Colombia were able to obtain landing rights in Colón, it was clear that American aviation interests would shortly dominate the Caribbean (see also El Diario Nacional, 1927; El Debate, 1927; Diario del Comercio, 1927).

The public campaign in support of Colombian interests did little to weaken American resolve. In fact, Secretary of State Kellogg informed Charles Hilles, vice chairman of the Republican National Committee, that Scadta's incitement to anti-Americanism was further reason to deny it entry to Panama. The American minister in Bogotá, Samuel Piles, who had so recently expressed confidence in von Bauer, informed the department at the height of the press campaign: "I heartily favor doing all we can consistently for Colombia but never through that company which I now regard as an absolute menace since it is viciously and publicly undertaking to incite a whole nation against us." Several days later, when Scadta began stamping patriotic slogans on all air mail it carried, Piles' hostility increased. "It is not Colombians who initiate attacks against us," he wrote on November 30, "but foreigners seeking favors who incite them." The American minister restricted his opposition to Scadta, however. He recommended that since Colombians viewed Scadta's petition as a national cause, some way might be found to grant landing rights in Panama to a "truly Colombian company."

> I am more than anxious to promote not only a friendly feeling here, but to do everything I can to advance the welfare and happiness of this people.... We are in a fight to counteract the open and insidious influences that are daily working to discredit us in these countries.... I am confident that ... nothing but ... persistent ... retaliation against such people will prove effective.[5]

In an effort to bring pressure to bear on Scadta, the State Department discussed the problem with the Colombian minister in Washington. Olaya was sympathetic to the department's position and promised to advise his government accordingly, but he expressed surprise at the company's action and pointed out that von Bauer was dependable and had made a major contribution in overcoming Colombia's national transportation obstacles. When Francis White was able to arrange a meeting the following month with Olaya and von Bauer, the Scadta president assured him that the press campaign had been the work of a subordinate, initiated during his absence from Bogotá, that he had dismissed the employee and would attempt to restore the damaged public image of the company (Ds 821.796 Sca 2/133, November 29, 1927; DS 821.796 Sca 2/160, November 28, 1927; DS 821.796 Sca 2/149, December 30, 1927).

The department was little impressed with von Bauer's professions of good intentions, but it is likely that American officials would have pursued a similar course had Scadta not attempted to use nationalist sentiment to soften American opposition to its presence in Central America. As chairman of the interdepartmental committee on aviation, Assistant Secretary of State Francis White was extremely influential in the articulation of a Latin American policy during both the Kellogg and the Stimson years. His support for what he viewed as benevolent interventionism in Haiti, Cuba, and the Dominican Republic was consistent with the type of aviation diplomacy he advocated. On December 19, 1927, White outlined the basis for an American aviation policy:

> these German interests have developed a net-work of lines over the Republic of Colombia so that they control aviation in that Republic. Germanic interests likewise are operating air lines in the Republic of Bolivia and in certain parts of Brazil. The French Parliament has just voted a large sum . . . for rapid mail service [to Brazil] . . . . This service will be an advantage to European competitors over those of the United States [sic] unless we likewise can reduce time by carrying mail to South America.
>
> The key to the situation is Panama, communication through Central America to there [sic] . . . . This work must be undertaken immediately . . . if American interests are to be able to get on that field at all.

The question of commercial aviation became one of the prominent topics at the Sixth International Conference of American States, which convened in Havana on January 16, 1928; although other issues, such as tariff reform and military intervention, occasioned by American involvement in Nicaragua, dominated the debates at the conference, the public and official discussion of commerical aviation the previous year had indicated that the question was another potential area of discord in U.S.-Latin American relations.

The Argument in 1928 and 1929

In the committee on Commercial Air Communication, a controversy developed between the United States and Colombia over an American-sponsored amendment to Article XXXI of the Projected Convention on Commercial Aviation drafted at the Washington meeting of the Inter-American Commercial Aviation Commission in May, 1927 (see Pan American Union, 1927: 751-758). In a lengthy memorandum of January 5 to the American delegation, the Secretary of State stressed the importance of revising the convention in a manner guaranteed to protect the position of the United States in the Caribbean (Foreign Relations, 1928a: 534-585). The department's proposed wording of Article XXXI was as follows:

> The right of any of the contracting States to enter into any convention or special agreement with any other State or States concerning international aerial navigation is recognized, so long as such convention or special agreement shall not impair the rights or obligations of any of the States party to this Convention, acquired or imposed herein; provided however that prohibited areas within their respective territories, and regulations pertaining thereto, may be agreed upon by two or more States for military reasons or in the interest of public safety. Such agreements, and all regulations pursuant thereto, shall be subject to the same conditions as those set forth in Article 5 of this Convention with respect to prohibited areas within the territory of a particular State (Foreign Relations, 1928a: 549; see also Informe del Ministro de Relaciones Exteriores, 1928).

The amendment was conspicuously designed to permit the United States to conclude agreements with Central American countries granting special status to the American government—as already existed in the Canal Zone and Guantánamo (New York Times, 1928a).

When the Colombian delegation, headed by Enrique Olaya Herrera, protested against the amendment submitted by Henry Fletcher, it received assurances that the United States had no intention of discriminating against Scadta's operations in the

Caribbean. Nevertheless, the American delegation was not prepared to include in the convention aircraft used for state functions, such as air mail service; this stipulation meant the exclusion of Scadta from the protection of the convention. Some months later, Francis White described the American objectives at the Havana Conference to the newly appointed Secretary of State, Henry Stimson. White's memorandum indicates the meaningless nature of the assurances given to the Colombians in 1928. Von Bauer, he informed Stimson, had continually urged the Colombian delegates to oppose the American position on commerical aviation. "It was necessary," White observed (in a memorandum to Stimson of April 25, 1929), "to speak very plainly to the Colombian delegates and tell them that unless those provisions [in the convention unfavorable to U.S. interests in Panama] were eliminated the United States would sign the Convention with reservation."

Under this pressure, Olaya was able to achieve no more than a slight rephrasing of the Fletcher amendment, which became Article XXX in the final document. The clauses which delineated the basis of the Colombian-American compromise did not weaken the effectiveness of the convention from the American perspective.

> These regulations shall in no case prevent the establishment and operation of practicable inter-American aerial lines and terminals. These regulations shall guarantee equality of treatment of the aircraft of each and every one of the countracting states and shall be subject to the same conditions as are set forth in Article 5 of this Convention with respect to prohibited areas within the territory of a particular state. (Foreign Relations, 1928a: 593; New York Times, 1928b, 1928c; Sixth International Conference of American States, 1928; Delegates of the United States of America, 1928: esp. 33-35).

There was small justification for *El Tiempo's* interpretation of the events at Havana as a partial victory for Colombian aviation interests (El Tiempo, 1928a, 1928b, 1928c). A more accurate indication of the future trend of interamerican aviation was Charles Lindbergh's very timely flight to Havana during the conference and to Cartagena and Bogotá on January 27; in both countries, he received a hero's welcome (Pan American Union, 1928: 333-350).

The State Department, interpreting the compliance of Latin American delegations as an indication of support, viewed the Inter-American Conference as a success. In a memorandum circulated to all American missions in Latin America early in March, Francis White (in a memorandum of March 2, 1928, to Dana G. Munro) outlined the basis for the department's enthusiasm:

> It showed the inherent strength of our position when ably and candidly presented by such an able and inspiring personality as Mr. [Charles Evans] Hughes. It showed no real united animosity against us, a comprehension of our difficulties in the Caribbean and a realization of our non-aggressive, non-imperialistic purposes. It also showed the number of friends we can count upon in Latin America.
>
> Except on the question of aviation, which they were ably coached by the German and Austrian crowd who run aviation in Colombia, the Colombians came to battle for us and even in the matter of aviation they finally agreed upon the wording of the convention that would suit us.

Following the Havana Conference, the United States intensified its efforts to extend air service into Latin America. In July 1928, Postmaster General Harry S. New announced that the government had granted an air mail contract, under the provisions of the Foreign Air Mail Act of March 2, to Pan American Airways from Key West to the Panama Canal. Even at this early juncture, it was evident that the route to Panama was only one stage in an expansion which officials hoped would soon extend down both coasts of South America (New York Times, 1928d, 1928e). Following the stabilization of the Panama situation, Scadta assumed an increasingly important place in Pan American's future plans. With the aid of the U.S. government, Pan American had prevented Scadta from engaging in effective competition to the north; but in 1928 the company continued to dominate Colombian aviation and to hold the key to through routes to Ecuador, Peru, and Chile.

When Scadta sent representatives to Guayaquil and Quito in an attempt to obtain landing rights from the Ecuadorean government, the State Department moved quickly to prevent the Colombian company from blocking Pan American Airways. On June 15, the Secretary of State (Stimson, 1928) cabled the American delegation in Quito:

> A concession has just been granted by the Peruvian Government to American interests for the establishment of an air mail and passenger line in Peru and it is of the utmost importance that American interests should not be prevented from obtaining similar concessions in Ecuador, to connect the service in Peru with the United States.[7]

The Americans were particularly vulnerable to Scadta's competition in Ecuador early in 1928 because President Ayora resented the failure of the United States to recognize his regime following the *golpe de estado* of July 9, 1925. In July, the Ecuadorean government issued a contract to Scadta for coastal mail service from Buenaventura to Guayaquil. "It is known to the legation," the American minister in Quito, G. A. Bading, observed, "that the German minister here has been exceedingly active in advocating the Scadta Company contract." Significantly, on August 14, the United States granted de jure recognition to the Ayora government (DS 821.796 Sca 2/176, July 6, 1928; Foreign Relations, 1928b: 742).

Undeterred by American opposition, Scadta also continued to press for concessions throughout Central America. In Honduras, the representative of Pan American found that the press identified Pan American with the United Fruit Company, and he was consequently unable to obtain an air contract. Both Juan Trippe and the State Department blamed "German" aviation interests for agitating against the United States; when a similar problem arose in Cuba in July, 1928, Francis White (in a communique of July 12, 1928, to the counselor of the embassy in Havana) outlined the objectives of American policy:

> We are most anxious here to have American aviation as prominent as possible in the Caribbean region and for that reason this Department

> did everything possible to favor the bill that was enacted by Congress at its last session authorizing the Post Office Department to give subventions for the carrying of mails in the Caribbean region. The Pan American Airways is a hundred percent American owned and managed company (see also, Foreign Relations, 1928a: 786-788).

Simultaneous with its establishment of service to Guayaquil and its continued efforts in Central America, Scadta obtained permission from the Republic of Panama to establish a temporary base for its hydroplanes near Porto Bello (about twenty miles from the canal's Atlantic entrance) to conduct an aerial survey of the Colombian-Panamanian border for the Colombian government. The U.S. War Department immediately protested against the Panamanian action. "From every viewpoint," Dwight Davis wrote the Secretary of State on July 21, "the establishment of this base at Porto Bello is objectionable and should be prevented." The Department of War admitted the innocent nature of the Scadta survey, but recommended, first, that the American government offer to perform the service for Panama, and, second, that all airports in Panamanian territory be placed under joint United States-Panamanian control with no independent commercial bases.[8]

President Coolidge responded to the situation by issuing Executive Order 4971 in September 1928, conferring full powers on the Secretary of State to control foreign commercial airline operations to the Canal Zone. The following spring, the United States and Panama concluded an arrangement for the establishment of a Joint Aviation Board with complete control over the movement of aircraft and establishment of airfields in the Republic of Panama. The members of the Aviation Board were to be appointed by the President of Panama, three on the designation of the United States (DS 821.796/36; communique from J. D. Arosemena of April 22, 1929, to the American minister; Foreign Relations, 1929a: 728-729).

The American government was particularly concerned that Scadta would come under the control of Lufthansa and thus give the larger German company a foothold in the Caribbean. In September of 1928, the Vice President of Pan American, John Hambleton, informed Francis White that the company had the impression from recent discussions with Scadta that it had received capital support from Lufthansa. "The Company's policy has changed considerably," Hambleton (in a communique to White of September 12, 1928) noted, "and I feel they will attempt to expand as rapidly as possible throughout South America and that we can expect very little co-operation from them in the immediate future." Disturbed by the possibility of Scadta's expansion, White (see DS 821.796 Sca 2/204a, October 2, 1928) instructed the American chargé in Berlin, De Witt C. Poole, to observe the activities of the company's representatives and to assist Pan American officials in their efforts to purchase a controlling interest in the Colombian enterprise. Pan American's overtures remained unreciprocated for the moment, however, and the American government was obliged to implement a more direct policy.

On February 23, 1929, Secretary of State Kellogg and the Colombian minister in Washington, Enrique Olaya Herrera, signed an agreement providing for reciprocal landing privileges on the coasts of Colombia and the United States and the right to fly over Colombian territory, the United States, and the Canal Zone (Colombian Ministro de Relaciones Exteriores, 1929: 50-53). The Kellogg-Olaya agreement was evidence of the American determination to open the west coast of South America to Pan American service. The Post Office Department had called for bids on air mail service to Chile, and applicants were required to furnish evidence that they possessed the right to operate across intervening territory, a right which Scadta's monopoly and Colombia's insistence on air sovereignty had denied. To obtain the Chilean contract for Pan American, the State Department was willing to concede permission to Colombian planes to land in American territory; but, confident that they could now control aviation in the Caribbean, American officials considered the agreement with Colombia a minor sacrifice.[9] In fact, Francis White (in a communique of April 8,

1929 to Henry Stimson) argued that the Colombian-American exchange of notes had "regularized" the situation in the Isthmus. On March 2, little more than a week after the conclusion of the Kellogg-Olaya agreement, the Post Office Department granted the air mail contract for Panama-Chile service to Pan American-Grace Airways; but the highest bid had been placed by American International Airways of New York, which proceeded to file a protest against the decision. The Post Office Department argued that it had accepted the offer of the company best prepared to undertake the service, and American International had no operating lines in the area, simply the promise of financial backing and an operating contract with Scadta in the event it received the contract.

Although Pan American's contract was subsequently upheld, the delay in implementing the Chilean service enabled Scadta to expand its Ecuadorean line and to extend its service to the port of Paíta in Peru by June of 1929. Moreover, in token recognition of the Kellogg-Olaya agreement, Scadta sent a flight to the Canal Zone on March 27, thus culminating several years of fruitless petitioning for land rights in Panama. At the same time, von Bauer was thwarted in an attempt to obtain better subsidy arrangements with the Colombian government; he argued that such assistance would enable him to compete more effectively with Pan American (White memorandum of April 25, 1929 to the Secretary of State; New York Times, 1929b, 1929c; see von Bauer, 1929; DS 821.796 Sca 2/226 and 263).

The State Department was disturbed by Scadta's ability to strengthen its lines to Ecuador and Peru. Assistant Secretary Francis White (in a communique of July 6, 1929, to Stimson) observed to the Secretary of State on April 25: "If this German company gets into Peru it will then easily link up with the German companies already operating in Bolivia, and perhaps will be able to extend its services on to Buenos Aires and to Chile."

The resistance of Scadta and other non-American lines to Pan American expansion led the State Department to a redefinition of its policy toward U.S. airline companies operating in Latin

America. The department had consistently lent unofficial support to Pan American Airways, but with the encouragement of the Post Office Department it now debated the feasibility of granting diplomatic assistance to companies holding U.S. international air mail contracts; in Latin America, this would mean giving official sanction to the near-monopoly operations of Pan American and Pan American-Grace Airways. Assistant Secretary Francis White was particularly in favor of implementing the Post Office Department's request. He suggested that, for strategic reasons in the Caribbean, it was essential for U.S. mail to be on American carriers. He argued that because the French and German governments were active in Latin American aviation the United States needed to provide equal support to its own nationals. "If the United States," White suggested to the Secretary of State on July 6, 1929, "keeps hands off and lets American companies fight one another indiscriminately for concessions in Latin America, all Americans are apt to lose out." He conceded that the announcement of such a policy would invite criticism, but thought this was a light burden to carry in defense of American interests.

At White's suggestion, Stimson raised the issue at a Cabinet session on July 12, 1929. President Hoover was reluctant to support a policy which would encourage monopoly conditions but he approved the recommendation. The State Department promptly instructed heads of mission in Latin America to give full diplomatic support to Pan American Airways (Foreign Relations, 1929c: 542).

The loosening of Scadta's grip on domestic aviation in Colombia promised to be a more delicate operation than blocking the company's international expansion. In 1929, Juan Trippe developed a new line in Colombia to compete with Scadta; but the Sociedad Anónima Colombo-Americana de Aviación experienced little success, primarily because Pan American failed to take sufficient interest in local aviation developments. Although the American Legation in Bogotá gave enthusiastic support to the new enterprise in its efforts to obtain operating rights, Pan American officials appeared to consider the line more useful as a nuisance to von Bauer. When the Colombian government expressed the desire to develop air service between Bogotá and Buenaventura the local representative of Pan American, H. Case Wilcox, received no encouragement from the head office to place a bid. While Pan American procrastinated, Scadta obtained the contract and began survey flights over the route (see DS 821.746/41, DS 821.796 Sca 2/275, July 18, 1929).

American interests in Colombia, moreover, were not unanimously opposed to Scadta's operations. J. C. Luitweiler of Baker, Kellogg, and Company, president of the recently organized North and South American Corporation of New Jersey, objected to the decision of the American government to render diplomatic protection to Pan American; he pointed out to Caffery that the Colombian subsidiary of Baker, Kellogg, the Compañía Colombiana de Inversiones, did not consider Scadta a threat to American interests and intended to provide the company with much-needed capital support.[10]

The State Department was, of course, opposed to injecting new financial blood into the Colombian company. Francis White (in a communique of October 26, 1929, to the American minister in Bogota) suggested to Caffery that, in light of the deterioration of Scadta's operating equipment, the closing off of American sources of capital would make the company more inclined to submit to financial control.

> If he [von Bauer] can now get funds from the United States . . . he will . . . be again in a good strategic position to cause American companies a good deal of difficulty. I am, therefore, not in favour of giving him American capital to do so. If he will sell out to an American company . . . a big thorn will be removed in the development of our air lines to South America.

Significantly, the poor state of Scadta's equipment in 1929 casts considerable doubt on the State Department's earlier contention that Lufthansa was financing the Colombian company.

Well aware of Scadta's financial difficulties, Trippe attempted to force a "showdown" with von Bauer. Several times the latter had tested Pan American's willingness to purchase the Colombian line, but on each occasion he had halted short of a definite commitment. Late in November 1929, Pan American sent a representative to Bogotá with instructions either to purchase Scadta directly or obtain an air mail contract for the Pan American subsidiary from the Colombian government (a White communique of November 14, 1929, to Caffrey). The American initiative led to an operating agreement between the two companies, but once again the elusive von Bauer retained his control over Scadta.

The Early 1930s

In their international rivalry, Pan American and Scadta concluded an agreement in October 1929 coordinating their air mail routes on the west coast of South America. Under the provisions of the agreement, Pan American transferred to Scadta all mail destined for Colombia at Buenaventura, and Scadta transferred to Pan American-Grace Airways mail destined for Peru. In effect, this agreement ended their rivalry over the Peruvian service in a manner favorable to the American company and was an indication of the progress American representatives had made in guiding President Leguía away from an anti-American course. Trippe considered the October agreement, supplemented by cooperation at Colón and Barranquilla early in 1930, as "one of the first steps toward a settlement of the international rivalry for supremacy in South American air transportation" (Foreign Relations, 1929d; New York Times, 1930b).

It was not until 1931 that the protracted negotiations between Scadta and Pan American resulted in the financial takeover of the Colombian company. Scadta's need for capital and its inability to compete with Pan American outside Colombia, where it had enjoyed a monopoly on air mail transport, facilitated the transfer of 84 percent of the stock to the American company. The acquisition of Scadta was given little publicity at the time; the absence of publicity, plus the fact that there was no immediate management change, meant that even some Colombian officials were unaware of the American takeover. Nevertheless, the few Colombian newspapers which took note of the negotiations between the companies responsed favorably (e.g., Mundo al Dia, 1931; DS 810.79611 Pan American Airways 1000 and 1001).

The State Department was particularly gratified by the results of Pan American's sustained effort to purchase Scadta and recognized the value of not effecting a management reorganization of the company at that time; it anticipated, however, that within a few years Scadta would be entirely Americanized. It was the failure to implement Americanization of personnel which led to difficulties immediately prior to the outbreak of war in Europe. In the interval, Pan American and the State Department were content to allow Scadta to continue to function under its air mail contracts with the Colombian government, particularly in view of the fact that in February of 1931 the government placed civil aviation under the control of a Civil Aviation Section in the Ministry of Industries. The government's action combined with expressions of good faith from Scadta management satisfied the State Department that a minimum of supervision from the parent company was adequate for the moment (see DS 821.796 Sca 2/316, March 19, 1931; DS 821.796 Sca 2/314, February 9, 1931; DS 821-796 Sca 2/321; Diario Oficial, n.d.: 818; Colombian ministerio de Relaciones Exteriores, 1932: 75; DS 821.796 Sca 2/314; January 31, 1931). Certainly the American government no longer viewed Scadta's operations as a threat; early in June, the Post Office Department, with Pan American's encouragement, signed an air mail contract with Scadta for U.S. mail service from Barranquilla to Bogotá.

That Pan American had little intention of working through Scadta in Colombia became apparent when, after concluding the financial arrangement with Scadta, it established another subsidiary, the Urabá, Medellín, and Central Airways, Inc. (UMCA). Pan American provided the technical personnel, and its representative in Colombia, Allan Winslow, was given the presidency of the new company. On July 9, 1932, UMCA inaugurated Colombian air mail service between Colón and Medellín (Winslow memorandum of May 27, 1932 to the Secretary of State; Young communique of September 11, 1931 to White; White communique of June 3, 1932 to Young).

The conflict which erupted in September of that year between Colombia and Peru over control of Leticia, the Colombian port on the Amazon, added a new dimension to the aviation rivalry in Colombia. When fighting broke out in Leticia, the Colombian government found itself entirely dependent on Scadta planes and personnel. The government placed Scadta under the jurisdiction of the Ministry of War; but, determined to maintain the company's commercial service, it was compelled to look abroad for new aircraft. American, British, and German interests took advantage of Colombia's need to expand her own commerce.

Initially it appeared that Scadta's predominance in Colombian aviation would work to the disadvantage of American manufacturers. Scadta's manager, Hermann Kuehl, became government adviser on military aviation, but in spite of the charges that he was partial to German interests, by the end of 1932 the government had purchased 48 planes in the United States and only 9 in Germany. During 1933, however, there were indications that the government would distribute its contracts more liberally in Europe. The American planes had not performed well in contrast with either Scadta's older German models or the British planes used by the Peruvians. Moreover, the appointment as Minister of War of Alfonso Araujo, and of Herbert Boy, a distinguished Scadta pilot, as inspector-in-chief of the ministry's air branch, placed two talented individuals in a position where they could influence the government's contracts. Boy immediately obtained President Olaya's permission for a purchasing trip to Europe in late 1933 (F.O. A/8758/1658/11, December 13, 1932; F.O. 371,A/395/395/11, December 18, 1933).[12]

In Boy's absence from Bogotá, American interests returned to the offensive. American manufacturers had long been attracted by the potential of Latin America as a market for aviation equipment and viewed the hostilities between Colombia and Peru as an opportunity to establish contacts.[13] The Curtiss Aeroplane and Motor Co., Inc., now dispatched to Bogotá one of its vice presidents and a recently retired U.S. Navy Commander, James P. Strong, to strengthen the American position.

While still with the Navy Department in 1932, Strong had worked closely with the Colombian Consul General in New York to facilitate armament purchases for the Colombian government and to prepare a Colombian defense plan. Following his retirement from the Navy, Strong became a valuable asset to private industry anxious to increase sales in Latin America. In late 1933, he obtained a position in the Colombian Ministry of War as assessor for aircraft purchases and shortly impressed on Olaya the advantages of placing aircraft orders in the United States. Largely as a result of Strong's influence, in March 1934, President Olaya cabled Boy in London informing him that in order to maintain unity of type and prompt delivery his government had decided to cancel European orders.[14]

Strong's fortunes shortly met with a sharp reversal, however. His unpopularity with the American legation and his aggressiveness in obtaining contracts for American companies alienated his Colombian associates, and the Colombian government dismissed him. "It's the old story," the British minister (F.O. 371, A/5828/395/11, June 18, 1934) commented;

> The United States does not send first-class men to these countries. The inferior men they send gather that business has to be got by graft, but they do not realize that graft or no graft, they must deliver the goods. Strong placed orders for aircraft right and left in the States, incompetently, unscrupulously. Now these orders are being cancelled as fast as possible.

The Strong incident did little to effect a marked shift of the Colombian government away from American aviation interests.

Under the subsequent liberal administration of Alfonso López, Scadta once again found itself the target of criticism. In June 1935, a serious accident involving a Scadta and a Saco (Servicio Aéreo Colombiano) plane at the Medellín airport claimed the lives of some sixteen people, among whom were Ernesto Samper Mendoza, a noted Colombian aviator from a prominent Medellín family, and Carlos Gardel, the popular Argentine singer. Public reaction to the crash was hostile to Scadta, in spite of the uncertain cause of the mishap; when Scadta officials, in an effort to correct the distorted press accounts, issued a public statement prior to the government investigation, they received immediate criticism from President López.

The Late 1930s

In the aftermath of this friction between the company and the government, there was some speculation that López intended to nationalize civil aviation. For the moment, he took no action. What the incident revealed, however, was that the personal popularity of some of the Scadta officials, particularly Herbert Boy, was not sufficient to erase the public identification of Scadta as a foreign enterprise. It is in this light that one should view the indignation that arose in the Colombian press several years later when it was revealed that the State Department was using Pan American's financial control of Scadta to "de-Germanize" the latter's operations (compare El Diario Nacional, 1935; El Espectador, 1935a, 1935b, 1935c, 1935d, 1935e, 1935f, 1935g, 1935h, 1935i, 1935j; Colombia Nacionalista, 1935a, 1935b, 1935c, 1935d, 1935e; see also DS 821.7965/2, June 26, 1935; DS 821.796 Sca 2/383, March 21, 1936).

By 1938, the State Department was convinced that greater supervision of Scadta's activities was essential to American security. Pan American's financial control now served as a convenient diplomatic weapon, and the conclusion of agreements in 1938 with the liberal government of Eduardo Santos providing for U.S. naval and aviation missions further strengthened the American position (Bushnell, 1967: 9-11; El Tiempo, 1938; U.S. Military Mission, 1939). When Trippe informed the State Department that von Bauer was under pressure from Berlin to regain the stock held by Pan American, the department urged Trippe to assume more positive direction of Scadta's operations (DS 810.79611 Pan American Airways/1622, April 26, 1938; Josephson, n.d.: 157-158; Boy, 1963: 239-242). The Colombian press reacted defensively to the news that the American government was opposed to the continuation of Scadta in its present form. *El Tiempo* commented on February 24, 1939:

> Although at first glance it might appear otherwise, we need attach little importance to the sensational cablegram in which the United Press informs us of the uneasiness in military and industrial circles in the United States about the preponderance of Italo-German aviation in South America, and especially Scadta in Colombia.
>
> Colombians know very well what Scadta is . . . the major contributions which it has given us on all occasions, in time of peace and war; and how it is perfectly controlled by the national government. At a time when the United States had given no thought to developing air lines, Scadta established itself in Colombia and within a few years organized the best air transport in the world.
>
> Admittedly, there is a high percentage of German pilots. . . . But it is injudicious and somewhat absurd to believe that fifty commercial airplanes, controlled by the Colombian Government, can constitute a threat to the Panama Canal (see also DS 821.796 Sca 2/495, March 3, 1939; DS 821.796 Sca 2/408; March 9, 1939).

Although *El Tiempo's* editorial indicated that Colombians continued to maintain respect for Scadta, the American ambassador was confident that President Santos would assist the State Department in eliminating the company's German personnel. Santos was concerned only that the action not become a public issue. "President Santos," Braden commented, "does not want to be embarrassed by enquiry but only to be told a *fait accompli*" (DS 821.796 Avianca/20, December 31, 1939). In his message to Congress in July 1939, the Colombian

President referred briefly to the necessity of assuming greater national direction of the aviation industry and recommended the establishment of a national airline absorbing both Scadta and Saco (El Tiempo, 1939; DS 821.796/108, July 26, 1939).

Legislation passed late in the López administration provided the vehicle for the elimination of Scadta. Law 89 of 1938 required 51 percent Colombian ownership, either private or government, of aviation companies operating in Colombia. It was a potential instrument of economic nationalism and had been designed as such by the López government; but under his successor it functioned as a two-edged weapon, serving as the basis for the establishment of Avianca (Aerovías Nacionales de Colombia) and allowing the Colombian government to comply with the State Department's request that Scadta be eliminated in the interest of interamerican security (Leyes, 1938).[15]

To the State Department, the proposed creation of Avianca was a mixed blessing. Although the reorganization of Colombian aviation promised to remove Scadta from the field, it would also reduce Pan American influence; as a result, there would be no guarantee that the Colombian government would carry out the elimination of former Scadta officials and personnel in accordance with U.S. policy. Immediately prior to the final organizational meeting of Avianca, the State Department wired Braden that it opposed the creation of a Colombian company in which Pan American Airways did not possess ultimate control (Foreign Relations, 1940: 723-726). In the compromise solution devised during the spring of 1940, Pan American retained financial control; the Colombian government was given an option to purchase 40 percent of the stock; an additional 20 percent of the stock was reserved for Colombian nationals (Foreign Relations, 1940: 730-733; Bushnell, 1967: 23; El Tiempo, 1940).[16]

Before the creation of Avianca on June 8, 1940, Pan American and the American Embassy, with the cooperation of the Colombian government, had succeeded in eliminating the German directors of Scadta. On February 7, Hermann Kuehl resigned as general manager; on February 23, Albert Tietjan, one of the original founders of the company, who had been elected president a month earlier, resigned along with Herbert Boy, operations manager. On May 27, Braden, while on a two-month trip to the United States, surveyed the Colombian situation in a memorandum for Laurence Duggan, Chief of the Division of American Republics, and Herbert Feis, Adviser on International Economic Affairs:

> In addition to measures already taken, all of the German pilots and ground personnel in Scadta are to be replaced on June 15 by Americans or native-born Colombians. This substitution and other phases of the aviation situation are progressing sufficiently well to indicate that all danger to the Canal . . . will be eliminated in so far as Scadta is concerned within the near future (Foreign Relations, 1940: 729-730).

An analysis of Colombian-U.S. aviation relations demonstrates a continuity of the objectives of American policy in the decade preceding World War II. It indicates that both strategic and commercial factors were instrumental in shaping the response of the United States to potential rivals, such as Scadta in the Colombian instance. Both considerations were apparent in the State Department's refusal to grant Scadta landing rights in Panama in 1927; they were in evidence during the debate at the Havana Conference of American States in 1928, in the conclusion of the Kellogg-Olaya agreement in 1929, and the official support granted to Pan American Airways later in the same year. The Department of State, particularly in the Hoover-Stimson years, took every opportunity to obtain privileges it wanted to deny Scadta for Pan American in Central America, Ecuador, Peru, and Chile. In Colombia itself, the American legation lent considerable support to Pan American and its subsidiaries in obtaining operating rights, and it was instrumental in making possible the transfer of ownership of Scadta to the Pan American system in 1931.

Pan American Airways became, in fact, a convenient instrument of American imperialism in Latin America before and during World War II. Its financial control of lines such as Scadta enabled the State Department to strengthen American commercial and political control while at the same time reducing the ability of European interests to compete. The preoccupation of department officials with the presence of a potential strategic threat, in the form of German pilots employed by Scadta, is understandable; but the evidence suggests that Scadta officials and Colombian authorities were consistently prepared to cooperate with the United States, making unnecessary the rather ruthless dismissal of Scadta personnel, who had performed yeoman service in the establishment of effective aviation communications in the Americas and had been instrumental in providing Colombia with a means by which she could overcome her severe transportation obstacles. What, in fact, the story of interamerican aviation rivalry suggests is the narrow, sphere-of-influence orientation of U.S. Open Door policy in Latin America in the 1920s and 1930s.

NOTES

1. In 1928, European-controlled companies operated 8,520 miles of air routes in Latin America while the U.S. foreign air mail system extended 252 miles. In 1933, the figures were 9,924 and 13,745, respectively. (See DS 810.79611 Pan American Airways/1306. All future references to Department of State Papers, National Archives, are from Record Group 59.)

2. Scadta was formed in 1919 by a group of prominent German-Colombians in Barranquilla. For its early history, see Newton (1965), and Boy (1963), who was one of Scadta's leading pilots and operations manager when he resigned in 1940. Matthew Josephson (1944) outlines the development of Pan American's system.

3. See the memorandum from J. Butler Wright, Assistant Secretary of State, of December 6, 1926, DS 821796 Sca 2/106. It is interesting at this junction that the American minister in Bogatá, Samuel Piles, was impressed with the sincerity of Scadta's president (DS 821.796 Sca 2/106, April 23, 1927).

4. John Baxter, the editor of The Panama American, was responsible for much of the business agitation at that time (see his editorial of November 19, 1927; DS 821.796 Sca 2/134, November 19, 1927). At the invitation of Aeromarítima's manager, Bogota business interests met in the company's offices and subsequently cabled James H. Furay, a vice president of United Press, in the hope of obtaining American press support for the Colombian petition. Shortly thereafter, the Bogota Chamber of Commerce wrote to the Colombian Foreign Minister suggesting that the government adopt a positive position (see DS 821.796 Sca 2/131, November 23, 1927; El Tiempo, 1927a).

5. See DS 821.796 Sca 2/130, November 29, 1927; DS 821.796 Sca 2/135, November 30, 1927; DS 821.796 Sca 2/143, November 28, 1927. Scadta's manager, Hermann Kuehl, was unable to convince Piles that the company considered itself Colombian and that it had no intention to expand beyond Colon.

6. For White's defense of intervention, see New York Times (1930a). It is significant that when Franklin Roosevelt came to office, White was appointed minister to Czechoslavakia as part of the general good neighbor facelift given the department after 1933.

7. See DS 821.796 Sca 2/165, June 15, 1928. A copy of the Lima report on aviation rivalry was sent to the postmaster general, Pan American Airways, and the Department of War, Commerce, and Navy.

8. See DS 821.796 Sca 2/171, July 21, 1928; DS 821.796 Sca 2/178, August 7, 1928. The Department of the Navy shared the opposition to the Panamanian agreement with Scadta (see also DS 821.796 Sca 2/177, August 6, 1928).

9. See Foreign Relations, 1929b; New York Times, 1929a; the White Memorandum of April 25, 1929. Prior to conclusion of the agreement, the American minister in Bogota noted that Scadta had increased its advertising in the press and movie houses to ward off Pan American competition (see also DS 821.796 Sca 2/226, February 13, 1929).

10. See DS 821.796 Sca 2/285, September 12, 1929. Baker, Kellogg and Company had considerable financial interests in Colombia. It had floated loans totalling some $30,000,000 in Colombian government and banking securities between 1926 and 1928, and its subsidiary had interests in automobile marketing, a flour mill, bakery, chicken farm, brewery, and construction company (see also DS 821.796 Sca 2/290, September 25, 1929).

11. See DS 821.796 Sca 2/323 and 324.

12. The best general account of the dispute is Wood (1966: 169-255).

13. Leighton Rogers of the Department of Commerce commented to Francis White on September 28, 1927 that "the Department of Commerce feels that South America is our greatest field for the sale of aviation equipment."

14. See the Olaya Memorandum of the British legation in Bogota, January 7, 1935, F.O. 371, A/1072/1072/11. Olaya had expressed annoyance at the face that Scadta had charged excessively for equipment it had turned over to the government, and, late in 1933, the president questioned the American minister on the possibility of Pan American assuming management responsibilities more commensurate with its financial interest in Scadta. (See DS 821.796 Sca 2/345, June 2, 1933; DS 821.796 Sca 2/351, December 13, 1933; New York Times, 1934a, 1934b.)

15. See Leyes, 1938. Scadta officials had not been averse to Law 89 since they believed that national control promised to operate in their favor against both Pan American and German influence. In March 1939, von Bauer assured the American ambassador that as an Austrian his political views were not the same as those held by the Germans and that he would dismiss the few Nazi sympathizers in Scadta's employ. Von Bauer himself had just received Colombian citizenship (see DS 821.796 Sca 2/408, March 9, 1939).

16. See DS 821.796 Avianca /4.

REFERENCES

BOY, H. (1963) Una Historia con Alas. Bogotá.

BURDEN, W. A. (1943) The Struggle for Airways in Latin America. New York.

BUSHNELL, D. (1967) Eduardo Santos and the Good Neighbor. Gainsville: Univ. of Florida Press.

Colombian Ministro de Relaciones Exteriores (1932) Memoria: 75.

--- (1929) Memoria: 50-53.

Colombia Nacionalista (1935a) March 2.

--- (1935b) June 27.

--- (1935c) June 28.

--- (1935d) June 29.

--- (1935e) June 30.

CONN, S. and B. FAIRCHILD (1960) The United States Army in World War II: The Western Hemisphere. Volume 1. Washington, D.C.

El Debate (1927) November 23.

Delegates of the United States of America (1928) Report to the Sixth International Conference of American States. Washington, D.C.

Diario del Comercio (1927) November 23 (Cartagena).

El Diario Nacional (1935) June 25.

--- (1927) "In defense of Colombian aviation." November 23.

Diario Oficial (n.d.) 21,793.

El Espectador (1935a) June 20.

--- (1935b) June 24.

--- (1935c) June 26.

--- (1935d) June 28.

--- (1935e) June 29.

--- (1935f) June 30.

--- (1935g) July 1.

--- (1935h) July 2.

--- (1935i) July 3.

Foreign Relations (1940) Volume 5: 723-733.

--- (1929a) Volume 3: 728-729.

--- (1929b) Volume 2: 879-880.

--- (1929c) Volume 1: 542.

--- (1929d) Volume 1: 601.

--- (1928a) Volume 1: 534-585.

--- (1928b) Volume 2: 742.

Informe del Ministro de Relaciones Exteriores (1928): 199-205.

JOSEPHSON, M. (1944) Empire of the Air: Juan Trippe and the Struggle for World Airways. New York.

McCANN, F. D. (1968) "Aviation diplomacy: the United States and Brazil, 1939-1941." Inter-American Economic Affairs 21 (Spring): 35-50.

Mundo al Día (1931) April 27.

New York Times (1930a) May 18, part 2: 6.

--- (1930b) March 3, part 10: 4.

--- (1929a) February 24, part 14: 3.

--- (1929b) March 28, part 30: 1.

--- (1929c) April 18, part 2: 5.

--- (1928a) January 25, part 3: 1.

--- (1928b) January 27, part 4: 5.

--- (1928c) February 8, part 4: 3.

--- (1928d) July 11, part 12: 1.

--- (1928e) July 12, part 5: 3.

NEWTON, W. P. (1965) "International aviation rivalry in Latin America, 1919-1927." J. of Interamerican Studies 7 (July): 345-356.

Pan American Union (1928) Bulletin 62 (April): 333-350.

——— (1927) Bulletin 61 (August): 751-758.

El Porvenir (1927) November 29 (Cartegena).

Sixth International Conference of American States (1928) Final Act, Motions, Agreements, Resolutions, and Conventions. Havana.

El Tiempo (1939) July 21.

——— (1938) November 27.

——— (1928a) February 10.

——— (1928b) February 1.

——— (1928c) February 14.

——— (1927a) November 28.

——— (1927b) November 23.

U.S. Military Mission (1939) Agreement between the United States of America and Colombia. Washington, D.C.: Executive Agreement Series.

VON BAUER, P. (1929) Letter to El Porvenir (Barranquilla) June 27.

WOOD, B. (1966) The United States and Latin American Wars, 1932-1942. New York: Columbia Univ. Press.

ROLAND H. EBEL
Department of Political Science
Newcomb College
Tulane University
New Orleans, Louisiana

GOVERNING THE CITY-STATE
Notes on the Politics of the Small Latin American Countries

One of the fundamental difficulties in the study of Latin American politics by North American scholars has been the attempt to apply the political experience of the United States (and, to a lesser extent, that of the developed countries of Europe and Asia) to that region. In attempting to interpret Latin America's political patterns and understand her political difficulties, emphasis has been placed historically on such visible features as the instability of national governments, the lack of adequate party systems, the dysfunctional role of the military, inadequate constitutions, hierarchic social structures and a variety of deficiencies in the region's political culture. In proceeding along these lines, analysts have been working from the implicit, although I believe unconscious, assumption that the Latin American nation-state constitutes a large, geographically dispersed polity. Until recently there has been very little effort to even study the political processes of the Latin American city, much less attempt to understand national politics in light of the region's peculiar urban culture.

The purpose of this paper is, hopefully, to stimulate a reexamination of Latin American politics by postulating that in many of these countries what we traditionally call "national" politics is really "city" politics, and that the nation-state, in a number of cases, can be more accurately conceived of as a city-state. It is further postulated that many of the particular political patterns of the region can be more adequately understood in this light.

In what sense can the nations of Latin America be considered city-states? In the first place the majority of these nations are small. As Table 1 reveals, the average size (34,834 sq. mi.) of half the Latin American states–Uruguay, Nicaragua, Guatemala,

TABLE 1

THE DIMENSIONS OF THE LATIN AMERICAN CITY STATE

Ranking by Size	*Square Miles*	*Comparable U.S. States*	*Square Miles*	*Rank*
Group I				
1. Brazil	3,285,170			
2. Argentina	1,078,266			
3. Mexico	760,373			
Group II				
4. Peru	513,000	Alaska	586,400	1
5. Colombia	429,828			
6. Bolivia	412,777			
7. Venezuela	352,143			
8. Chile	286,396	Texas	267,339	2
Group III				
9. Paraguay	150,518	Montana	147,138	4
10. Ecuador	115,000			
Group IV				
11. Uruguay	72,172	N. Dakota	70,665	17
12. Nicaragua	57,143			
13. Guatemala	45,452	Pennsylvania	45,333	33
14. Honduras	45,000			
15. Cuba	42,857			
16. Panama	28,575	Maine	33,215	39
Group V				
17. Costa Rica	19,238			
18. Dominican Republic	19,129			
19. Haiti	10,714			
20. El Salvador	8,060	Massachusetts	8,265	45

SOURCE: *Hammond Contemporary World Atlas* (Garden City, N.Y.: Doubleday, 1969).

TABLE 2
THE PRIMATE CITY IN LATIN AMERICA

	Population of Largest Metropolitan Area as % of Nation (1961-1964)	*All Urban Regions as % of Nation (1965)*	*Ratio of All Urban Regions to Largest Metropolitan Area*
Group I			
Brazil	20.9 (est.)	49.3	2½–1
Argentina	44.5	74.1	1½–1
Mexico	14.4	54.7	4 –1
Group II			
Peru	17.3	46.6	2½–1
Colombia	14.7	53.1	3½–1
Bolivia	33.2	35.0	1 –1
Venezuela	23.4	67.4	3 –1
Chile	32.9	68.7	2 –1
Group III			
Paraguay	16.8	35.6	2 –1
Ecuador	11.0	38.2	3½–1
Group IV			
Uruguay	46.5	72.5	1½–1
Nicaragua	17.3	41.7	2½–1
Guatemala	13.4	34.3	2½–1
Honduras	7.7	23.2	3 –1
Cuba	28.0	–	––
Panama	25.4	40.9	1½–1
Group V			
Costa Rica	36.4	34.8	1 –1
Dominican Republic	15.3	33.3	2 –1
Haiti	6.3	15.9	2½–1
El Salvador	10.2	39.3	4 –1

SOURCE: Irving Louis Horowitz, "Electoral Politics, Urbanization, and Social Development," in Horowitz et al., *Latin American Radicalism* (New York: Vintage Books, 1969), Table I.

Honduras, Cuba, Panama, Costa Rica, the Dominican Republic, Haiti, and El Salvador—approximates the size of the state of Maine. Second, although countries like Argentina, Brazil, Bolivia, and Chile are considerably larger, they are, nevertheless, dominated by a single city (see Table 2). In fact, the only countries that exhibit the twin characteristics of reasonably large size and a dispersed urban population (countries with a ratio of urban population to metropolitan population of over 3 to 1) are Mexico, Colombia, and Venezuela, with Ecuador conforming marginally to these criteria. Even though the small, less-economically-developed countries are more rural, their primate cities represent from 10 to 45 percent of the population. Only Haiti and Honduras deviate from this pattern. Even the latter country, however, does have a fairly high level of urbanization (23.2 percent); it is just not concentrated in a single primate city.

What follows, then, is a series of propositions about the patterns of politics in what I have called the Latin American city-state. The analysis is focused upon the ten smallest Latin American countries (groups IV and V) concentrated for the most part within Central America and the Caribbean, although a number of these generalizations can be applied to the larger ones, either because they are not that large or because they contain a densely populated primate city.

The Power Structure of the Latin American City-State

The first proposition to be put forward is that, other things being equal, the size of a country will have a direct bearing upon the kind of power structure that will develop there. To be more specific, the smaller the country, the more concentrated its power structure is likely to be.[1] Let us analyze this proposition first from an economic point of view. The Latin American city-states are small economies with extremely restricted internal markets. This fact places severe limitations on the number of economic enterprises of any size that can successfully compete within the national economy. Thus, although the traditional economic structure may be composed of a great many petty entrepreneurs and suppliers, industrial development tends very quickly to concentrate economic power in the hands of the one or two enterprises within a given field which, because of their relative efficiency, can survive in a limited market. This, in turn, gives these companies considerable control over the country's natural resources and its human resources and skills as well. Thus, the small country with limited resources and a restricted market is tailor-made for the "fourteen family" syndrome. The emergence of *catorces grandes*—investor families who, because of their economic resources, superior skills, and links with the international business community, achieve a position of economic dominance—is a natural socioeconomic phenomenon in countries where resources and population size severely limit the remunerative application of capital and technology.

In addition to producing a concentration of power, the small economy tends to reinforce the historic Hispanic-American "corporative" pattern of socioeconomic organization. During the colonial period, the major societal organizations—the church, the craft guilds, the haciendas, the universities, the Indian communities, and, to some extent, the municipalities—were quasi-corporate groups which exercised substantial control over the recruitment and decision-making processes within their respective domains (Beezley, 1969: 347; for an extended disucssion of the corporate structure of Latin America, see Newton, 1970). Furthermore, because of the geographic isolation within the Spanish colonial dominions, they were relatively free from outside pressure. Since independence, many of these same prerogatives have been granted other emerging groups, such as the military, the higher professions, the commercial agricultural producers, the universities, industrialists, and, to a limited extent, the trade unions (see Scott, 1967). Probably the most visible of Latin America's "corporate states" is Mexico, where the pattern of integrating the major interest groups into the labor, agrarian, and popular sectors of PRI or into the powerful chambers of commerce (CONCANACO) and industry (CONCAMIN) are well known. As Kalman Silvert states, for the Latin syndicalist (corporativist), the good society is one in which "mass man is tamed by being herded into institutional kennels, safely under the tutelage of the leader" (Macridis and Brown, 1968: 567). In such mini-states as Guatemala and El

Salvador, decisions affecting the financing, marketing, and pricing of the major segments of the export economy–i.e., coffee and cotton–are made by quasi-public interest groups substantially outside the direct influence of the nations' representative institutions. These corporate organizations, controlled by the economic elite and relatively immune from the influence of the society at large, take on an added significance in the light of their predominant position in the small-scale economies of their societies.

Because of the self-limiting character of the small economy, economic activity is likely to be concentrated in a single primate city. For one thing, except for the extractive industries, there is relatively little reason for light industry to be dispersed throughout the country. Transportation facilities, power, technological skills, and financial institutions are all likely to be located in the capital city. The urban center also constitutes the largest and most accessible market. Thus, unless the location of a particular resource exercises a compelling influence upon an industry to cause it to locate elsewhere, the national metropolis draws new business ventures like a magnet. Furthermore, the historic urban bias in the Latin American culture reinforces the attractions of the primate city for both the economic elite and the aspiring middle classes who view residence outside the capital city as a form of social demotion. Thus, for both economic and sociocultural reasons, urbanization tends to be centralized rather than dispersed.

A third and obvious point concerning the mini-economy requiring brief mention is that little economies tend to be weak economies. Those enterprises that are concerned with supplying primary products to the world market are acutely subject to its instability while manufacturing, almost always of the import substitution variety, is inherently inelastic and greatly affected by the decisions made in the industrial and financial capitals of the world. Thus, the entire socioeconomic structure of the urban-industrial sector of the society is extremely fragile and, particularly for the middle classes, shot through with a nagging sense of insecurity and, at times, helplessness–feelings that are only intensified by the sense of dependence produced by urban life generally.

The economic concentration that naturally develops in the Latin American mini-state—particularly during the early stages of economic development—inevitably translates into political power. To begin with, the emergence of nascent industry, be it light manufacturing or commercial agriculture, spawns a parallel tertiary sector composed of suppliers, service businesses, and technocrats largely dependent upon the capacity and good will of a few entrepreneurial families. This relative handful of powerful families and interests control the mobility of the aspiring middle sectors. University students, most of whom come from the middle and lower-middle classes, feel particularly the impact of this situation. A student's future career—whether it be in law, journalism, engineering, or banking—will be largely determined by the kinds of contacts he has linking him with members of powerful families or their organizations or whether or not he can break into a successful mutual support group or *panelinha* (for a discussion of panelinha, see Leeds, 1965). Furthermore, as the urban service and technocratic class expands, a public service sector composed of bureaucrats, school teachers, postmen, and utility and transport workers, most of whom are dependent upon government revenues for their livelihood, also develops. These groups are in a socially and economically insecure position. Withdrawal of support or sheer adversity on the part of one or two industries can paralyze the entire structure of public services. For example, a drop of two or three cents in the price of coffee may mean that hundreds of Salvadoran government clerks, postmen, and school teachers will go without their salaries for weeks or even months at a time. On the other hand, these same groups are likely to be among the best-organized segments of the political infrastructure and constitute the only sources of countervailing power to the investor families and international businesses. Thus, a strike on the docks of Puerto Barrios not only poses a threat to Guatemala's cotton and coffee growers, but it also has major economic impact upon the middle sectors as well—a circumstance that more than once has undermined the stability of the incumbent government.

A second way in which economic concentration can be translated into political power has to do with intraelite relations. With major segments of the nation's economy in the hands of powerful families or interests, it is relatively easy for coalitions of economic elites to bring pressure to bear upon a recalcitrant company by threatening to withhold resources, credit, or contracts which only they control (see Bourricaud, 1966: 23-25). In addition, preferential political contacts with governmental licensing agencies are also used to freeze out competitors.

Third, the politician, whatever his ideological proclivities, will feel compelled to give at least minimal support to the economic powers that be. He knows that whatever business or professional aspirations he has require that he retain allies in a system of concentrated power and relatively few actors. Whether he has a law practice or a hardware store, he knows that his future and the security of his family depends upon his ability to do business with the "establishment." He also knows that his public career is ultimately dependent upon the stability and viability of the national economy. Recognition of these realities tends to set limits on the behavior of the politician. He knows that while he is "in" today, he will probably be "out" tomorrow and, thus, dependent upon others. Consequently, he is greatly motivated to take a live-and-let-live attitude toward the major economic, social, and political power groups, regardless of his rhetoric. The fact that the majority of these economic and political forces are concentrated in one—possibly two—urban centers only intensifies the pressures toward conformity.

The Politics of the Latin American City-State

A second proposition is that much of what in Latin America is considered to be national politics is, in reality, city politics.

Most of what goes on in Latin America goes on in the city. All of its universities, its publishing houses, libraries, and concert halls are there. Its newspapers, which subsequently radiate into the smaller cities and towns, are published there. Almost all of the schooling above the sixth grade available in the country must be obtained there. As a result, the cities of Latin America are like celestial bodies: they exert a profound gravitational pull upon the rest of the society.

This pattern is even more exaggerated in the area of politics and government. Most of the power and most of the services are to be found in the city—particularly the capital city. For one thing, political leadership in Latin America has historically been recruited from its urban, educated elite. Persons moving into the higher echelons of politics or government service will typically have either been born in a major city or have moved there by the time they reach the seventh grade. They will have completed a professional degree in the national university, will have established a business or a practice in the capital city and then will have begun to engage in political activity there. In many cases, a young professional is required to engage in multiple job-holding to adequately support himself and his activities. Such a person may well work in a government job from eight to twelve, practice law in the afternoon, teach in the university two nights per week, write articles for a national newspaper on the other evenings, and oversee on the weekends a small coffee finca which his family owns. All these activities, of course, put him into contact with other professionals, businessmen, and politicians, thereby enhancing his overall professional and political mobility. In this way, he gradually becomes a part of the political and professional elite centered in the national capital or other major city and, if he is lucky, will ascend within the sociopolitical pyramid, occupying increasingly higher positions in government, business, and politics.

It is from this political elite that most candidates for national and regional office are recruited. Rarely do the national legislators provide functional representation for the constituencies from which they are elected. Rather, they are sent by their parties to run in a given department or *municipio*. If, by chance, they live or own property in their constituency, chances are they were educated in the capital, practice law in the capital, and reside there most of the time. Legislators tend not to speak for their constituents, but rather for the party that nominated them. Thus, they are rarely concerned with local issues, but rather with ideological issues and the political rivalries that agitate the participatory segments of the national capital.

Administrative personnel and the services they control are also subject to the same influences. All of the nation's major ministries are centered in the capital city, and their personnel are recruited from its university-educated elite. Regional administrators also are either recruited from that elite or are selected from persons with higher education living in the regional urban centers. In any case, few of these administrators have had experience with the problems of the countryside—with the possible exception of commerical agriculture. A secondary political elite is comprised of interest group leaders. Again, because of the concentration of industry, commerce, and education in the principal cities, these leaders are overwhelmingly urban.

The factors described above have injected a particular quality into Latin American political life—namely, an overwhelmingly urban bias which manifests itself in a number of ways. First, there is a marked concern for the interests and problems of the city. Much of the social legislation, for example, applies primarily—if not exclusively—to urban populations. Most of the expenditures on local improvements are made in the capital city. Smaller communities are forced to come, hat in hand, to the national capital to acquire sufficient funds to make the most elementary repairs or improvements. Second, there is little radiation of governmental outputs to the rural areas. For example, ministries of agriculture typically have top-heavy staffs in the capital city, with only one or two technicians available for the inoculation of chickens or cattle in any given department or province.

Third, there develops in the capital city a political network composed of persons who move in and out of governmental and political positions and who are concerned primarily with the problems, gossip, and rivalries of the city. The national capital, in other words, *becomes a largely self-contained political system.* Although this system is periodically subjected to the intervention of rural voters, it tends to seal itself off again after elections.

Latin American cities are not only the centers of power and of governmental output, but also generate the dominant values of the society. Unlike the United States, Latin American folk heroes do not split rails or wear coonskin caps; nor have many of their political candidates claimed to have been born in log cabins—or have worked in filling stations, for that matter. (Rather, they write serious essays or attempt poetry.) Urbanity is the preferred life style of most Latin Americans.

More specifically, Latin America's urban-oriented culture has caused certain values to be particularly esteemed, and these are the values by which persons aspiring to leadership positions are judged. First is *hidalguia*—a striving after a genteel, aristocratic style of life. To wear fine clothes, be surrounded by books, and to have mundane tasks performed by others are the marks of gentility. Related to this is a tendency to downgrade manual labor as being worthy only of servants. Intellectual and artistic achievements are prized, particularly the ability to speak well, extemporaneously as well as formally. Upward mobility is a basic value. Mobility and personal achievement, however, have not always been directly associated with each other.

These values and life styles have had certain consequences for the attitudes of the elite. First, purposive economic and political activity tend to be downgraded. Style is more important than accomplishment, consumption more valued than investment. Furthermore, persons without style—that is, persons without *cultura,* or those who are forced to earn their living with the sweat of their brows—are viewed as inferior and less deserving of the outputs of the system. The genteel Latin American life style militates against the maintenance of the kind of instrumentally oriented bureaucratic or political organizations necessary to the task of development. Furthermore, it reduces interest in attempts to solve national problems which affect the workers, the peasants, or the unemployed.

These inherently urban values also impede the development of leadership outside the capital city. It is obvious that the bulk of Latin Americans do not possess the attributes the culture assigns to its political leaders. Furthermore, if one aspires to social mobility, he is less likely to cultivate the traits that would enable him to identify with the masses. As a consequnce, the tendency to limit national leadership to the urban elite and to focus attention on the demands and problems of the urban area is greatly reinforced.

In summary, we might conceptualize the sociopolitical structure of the Latin American city-state as a series of relatively isolated, backward communities linked through regional, urban subelites to a modernized, cosmopolitan urban core. *Resources flow from the periphery to the core for redistribution within it. Control flows outward from the core to the periphery.* The metropolitan elites are just that–*elites,* not an integrated oligarchy. Although situated at the apex of the social and political pyramid, they control varying resources and have different interests. Politics in the city-state is a struggle between elites for a particular allocation of goods and values. These elites tend to be organized corporatively. That is, the cotton growers, coffee planters, industrialists, the church, the military, and, to some extent, international business, seek to retain hegemony within their own domain and to ensure and control their "slice of the pie."

The Governance of the Latin American City-State

A third set of propositions has to do more directly with the patterns of governance within the city-state. One of the continuing enigmas encountered in the academic literature concerning Latin America is the confusion that exists concerning the precise nature of the region's decision-making structure. A fairly typical formulation has been to contend that Latin American governments are republican in form but autocratic in practice (for the classic statement, see Meecham, 1959; a more recent formulation has been advanced by Véliz, 1968). Advocates of this position point to such phenomena as strong executives, weak legislatures and courts, nonfunctioning federal systems, and the statist emphasis on government planning and the centralized control of everything from cotton subsidies to the price of movie tickets.

An alternative formulation that comes much closer to the truth would state that Latin American governments, while republican in form and autocratic in manifestation, are corporativist in actual operation. That is, the major decisions are made by the powerful corporate groups, sanctioned by the state and implemented by the executive. Representative institutions and other constitutional bodies such as courts[2] or municipalities are effectively bypassed. Hence, the paradox of the governmental process in Latin America: *decision-making power* is likely to be dispersed and decentralized while *administrative power* is highly centralized. Thus, while the *Presidente de la Republica* looks impressive, and from his office and those of his subordinates flow streams of *licencias, diligencias, permisos, avisos, prorogas,* and *tramites,* he is, in reality, something of a paper tiger. Much of the time he is performing a delicate balancing act in his attempt to coordinate the activities and harmonize the conflicting demands of such powerful interests as *algodoneros, bananeros, eclesiasticos, militares,* and *Norteamericanos.* In summary, the paradox of government in the Latin American city-state manifests itself in three ways: the overcentralization of administration, the decentralization of decision-making, and the circumvention of constitutional arrangements.

Administrative overcentralization. From the standpoint of its formal structure and the political theory underlying it, the

Spanish colonial empire was, as Richard Morse points out, a patrimonial state (see Hartz, 1964: 157-158). That is, the state is viewed as the ruler's private domain and is centrally administered as a part of his personal household or legacy. Patrimonial authority resists the development of autonomous centers of economic or political power, preferring simply to make temporary grants of such on a concessionary basis. However, over the course of the colonial period, two developments took place which modified the extreme centralism of the system. For one thing, a variety of channels of communication and access between the colonies and the crown emerged. Conflicting instructions were often submitted to regional and local officials through the viceregal, ecclesiastical, and financial bureaucracies (see Phelan, 1960-1961). Second, isolation and inefficient communications nurtured the development of the powerful local corporate groups noted earlier. As a result, the imperial political system was marked by a struggle between the formally centralized bureaucratic structures of the Spanish patrimonal state and the power residing in the hands of local administrators and the heads of the powerful corporate institutions and groups. "Obedezco, pero no cumplo"—"I obey, but do not execute"—became the governing formula under which administrators expressed their loyalty to the crown yet remained relatively free to achieve regional stability through a process of political bargaining. The formula also provided local officials with room to maneuver around what were often conflicting instructions. By the same token, however, because royal officials knew that the directives of their superiors could be selectively and arbitrarily enforced, particularly through a *visita* or a *residencia,* slavish compliance to administrative minutiae was often in their best interest. Thus, the Spanish colonial structure early manifested the paradoxical qualities that have colored Latin American government ever since—namely, the high degree of formal centralization, statism, and governmental interventionism, on the one hand, coupled with localism, lack of effective governmental penetration, and resistance to authority, on the other.

Although localism and decentralized decision-making were well advanced in the empire by the eighteenth century, these trends reached their culmination during the decades after independence, when only the regional caudillos had sufficient strength to temporarily integrate their societies by the substitution of naked power for the political legitimacy which had been lost through the severance of the ties with the crown (Beezley, 1969). Gradually, however, the economic concentration produced by modernization and development brought with it the conditions necessary for a recentralization of governmental administration.

To use Guatemala again as an example, this latter transformation took place in essentially three stages. First, the Liberal administrations of Justo Rufino Barrios (1873-1885) and his successors, in their desire to modernize the country by linking it to the world economy, not only began to integrate the country physically by building roads, railroads, and telegraph lines, but also through their land reform policies created a national elite who, although their resources were located in the countryside, were socially and culturally tied to the capital city. As communications improved and as the agrarian elite expanded into other industrial and commercial enterprises, what at an earlier data had been a rural and regional elite structure was transformed into an urban one (for a description of the development of the Guatemalan elite, see Adams, 1970: ch. 3).

The second stage resulted from the Revolution of 1944, which transferred a share of the power from the agrarian-based metropolitan elite to the urban middle classes and their allies, the working class. The demands of these groups converted the country from a laissez faire economy into a modified welfare state. This process saw the development of programs and agencies designed to service the two politically relevant segments of the society: the middle and lower-middle sectors whose economic and political demands had to be met, and the powerful economic groups whose well-being was essential to the viability of the nation. However, because both of these groups were urban, and because the countryside was relatively nonpoliticized, effective administration and the implementation of programs were largely limited to the metropolis.

The third stage in the development of administrative centralization flows from the second: the creation of a more ramified administrative apparatus headed by a chief executive who represents the dominant coalition of essentially urban forces. Whatever the potential electoral power of the countryside, the political organization of the Latin American city-state remains a creature of the capital city. As has already been pointed out, all of the political parties and other relevant political organizations are based there and almost all the candidates for public office—even congressional candidates representing rural districts—are city-based elites. The fact is, there exist neither the funds nor the skills among the campesinos to mount a campaign for independent candidates.

The recentralization of authority and its locus in the capital city has had at least three results. The first is that there are very few pressures on the national administration to act on behalf of the rural population, while the demands of the politicized urban dwellers are intense. And, given the relative smallness of the socioeconomic "pie" to begin with, the natural inclination of the government is to allocate its limited resources to meeting the needs of the more modernized, politicized urban population. Thus, the executive is strongly tempted to concentrate his efforts on the politically relevant population who live crowded together in one or two metropoli and who look with Hispanic single-mindedness to the state to meet the problems of its existence.

Second, not only does the government receive greater political pressure from the urbanized sectors of the population, their greater organization simplifies the task of administration. For example, it is much easier to implement a retirement program for organized postal workers than it is for tenant farmers. Thus, one of the central problems of the Latin American city-state is that it lacks both the political power base and the administrative capability to penetrate much beyond the confines of the city. This problem is exacerbated even further by the fact that the gravitational attraction of the capital city drains the local areas of much of their leadership talent. Local communities, because they lack a civic elite, find it difficult to solve community problems at the local level. Thus, the trend toward administrative centralization is further intensified. Occasionally, such secondary regional centers as Quezaltenango, Santa Ana, Cartago, or Leon may retain the remnants of their traditional civic elites, but increasingly these cities look to former residents living in the capital city to assist them in generating sufficient power and resources to attack local problems (see Shrawder, 1968: 38). In the newer developing cities, such as Escuintla and San Pedro Sula, local leadership is generally supplied by members of the national elite who have investments in the area.

Decentralization of decision-making. Overcentralization of administration cannot be fully understood without a comprehension of the decentralized character of political power and decision-making in the region. In Latin America's corporatively organized society, power tends to drain downward from the center into the hands of the major corporate groups—particularly those that have the capability of seriously affecting the functioning of the mini-economy. Corporative decision-making manifests itself in a number of ways: in government-negotiated quotas, prices, and subventions for agricultural products; in government-negotiated prices, exchange rates, duties, and tariffs for industrial goods; in government-negotiated wages for the workers; and, finally, in the licenses and charters under which the rights and obligations of officially recognized groups are specified or guaranteed. Each major group has its own specialized point of access to the decision-making process: a specific ministry, an autonomous institution, or a specialized court. In addition, it is not uncommon for important urban segments to have their own clubs, schools, banks, and housing projects.

Latin American corporativists proceed under the assumption that decisions affecting their sector should be made by them free of outside interference. Once the decision has been made, it is the government's responsibility to see that it is carried out.

Thus, the government has a twofold task: first, to shield the group from the claims of other groups by validating and legitimizing contracts negotiated between it and the corporate group; second, to extract sufficient resources from the society (such as money, credits, and labor) to implement the previously negotiated policy. *Corporativism, therefore, inevitibly leads to statism and centralized administration.*

To state that decision-making power tends to drain downward to the private sector is not to say that the government has no authority. However, much of its power is exercised through the process of creating or encouraging new corporate groups to counteract the power of others. In Guatemala, for example, a wheat growers' association *(Gremial de Trigueros)* was created by the Ydigoras administration to offset the power of the millers who had been given preferences by the administrations of Arevalo and Arbenz. The wheat growers were accorded a fixed price which the millers were required to pay until the national crop was exhausted. The motivation behind this was the potential political support of thousands of small wheat growers in the highlands (Adams, 1970: 342-343). It might be argued that the power to create groups such as this and provide them with competitive advantages means that power resides at the top. It is true that *legality* is largely a monopoly of the regime in power, provided it has the support of enough of the corporate groups—particularly the army. However, economic power lies predominantly in the hands of the producers, and this is of crucial importance in the delicate mini-economy so dependent upon the earnings of the export sector.

Circumvention of the constitution. The concentration of economic, social, and political power in relatively few hands, its organization in corporate form, and its location in a largely urban center help to explain the constitutionally deviant patterns of governance in the Latin American city-state. Latin America's formal constitutional system, patterned after North American and European models, is built around the principle of geographic representation. The actual system, however, provides primary access to the competitive elites which struggle with one another over the allocation of scarce resources. Each of these corporate groups seeks to maintain hegemony over the decision-making within their respective domains. This is done by making alliances and by threatening the employment of the political resources at their disposal–Charles Anderson's (1967: ch. 4) famous "power capabilities"–against the regime in power.

The democratic process is viewed as the method to select and legitimize the regime which will serve as the arbiter of group conflict and implementer of contracts arrived at. This involves a minimal sharing of power with other segments of the society–particularly the *campesinos*–through the electoral process. Democratically elected regimes are generally allowed to remain in power as long as the balance of forces is not too severely upset. When the balance is disturbed or when the government fails to keep the bargains ratified between the groups and itself, the rules of the political game permit the threatened groups to employ the resources at their disposal to restore an equilibrium. This usually involves an alliance with the military.

Corporativist decision-making is, by its very nature, *private decision-making.* This has at least two consequences. First, the groups involved seek to remove the major issues from the more open legislative forum. The major groups much prefer to negotiate with the relevant administrative agencies which are not only more sympathetic to their interests but also more susceptible to the pressures of the domains with which they work. Second, the preference for private decision-making reinforces the dominant position of the executive. The extensive use of executive decree power traditionally granted by Latin American constitutions means that corporate groups can most readily achieve their ends by keeping issues bottled up within the confines of the executive. Recourse to the legislature or to the press occurs only when constitutionally required or when the group feels that its interests cannot be achieved by limiting its activities to that one decision-making arena. Legislatures, thus, generally perform the latent function of providing access for groups outside the power structure.

Although corporativist decision-making enhances the executive branch at the expense of the legislative, the bureaucracy is relatively weak. For one thing, the corporate groups seek to "colonize" the administrative agencies with which they interact. The phenomenon of multiple job-holding by the technocratic middle class and the lack of a well-developed civil service tradition makes the bureaucracy vulnerable to this tactic. As a result, given the preponderant position of urban interests and urban values on the part of most bureaucrats, administrative agencies tend not to penetrate the rest of the society. Public administration tends to be weak and ineffective outside the capital city, except in areas where there are linkages with powerful rural corporate groups or political organizations.

The corporate organization of Latin American societies helps to explain the particular role of the military. The nature of the socioeconomic structure of these countries produces administrative centralization while, at the same time, often leaving the executive politically naked by not providing him with the support of well-developed autonomous national political and governmental institutions. As a result, the executive becomes dependent upon the military. Made up largely of middle- and upper-middle-class personnel with an urban orientation, under normal conditions the military allies itself with the urban sectors and directs its activities toward the control of the interior, the objective being to insulate the more modernized urban elites from the pressures of the countryside. However, at times the military is called upon to police the contract among the elites. Thus, the military often becomes a major aggregator of interests and, ultimately, the arbiter of the political struggle.

Conclusion

This paper has attempted to suggest some of the patterns of politics which flow from the particular kind of socioeconomic structure found in small Latin American countries with large primate cities; societies which for all intents and purposes can be considered city-states. The analysis does not purport to be a complete explanation. A number of these patterns are true of most of the Latin American nations regardless of size, a fact which must be attributed to the values and orientations of the region's political culture. What is posited, however, is that these general patterns are intensified and exacerbated in a city-state.

For a number of decades now, more of the research and writing (policy-making, too, for that matter) on Latin American politics have been carried on largely within the framework of a republican-pluralistic model. Deviations from the model were primarily viewed as aberrations rather than as patterns inherent in the socioeconomic and institutional structure of the societies themselves. Ultimately, what this essay suggests is that we employ alternative models against which to analyze Latin American political reality, namely, that of the corporate state and, for the smaller countries of the region, its variant, the Latin American city-state. It is not suggested here that we will find many examples of formally organized corporate states. However, we are likely to find a mix of republican and corporative institutions and practices which, when recognized and fully analyzed, will bring our understanding of Latin American decision-making a lot closer to reality.

NOTES

1. This is particularly true of countries undergoing the early stages of industrialization and development. Small industrialized countries such as Belgium and Switzerland are obvious exceptions.

2. With the exception of the specialized tribunals like labor courts which dispense justice to a particular segment of the society.

REFERENCES

ADAMS, R. N. (1970) Crucifixion by Power: Essays on Guatemalan Social Structure, 1944-1966. Austin: Univ. of Texas Press.

ANDERSON, C. (1967) Political and Economic Change in Latin America: The Governing of Restless Nations. Princeton, N.J.: D. Van Nostrand.

BEEZLEY, W. H. (1969) "Caudillismo: an interpretive note." J. of Inter-American Studies (July): 347-352.

BOURRICAUD, F. (1966) "Structure and function of the Peruvian oligarchy." Studies in Compartive International Development 2: 23-25.

HARTZ, L. (1964) "The heritage of Latin America," in The Founding of New Societies. New York: Harcourt, Brace & World.

LEEDS, A. (1965) "Brazilian careers and social structure: a case history and model," pp. 387-398 in D. B. Heath and R. N. Adams (eds.) Contemporary Cultures and Societies of Latin America. New York: Random House.

MACRIDIS, R. C. and B. E. BROWN (1968) Comparative Politics: Notes and Readings. Homewood, Ill.: Dorsey Press.

MEECHAM, J. L. (1959) "Latin American constitutions: nominal and real." J. of Politics 21 (May).

NEWTON, R. C. (1970) "On 'functional groups,' 'fragmentation,' and 'pluralism' in Spanish American political society." Hispanic Amer. Historical Rev. 1 (February): 1-29.

PHELAN, J. L. (1960-1961) "Authority and flexibility in the Spanish imperial bureaucracy." Administrative Sci. Q. 5 (June-March).

SCOTT, R. E. (1967) "Political elites and political modernization: the crisis of transition," in S. M. Lipset and A. Solari (eds.) Elites in Latin America. New York: Oxford Univ. Press.

SHRAWDER, C. (1968) "A decision-making study of Quezaltenango." M.A. thesis. Tulane University.

THOMAS V. GREER
Department of Business Administation
University of Maryland
College Park, Maryland

THE MERCANTILE POTPOURRI CALLED PANAMA

Panama is a land of trade. For four and a half centuries, it has been a funnel for exchange between Europe and the west coast of South America and between the Atlantic and the Pacific. This article examines the place of retail trade in the Panamanian economy, with an emphasis as much cultural and social as it is economic.

The First Census of Commerce

Panama's recent publication of its first census of commerce is a landmark in the evolution of economic information available on that nation. Despite some shortcomings in the census, it is a significant breakthrough. Required by a new 1960 law, the census was conducted in 1962 and used calendar 1961 as its reference year. A complete census was made of stores in which five or more persons were occupied. Only a stratified random sample totaling about 8.5 percent, however, was utilized on the smaller stores.

AUTHOR'S NOTE: The author gratefully acknowledges research grants from the Frost Foundation and the Louisiana State Foundation, which made possible a two-and-one-half-month residence in Panama.

The census told a story of a basic division between metropolitan and rural areas of the nation and of extremely small-scale retailing throughout.[1] The research showed that Panama Province, which includes Panama City and about 11,000 square kilometers of surrounding countryside, accounted for 62.9 percent of the retail sales in the nation in 1961. That province accounted for an even larger share, 76.6 percent, of the sales of stores having five or more persons occupied. Unfortunately the smallest unit in the geographical breakdown published was the province. Thus separate data on the principal urban area, Panama City, are not available. Panama City, however, has 73.4 percent of the population of Panama Province and probably transacts nearly 90 percent of the retail trade shown for that province and about 56 percent of the retail trade shown for the entire country.

The nation's 5,919 smaller retail establishments, constituting 92.7 percent of all stores, did only 45.7 percent of retail volume. The mean average sales volume per store was $20,644, while the corresponding figures for smaller (under five persons occupied) and larger stores were $10,267 and $141,267, respectively. Even the average for the larger stores was quite low and reflected the fact that retailing is still overwhelmingly a small family operation. Per capita annual retail sales ranged from $37.16 in Los Santos Province to $224.76 in Panama Province. The retail sales figures in the census do not include transactions in the public market places and thus understate the per capita in Panama Province by probably 9 or 10 percent and that of the rural areas by probably 40 to 45 percent. The fact remains, however, that most of the people of the interior, as the provinces away from the Canal Zone are called, are very poor and participate only to a limited degree in the money economy. Subsistence agriculture and barter are still common there.

The census revealed that only six stores in the nation had 50 or more persons occupied. The 17,013 persons occupied in retail stores included 9,008 paid employees (52.9%), 3,330 unpaid workers (19.6%), and 4,676 proprietors and active partners (27.5%). Thus the average store had only 1.4 paid workers. Paid male salespeople slightly outnumbered females. Individual proprietorships did only 58.2 percent of the sales volume, despite constituting 93.6 percent of the stores. The census also showed that only 25.5 percent of all stores had been operating longer than ten years, 24.5 percent for five to ten years, and 50.0 percent for under five years.

A large majority (76.5 percent) of the stores were engaged primarily in the foods and beverages category, while the second most numerous category–apparel, shoes, and textiles–included only 8.1 percent of the stores. Just 2.8 percent of the stores specialized in furniture, appliances, and other household articles. These three categories accounted for 45.8, 24.1, and 11.7 percent, respectively, of sales volume. One notes the small sales volume ($12,349) of the typical store selling foods and beverages. The census found 32 supermarkets, however, the mean average volume of which was $445,707.

The Rural Scene

Rural Panamanian towns are served by clusters of small shops around the ubiquitous tree-shaded plaza. In tiny villages, the stores are often at the edge of an elliptical village green and common pasture. In the Darien rain forest, the unitary riverine location predominates, but current extension of the Pan American highway into this region is a harbinger of change. Additional change is offered by the national government's program of constructing farmers' marketplaces in several small towns of the interior. Spartan but functional, these establishments emphasize sanitation and adequate physical facilities for wholesale and retail exchange. In Caribbean coastal areas, another form of rural interchange is the interaction of the Cuna Indians with townspeople. An isolated, gold-hoarding matrilineal society, their only regular contact with Panama's economic life is an occasional bartering or buying expedition from their islands to the small coastal towns.

Rural stores are poorly stocked and often on the verge of

financial disaster, but ability to establish the most modest store is a sign of great personal progress and much aspired to. Merchants have traditionally occupied a pivotal position as a link between the outside and the village worlds and still do so to a considerable extent. Trade and politics are very much interrelated. Merchants are often politicians, and politicians, merchants. Prices of food and medicines have legal ceilings but these are seldom observed. The political role of the merchant is intertwined with the enforcement and lack of enforcement of such price ceilings.

The author spent some time in one village which probably constitutes a good example of rural Panama.[2] San Felipe de Veraguas lies in the foothills of the Cordillera Central and boasts 800 residents close in and another 700 living within a densely populated belt about one mile wide around the village proper. Although the village is poor, no one is starving or going without shelter. The climate is hot and rainy most of the time, but temperate enough for a flourishing crop and cattle agricultural base which furnishes most of the jobs. Electricity is now available from 6 p.m. to 1 a.m.

San Felipe is a small-scale entrepôt. It serves the tiny villages higher up in the mountains from a network of rutted dirt roads passable in dry weather by jeep or landrover. In wet weather, airplanes are used by the most affluent and also to bring in the most basic goods from lowland points. When a plane visits one of the upper hill communities, it lands on the village green.

The dry-weather road from San Felipe to the provincial capital, Santiago, fifteen miles away and situated on the excellent Pan American highway, was recently paved, opening a new world for residents of San Felipe and the mountain people. Scheduled bus service has started, and trucking is becoming regularized. The two-hour trip in dry weather has yielded to a half-hour trip in any weather. The mountain communities are beginning to ask if the new paved road could not be extended to serve them better.

The village has a politically appointed mayor, Federico Tapias. A former worker in the Canal Zone, he returned to the area and invested $2,000 he won in the national lottery in a general store in the tiny hill village of San Benito, six miles away. Tapias spends Monday through Thursday in San Felipe on his official duties and the rest of the week minding his store in San Benito.

There are four general stores and two cantinas in San Felipe. All are run by locally born and reared people except Casa Ruíz, whose proprietor, Fernando Ruíz, was born some sixty miles away. He is still openly referred to by merchants and some townspeople as an outlander and, in terms of the operations of his store, a maverick.

One businessman, Ignacio Hernández, symbolizes in a myriad of ways the social, cultural, and economic structure which has characterized most of Latin America for several centuries. Moreover, his situation symbolizes much that is happening and much that is about to happen in Latin America. At age seventy, he is still a robust man. Not an artistocrat cultivating the title of "Don" or "Patrón," he is known simply as "Nacho" to everyone. He is a retailer, wholesaler, rancher, benefactor, and consummate politician.

Hernández claims that all his rather sizeable estate derived from the general store he operates just off the plaza. One of twelve children, he completed the sixth grade. Nacho's store is open from 7 a.m. to 7 p.m. seven days a week. He pays one of his two employees 19 cents an hour, although the legal minimum wage for this region of the country is 25 cents, and both work eleven hours a day seven days a week.

The sales area of the store is 18 by 35 feet and is topped with a vaulted roof from which hang rope, belts, harness, saddles, and kitchen utensils. Several glass cases hold good cloth and cosmetics. Groceries and other goods line the shelves. There are no display windows. Rolls of multicolored oilcloth lean into the street over saloon-type doors. A kerosene refrigerator holds soft drinks. Hernández also sells Shell gasoline and displays the familiar emblem on a pole outside. Behind the store but in the same building, the living quarters open into an enclosed patio. Here is located a small quesería, or place where Nacho makes by a very secret process the cheese he sells. Nacho says he cannot sell fresh meat, although one of his competitors sells it one-half day a week, but tinned sardines and tuna move well. He likes the higher markup on cloth and so does not push hard on selling canned items.

The store sells about $60,000 worth of merchandise a year, 60 percent of which is retail, the rest wholesale to smaller retailers in the mountain villages. For example, last year Nacho supplied Rodolfo Salazar in Santa Ynés with goods worth $3,489. Salazar paid his year's bill with coffee beans at harvest time. Bad debts average about 0.2 percent of sales. From 10 to 15 percent of retail sales each year are on credit, but the ratio is much higher for wholesale transactions. Nacho gets considerable amounts of merchandise from a brother who is a wholesaler in Panama City and the rest of his stock from other relatives and long-time friends.

"Donde Nacho" (literally "where Nacho") is the oldest establishment in the village. The other businessmen look to Nacho for guidance and endorsement. Occasional meetings are held by the four general store proprietors to decide on uniform prices. Legal maxima are not consistently observed. The government price inspector, Señora Luisa, is a reserved, shy woman who prefers not to rock the boat with questions.

Nacho Hernández is the political king of San Felipe. For almost 50 years he, his late father, one of his brothers, or his nephew has represented the district in the National Assembly. He holds political influence and loyalty through judicious utilization of credit, gifts, scholarships, employment on his extensive ranch, and economically useful advice. He believes he can be reelected easily if he chooses to run.

At long last, however, some people are beginning to question Nacho's informal rule over this little semi-feudal empire. Ruíz is restless about commercial practices as expressed in the traditional merchant alliances. A good many former customers now combine purchases with an otherwise necessary trip into Santiago on the new road. Nacho's own children are not as supportive as he might wish. Undoubtedly his authority will slip more and more as economic dependence on his good will decreases. San Felipe, like many other rural Panamanian villages, has begun its transition from fiefdom to integral unit in the national economy.

The Urban Scene

The urban areas are Panama City, Colón, and David.[3] Panama City is dominant and is the mecca for social and economic aspirants. The ecology of this city is interesting in that the shape and pattern of land use have been heavily influenced by the coastline, protection against pirates and military forces, the rainfall patterns, and the Panama Canal Zone. The presence and configuration of the Zone have not allowed normal spatial development and have vastly complicated physical distribution.

The central business district of Panama City lies on a narrow, fortified peninsula and focuses on Avenida Central, an old street punctuated by four attractive plazas. Through the years, retailers have abandoned the two lower plazas as the central business district has been shifting north and east off the peninsula, and it appears that the continuation of Avenida Central, called Vía España, will ultimately take over. A secondary contender for development, however, is the highway to Colón. Both thoroughfares take a sharp curve to the east as they leave the central business district, a twist necessitated by the boundary line of the Canal Zone, imposing a shape like a bent funnel on the city. Several miles out, Vía España shopping centers of four to eight small stores have begun operations. Small local chains of grocery and drug stores have arisen, but the family-owned store predominates.

The most striking factor in the pattern of ownership in Panama is racial, ethnic, and national background. Ever since the Isthmus was discovered, it has been one of the world's busiest crossing points and a demographic conglomeration of persons on their way to seek their fortunes. Many stayed to engage in trade in Panama. Today one finds Panamanians of

Spanish descent, Indians, Negroes from the West Indies, mestizos, zambos (mixed Indian and Negro), mulattos, Chinese, Pakistanis, Hindus from India, Arabs, Lebanese, and many others carrying on retail trade. In fact, in the central business district of Panama City, retailers with Spanish names are definitely in the minority. Some of the newer retailers in this nation are termed arrivistas (recent arrivals), but interestingly enough this label is reserved for Europeans. About one-half of the food trade is in the hands of two such men, a Greek and a Spaniard, who became Panamanian citizens only in recent years. The Chinese are very important in food and hardware, while Jewish persons of Spanish, French, and Dutch descent dominate the apparel trade. Persons from India and Pakistan operate most of the gift shops catering to tourists and are important in the sale of fabrics. Several well-known American mercantile names, such as Saks, Alden's, and Lerner's appear on stores but there is no connection with the U.S. firms.

Partly because of the apparently burgeoning population of non-Spanish persons and the sensitivity of blacks, all questions as to race have been dropped from all types of censuses in Panama. Businessmen and social scientists find this deletion regrettable, of course, but can expect this line of thought to affect census data of other countries in the future. Brazil has also taken this action.

On the narrow congested peninsula downtown lies the Mercado Grande, or central marketplace, for the metropolitan area.[4] As in all fast-growing, large Latin American cities, the relatively affluent are leaving the inner city for outlying areas. Increasingly, the central marketplace serves the poor and the lower-middle class. Yet the maids of the affluent still are often sent to shop the marketplace.

Unsanitary and woefully inadequate, the marketplace is still the principal food wholesaling center for the entire nation, as well as a large retail center. It is so important that the national government, rather than the municipal government, operates it, although the latter has asked for jurisdiction several times. The market buildings, constructed at the turn of the century, extend out over the Bay of Panama. Much of the waste from their operations is simply dropped, polluting the water below, an inconsistency for a city which generally scores higher than most other tropical cities on public health matters. The Agency for International Development rejected in 1967 a Panamanian application for funds to rebuild the market in the same location.

The Mercado Grande is a cornucopia of foods and a kaleidoscope of races. The two largest ethnic groups in the marketplace are third-generation Panamanian blacks, many of whom still speak the English of the British Caribbean islands, and Orientals. Analysis of local newspaper files of the past sixty years provides much evidence of a long-standing racial bias in Panamanian trade. This is by no means a thing of the past, for the government administrator of the central marketplace boasted to the author that he got rid of Oriental sellers at every opportunity. On another occasion a former member of the Panamanian Congress remarked to the author that "Every Chinese here is dishonest and wealthy."

Recent arrival of business people from Pakistan and India, some by way of Trinidad, is further complicating the mercantile situation. These traders are too large-scale to want stalls in the marketplace, but are causing unrest among owners of stores, including the numerous Orientals and Lebanese who are well established. A few of the Orientals, it should be noted, have no immigration papers and remain in the country only by allegedly bribing various government officials.

The American Presence

American private investment is accounted for principally by Singer and Sears, Roebuck and Company. Singer operates home appliance stores, two in Panama City, one in Colón, and four in the interior. Sears, the larger operation, has a downtown store and a suburban store in Panama City and one store in Colón. In the late 1950s the company operated a store in David, in extreme western Panama, for a brief time. The attempt was unsuccessful. Behind-the-scenes pressures were too much even for the North American giant. Sears' Central American headquarters is also in Panama City. Sears started in the 1930s with a catalog office in downtown Panama City and opened a retail store only in 1955. That store was closed in favor of a suburban location in 1959. However, the continued importance of the central business district caused Sears to open a store in 1965 on Avenida Central in the heart of downtown. Another attempt in David is planned "eventually," although a wealthy retailing family in that city is an active obstacle.

The citizenship aspect of Sears' image is very good for several reasons. Not only has the company assisted in the development of Panamanian shirt and furniture manufacturing, but it does a significant share of its sales volume in Panamanian-made goods. The share reached 34.7 percent in 1966. More important perhaps is that no store personnel are American, although Panamanian law generously allows 25 percent of employees to be foreign. The four Americans working for the company in Panama are all in the Central American headquarters office. The well-known story of the protection of Sears property by Panamanian employees during the 1964 anti-American riots, often regarded as apocryphal, actually occurred.

Another institution in the American retailing presence is the Canal Zone stores, which have a current annual sales volume of about $28 million. A major source of American-Panamanian friction ever since the Canal was built, these stores offer the advantages of generally lower prices, higher quality, wider assortments, and a lower frequency of out-of-stock conditions. These stores maintain buying offices in New Orleans, Louisiana. They purchase very little from Panamanian or other Latin American suppliers.

Table 1 shows the net sales and net income of the stores by year for the period 1963 through 1970. If price inflation is considered, the growth in sales has been modest. In seven of those eight years, the stores operated at a net loss. In the late 1960s, substantial amounts were spent to modernize many of the retail facilities.

TABLE 1
RETAILING OPERATIONS, PANAMA CANAL COMPANY
1963-1970

Year	*Net Sales*	*Income (or loss)*
1970	$27,988,744	($1,279,009)
1969	27,836,102	(66,579)
1968	25,552,212	(241,347)
1967	23,768,771	(256,410)
1966	23,119,973	100,388
1965	22,932,537	(350,544)
1964	21,958,972	(192,843)
1963	20,201,784	(36,261)

SOURCE: *Annual Reports,* Panama Canal Company (Balboa: Panama Canal Co., various dates).

As a concession to Panama City retailers, the treaty revision of 1955 cancelled commissary privileges of Panamanians who did not live in the Zone. Panama City merchants, however, would like to see the commissaries closed, for this would bring them from 25 to 35 percent more volume, depending on the price levels they set.

Traditionally and today, much merchandise "walks" out of the Zone, as the Panamanians say. The contraband articles are chiefly food, tobacco products, and shoes and they are not hard to buy in Panama. Little of significance is done to stop the smuggling, and it is often alleged that the Panamanian police are active middlemen in this illicit commerce.

The proposed new treaty between Panama and the United States concerning the Canal would not remedy this problem. The treaty calls for leasing the Zone stores to private enterprise. At least this change would remove the U.S. government as a competitor of private Panamanian merchants. However, leasing to North American companies, a likely event, would still arouse great antagonism. Sears is quite interested in the lease if the treaty is adopted and believes it is the best-qualified organization to manage the stores. The labor unions of the Canal Zone are studying the possibility of turning the retail facilities into cooperatives.

Other Developments Affecting Retailing

Consumer cooperative stores have made little place for themselves in Panama, but the movement is far from moribund. Eighteen of the 25 stores of this type in the Republic are on the United Fruit Company plantations in western Panama and came into being when the company divested itself of retail operations. Three cooperative stores have developed in Panama City, one of them a general store at the edge of the city in a low-income area and unofficially sponsored by the Catholic Church. However, the Catholic Church in Panama continues to place more emphasis on other types of cooperatives, such as credit, than on retailing. One of the more provocative views expressed to the author by a priest doing social work with the poor was that the wealthy and powerful retailing and wholesaling interests would refrain from opposing cooperative stores in the years ahead in the hope that attention would be diverted from land reform. The reason for this prediction is that ownership in distribution and agriculture overlap to a considerable extent.

The issue of a new sea-level canal to replace or at least supplement the famous Panama Canal has caused great anxiety in that country among retailers, wholesalers, owners of office buildings, and other investors, especially in Panama City. Canal operations and related services are the largest single element in the national economy. Possible routes in Colombia, Nicaragua, and Mexico have been studied. They announced preference of the United States for a route in Panama very near the present waterway is, however, now reducing the apprehension.

Conclusion

In summary, it appears that the moving spirit behind present trends in Panamanian retailing is nationalism. This growing consciousness explains the incipient integration of the rural consumer into the larger economy, the racial and ethnic prejudices in urban retailing, and the antagonism toward foreign encroachments such as the former United Fruit Company stores and the Canal Zone commissaries. Panama could undoubtedly make faster strides by cooperating with, rather than thwarting, her gargantuan house guest in the Zone. However, the callous attitudes of most Zone residents and officials toward Panamanian feelings have done little to smooth the way for American investment. On the other hand, at least two American firms have gained success.

The diverse types engaged in Panamanian trade have infused values and practices stimulating to the development and modernization of trade. The polyglot community of Panamanian merchants has never found commerce dull, and the rudimentary information now available to them in the census will undoubtedly spark self-criticism and planning to further stimulate retailing development through their own resources.

NOTES

1. Census data are taken from, or in most instances calculated from the following: *Censos Nacionales de 1960 Panamá, Primer Censo Industrial, Comercial y de Servicios* (Panamá: Dirección de Estadística y Censo, n.d.); and *Censos Nacionales de 1960 Panamá, Directorio de Establecimientos–Comercio y Servicio* (Panama: Dirección de Estadística y Censo, n.d.).

2. The names of the village and individual villagers have been changed.

3. Helpful background on life styles, especially in urban areas, can be found in Biesanz and Biesanz (1955).

4. There are extremely few published studies on urban marketplaces in Latin America. A worthwhile behavioral study is Richard W. Patch, *La Parada, Lima's Market, American Universities Field Staff Reports Service, West Coast South America Series,* Vol. 14, No. 1, No. 2, and No. 3, 1967.

REFERENCES

BIESANZ, J. and M. BIESANZ (1955) The People of Panama. New York: Columbia Univ. Press.

PATCH, R. W. (1967) "La Parada, Lima's market." American Universities Field Staff Reports Service West Coast South America Series 14, 1, 2, 3.

"This is an intellectually stimulating book. Its systematic treatment of problems in international organization politics is refreshing. It is well written and clearly argued."

—Annals of the American Academy of Political and Social Science

THE MAJORITY OF ONE

Towards a Theory of Regional Compatibility

by MINERVA M. ETZIONI, *with a Preface by* RICHARD A. FALK

This book is a study of relations established over the last twenty years in the handling of political and security matters between a universal and a regional international organization——the United Nations and the Organization of American States. The unusual quality of this particular regional organization is expressed in the Latin American quotation that the OAS is governed by "the majority of one . . . the minority of twenty"—a reflection of the strength of United States influence.

"*The Majority of One* is an illuminating study in the use of regional institutions as a comtemporary vehicle of great-power diplomacy. The book reveals, in its analysis of principal incidents of peaceful settlement and enforcement, the extent to which American foreign-policy-makers have succeeded in using the OAS to legitimate more or less unilateral uses of force in the Western Hemisphere in such a fashion as to contradict UN purposes and to defeat the indended jurisdiction of the world organization." ——from the Preface by RICHARD A. FALK

Table of Contents

Preface by RICHARD A. FALK

I. Towards a New Theory of International Organization

II. Regional and Universal Forces at the Founding of the United Nations

III. The United Nations Charter: *Regional and Universal Clauses*

IV. The Cold War and the Rise of Incompatible Regionalism: *Tendencies After San Francisco*

V. Incompatibility in the Peaceful Settlement of Disputes at the Regional Level

VI. Incompatibility in the Adoption of Enforcement Action at the Regional Level

ISBN 0-8039-0042-2 **1969** **238 pages** **$7.50**

L.C. 78-84220 **Market: World**

SAGE PUBLICATIONS, INC.
275 S. Beverly Dr. / Beverly Hills, CA. 90212

SAGE PUBLICATIONS LTD
44 Hatton Garden, London E C 1

BOOKS RECEIVED

GENERAL AND REGIONAL LATIN AMERICA

Burns, E. Bradford, LATIN AMERICA: A CONCISE INTERPRETIVE HISTORY. Englewood Cliffs, New Jersey: Prentice-Hall, 1972. Preface, acknowledgements, statistical tables, glossary, guide to paperback literature in English, index, list of maps. xiv + 272 pp.

Cline, William R., POTENTIAL EFFECTS OF INCOME REDISTRIBUTION ON THE ECONOMIC GROWTH: LATIN AMERICAN CASE (Praeger Special Studies in International Economics and Development). New York: Praeger Publishers, 1972. Acknowledgments, tables, figures, abbreviations, appendix, bibliography. xvii + 242 pp. $12.50.

Delpar, Helen, ed., THE BORZOI READER IN LATIN AMERICAN HISTORY, Volume 2. New York: Alfred A. Knopf, 1972. Foreword, contents, bibliography, glossary. ix + 294 pp.

Dorn, Georgette M., compiler, LATIN AMERICA, SPAIN, AND PORTUGAL: AN ANNOTATED BIBLIOGRAPHY OF PAPERBACK BOOKS. Washington: Library of Congress, 1971. Introduction, subject, index. 180 pp. $.75.

Dorner, Peter, ed., LAND REFORM IN LATIN AMERICA: ISSUES AND CASES (Land Economics Monographs Number 3). Madison, Wisconsin: Land Economics, University of Wisconsin–Madison, 1971. Acknowledgements, foreword, introduction. xx + 276 pp. $3.95.

Dunn, John, MODERN REVOLUTIONS: AN INTRODUCTION TO THE ANALYSIS OF A POLITICAL PHENOMENON. Cambridge, England: Cambridge University Press, 1972. Preface, introduction, conclusion, bibliography, index. xiii + 346 pp. $14.50.

Fitzgibbon, Russell H., LATIN AMERICA–A PANORAMA OF CONTEMPORARY POLITICS. New York: Meredith Corporation, 1971. Preface, glossaries, bibliography, index. x + 546 pp.

Latin American Urban Policies and the Social Sciences

Edited by JOHN MILLER *and* RALPH A. GAKENHEIMER

Accelerated urbanization and rapid population growth have drawn particular attention to Latin American in recent years. Current statistics on the growth rate of the nations of South America indicate the highest continental growth rate in the world, and there is no evidence that it may decelerate significantly..

Editors Miller and Gakenheimer have addressed various policy issues related to urban development in Latin America at international, national, and local levels from the points of view of different social sciences. The problems and potentials generated by rapid urbanization and the use of the social sciences for understanding and guiding urbanization and the process of national growth are treated extensively.

This volume is based on the Jahuel, Chile, Conference sponsored by the Ford Foundation—at which eminent scholars from both North and South America met to discuss Latin American Urban Policies.

Table of Contents

I. The New Urban Era in Latin America: A Challenge—The Urban Phase: Raison d'étre for Policy, **John Miller**

II. Integrating Urban-Regional Policies Among Nations—The Rapprochement of Nations with Contiguous Regions, **John Miller** / Economic Integration and the Spatial Development of South America, **Paul Ove Pederson** and **Walter Stohr**

III. Urban Growth Policies for the Nation—Channeling National Urban Growth in Latin America, **John Miller** / The Role of Cities in National Development, **John Friedmann** / Planning, History, Politics: Reflections on John Friedmann's 'The Role of Cities in National Development,' **Richard M. Morse** / Rejoinder to Richard M. Morse, **John Friedmann**

IV. Political Development Vis-a-vis Urban Growth—The Distribution of Political and Governmental Power in the Context of Urbanization, **John Miller** / Urbanization Policy and Political Development in Latin America, **Robert T. Daland**

V. Metropolitan Policy for the Squatter Settlements—Three Proposals Regarding Accelerated Urbanization Problems in Metropolitan Areas: The Lima Case, **Carlos Delgado**

VI. A Future Role for the Social Sciences: Policy and Action—The Contribution of the Social Sciences to Urban Policy Formulation in Latin America, **John Miller**

Appendix: Jahuel Seminar Summary, **Kalman H. Silvert**

ISBN 0-8039-0056-2 **1971** **384 pages** **$12.50**
L.C. 70-103481 **Market: World**

SAGE PUBLICATIONS, INC.
275 S. Beverly Dr. / Beverly Hills, CA. 90212

SAGE PUBLICATIONS LTD
44 Hatton Garden, London E C 1

Goldhamer, Herbert, THE FOREIGN POWERS IN LATIN AMERICA. Princeton, New Jersey: Princeton University Press, 1972. Preface, tables, index. xiii + 321 pp. $10.00.

Harowitz, Michael M., ed., PEOPLES AND CULTURES OF THE CARIBBEAN. New York: The Natural History Press (division of Doubleday & Company), 1971. Introductory essay. xi + 606 pp. $4.50.

Hudgens Watson, Gayle, COLOMBIA, ECUADOR, AND VENEZUELA: AN ANNOTATED GUIDE TO REFERENCE MATERIALS IN THE HUMANITIES AND SOCIAL SCIENCES. Metuchen, New Jersey: The Scarecrow Press, 1971. Acknowledgments, introduction, evaluation, main entry index, bibliography. vii + 279 pp. $7.50.

Lambert, D. C. and Martin, J. M., L'AMERIQUE LATINE ECONOMIES ET SOCIETES (Series "Sciences Economiques et Gestion"). Paris: Librarie Armand Collin, 1971. Preface. 411 pp. 34,00 F.

Leonard, Irving A., ed., COLONIAL TRAVELERS IN LATIN AMERICA. New York: Alfred A. Knopf, 1972. Introduction, related reading, glossary. x + 235 pp.

Liss, Sheldon B. and Liss, Peggy K., eds., MAN, STATE AND SOCIETY IN LATIN AMERICAN HISTORY. New York: Praeger Publishers, 1972. Preface, introduction, epilogue, maps, glossary, paperback bibliography, index. xvi + 456 pp. $12.50.

McClelland, Donald H., THE CENTRAL AMERICAN COMMON MARKET: ECONOMIC POLICIES, ECONOMIC GROWTH, AND CHOICES FOR THE FUTURE (Praeger Special Studies in International Economics and Development). New York: Praeger Publishers, 1972. Preface, tables, charts, appendix. xiii + 243 pp. $15.00.

Morse, Richard M., ed., THE URBAN DEVELOPMENT OF LATIN AMERICA 1750-1920. Stanford: California: Center for Latin American Studies, Stanford University, 1971. Acknowledgements, maps. 129 pp. $1.00.

Odle, Maurice A., THE SIGNIFICANCE OF NON-BANK FINANCIAL INTERMEDIARIES IN THE CARIBBEAN. Jamaica: Institute of Social and Economic Research, 1972. Preface, index. xiv + 212 pp. $2.50 J.

Parry, J. H. and Sherlock, Phillip, A SHORT HISTORY OF THE WEST INDIES, (Third edition). New York: St. Martin's Press, 1971. Introduction, author's note, illustrations, suggestions for further reading, index. xiii + 337 pp. $5.95.

Ratliff, William E., ed., 1971 YEARBOOK ON LATIN AMERICAN COMMUNIST AFFAIRS. Stanford: California: Hoover Institution Press, Stanford University, 1971. Foreword, preface, note on abbreviations, introduction, chronology, bibliography, index, index to Marxist-Leninist periodicals. xii + 194 pp. $4.50.

Schmitt, Karl M., ed., THE ROMAN CATHOLIC CHURCH IN MODERN LATIN AMERICA. New York: Alfred A. Knopf, 1972. Preface, introduction, selected readings. x + 225 pp.

Sullivan, Edward D., ed., CHANGE OR REVOLUTION? New York: Institute of Life Insurance, 1971. Contributors, foreword, introduction. 121 pp. $1.00.

Thomas, Clive Y., THE STRUCTURE PERFORMANCE AND PROSPECTS OF CENTRAL BANKING IN THE CARIBBEAN. Jamaica: Institute of Social and Economic Research, 1972. Preface, tables, appendix, index. 77 pp. $2.00 J.

COUNTRIES OF LATIN AMERICA

Argentina

Kirkpatrick, Jean, LEADER AND VANGUARD IN MASS SOCIETY: A STUDY OF PERONIST ARGENTINA. Cambridge, Mass.: M.I.T. Press, 1971. Foreword, preface, epilogue, appendixes, index. xxii + 262 pp. $12.50.

Bolivia

Fifer, Valerie J., BOLIVIA: LAND, LOCATION, AND POLITICS SINCE 1825 (Cambridge Latin American Studies). Cambridge, England: Cambridge University Press, 1972. Maps, plates, acknowledgements, abbreviations, introduction, sources, index. xiii + 301 pp. $23.50.

Brazil

Rosenbaum, H. Jon and Tyler, William G., eds., CONTEMPORARY BRAZIL: ISSUES IN ECONOMIC AND POLITICAL DEVELOPMENT. New York: Praeger Publishers, 1972. Preface, tables, figures, about the editors and contributors. xviii + 438 pp. $20.00.

Caribbean Region

Brathwaite, Edward, THE DEVELOPMENT OF CREOLE SOCIETY IN JAMAICA, 1770-1820. New York: Oxford University Press, 1971. Maps, introduction, bibliography, index. xvi + 374 pp. $16.00.

Girvan, Norman, FOREIGN CAPITAL AND ECONOMIC UNDERDEVELOPMENT IN JAMAICA. Jamaica: Institute of Social and Economic Research, 1972. Tables, figures, preface, acknowledgments, explanations and terms, bibliography, statistical sources, index. xvii + 282 pp. $3.50 J.

Jefferson, Owen, THE POST-WAR ECONOMIC DEVELOPMENT OF JAMAICA. Jamaica: University of West Indies, 1972. Tables and maps, notes on currency units, preface, introduction, frontispiece (map), conclusion, select bibliography, index. xv + 302 pp. $3.50.

Moore, O. Ernest, HAITI: ITS STAGNANT SOCIETY AND SHACKLED ECONOMY. Jericho, New York: Exposition Press, 1972. Preface, notes. x + 281 pp. $8.00.

Munroe, Trevor, THE POLITICS OF CONSTITUTIONAL DECOLONIZATION: JAMAICA 1944-62. Jamaica: Institure of Social and Economic Research, 1972. Preface, abbreviations, tables, bibliography, index. xiv + 239 pp. $3.50 J.

Colombia

McGreevey, William Paul, AN ECONOMIC HISTORY OF COLOMBIA, 1845-1930. Cambridge, England: Cambridge University Press, 1971. Tables, figures, maps, acknowledgements, note on sources, list of works on Colombia cited, index. xiv + 330 pp. $10.95.

Mexico

Bakewell, P. J., SILVER MINING AND SOCIETY IN COLONIAL MEXICO, ZACATECAS, 1546-1700 (Cambridge Latin American Studies No. 15). Cambridge, England: Cambridge University Press, 1971. Tables, Illustrations, acknowledgements, abbreviations and conventions, graphs, plans, appendixes, glossary on primary sources, select bibliography, index. xiii + 294 pp. $13.50.

Hanna, Alfred Jackson and Hanna, Kathryn Abbey, NAPOLEON III AND MEXICO. Chapel Hill, N.C.: University of North Carolina Press, 1971. Acknowledgements, prologue, abbreviations, bibliography, index. xii + 350 pp. $11.25.

Rutheford, John, MEXICAN SOCIETY DURING THE REVOLUTION. Oxford, England: Oxford University Press, 1971. Preface, conclusion, bibliography, index. x + 347 pp. $13.00.

Taylor, William B., LANDLORD AND PEASANT IN COLONIAL OAXACA. Standord, California: Stanford University Press, 1972. Preface, introduction, conclusion, appendixes, notes, glossary, bibliography, index. x + 287 pp. $10.00.

Peru

Baines, John M., REVOLUTION IN PERU: MARIATEGUI AND THE MYTH. Alabama: The University of Alabama Press, 1972. Introduction by Juan Mejia Baca, preface, appendixes, notes, bibliography, index. x + 206 pp. $7.50.

Purser, W.F.C., METAL MINING IN PERU, PAST AND PRESENT. New York: Praeger Publishers, 1971. Preface, maps and tables, appendix, index, about the author. xi + 339 pp. $18.50.

INTER-AMERICAN RELATIONS

Atkins, G. Pope and Wilson, Larman C., THE UNITED STATES AND THE TRUJILLO REGIME. New Brunswick, New Jersey: Rutgers University Press, 1972. Preface, references, bibliography, index. viii + 245 pp. $10.00.

Lowenthal, Abraham F., THE DOMINICAN INTERVENTION. Cambridge, Mass.: Harvard University Press, 1972. Preface, introduction, appendixes, notes, bibliography, index. x + 246 pp. $10.95.

Smith, Robert Freeman, THE UNITED STATES AND REVOLUTIONARY NATIONALISM IN MEXICO, 1916-1932. Chicago: The University of Chicago Press, 1972. Preface, appendix, bibliography, index. xv + 288 pp. $12.00.

Wolpin, Miles D., CUBAN FOREIGN POLICY AND CHILEAN POLITICS. Mass.: D. C. Heath and Company, 1972. Tables, acknowledgements, appendixes, notes, bibliography, index, about the author. xv + 414 pp. $15.00.

MISCELLANEOUS

Andrews, Kenneth R., ed., THE LAST VOYAGE OF DRAKE AND HAWKINS. Cambridge, England: Cambridge University Press, 1972. Plates and maps, preface, notes on presentation, introduction, appendix, bibliography, index. xiv + 283 pp. $17.50.

Lavoie, Yolande, L'EMIGRATION DES CANADIENS AUX ETATS-UNIS AVANT 1930. Canada: Les Presses de L'Universite de Montreal, 1972. Introduction, bibliography, tables, graphs. 87 pp. $3.00.

Schwartz, Kessel, A NEW HISTORY OF SPANISH AMERICAN FICTION, Vol. I (From Colonial Times to the Mexican Revolution and Beyond). Coral Gables,

Peasants, Power, and Applied Social Change

Vicos as a Model

Edited by HENRY F. DOBYNS, Prescott College
PAUL L. DOUGHTY, Indiana University
HAROLD D. LASSWELL, Yale University

Analyzes one of the most exciting instances of planned social intervention in the history of modern social science—the fifteen years during which the Cornell Peru Project (under the leadership of the late Allan R. Holmberg) undertook to assist in the self-transformation of a group of peasants in the village of Vicos, from what was essentially a fifteenty-century condition of serfdom to a late-nineteenth-century stage of economic, political and social development. The theoretical framework of this report is based upon a value-institutional system developed in large measure by one of the volume's co-editors (Harold Lasswell) and lays heavy emphasis upon the power variable . . . which is seen as the key to obtaining positive change effects. The relevance of this study to contemporary trends in anthropology is also underscored.

Based on the March 1965 issue of the American Behavioral Scientist.

Table of Contents

Introduction—Henry F. Dobyns, Paul L. Doughty, Harold D. Lasswell
A Note to Anthropologists—Henry F. Dobyns and Paul L. Doughty
I. Experimental Intervention in the Field—**Allan R. Holmberg**
II. The Role of Power in Changing Values and Institutions—**Allan R. Holmberg**
III. The Interplay between Power and Wealth—**Mario C. Vazquez**
IV. Human Relations: Affection, Rectitude, and Respect—**Paul L. Doughty**
V. Well Being—**J. Oscar Alers**
VI. Enlightenment and Skill Foundations of Power—**Henry F. Dobyns**
VII. The Transferability of Vicos Strategy—**Harold D. Lasswell**
VIII. The Significance of Vicos for the Emerging Policy Sciences—**Harold D. Lasswell**
Appendix A: Vicos Area and Population Growth—**J. Oscar Alers**
Appendix B: Local and National Power Structure in Relation to Vicos—**Paul L. Doughty**
Select Bibliography of Cornell Peru Project Publications
General Bibliography / Index

ISBN 0-8039-0049-x **1971** **224 pages** **$10.00**
Market: World

SAGE PUBLICATIONS, INC.
275 S. Beverly Dr. / Beverly Hills, CA. 90212

SAGE PUBLICATIONS LTD
44 Hatton Garden, London E C 1

Florida: University of Miami Press, 1972. Preface, bibliography, index of authors, index of titles. xii + 436 pp.

Schwartz, Kessel, A NEW HISTORY OF SPANISH AMERICAN FICTION Vol. II (Social Concern, Universalism, and the New Novel). Coral Gables, Florida: University of Miami Press, 1972. Preface, bibliography, index of authors, index of titles. x + 445 pp.

Weber, Ralph E., ed., AS OTHERS SEE US: AMERICAN HISTORY IN THE FOREIGN PRESS. New York: Holt, Rinehart and Winston, 1972. Preface, introduction, index. xii + 361 pp.

White, John, REGIONAL DEVELOPMENT BANKS–THE ASIAN, AFRICAN AND INTER-AMERICAN DEVELOPMENT BANKS. New York: Praeger Publishers, 1972. Preface, introduction, tables. vii + 204 pp. $12.50.

Vol. 14 No. 4
November 1972

JOURNAL OF INTERAMERICAN STUDIES

and WORLD AFFAIRS

A Publication of the Center for Advanced International Studies.
The University of Miami

Journal of
INTERAMERICAN
STUDIES
and WORLD AFFAIRS

Vol. 14
No. 4
November
1972

CONTENTS

This issue devoted to:
MILITARY AND REFORM GOVERNMENTS IN LATIN AMERICA

The Armed Forces in Latin America: Potential for Changes in Political and Social Functions
MANFRED KOSSOK 375

Military Institutional Development and Sociopolitical Change: The Bolivian Case
CHARLES D. CORBETT 399

Peru Before and After the Coup of 1968
JAMES M. MALLOY 437

An Approach to the Study of the Latin American Military
THOMAS I. DICKSON, Jr. 455

U.S. Military Assistance to Latin America: An Assessment
JOHN M. BAINES 469

Review Essay

Culture and Colonialism in the West Indies
JAMES W. GREEN 489

Books Received 497

Beverly Hills *SAGE PUBLICATIONS* *London*

JOURNAL OF INTERAMERICAN STUDIES AND WORLD AFFAIRS is published four times annually–in February, May, August, and November.

Journal of INTERAMERICAN STUDIES *and* WORLD AFFAIRS

Published quarterly by SAGE PUBLICATIONS
Sara Miller McCune, *Publisher*
Constance U. Greaser, *Editorial Director–Journals*
Rhoda Blecker, *Production Editor*

POLICY: *The Journal of Interamerican Studies and World Affairs* reflects the interests of the scholarly community and interested public concerned with the social, economic, political, and cultural aspects of life in Latin America (including the Caribbean); particularly in those instances where the subject is of concern to more than one of the traditional disciplines. As these concerns change, so will the content of the journal. ¶ Articles which have special relevance for interrelationships between American nations and of those nations with the rest of the world will be given special consideration. An effort will be made to include occasional articles that state an unusual or even discordant position on a subject of broad interest to be supplemented by critical comments of authorities representing differing positions on the topic. The editors continue to welcome articles by scholars from all parts of the world.

MANUSCRIPTS: Manuscripts should be submitted in duplicate to: Editor, *Journal of Interamerican Studies and World Affairs,* Box 8134, University of Miami, Coral Gables, Florida 33124. ¶ Correspondence regarding book reviews should be sent directly to: Book Review Editor, *Journal of Interamerican Studies and World Affairs,* Box 8123, University of Miami, Coral Gables, Florida 33124.

Subscriptions: Regular institutional rate $15.00 per year. Professionals and teachers may deduct one-third from the regular institutional rate (one-year rate $10.00); full-time college and university students may subscribe at $8.00. Add $1.50 for subscriptions outside the U.S., Canada and Latin America. No student discounts outside the U.S., Canada and Latin America. Orders from U.K., Europe, the Middle East, and Africa may be placed at £7.00 annually (£4.70 to individuals), and should be sent to the London office (address below). Non-institutional orders **must** be paid by personal check.

Application to mail at second-class postage rates is pending at Beverly Hills, Calif.

Inquiries: Address all correspondence and permissions requests to SAGE PUBLICATIONS, INC., 275 South Beverly Drive, Beverly Hills, California 90212. Inquiries and subscriptions from U.K., Europe, the Middle East, and Africa should be sent to SAGE PUBLICATIONS LTD, St George's House, 44 Hatton Garden, London EC1N 8ER. Other orders should be sent to the Beverly Hills office. ¶ **Exclusive Advertising Representatives:** R. K. Armstrong & Associates, Inc., 11661 San Vicente Boulevard, Suite 210, Los Angeles, California 90049.

Back Issues: Single copies of issues are available at $5.00 each. Orders for 10 or more copies of a single issue for course adoption will be billed at $2.50 per copy. Sterling prices available upon request from the London office. Prior to Volume 10, back issues published are available through Swets & Zeitlinger N.V., Keizersgracht 471 and 487, Amsterdam, Holland. ¶ **Claims for undelivered copies** must be made no later than three months following month of publication. The publisher will supply missing copies when losses have been sustained in transit and where the reserve stock will permit. ¶ **Change of Address:** Six weeks' advance notice must be given when notifying of change of address. Please send old address label along with the new address to insure proper identification. Please specify name of journal.

MANFRED KOSSOK
Department of History
Karl Marx University–Leipzig
701 Leipzig
Petersteinweg 8

THE ARMED FORCES IN LATIN AMERICA

Potential for Changes in Political and Social Functions

At the beginning of this study of military dictatorship and the political role of the intellectuals in Latin America, Florestan Fernandes (1970: 1) makes the following statement: "The idea that Latin America is a region in which the coups d'état are a political routine has become a commonplace." Without doubt, such an opinion is justified and also explains—at least to a certain extent—the wealth of "routine" verdicts on the function of the military in Latin America. A contradiction, however, seems evident at this point: while the number of publications on the political and social position of the armed forces is rapidly increasing (McAlister, 1966; Rouquié, 1969), there is an evident lack of comprehensive analyses that go beyond detailed description, and which explain in a reliable and sound manner the phenomenon of the cyclically increasing militarization of politics. It cannot be overlooked that research on the role of the military in Latin America is in a really critical situation which calls for a reexamination of the facts according to new criteria. At the same time, this represents one of the starting points for the commitment on a greater scale of Marxist scholars (Klassen und Klassenkampf in den Entwicklungsländern, 1967-1969:

259-278). The outward indication of this critical situation is the fact that, as a consequence of developments since 1962, a series of "doctrines" which had been regarded as valid and indisputable have now been refuted or seriously questioned in fundamental points, among which the following are the most important:

(1) The hypothesis that militarism had been replaced by the progressive democratization of the armed forces, so popular after the 1955 collapse of the Perón dictatorship, was quickly followed by the overthrow of dictators in Colombia, Venezuela, Cuba, and the Dominican Republic and has been proven incorrect. Since 1962, a situation has existed which Lieuwen (1964) has aptly characterized as "neomilitarism."

(2) The attempts to group the countries of Latin America into categories, according to the degree of their susceptibility or nonsusceptibility to coups d'état (e.g., "countries in which the armed forces dominate politics," "countries in which the armed forces are nonpolitical," and so on), have also proven untenable. In the meantime, political practice–reflecting the situation of social conflict of the region in an impressive manner–has made it clear that, at a given moment, all Latin American countries are potentially confronted with the problem of the intervention by the armed forces.

(3) The efforts to establish a relation between the frequency and the character of the coups d'état and certain indicators (which were, moreover, schematically and statistically interpreted) such as per capita income or degree of literacy and so on, have proven just as unconvincing. On the contrary, the statistics show an extreme degree of spread which, when superficially considered for the period from 1930 to 1966, equates, for instance, Argentina with Paraguay and Brazil with Haiti (Lambert, 1964: 372-375).

(4) Also, the "wholesale" critique of militarism, by the liberal-positivist school of history and sociology, which views the politically committed armed forces as solely the defenders of the status quo, can no longer be maintained in its original undifferentiated form, in view of the revolutionary and reform-

ist tendencies which have appeared since 1962 in Venezuela, Guatemala, Ecuador, the Dominican Republic, Panama, and Peru.

(5) The view that a "depoliticization" of the armed forces must set in as an inevitable consequence of the establishment of the officer corps on a professional basis (growth of professionalism), and with the increasing technocratic penetration of the leading circles as a result of the (imported) scientific and technological revolution, the concrete facts indicate that the contrary is the case.

The Military and the State

The attempt to determine the tendencies in the change of the politicosocial function of the armed forces in Latin America (and not only in this region), in more detail assumes an analysis of the economic, social and politicoinstitutional structure, within which the armed forces operate as the specific and best-organized form of extra-economic violence. It is through the interrelations within this larger structure that the actions of the armed forces are determined to a decisive extent. "There is no autonomous military phenomenon which could be studied without regard to the other phenomenon [sic] of a given society." The thesis formulated by Hamon (1966: 385) in this connection of the "noninsularité de l'Armée" will find support from another point of view as well. For some years now, an intensive development of military sociology has become evident as regards Latin America, and this is gradually reducing the lead of the scholars working in the field of the political sciences. Due to the complicated problems which arise, the positive impulses which should follow from such an approach (i.e., that of the military sociology) often experience a negative turn, since the necessary relation with the dominating social reality is ignored or misinterpreted from a psychological point of view (Lombardi, 1966). From the complexity and multilevel nature of the relations, there results the necessity for cooperation between the most diverse fields of science, ranging from sociology, historiography, and economics to jurisprudence, political and military science, demography, and ethnography.

The history and present position of Latin America fully confirm the statement formulated by Marx in 1854 from the example of Spain: "Under revolutionary conditions—even more than in normal times—the destinies of the armies reflect the true nature of the civil government" (Marx and Engels, 1961: 449). The "hegemony crisis" discussed in detail by Nún (1969; 1967) and its military implications in Latin America have, since 1962, achieved dimensions and experienced forms of institutionalization which necessitate the formulation of a differentiated approach to the problem for further research and discussion. Of course, the thoughts outlined here do not claim to close the gaps in research—it is rather a matter of raising some questions which could help to clarify the largely common methodological and theoretical basic concern regarding the sociology and the writing of history in this field. From this viewpoint, it is the following groups of problems which merit attention:

The specific features of the socioeconomic and political development of Latin America: Within the circle of the developing countries, Latin America occupies a place which permits only a relative comparison with apparently analogous and parallel processes and experiences in Asia and Africa. In the preliminary work on his theory of imperialism, Lenin (1965: 746-747) stressed the "middle position" of Latin America and compared the status of these countries with the development of Eastern and Southeastern Europe before World War I. This methodological viewpoint is of major importance for a critique of the tendency to reduce the problems of Asia, Africa, and Latin America in an ahistorical manner to a common denominator (Kossok, 1968a). This applies, in particular, to the role of the military. The question of a possible "Latin Americanization" of certain countries or groups of countries in Africa and Asia (Klassen und Klassenkampf in den Entwicklungsländern, 1967-1969: 241), which became topical at the beginning of the sixties and is certainly justified, can only be answered by accepting a balanced examination of the possibilities and limitations of comparative analysis as a basic condition. It is precisely on this point that the sociologist needs to cooperate with the historian (Hamon, 1966: 385, 389).

The relationship of the military, society, and the state: Without doubt, it is here that the cardinal problem lies. In the first place, it is a question of identifying the sum of the factors of that structural and institutional instability which is typical of Latin America and which results in a quasi-permanent intervention of the armed forces (and not, as is often asserted, in regarding this as the cause or basic condition). Marx noted that the armies, in their politicoinstitutional function, can be both an instrument of revolutionary initiative and also a praetorial element. Thus, it always remains a question of investigating under which conditions one or the other of these two basic tendencies will predominate. For Latin America, the second tendency still continues to dominate the situation. This, in turn, leads to the question of the qualitatively new elements in the political attitude of the armed forces. Even a superficial historical and sociological comparison will show that the renewed militarization of politics since 1962—without completely excluding continuities—is not a mere return to or repetition of certain experiences of the 1930s and 1950s. With the change in the structure of the armed forces themselves, the importance of their position in the system of postwar politics and social relationships has visibly altered. To a much greater and more sensitive extent than other institutions, the armed forces have become the barometer of the generally acknowledged crisis situation. In their fashion, all the social forces are waging the "struggle for the army" in an intensive and deliberate manner (Lenin, 1966: 162).

Forms and specific features of rule by the military: The sum of the coups d'état and military regimes can no longer, even nominally, be restricted to the simple term "military dictatorships." The politicosocial attitude of the military, in a noteworthy analogy (even if this is certainly not absolute) with the strategic and tactical reorientation of the church, reveals tendencies toward an increasing differentiation which, it is true, does not yet outweigh the negative overall balance but is, nevertheless, important for an attempt to elaborate a prognosis of developments in Latin America. (It may be mentioned, in passing, that the comparative analysis of the developmental trends, which the army and the church have or do not have in common, still constitutes one of the most urgent research desiderata; Klassen und Klassenkampf in den Entwicklungsländern, 1967-1969: 268-270). As with every scientific prognosis of society (Hahn, 1970), in the case of the initial differentiation within the armed forces, the major difficulty is in drawing a clear distinction between trends which dominate for a certain time and lasting development based on underlying conditions. The often contradictory situation on the surface, in which secondary aspects obscure the long-term primary factors in a complicated and confusing manner, is one explanation for the rather unsatisfactory results to date of efforts to predict "the possible attitude of the military sector" (Arismendi, 1964: 1).

Common features of and differences between military and civil reformism: With the events in Peru since October 1968, the center of attention is again occupied by the question of the historical location and the prospects of development of a national reformist policy operated by progressive military forces. This phenomenon is not new for Latin America. A historical retrospective since World War I makes it clear that the climaxes of social and economic crisis-situations were always associated with the emergence of national revolutionary and national reformist movements in the armed forces. The chain of examples extends from Tenentismo in Brazil, the government of Franco in Paraguay, and the "military socialism" of Busch, Toro, and Villarroel in Bolivia to the beginnings of the government of Arévalo in Guatemala (Kossok, 1966: 160-161). For the present, the new aspects are indicated by the following questions: Can and will military reformism compensate for the failure of "civilian" reformism—i.e., of the bourgeois national reform parties of the type of APRA, MNR, or Acción Democrática? To what extent do the changed internal and external conditions offer the potential that national-reformist military regimes do not remain mere episodes, but establish themselves for a fairly long time and initiate genuine structural reforms of an anti-imperialist and anti-oligarchical character? In the analysis of these processes, which are extremely contradictory as a rule, exact definitions are required. New terms, attractive as they may be—such as "Revolución Militar" (Ceresole, 1969)—can scarcely give the necessary lead for reliable assessments.

Influence of the Military

A basic law can be formulated for the capability and radius of action of the armed forces in the developing countries: The relative independence and the capacity of the armed forces as a political factor increase, in proportion to the immaturity or instability of the class relations and of the general social situation—i.e., the dialectic of army and society cannot be schematically reduced to a unilateral, linear subordinate or causal relationship. The armed forces are neither indifferent to class (which certainly includes a commitment for different class-interests at different times), nor are they the mere sum of the social components of a particular society (Mirski, 1970: 140-143; 1969: 83).

For the comparison of the position of Asia and Africa with that of Latin America, an essential difference needs to be stressed: in the case of Latin America, the integration of the armed forces in the overall existing social system is considerably more advanced and intensive. This integration is the expression of the historical lead and of the historical maturity under the conditions of an emancipation completed as far back as the beginning of the nineteenth century—an emancipation which had the character of an incomplete and a posteriori deformed bourgeois revolution (Kossok, 1961). If one follows the interpretation of Nún (1969: 328), the final constituting of the armed forces of Latin America already comes within the phase of the "professional revolution"; since then, they have achieved a high degree of homogeneity in development, character, and function. For modern Latin America, the question of the "type" of army–i.e., the forms and processes of its emergence, is of subordinate importance in contrast to the position in Asia and Africa (Klassen und Klassenkampf in den Entwicklungsländern, 1967-1969: 261). (The problem of radical reconstitution as the consequence of revolutionary transformations–Mexico, Bolivia, Cuba–comes within a different framework.)

The principal feature of the "middle position" of Latin America is the general predominance of capitalism as the determining social formation, despite the existence of underdevelopment, deformation, and dependence. A fairly mature class structure (development and degree of organization of the working class, broad basis of the petit bourgeoisie and other intermediate strata, elements of a native system of monopoly capitalism, and the fairly unstable political position of the national bourgeoisie) corresponds to the historically advanced level of the productive forces (industrialization) and of the relations of the factors of production (rudimentary significance of precapitalist forms).

In conformity with the socioeconomic level of development achieved, it is no longer usual for the armed forces to be the exclusive instrument of force of the big landowners whose political hegemony has been cut down as a result of the accelerated defeudalization of the economy and society which has been carried out since World War I (Kossok, 1967). The staff officers of the armed forces reflect to a relatively exact degree the specific features of capitalist development in Latin America. As far as statistics are available, they show a preponderance of bourgeois and petit bourgeois elements in the officer corps (Imaz, 1964: 43; Nún, 1969: 336). In the interpretation of the consequences which result for the political position of the armed forces from the "bourgeois penetration," which, without doubt, represents a genuine, qualitative change in structure, the historian will perhaps be more cautious than the sociologist. From the historical viewpoint, it would seem that two observations have to be made:

(1) The social structure of an army and especially of its commanders is an essential factor, but more important is the decisive fact that, in the first place, "the character of the armed forces [is marked] by the social nature of the state and its policy" (Soviet Encyclopedia, 1963: 697); i.e., changes in the social structure of the army cancel out neither the class-character of the state nor the function of the armed forces which this prescribes. In the case of Latin America, a relatively synchronous development in the process of the evolutionary bourgeois penetration of state and army can be identified for the majority of countries. Here it should be stressed that this process was marked by the typical features of the "Prussian way": from the fusion of the big landowners and the bourgeoisie, there developed an economically and politically predominant oligarchy in which the essential features of a pure bourgeois class-rule are lacking.

(2) With different accents, but with the same direction of interpretation, Nún and Fernandes have attempted to establish a close connection between military interventionism and the constitution of the bourgeoisie as the ruling class. The basic idea of the middle-class military coup is expressed by Nún (1969: 359): "Interventionism . . . represents the middle class and serves to compensate for its inability to constitute itself as the ruling class." Thus, to take a concrete example, all the coups d'état in Argentina (with the exception of the overthrow of Yrigoyen in 1930) are explained by the commitment of the military "to the interests and values of the middle class." This thesis is weighty enough to justify comprehensive discussion—precisely in the form of a dialogue between historians and sociologists.

First, it is a question of the absolute negation of the liberal model, which places the military as a tool of the reactionary feudal-aristocrat. At the same time—and this also is certainly justified—the developmental model, which is valid for a series of Afro-Asian states, is rejected. In Latin America, for example, the army is the institution that, of necessity, compensated for the political weakness of a bourgeoisie unable to constitute itself as a class as such (Nún, 1969: 359). Beginning with Argentina since 1890, history contains a wealth of examples of the attempts of the petit bourgeois revolutionary opposition and also the bourgeois liberal opposition to assert their interests in alliance with the armed forces. A theoretical generalization and historical-political assessment of these tendencies should, however, be carried out on a more comprehensive and differentiated basis than has been attempted in the descriptions of Nún and Fernandes.

A major difficulty is the exact definition these authors provide for middle sector (or middle class) and bourgeoisie, which limits them in their relationship to oligarchy. The amorphous term middle class, in particular, scarcely permits an exact definition of social status. No less complicated is the fixing of the historical location of the bourgeoisie in the overall process of the social development of Latin America from the end of the nineteenth century to the present. Before a national bourgeoisie, as the potential instrument of an anti-imperialist and anti-oligarchical movement, could fully emancipate and consolidate itself as a class, the fusion with the big landowners began; the landowners themselves assuming capitalist functions (and not only in the agrarian sector). This specific feature in association with the more marked form of the basic antagonism between capital and labor (bourgeoisie versus the proletariat) explains why the progressive potentialities of the national bourgeoisie of Latin America have been less and more unstable than in the countries of Asia and Africa. For the assessment of the relationship of the army and bourgeoisie, the concrete historical situation and the character of the particular class-confrontation are of preeminent importance. The following courses of action emerge as relevant:

(a) Orientation toward intervention by the armed forces in view of the lack of an organized popular movement under the leadership of the bourgeoisie. (In its tendencies, this attitude was already evident in the "liberal caudillism" of the nineteenth century, which sought to defeat the dominance of the big landowners and the clergy with their own weapons, as it were.) Example: beginnings of radicalism in Argentina up to the accession of power by Yrigoyen in 1916.

(b) Alliance of the bourgeoisie with the armed forces in order to carry out preventive neutralization of an independent movement, which usually is already proletarian and which is no longer subject to the political hegemony of the bourgeoisie. Example: the change in the position of Acción Democrática in Venezuela in relation to the progressive military element in 1945.

(c) The appeal certain groups of the bourgeoisie made to the armed forces to assert, more effectively, the position of particular special interest groups within the ruling class. Example: the beginnings of the Perón dictatorship.

(d) Intervention of the armed forces as the instrument of power of the ruling class as a block–bourgeoisie and big landowners united–in order to maintain the status quo at a time when the crisis in the general structure of Latin American society was being radically sharpened. This was the objective of most of the coups d'état since 1962, which are also clearly marked by the trauma of the possible "Cubanization" of the subcontinent.

The sum total of this is that the bourgeois components of the coup d'état have a range of variation of which the complexity cannot be reduced only to the concept of the middle-class military coup. In passing, it may be mentioned that the attempt to formulate a theory of the coups d'état in Latin America should also take into account the differences in national and regional development which have evolved in the course of history and which are being accentuated at the present time.

Functions of the Military

The ability of the armed forces to take independent political action and the fact of their relative institutional independence reflect the degree of divergence between the supreme power and society. Marx (and Engels, 1960: 113-207) has described the partial alienation and the separation of the state and military power from the society in a detailed examination of the phenomenon of Bonapartism. In his publications on the political role of the army in Asia and Africa, Mirski (1969: 80-82) stresses the basic significance of the theses of Marx and Engels (1962: 405-465) on Bonapartism for understanding the special position of armed force in the developing countries. "This tendency [of the relative independence of the state military power] can occur in a transitional period in the development of the society or when there is a clash between two epochs when a relative equilibrium or weakness is evident in the principal classes" (Mirski, 1969: 80).

At the present time, two kinds of transitional periods are characteristic of all developing countries:

First, the majority of the Afro-Asian states are passing through an unstable socioeconomic and politicoinstitutional situation in which the choice of the development path to be taken has become the cardinal question for the successful defense and consolidation of the economic and social content of anti-colonial emancipation. This position favors the considerable technical, organizational, and politicoinstitutional lead of the armed forces and their marked preponderance in comparison with the civil organs of power of the state. Above all, the lack of a power equivalent in the form of parties and an effective parliamentary system places the armies in a situation which offers them the opportunity to become the active instrument and the mobilizing driving force of a new order instead of reflecting the power relations established with state and political independence as the sole objective. Contrary to many premature conclusions which have been drawn, there is still a need for detailed discussions of the question whether and under what concrete conditions the armies could become the vehicle of that energetic dictatorship through which Marx considered every genuine revolution had to pass. This opinion by Marx, however, carries a qualitatively completely different accent than the widely propagated thesis of the "developmental dictatorship" (Johnson, 1962), according to which the process of anti-colonial emancipation in Asia and Africa is being "militarized" as the result of an objective law, as it were.

Finally, the different function of the armed forces before and after the victory of the revolution is of significance (Markov, 1961: 21-22). Under certain conditions, an army can certainly initiate an anti-colonial revolution, direct it, and, for a certain time, determine its character. In the postemancipation period, however, the narrow basis of military rule is not sufficient for the consolidation of the sovereignty achieved which, in turn, can be the result only of a total revolutionization of the relations obtaining as starting conditions. Sooner or later, the dynamics of the internal and external power relations confront the armed forces with the necessity of making the decision to become an instrument of the revolutionary initiative on the side and under the hegemony of the popular forces or of changing over to a praetorial status, which more and more tends to be collated with the compromise character of the right wing of the national bourgeoisie. This is illustrated by the political situation in the Arab (Algeria, the UAR, Syria, Iraq, Sudan, and Libya) and Asian (Burma, Indonesia, and Pakistan) states and various sub-Saharan states. The transition between the two alternative directions is fluid and certainly reversible (Kossok, 1966: 137; Mährdel, 1967; Rathmann, 1968). Even armies with a mainly petit bourgeois and peasant staff nucleus do not necessarily have to opt for a "Jacobin" position. Since the petit bourgeoisie is "a transitional class in which the interests of two classes are blunted at the same time" (Marx and Engels, 1960: 144), it can become the carrier of completely divergent interests—and it is here again that the comparison with Latin America is justified.

Second, Latin America is in a far-reaching social and political structural crisis which has led to the development of a "general revolutionary situation" (Arismendi, 1964), although with marked regional differences. The degree of politicosocial polarization and the character of the objective and subjective conditions of the revolutionizing process (as demonstrated in practice by Cuba) make the expectation of links between the national democratic and the socialist revolutions closer for Latin America than for Asia and Africa. As a consequence of the manifest failure of civil palliatives, the armed forces are dominating the field of political action. Expressed as a formula, it can be said: In Africa and Asia, armed force mostly shows itself as prima ratio; but in Latin America, usually as ultima ratio, in order to master qualitatively incommensurable transitional or crisis situations. For the development since 1962, it is characteristic that the intervention of the armed forces certainly does not take place only at the climax of a crisis, but is carried out to an increasing degree as a preventive measure, so as to avoid such a situation as far as possible or to bring it under control in good time. Ideologically, this kind of action is reflected in the claim of maintaining or restoring the constitutional state of affairs. However, the concept of defense of the status quo should not be interpreted in too narrow or schematic a manner. Every attempt, on a long-term basis, to stabilize the existing socioeconomic conditions and power relations is bound to a minimum of reforms–both from the viewpoint of the ruling classes and from that of the U.S. Program of the Alliance for Progress (Kübler, 1967). Even conservative dictatorships are practicing a canalized "desarrollismo" in controlled proportions which, in turn, means that reformist tendencies, usually containing a nationalist element, in the political interventionism of the armed forces, are not per se a sign of progressive orientation. They can just as well be the expression of divergences within the ruling classes concerning the direction and methods of development. For certain sectors of the Latin American bourgeoisie, the armed forces are the determining guarantee for the institutional safeguarding of a reform policy (and, if necessary, for carrying it through in the face of the short-sighted intransigence of the rival groups in the ruling block). Fernandes (1970: 5,7) has aptly described this state of affairs, although with the unacceptable interpretation that it is a variation of the bourgeois revolution.

Military Intervention in Society

The interventionism of the armed forces in Latin America is expressed in a direct or an indirect form. Three main variations are characteristic:

(1) Open military dictatorship with complete or very far-reaching loss of power by the parliamentary and civil institutions.

(2) Military dictatorships, as a limited transitional solution, with the aim of removing or reorganizing civil governments which are incapable of handling a given situation.

(3) Indirect control for the implementation of the line desired in internal and foreign affairs (the role of the armed forces as a permanent pressure group). Particularly, in association with the second and third variations, the elements of a parallel system of military and civil power–i.e., a kind of dual rule has emerged in a series of countries–examples: Guatemala (Adams, 1968-1969),[1] the Dominican Republic, and Colombia.

An essential point which explains why there are often considerable difficulties in adequately defining the connection between military interventionism and certain class and group interests consists in the fact that "the army cannot be designated simply as the armed force, the instrument of power of the ruling class, for it is also part of the ruling class itself" (Klassen und Klassenkampf in den Entwicklungsländern, 1967-1969: 267). Consideration of only the political aspect (e.g., the role of high-ranking officers as leading politicians) would present too narrow a view of the problem, because the economic and social sides of the problem are equally important. The institutional weight of the armed forces results from the combination and fusion of their military, political, and economic potentials. In the most advanced countries (especially in Argentina and Brazil), the beginnings of a military-economic complex have emerged from the increasing links between the army and the economy. Both in Argentina and in Brazil, the army not only functions as an instrument, agent, or mere executive force, but also represents extensive interests of its own. The class-content of the armed forces certainly conforms to the dominant interests, but, at the same time, the army is an important element in the confrontations between the different groups within the ruling oligarchy. The role of the armed forces, as an economic power factor in Latin America (Kossok, 1968b), is the most important part of the equation explaining its relative independence in position and action. This is becoming increasingly true throughout Latin America and is not confined to the more developed countries.

Increasing attention is being given the question of where the armed forces fit within the overall social structure. Insofar as the economic potential of the armed forces is linked with the emergence of a state capitalist economic sector, a partial fusion develops at the same time between the leadership of the army and the bureaucratic bourgeoisie (in structure and interests clearly separated from the traditional bourgeoisie) which extends as far as direct personal union (Klassen und Klassenkampf in den Entwicklungsländern, 1967-1969: 125-211). From the historical-political ambivalence of the petit bourgeoisie, in turn, there results the possibility that even army staffs with a socially progressive structure can be absorbed by the ruling classes and a reversal of function brought about. It is enough to refer to the origins and development of Batista, the subsequent options of Tenentes who once belonged to the "Prestes Column," and the negative change in function of the new Bolivian army between 1954 and 1964. The degree of institutionalization and professionalism, discipline, esprit de corps and caste feeling, social and political assimilation, and absorption potential (which, via educational policy, can also cover the basic peasant element of the army) on the one hand, and the intensity of the polarization of the general politicosocial power relations on the other, have proven to be the decisive corrective factors (Klassen und Klassenkampf in den Entwicklungsländern, 1967-1969: 260).

In connection with the development of Peru since 1968, there arises the problem of the nature and the role of the military intelligentsia. Janowitz (1964: 122-125) has rightly insisted that the intellectual element should be understood as a qualitatively new aspect of the "military mind." A considerable part of the young officer generation, which has passed through the military academies where there is a clear orientation toward development policies (the Peruvian Centro de Altos Estudios Militares, CAEM, may be regarded as the prototype for these), has the characteristics of an intelligentsia which understands the problems of technology, economics, and the social sciences (Lindenberg, 1969; Villanueva, 1969: 191-194). This group of the military intelligentsia shows a high degree of understanding for developmental problems which—in conjunction with progressive nationalism—provides the substratum of national reformist military regimes. Consequently, the political commitment of the armed forces is subject to a multilayered, diverging, and unstable state of affairs; the main coordinates of which also include the state of tension between the upper-class landowning oligarchy, the bureaucratic bourgeoisie, and the petit bourgeoisie with the intellectual military sector and the revolutionary popular movement.

Summary and Conclusions

It follows from the essential differences in the basic politicosocial behavior of the armed forces (see above) that a differentiation must be made between the various types of military dictatorships. There are differences both between countries and within an individual country (e.g., Bolivia, 1936-1943 and 1964-1969). The value of the terms military dictatorship or military regime is not very high, since every form of military rule has certain objectives, external features in common with all others, due to the specific institutional characteristics of armed forces (Lieuwen, 1960). Thus, there is a need for additional qualification. Affinities in the technique of the coup d'état and in the form of the exercise of power by the army appear (but *only* appear) to substantiate the impression that there is *the* coup d'état or *the* military dictatorship. When special account is taken of developments since World War II, it seems that four "models" or "types" can be derived from the multiplicity of political interventions by the armed forces.

(1) Traditional dictatorships with marked elements of caudillism. In the system of types, these represent residual forms, which, although historically outdated, continue to exist under the specific conditions of certain countries, of dictatorships occupying a dominating position up to about the time of the world economic crisis. Examples: the Somoza rule in Nicaragua; the Stroessner regime in Paraguay. The Duvalier dictatorship (Thebaud, n.d.) contains features of a special nature through the hegemony of the tonton macoutes over the army, which has lost its significance.)

(2) Reactionary military regimes, using modern forms to a great extent in structure, mode of operation and methods for the maintenance of the upper-class, oligarchical, ruling system. The suppression of the democratic opposition, especially of the organized working-class movement, is linked with the simultaneous development, in a systematic manner, of capitalism within the framework of a canalized desarrollismo. Outwardly, these regimes appear as collective dictatorships–i.e., with a marked anti-caudillistic accent. This form of the collective exercise of power (representatives of the army, air force, and navy) is not used because of the political image (demonstration of unity and of the role of a "national" institution), but rather to balance out the tactical differences within their own camp–linha dura versus linha branda; Blancos versus Azules; and so on. Examples: Brazil since 1964, Argentina since 1966. Especially in connection with the development of Brazil since 1964, the problem of the tendency to fascism is of topical interest (Fernandes, 1970: 3). The question remains open as to the extent that, not only fascistic techniques of maintaining supremacy could emerge; but, also, the structural elements necessary for an independent fascist development, given the consolidation of domestic monopoly capitalism, at a time when

the politicosocial class structure is becoming increasingly polarized.

In the case of the dictatorships belonging to types 1 and 2, the principal indication of the praetorial function, as characteristic of Latin American armed forces, is the primacy of the internal—over the external or defense function—which attains its most extreme form with the de facto fusion of the state, military, and police powers (Kossok, 1966: 148-149). The character and dimensions of this tendency, which has a lasting effect on the political profile of the armed forces, have been determined since 1961/62 by the orientation toward the "anti-subversive preventive war," the struggle against the actual or potential rural or urban guerrillas and the variations of the Military Civic Action corresponding to this (Lieuwen, 1967: 20-21).

(3) National reformist military regimes of which the domestic and foreign policies are directed toward the implementation of national economic and political interests on the basis of comprehensive structural reforms. From an objective standpoint, these regimes are moving toward a confrontation with the foreign monopolies (nationalization measures) and with certain groups of the national oligarchy (expropriation of the big landowners, agrarian reform). Neither the experience gained in Peru and certain developmental starting points in Bolivia under the Ovando government nor the inadequate analysis, so far, of the earlier reformist regimes already mentioned, permits a definitive evaluation of this phenomenon. This is all the more reason for raising some questions, as regards these problems, as a contribution to the formulation of the desiderata for future efforts in research.

For the sake of clear definition, it should just be stressed that one can only refer to national reformist military regimes when a policy of reform, in the broad sense of the term, is the aim or is being put into effect. Individual and partial reforms are certainly not an adequate criterion for classifying a military dictatorship as national-reformist; it is a well-known fact that there is practically no military dictatorship since the 1950s which has not passed laws of agrarian reform. It is only from the overall review of the motive forces, character, nature of the structural reforms, relationship with the popular movement, and so on that one can venture a definition of this kind. The question of the relationship between military and civil reformism is particularly complicated for Latin America. On the other hand, reference has justifiably been made to the disproportionately weaker anti-capitalist potentials of the armed forces of Latin America in comparison with the role of the "young officers" in the Afro-Asian area (Klassen und Klassenkampf in den Entwicklungsländern, 1967-1969: 275). It would appear premature, nevertheless, to conclude that, with the fiasco of bourgeois reformism, as institutionalized in parties, the army has also lost its importance as the motive power of social reforms (Kossok and Kübler, 1970). The connecting threads and the possibilities of comparison between civil and military reformism are manifold and, in the final analysis, are subject to the same laws of development. Nevertheless, the limits and differences between the reformism of a bourgeoisie, which is increasingly moving toward a compromise with foreign monopoly interests and the national progressive concepts of development of a petit bourgeois, and intellectual military elite should not be left out of account. Equally unfounded is the contrary conclusion, which provides the rationale for the "Revolución Militar." According to this thesis, the civil reformism is now being generally succeeded by military reformism as the variation of the policy of reform, which will predominate in the future—or as the only version with a prospect of success. The maturity of the Latin American situation (contrary to the hopes of the Rockefeller Report) no longer permits a military solution. In Latin America, more rapidly than in Asia and Africa, a policy of reform, inaugurated and institutionalized by the army, is moving to the critical turning point, where the decision has to be made: (1) as to whether the progressive officers (or at least some of them) integrate themselves with a popular revolution; or (2) if the regime, under the pressure of right-wing forces (national and foreign), evolves the movement into a dictatorship "type" (described above under 2). The Perón and the Vargas regimes provide two examples of dictators at the center of power of both forms (Rowe, 1966; Johnson, 1966). On the historical average, the tendency to associate with the conservative element is, without doubt, more marked than the possibility of commitment for a revolutionary democratic development.

The earlier and contemporary indications of military reformism contain a regional and national differentiation, which scarcely permits generalizations on a continental scale. The best objective conditions for the emergence of national reformist tendencies in the interventionism of the armed forces exist in the states with a predominant agrarian structure and a primarily extractive industry (the majority of the states of Central America and the Andes). Despite the greater affinity between these countries and Afro-Asian problems of development, the historical-political and socioeconomic conditions for the role of the armies are divergent enough to greatly reduce or nullify the usefulness of the often-attempted transference of certain terms, such as "Nasserism," to Latin American conditions (Lindenberg, 1969; Lieuwen, 1964: 136-144).

(4) Emergence of national revolutionary tendencies in the armed forces and the formation of a military left-wing. The historical framework for the analysis of this process is limited by the most radical representatives of Tenentismo (Werneck Sodré, 1965: 198-236) and by the movement led by Colonel Caamaño in the Dominican Republic (Drechsler, 1965). The oft-quoted example of the Guatemalan Revolution in this connection must be evaluated differently. In the events of 1944, the progressive military sector, first of all, played a key role; however, under the government of Arbenz–i.e., in the critical phase of the transition to a policy of revolutionary democratic reform, the army took up a markedly neutral–or at least noncommitted–position (Adams, 1968-1969: 110).

In view of the specific conditions of Latin America, the possibilities for the institutionalization of a revolutionary democratic dictatorship, under the hegemony of progressive officers, are extremely limited and represent a historial exception (Klassen und Klassenkampf in den Entwicklungsländern, 1967-1969: 267). As a rule, national revolutionary tendencies emerge under conditions which, mostly, do not permit the protagonists to maintain their position within the army, or even to carry along the rank and file. The necessity to take offensive action in isolated instances (rebellions of Carápano and Puerto Cabello in Venezuela in 1962; Lieuwen, 1965: 193) or to seek links with the guerrilla movement (Guatemala) underlines the objective impossibility of revolutionizing the important parts of the armed forces from the inside (Fernández, 1968). Thus, the field of action for progressive activity on the part of the armed forces, as a potential motive force of politicosocial change in Latin America, is largely restricted to national reformist tendencies. A spontaneous reversal of direction, however, is conceivable under exceptional conditions, which could include intervention or the fusion of an organized, revolutionary popular movement with the radical nationalism of a progressive military sector. When Hamon (1966: 410) states that the revolutionary potential of an army is dependent on its ability "to have a revolution against right-wing elements without becoming the prisoner of the left," the dialectic of the relationship between the army and the revolution presents rather a picture to the contrary. The revolutionary military element gains historical effectiveness to the same degree it succeeds in emerging from its own institutional "captivity"–i.e., of isolated action and in regarding the integrating itself as a component of a comprehensive revolutionary popular movement.

In the efforts of historians and sociologists to unravel the complex reality of Latin America, the military question and the need to evaluate it in a differentiated manner remain one of the great tasks which have to be tackled.

NOTE

1. A more consecutively complete version of the article cited is Adams (1970).–Ed.

REFERENCES

ADAMS, R. N. (1970) "The development of the military," in Crucifixion by Power: Essays on Guatemalan National Social Structure, 1944-1966. Austin, Texas.

--- (1968-1969) "The development of the Guatemalan military." Studies in Comparative International Development 4, 5.

ARISMENDI, R. (1964) "Anotaciones acerca de la tática del movimiento obrero y popular después del golpe en Brasil." Estudios, Montevideo 29.

CERESOLE, N. (1969) Perú: Una revolución nacionalista. Buenos Aires.

DRECHSLER, H. (1965) "Die USA–Intervention in der Dominikanischen Republik." Lateinamerika. Semesterbericht, Rostock.

FERNANDES, F. (1970) "The military dictatorship and the political roles of the intellectual in Latin America." (mimeo)

FERNANDEZ, O. (1968) Turcios Lima. Habana.

HAHN, E. (1970) No title. Presented to the plenary session of the Seventh World Congress of Sociology, Vama.

HAMON, L. [ed.] (1966) Le róle extra-militaire de l'Armée dans le tiers monde. Paris.

IMAZ, J. L. de (1964) "Los que mandan: las fuerzas armadas en Argentina." América Latina 4.

JANOWITZ, M. (1964) The Military in the Political Development of New Nations. Chicago-London.

JOHNSON, J. (1966) "The Military in Brazil," pp. 482-497 in R. D. Tomasek (ed.) Latin American Politics. New York.

--- (1962) [ed.] The Role of the Military in Underdeveloped Countries. Princeton.

Klassen und Klassenkampf in den Entwicklungsländern (1967-1969) Berlin. (German translation of a three-volume collection of essays prepared by the Institute of World Economy and International Relations of the Academy of Science, Moscow.)

KOSSOK, M. (1968a) "Der antiimperialistische befreiungskampf der völker Afrikas, Asiens und Lateinamerikas für die errichtung der nationalen demokratie." Zeitschrift für Geschichtswissenschaft, Berlin 8: 1186-1203.

--- (1968b) "Zur politischen funktion der armeen in Lateinamerika (aktuelle und historische Aspekte)." Zeitschrift für Militärgeschichte.

--- (1967) "Aktuelle probleme der befreiungsbewegung in Lateinamerika." Zeitschrift für Geschichtswissenschaft 8: 1321-1322.

--- (1966) "Armee und politik in Lateinamerika." Die nationale Befreiungsbewegung 1965, Leipzig.

--- (1961) "Revolution und bourgeoisie in Lateinamerika." Zeitschrift für Geschichtswissenschaft: 123-143.

KOSSOK, M. and J. KUBLER (1970) "Entwicklung und gegenwärtige funktion der reformparteien in Lateinamerika." Asien-Afrika-Lateinamerika. Bilanz, Berichte, Chronik. Berlin (im Druck).

KUBLER, J. (1967) "Die 'Allianz für den Fortschritt': wurzeln und miberfolg der strategisch-taktischen neuorientierung in der Lateinamerikapolitik der USA unter J. F. Kennedy." Zeitschrift für Geschichtswissenschaft 8: 1436-1459.

LAMBERT, J. (1964) América Latina: Estructuras Sociales e Instituciones Políticas. Barcelona-Caracas.

LENIN, W. (1966) Werke. Volume 11. Berlin.

——— (1965) Werke. Volume 39. Berlin.

LIEUWEN, E. (1967) The Latin American Military. Washington.

——— (1965) Venezuela. London.

——— (1964) Generals vs. Presidents: Neomilitarism in Latin America. New York.

——— (1960) Arms and Politics in Latin America. New York.

LINDENBERG, K. (1969) "Nasserismus in Lateinamerika? der fall Peru." Vierteljahresberichte. Forschungsinstitut der Friedrich-Ebert-Stiftung. Hannover 37: 289-314.

LOMBARDI, M. (1966) "Función social de las fuerzas armadas." Problemas de Economía 20: 27-41. (With critical remarks on B. Rattenbach's Sociologia Militar, Buenos Aires, 1959.)

McALISTER, L. (1966) "Recent research and writing on the role of the military in Latin America." Latin Amer. Research Rev. (Fall): 5-36.

MAHRDEL, C. (1967) "Die role der armee in der nationalen befreiungsrevolution Afrikanischer Völker." Zeitschrift fur Geschichtswissenschaft 8: 1406-1421.

MARKOV, W. (1961) Arbeiterklasse und Bourgeoisie im Nationalen Befreiungskampf. Leipzig.

MARX, K. and F. ENGELS (1962) Werke. Volume 20. Berlin.

——— (1961) Werke. Volume 10. Berlin.

——— (1960) Werke. Volume 8. Berlin.

MIRSKI, G. (1970) Armija i politika Va stranach Azii i Afriki. Moscow. (Reviewed by K. Majdanik in 1970 in Mirovaja Ekonomika i Mezdunarodnye Otnosenija. Moscow 5: 140-143.)

——— (1969) "Papel político del ejército en los países de Asia y Africa." Ciencias Sociales Contemporáneas 5. Moscow.

NUN, J. (1969) "Lateinamerika: die hegemoniekreise und der militärische staatsstreich." Aspekte der Entwicklungssoziologie 13. Köln-Opladen: 328-366.

——— (1967) "The middle class military coup," pp. 66-118 in C. Veliz (ed.) The Politics of Conformity in Latin America. London.

RATHMANN, L. (1968) "Uber die rolle der armee in der Agyptischen revolution." Zeitschrift für Militärgeschichte 2: 167-182.

ROUQUIE, A. (1969) "Le rôle politique des forces armées en Amérique Latine: etats des traveaux." Revue Francaise de Science Politique 19 (August): 862-886.

ROWE, J. (1966) "Argentina's restless military," pp. 439-466 in R. D. Tomasek (ed.) Latin American Politics. New York.

Soviet Encyclopedia (1963) Moscow.

THEBAUD, F. (n.d.) "Katholizismus, vaudou und ideologies im soziokulturellen entwicklungsprozeb der republik Haiti." Aspekte der Entwicklungssoziologie: 122-135.

VILLANUEVA, V. (1969) Nueva Mentalidad Militar en el Perú? Lima.

WERNECK SODRE, N. (1965) Historia Militar de Brasil. Rio de Janeiro.

CHARLES D. CORBETT
Center for Advanced International Studies
University of Miami
Miami, Florida

MILITARY INSTITUTIONAL DEVELOPMENT AND SOCIOPOLITICAL CHANGE

The Bolivian Case

The Latin American military is a complex institution in a complex society. It probably has always been, but in the past the dynamics acting upon the change versus order equation have allowed new structural relationships to be worked out over extended periods of time, relatively free from ideological passions and exogenous influences. That time has passed. Probably in no other region of the world are military establishments undergoing the degree of institutional self-examination and mission redefinition as are the armies of Latin America today. They have neither the development-oriented self-confidence of the armies of the "new" nations, nor the threat-oriented *Weltanschauung* of the military in the established countries. Previously acceptable roles—as moderators in the political process or guarantors of their own image of the

AUTHOR'S NOTE: This article is adapted from a more comprehensive monograph written during the year the author spent at the Center for Advanced International Studies of the University of Miami as a U.S. Army War College Research Associate. But all research reported here is private, having nothing to do with official responsibilities. The author was in Bolivia for varying periods in 1963, 1967, and 1970. He is fortunate to count as friends a large number of Bolivian officers of all ranks. The article draws heavily on numerous conversations and a few loosely country's traditions–are under examination not only in the society at large but in the heart of the military institutions.

There is much talk of a "new military" in the region. The radical reformist junta in Peru, the three more conservative but self-styled "revolutionary" military governments in Brazil since 1964, and the Onganía-Levingstone-Lanusse succession since 1966 in Argentina are all manifestations of change *within* the military institution. These are giants in the regional context, but the Torrijos regime in Panama and the Ovando-Torres interlude in Bolivia between 1969-1971 indicate that the trend extends to smaller countries.

In the latter case, there are many aspects to military institutional development in that heartland country of the subcontinent that transcend its relative obscurity on the world or even on the hemispheric stage.

After a stormy and chaotic political history that saw 179 military coups in 126 years of existence as an independent state, Bolivia underwent a true revolution in 1952, described by one authority (Alexander, 1956: vii) as "the most profound movement for social change which has swept any Latin American country since the Mexican Revolution of 1910." The country was dominated for the next 12 years by the authors of the April 1952 insurrection, the Movimiento Nacionalista Revolucionario (MNR).

The overthrow of the MNR regime in 1964 plunged the Bolivian military back into politics after 12 years of civilian government. After a period of junta rule, constitutional process was reestablished with the election of General René Barrientos

---

structured interviews with many of them over the years. The reader hopefully will understand that, in view of the bitterness engendered within the military by recent events, identification of individuals is inadvisable even though they agreed to that procedure in interviews before 1970. The principal documentary source was the *Revista Militar,* a remarkable military "house organ" that has been published, with some interruptions, since 1885. The *Revista* contains social items, promotion lists, biographical sketches, and occasional exhortations from the high command to the officer corps, in addition to the usual professionally related articles of any military journal. It normally has appeared as a quarterly. Other primary sources included the La Paz newspapers and a Cochabamba daily, *Los Tiempos,* which carries considerable military coverage because of the proximity of the military school complex and other important installations.

Ortuño, who had led the 1964 coup, to the presidency in 1966. Military support, or at least political neutrality on the part of the army was critical to the survival of his regime, but the military institution did not assume the full weight of responsibility for the direction of national policy until Barrientos was killed in a helicopter crash in April 1969. That event set off a protracted political crisis that has seen three successful coups in two years and a kaleidoscopic shift in national orientation from Barrientos' generally laissez faire stance to a populist-leftist position to what is now described as a rightist-nationalist regime. During the radical phase, private U.S. interests were nationalized, the Peace Corps was expelled, diplomatic relations were established with the Soviet Union, and a "popular assembly" advocating Cuban-style reforms dominated the news for much of 1971; the latter despite the fact that Fidel Castro had selected Bolivia as the first of his "many Vietnams" in Latin America, and supported Che Guevara in a serious insurgency attempt in 1967.

Understanding these phenomena requires something more than a resurrection of the debate over *civilismo* versus *militarismo* or the dissection of military motivations for political intervention. More attention must be focused, in Robert Potash's (1969: vii) words, "on the real-life figures who have led the armed forces, on the details of institutional development, and on a broader spectrum of political behavior than the occasional coup."

Attention is concentrated on the army, because of its dominance. A separate air force was formed in the fifties, and an army unit was converted to a river and lake force in 1963, but the army outnumbers the other forces by a ratio of about ten to one, and, more importantly, army officers invariably control the armed forces general staff and most elements of the institutional military structure.

Early History

The Bolivian army's supreme hero, General Andres Santa Cruz, was second in command to Bolivar's lieutenant and the founder of Bolivia, General Antonio Sucre. The army traces its heritage through the half-century of anarchy and civil strife that followed Santa Cruz' downfall in 1839 after the failure of his Peruvian-Bolivian Confederation. A new attempt at forcible union, led this time by the president of Peru, was defeated by the Bolivian army in the only successful major battle it ever fought, at Ingavi, in 1841. A campaign against Chile in the 1879 War of the Pacific was disastrous and sealed Chilean sovereignty over the Pacific littoral (for descriptions of the battles in the nineteenth century, with maps and troop lists, see Wilde, 1963).

A liberal regime came to power as the century closed, and, in the fifty years of internal and external peace that preceded the Chaco War of the 1930s, some steps were taken to professionalize the army. A military academy was formally opened in Sucre in 1891, under the direction of a Bolivian officer who had graduated from the French Ecole de Guerre. After graduating its first class of 11 *subtentienties*, the academy was moved to Oruro, and then finally to La Paz in 1899 as a part of the reforms carried out by the newly ascendant Liberals. A German officer, Major Friedrich Muther, was appointed director in 1911 and for the first time established a fixed curriculum and program of studies for the school. Except for an interregnum during the Chaco War, it has remained in business since 1891. There have been no other foreign commandants.[1] The only important organizational reform was the formation of a general staff in the army in 1905, with the assistance of a French mission.

These reforms did not save the army from disaster in the Chaco War of 1931-1935, although the general ineptitude was relieved by many acts of individual heroism and small unit initiative. The general staff badly bungled the management of resources during the war, and a Superior War School was established in 1938 to train officers in general staff procedures and techniques. An Italian military mission was brought to Cochabamba to organize the school, and operated it until 1944, when Bolivian graduates took it over. The school has been in continuous operation since its founding, although the name was changed to Command and General Staff School (ECEM) in 1950. With its inauguration, the army adopted the European system of distinguishing general staff officers *(diplomados de estado mayor)* from other line officers.[2]

Mid-level officers were prominent among the disillusioned intellectuals who sought social and political reforms in the postwar period. Two of them, Lieutenant Colonels David Toro and Germán Busch, headed juntas with vaguely socialistic aims between 1936 and 1939, but it was not until 1943 that the officer corps as an institution involved itself seriously in reform politics. At least two officer "lodges" joined forces with the new Movimiento Nacionalista Revolucionario in that year for a successful coup, and Major Gualberto Villarroel found himself a compromise choice for president. The commercial and mining establishment's (called *La Rosca* by Bolivians) virtual autonomy threatened by new taxes and financial controls, regained control in 1946 when Villarroel's government was overthrown and the president killed (Alexander, 1956; Osborne, 1964).[3]

In a precedent-shattering action, more than a hundred junior and mid-level officers were tried by military courts for their actions during the previous regime. Some went into exile with Paz and the MNR nucleus (Silva, 1968). Others formed conspiratorial cells that planned and guided the "civil war" of 1949. Despite local successes, that insurrection failed, and again the officer corps was subjected to a widespread purge.[4]

The MNR tried for power legally in the elections of 1951. A military junta barred the party from office on a technicality, and in a short, intense fight between April 9-11, 1952, party militants defeated the troops of the La Paz garrison and gained power. General Antonio Seleme, a junta member, abetted the victory by collusion, but sought asylum in mid-fight, so that the party gained power with no debt to the standing army.[5]

Popular opinion to the contrary, Paz did not destroy the army following the MNR victory. About two-thirds of the one-year Indian conscripts were released from the eighteen to twenty thousand man force, but probably no more than 250 of the twelve to thirteen hundred officers were discharged or exiled, and most of them were from the top ranks. Their places were filled by officers who had been in the Villarroel government and on the rebel side in the 1949 insurrection.[6]

To placate the left wing, the party and miner militias were left intact and given many of the army's responsibilities, and a desultory effort was made to change the class structure of the officer corps by modifying, entrance requirements for the Military Academy when it reopened in late 1953. The first, and only, class of "MNR cadets" graduated in August 1954, and Paz congratulated them in the commissioning ceremony as being representatives of the common people *(hijos del pueblo)* as well as the *"burguesía y clase media."*[7] The military budget was halved.[8] General Ovando in later years wrote bitterly of this period, when officers were refused admittance to their old installations by militiamen, when army vehicles had to be parked downhill so they could be restarted because of a lack of batteries, when officers had to live "in rented garages" and share their rations with their entire families, and when official correspondence had to be posted in envelopes used on both sides for lack of office supplies.[9]

The institutional core persisted and survived. All the career schools were kept open, although the students devoted much time to repairing facilities and scrounging materials, and ambitious officers often defrayed many of their expenses from their own pockets to win the coveted diplomas.[10] Study abroad was dependent upon the generosity of the host government, but continued. Seven officers attended the U.S. Army School of the Americas in 1954, and the number increased annually thereafter.[11]

Improving Fortunes

Army fortunes improved somewhat under the MNR's second administration from 1956-1960. President Siles Zuazo's regime is seen as a Jacobin phase in the revolution by most observers (see, e.g., Malloy, 1970: 216-280), and he was less doctrinaire about the military's role, putting greater emphasis on the army's traditional image as a symbol of national sovereignty and defender of the nation's interests.

He undertook to reduce the raging inflation and to impose some discipline on the labor sector that had been Paz' chief support. The army was increased in strength only slightly during the period, but its prestige and importance rose enormously with the new functions it was given after 1957. Siles' reforms were largely at the expense of labor, and he lost the support of the miner militia. Guillermo Bedregal (1966), a leading MNR figure, dates the political resurgence of the army from 1957:

> The breakdown in the revolutionary front that occurred in 1957, during the unsuccessful general strike of the Bolivian Workers Central, produced the determining initiative for the reinforcement of the power of the armed forces. The government, deeply involved in the anti-inflationary fight . . . at the mercy of the unchecked rush of politically inspired and anarchic strikes, fomented by the labor leadership, had recourse to the simple expedient of strengthening the armed forces as a counterbalance, seeking by this artificial and risky path the maintenance of order within the revolution.

Siles also sought to divide the armed peasant leagues that appeared in the East, and in the ensuing struggle found it necessary to establish a military zone in the Cochabamba Valley and developed a considerable dependence upon the army for the maintenance of peace there. Bedregal says this move let the army into the party's decision-making councils for the first time, and that its influence began to grow at the expense of the other sectors. The army was not strong enough to disarm the peasant bands and depended largely on negotiation to maintain peace between them. The task became more difficult as the 1960 elections approached, and the varying factions of the MNR sought support from the peasant chieftains and other irregular armed elements (for an account of the early years of peasant league organization by someone who has written extensively on campesino affairs, see Patch, 1960).

The victory went to Paz again, and he opted for a state-capitalist model of development with the support of the Alliance for Progress. That decision, and the changes in U.S. hemispheric security policy that the Kennedy administration instituted in response to the Cuban experience, opened new horizons for the army.

New Horizons

The Kennedy administration's hemispheric security policy had far-reaching effects on the Bolivian army. The military civic action doctrine was completely compatible with the "productive" role it had been assigned by the MNR, and counterinsurgency was an acceptable mission that brought with it the kind of equipment the army wanted and could most easily absorb. The rise in U.S. military aid is indicated by Table 1.

Training in U.S. facilities also showed a sharp rise, from about 25 officers per year during the fifties to an average of 160 during the early sixties. According to one study (Barber and Ronning, 1969: 149), by the end of 1963, Bolivia had more graduates of the U.S. Army Special Warfare School at Fort Bragg than any other Latin American country.

There was also a steady rise in Bolivian government defense expenditures during the period, although they remained quite low in absolute terms. Army strength, meanwhile, had risen from a low of 5,000 in January 1953 to about 12,000.[12]

Military interest and leverage in political matters were expanded by a steady broadening of the concept of national security during the early sixties and by the army's almost sovereign administration of the military zones established in Cochabamba and Santa Cruz to keep a lid on the endemic campesino violence there.

TABLE 1

U.S. NET FINANCIAL COMMITMENTS (disbursements in millions of dollars)[a]

1958	.1	1962	2.2
1959	.3	1963	2.4
1960	–	1964	3.2
1961	.4		

SOURCE: Wilkie, 1969: 60-61, tables.

a. The AID's 1968 *Economic Data Book* lists on page 10 total military assistance for the 1946-1967 period as $18.7 million, but yearly totals are given only for 1966 ($2.4 million) and 1967 ($2.9 million).

The establishment of a School of Higher Military Studies[13] in 1960 to educate "the high level civilian and military hierarchy about problems of a strategic nature," and a Supreme Council for National Defense in 1961 institutionalized the broader concerns of national defense policy. The latter body was formalized in a presidential decree of December 1961 as the "highest advisory body charged with problems of national defense," and it had as its members the president, vice president, minister of defense, all cabinet members, the chairmen of the congressional committees on foreign relations and defense, the commander in chief of the armed forces, and each of the service commanders. An army general has always served as permanent secretary of the council. The charter gave the council responsibility to direct, orient, and resolve matters dealing with international defense policy, economic and financial planning that affected defense, mobilization, and coordination of the participation in national defense matters by other elements of the government. Under the emerging broad definitions of national defense, the council structure gave the military, through the permanent secretariat, Supreme Decree 0741-65, a legal national forum for presentation of the army viewpoint on almost any question.

General Alfredo Ovando Candía became the second most powerful officer in the military establishment with his appointment as army commander in 1960. He was to move up to armed forces commander in 1963 and exercise great influence for a decade.

Ovando reminisced about the early sixties in a remarkable open letter to the officers of the armed forces in 1968, published in the April-June edition of *Revista Militar.* He traces the evolution of the army from colonial days and underlines the importance of the Chaco War and its aftermath in awakening a social consciousness among officers. He gives credit to Busch, Villarroel, and the 1943-1946 MNR for having "opened the road for the national revolution" by weakening the walls of reaction with their economic and social reforms. He indicates that, after its return to power in 1952, the MNR turned its back on the military institution, making of it a simple cell in the party structure and entrusting the coercive power of the state to an armed rabble. Ovando says "the resistance" formed among members of the general staff and the improvements in the army were carried out "behind the back of the president and of the MNR generals." He ridicules the MNR claim that it created the prestigious Center of Instruction for Special Troops (CITE), saying it was formed through the sweat of the army and the assistance of "comrades in arms who in secret gave us parachutes and invaluable technical assistance," without a cent being allocated in the budget.[14] Ovando goes on to claim that he "singlehandedly" procured vehicles abroad to motorize a battalion, and delivered them by air to the La Paz airport "before the astonishment and surprise of the then Secretary of Defense." He also attacks the MNR claim that it organized the River and Lake Force in 1963, saying that officers who formed it had to study abroad surreptitiously to make it possible. He says, however, that "it was necessary to offer its command to an MNR general in order to get the signature on the decree legalizing its creation."[15]

An enigmatic, taciturn man, Ovando had few close confidantes. Most interviewers who talked with him before 1969 came away with the impression of a dedicated professional soldier with an almost obsessive drive to professionalize the army and keep it out of political squabbles. There were, however, occasional references to Kemal Ataturk in his conversations, and in the open letter mentioned above he prescribes for Bolivia "governmental action, or revolution, as remoralizing *(moralizadora)* as that of José María Linares and as constructive and nationalistic as that of Kemal Ataturk in Turkey." Nobody doubted who was to play Ataturk.[16]

The 1964 Coup

Paz' decision in 1963 to seek the presidency for a second consecutive term split the MNR, and its squabbling factions sought support wherever it was to be found. The prize was the vice presidency and a share of control in top party councils, since Paz was unbeatable. The military cell of the MNR, apparently dominated by the old "party generals," proposed General René Barrientos for the vice presidency and launched a vigorous campaign in his behalf. Despite their best efforts, Paz selected a party wheelhorse, but after a dramatic assassination attempt on Barrientos added to his already widespread popularity, Paz changed his mind and accepted the ambitious officer as his running mate.

Ovando's principle concern during this period appeared to be that of preventing a split in the army over the election issue. He apparently did not take an active part in the military cell of the party and certainly never gave warm support to Barrientos' candidacy. In a setting of nationwide student and teacher strikes, disarray in the MNR, and a general feeling that Paz' violation of the tradition of "no continuismo" cast a doubt of legality on his election, both men apparently began separately to plot Paz' overthrow almost immediately after his inauguration in August (for interviews to this effect with Barrientos and two colonels from Ovando's staff, see Brill, 1967: 23-29). Characteristically Ovando's moves were covert, ambiguous, and tentative while Barrientos openly championed the causes of dissenters of any hue to intensify dissatisfaction with the government. He breathed new life into the now mythologized concept that social concern had been introduced into Bolivian history by the military "martyrs" Busch and Villarroel. He was a peripatetic figure, whose political office and military status gave him a forum on any subject and entree into any garrison. His long association with Cochabamba gave him allies among the peasant leagues there and support in the key Seventh Division with its CITE unit and schools command. It was from there that Barrientos called for Paz' resignation on November 3 after the Seventh Division declared itself in rebellion.

The weight of the circumstancial evidence indicates that Ovando had given no commitment of support to Barrientos before his *pronunciamiento.* There was a noticeable lack of coordination among army units after the Cochabamba garrison pronounced itself against the government, and Ovando himself issued no public proclamations. He closeted himself with the army general staff in the Miraflores headquarters on the third and emerged the following day to escort Paz to the airport on his journey into exile. The Miraflores complex houses the military communications center, and no doubt key commanders were polled during the momentous interval. Most of the important provincial garrisons had declared for Barrientos by the afternoon of the fourth, and, on the fifth, having reached an accord, Ovando and Barrientos announced that they would serve as co-presidents, but after the former was subjected to a cacophony of catcalls and jeers when they appeared together on the balcony of the *Palacio Quemado,* Ovando withdrew as co-president.

To seek the underlying motivations for a resurgence of military rule–after 12 years of revolutionary civilian government–in the nature and character of the military institution is to encounter frustration. There was no threat to its corporate structure or interests in 1964; neither communism nor other radical doctrines were involved, and the junta continued most of Paz' economic policies. There was no hint of reversing "revolutionary" gains. Barrientos told army leaders in a January 1965 speech that his government would make "a revolution within the revolution," and that the "grand social conquests," including universal suffrage, agrarian and educational reform, and nationalized mines would be maintained (reported in *Revista Militar* for February/March of 1967). It would be safe to say that the 1964 coup was probably pushed more by pressures internal to the military than pulled by political factors external to the institution, although the latter were present. As has occurred so frequently in Bolivia, events turned principally on the driving ambitions of strong men. One insisted on holding power in the face of a tradition that prohibited consecutive second terms, splitting his machine, alienating powerful supporters, and putting himself temporarily at a power disadvantage; the other two had at hand the power to seize control, and were able to reach an accord on how to divide it. Neither felt any loyalty to the party of the revolution, and both were willing to divide power to prevent damage to *la Institución.* The enormous prestige of Ovando and the early commitment to elections were sufficient to keep opposition elements in the military neutral. These elements, however, were to play a much more active role in succeeding events.

Ovando did not remain long in the shadows. Barrientos sent the army into the mines in May of 1965 to break strikes. Several days of open warfare ensued, resulting in several dozen deaths and numerous exiles. Ovando, as armed forces chief, negotiated a truce with the new mine leaders, and the following month was again named co-president. This time there were no complaints.

The Professional Elite

When the military took power in 1964, an elite nucleus of officers groomed for leadership under Ovando's watchful eye was approaching positions of institutional power. Having graduated from the *Colegio Militar* between 1941 and 1944, they were too young to participate in any important way in the Villarroel regime and were lieutenants or captains when the revolution of 1952 brought the MNR to power. With few exceptions, they escaped the army purge that followed and devoted themselves to institutional concerns and educational development in the lean years of MNR rule. Nineteen of the most successful comprised the unusually large promotion lists to brigadier general of 1967 and 1968, and, to a remarkable degree, they provided the governmental and armed forces leadership at operational levels after 1964.[17]

The educational background of this group is impressive. Three were at the top of their *Colegio Militar* class. All completed the career schools of the army, and all but three are graduates of the higher military studies course. (Two of the nongraduates are engineers; the other is a rehabilitated officer who was cashiered for political reasons in 1952.) Thirteen studied abroad at mid-career and higher-level military schools; seven in the United States, the others in France, Germany, Argentina, Peru, and Brazil.[18]

Since 1964, twelve of these officers have occupied cabinet

posts in the government, six on two or more occasions. (Not including the Ministry of Defense, a traditional military post. Interestingly, only one occupied that post during the period.) The group also provided four ambassadors.

They dominated the army institutional structure below the high command level, serving as commanders or operations chiefs of the ten divisions and the engineer command, commandants or directors of studies in the military academy and career schools, and as principal officers of the army general staff. The traditional practice of reassigning top officers annually gave them opportunities for a variety of jobs.[19]

Events connected with the repression of the Che Guevara guerrilla band in 1967 proved beneficial to most of this group. Two directed the counter-guerrilla operation as division commanders, and two others gained wide notice as judge and prosecutor in the trial of French revolutionary theoretician Regis Debray who was captured in the operation zone. Others won acclaim in planning and logistics jobs connected with the training of new units and the administration of outside military assistance that increased considerably during the emergency. Following that crisis, members of this group moved for the first time into the high command. General Marcos Vásquez Sempertegui, top graduate in his Colegio class of 1942, became army chief of staff in 1968, and General Ruíz Velarde was named chief of staff of the armed forces under Ovando.

Diverging Views

The increasingly divergent views between Ovando and the professional elite had much to do with shaping the events of the next few years. The differences fell into two main areas: the politics of development, and the role of the military in a developing society. There is no evidence that Ovando had expressed himself in a substantive fashion on the former before 1968, and there is every indication that the elite group, and most foreign observers, believed him to favor a relatively apolitical, traditionally organized force in the second area.

There are few clues to the development of Ovando's political philosophy. One acquaintance holds that his unpopularity following the 1964 coup, in contrast with the acclaim afforded Barrientos, convinced him that an espousal of popular causes was necessary to political success. The same source believes that circumstances surrounding the Guevara incursion awakened Ovando to an "anti-imperialist," nationalist sentiment with deep roots in Bolivia that could be exploited politically.

The first public airing of his political beliefs appeared in early 1968 in the long and completely uncharacteristic open letter previously cited, which he sent to senior officers in all three services before it was published.

In the letter, he listed the principles that guided his political thought:

> in order that the country be ours, the basic industries must belong to the state *[deben ser estatales]*. The highest priority must go to metallurgy, without which we can never break the barriers of backwardness and integrate outselves economically into the reality of a continent undergoing change. There cannot be a strong army without the complement of a strong heavy industry. Natural resources, and the terms of their exploitation, also constitute an inseparable part of national sovereignty. The country must move toward the control of their full exploitation through its own resources and entities.

He sketched a role for private enterprise in the derivative industries, a vast plan for state assistance to agricultural development, and a rationalization of university education to support the grand scheme, and came down hard on foreign oil companies:

> There are other aspects that I would like to emphasize strictly and concretely. With reference to petroleum, the Code Davenport must be annulled as soon as possible, and a tax established that reaches 50 percent of the gross production; special regulations for gas must be established; and control for the state obtained over its refining transport, marketing and industrialization through YPEB.[20]

He stressed the importance of in-country smelters, and hinted that the Barrientos government had failed to follow the intent of the military junta in its dealings with mining concessions. Ovando was extremely sensitive to nationalist criticism that the Barrientos government was dealing with the "economic imperialists" and that his position made him at least a tacit supporter of these policies.

On the military's role, Ovando said the military institution is not and must never be an armed political party, but:

> in the full use of its constitutional rights and under the most expansive interpretation of the principles that govern its existence, it must insure that the decisions of the people are respected and complied with and reserve the national patrimony and the resources that it contains. The best committee for the defense of the natural resources, and the most legitimate, is that constituted by the people and their armed expression, the national army.

When these opinions were made public in mid-1968, the political situation was more muddled than usual. The Cuban-supported guerilla band had been eliminated with U.S. training and material assistance, but the incident left great domestic turmoil in its aftermath. Conflicting stories on the circumstances of Che Guevara's death damaged the credibility of army spokesmen, and an attempt by the high command to sell exclusive publication rights to his diary precipitated suspicion of private gain in high places. Debray's trial brought an influx of foreign reporters and some diplomatic pressure from France, where his family was prominent. There were sensational charges of CIA infiltration of the highest levels in the government, and a major scandal developed around the delivery of a copy of Guevara's diary to Fidel Castro by the interior minister.[21] Rumors of new guerrilla bands, forming or in action, were rampant, and government announcements gave credence to some of them.

The government suffered chronic budget deficits, and violence and strikes in the mines reversed the annual growth rate of about seven percent that sector had enjoyed between

1961-1966. Oil had become an important source of foreign exchange for the first time in 1966 with the development of the Santa Cruz fields and completion of a pipeline to the Chilean coast in 1967, but nationalist opposition to rumored processing plants on the coast made the issue a source of great dissension. The cost of the anti-guerrilla war and U.S. refusal of a $12 million "stability loan" precipitated a sharp financial crisis in early 1968.

Barrientos responded by appointing an all-military cabinet in July of 1968, provoking an open quarrel with Ovando, who maintained that the armed forces could not spare top officers from their duties to serve in the cabinet.

The feud between the two leaders and the scandals rocking the government were highly disturbing to the army general staff, and when Ovando began openly to campaign for the presidency among the peasant leagues in the East, General Vásquez joined with spokesmen of the MNR and the Socialist Falange (FSB) in urging him to resign his post (see *Presencia* for May 24, 1968, and Roca, 1968). Ovando responded by firing Vásquez as chief of the army general staff on August 10. General Juan José Torres, chief of the armed forces general staff, was dismissed at the same time for reasons that are not clear, although it may have been at Barrientos' insistence in retribution for Torres' vehement, public opposition to any processing of Bolivian petroleum on Chilean territory. On August 20, Vásquez failed in a coup attempt that had the support of important elements of the MNR and the FSB. Vásquez had been the top graduate in his 1942 Colegio class and was probably the most respected member of the elite nucleus. He explained his actions in a message addressed to the armed forces from exile, and printed in *Los Tiempos* of Cochabamba on May 8, 1969:

> There is nothing more pernicious and corrosive for an institution like ours than to allow it to be dragged into political turbulence and to be asked to employ weapons in defense of a certain person. I unsheathed my sword so that the armed forces of the nation could return to their barracks with honor and dignity. . . . I shall devote

> my every effort and also my life, if necessary, to prevent their use against the people once again, or to prevent their being used as a pawn by anyone whose ambition is to climb to power and whose only qualification is the fact that he wears a uniform and whose only right is military might.

This justification for the August 1968 coup was written one month after Barrientos' death in a helicopter crash in April 1969, and the article was widely interpreted as an attack on and warning to Ovando.

The 1969 Coup

Ovando was out of the country when Barrientos was killed in April 1969. General Ruíz Velarde, acting armed forces chief, acquiesced in the accession of Vice President Siles. Siles' cabinet included only two military men. General Eduardo Gallardo Ballesteros was kept on as defense minister, and Colonel Eufronio Padilla Caero was appointed minister of the interior.

General Torres was appointed by Ovando to the largely honorary post of president of the Supreme Tribunal of Military Justice.

Ovando, looking to the 1970 elections, moved to gain the support of the peasant leagues that had backed Barrientos and, to a large degree, inherited it by default. His main opposition came from General Armando Escobar Uria, the popular mayor of La Paz and a famous Chaco War hero, but Ovando was able to restrict the latter's activities through control of the military prefects and mayors appointed by Colonel Padilla.

Siles' attempts to replace these officers with civilians, Escobar's growing popularity in La Paz, and the return of many old-line party leaders probably contributed greatly to Ovando's decision to depose the president rather than taking a chance in the June elections. The activities of General Vásquez, who had been allowed to return by Siles, were particularly worrisome; he continued to enjoy great support within the army elite, spoke out strongly in support of Siles and for a nonpolitical stance on the part of the army. The fear of losing control of the army in the eight months remaining before the election was probably the factor that weighed heaviest. Ovando had Siles arrested and flown to Chile while the latter was touring in Santa Cruz on September 26. There was no bloodshed.

Ovando announced that he had taken power to avoid the dangers of "anarchy, capitulation, and disorder." He pledged to secure national sovereignty over the means of production, improve the mining sector, promote heavy industry, enhance the rights of workers, and establish a nationalist economic policy (New York Times, 1969).

Within the next few weeks, the government announced that it would establish relations with Communist nations, including Cuba. Relations were established with Rumania in October, and the first Bolivian ambassador to Moscow was dispatched in December.

Corporate Concerns

Ovando appointed a mixed civilian-military cabinet and proceeded to implement the program he had outlined in 1968, nullifying the petroleum code and a few months later nationalizing the Gulf Oil operations. These moves and the inflammatory, revolutionary rhetoric of some of his cabinet ministers found resistance among the professional elite of the army. General Torres had been brought back into the high command as armed forces commander, replacing Ovando, but all the other positions had gone to members of the elite.

Early opposition to the nationalization plans apparently caused the ambassadorial "exile" to Great Britain of General Juan Lechín Suárez. Later diplomatic exiles included Generals Remberto Iriarte Paz and Joaquín Zenteno Anaya, ambassadors to Argentina and Peru respectively.

Institutional concerns, however, prompted the first countermoves. In a remarkable interview with a reporter-friend from the leftist magazine *Marcha* of Montevideo of December 19,

1969, Ovando indicated that the future role of the army would be almost entirely that of an instrument of production and development, with dependence on a "guerrilla strategy" for the external defense mission. He answered affirmatively when the reporter asked whether Bolivia should pull out of the Inter-American Defense Board, cancel its arms agreements with the United States, and quit training its people abroad.[22]

This interview raised a great alarm among the "professionalist" officers, coming as it did hard on the heels of an attack by General Torres on the "professional" mystique of the elite before the visiting Inter-American Defense Board in November, 1969.[23] Torres told the visitors that the armed forces of Bolivia had begun to consider the problems of defense in terms of economic and social development tasks that could no longer be postponed.

> The armed forces do not have to be . . . typecast as organizations exclusively dedicated to checking the political phenomenon of international communism, but fundamentally as co-participants and efficient agents of the battle . . . economic underdevelopment from which follow the elements that later go to make up the political setting that has set off the subversive struggle in the continent. . . . The arch conservatives see in the armed forces an exceedingly efficient instrument to return to the night of the past while they remain allied with the foreign monopolies. For their part, the popular classes look at the armed forces as the truest instrument of redemption since they [the armed forces] will no longer accept the role of simple wardens in an unjust order.

Torres went on in the same discourse to attack the conventional view of the historical process in Bolivia. He said the debate over military or civilian control of the government was artificial and irrelevant, because the true problem "consisted in deciding whether the aristocracy or the bourgoisie was going to control the armed forces." What is truly important is to know what interests the armed forces are protecting or alternatively, what interests are affected by the actions of the armed forces (for a report of a strikingly similar formulation made by a sociologist adviser to the military regime in Peru in 1971, see Einaudi, 1971: 62). He scandalized the army hierarchy by openly criticizing the Inter-American Defense Board, implying that it was anachronistic because of its exaggerated stress on the communist threat to the hemisphere, and telling the members that the Board had lost respect in many quarters.

Another threat to la Institución surfaced with the word that there was to be a reduction in army strength. Around a million dollars normally devoted to the annual conscription program was to be applied instead to a national literacy campaign, and the army was to carry the brunt of the campaign as well as suffering the costs (see *El Diario* of La Paz for December 16, 1969).

Another point of difference developed out of the visit of the Rockefeller presidential mission. The general staff reacted favorably to what it interpreted as sympathy for continued military assistance, but, according to Richard Patch (1969), Ovando told Rockefeller that water-drilling rigs, tractors, agricultural machinery, and road-building equipment were more appropriate items of U.S. aid to Latin America than arms. In a published government response to President Nixon's major policy speech on Latin America of October 31, 1969, the government publicly criticized the military recommendations of the Rockefeller Report, accusing him of "waving the bloody threat of imminent communist takeover," and declaring that the government "can take care of itself and if the United States wishes to give effective aid, plows would be better than bayonets" (Patch, 1969).

Influential members of the professional elite saw these policies as a challenge to their perception of the security threat and of the armed forces' mission, and they intensified their opposition. They did not feel strong enough to challenge Ovando directly at the time, but they induced him in July 1970 to abolish Torres' position and replace it with a superior council of the armed forces, chairmanship of which was to be rotated among the army, navy, and air force commanders.

The position of commander in chief of the armed forces had always been an organizational anomaly, representing in effect a second army high command, given the overwhelming preponderance of that service. The political effect of the second headquarters was to divide or dilute army influence. Establishment of the superior council represented an attempt to consolidate army influence and simultaneously to remove Torres from the leadership of a radical faction of younger officers. It was a setback for Ovando, but, in his search for popular bases of support, he continued to hold out against army demands for stronger action against the warring student factions that had made a battleground of the downtown San Andrés University, and for a concerted attack against a band of guerrillas, that included students, who attacked a U.S.-financed mining operation at Teoponte in the Northwest. The antagonism between Ovando and General Rogelio Miranda, army commander and president of the superior council, was an open secret in the last half of 1970.

Ovando's selection of Miranda as army commander had temporarily neutralized more popular officers with large personal followings, like Generals Zenteno and Lechín, and had divided his opposition among the elite. Miranda's inability to rally a majority of key officers behind his coup plans did not save Ovando in the end, but it did open the path for Torres to preempt the movement.

A move against Ovando was almost certainly planned for July, but the death of his son in an airplane crash that month led to nationwide sympathy for the family. Torres, meanwhile, with no legal base, found his situation precarious as sides were formed and had to seek refuge in Ovando's house when Minister of Interior Colonel Juan Ayoroa lined up with the Miranda faction and sent the political police to arrest him.

Miranda made his move in early October, calling upon Ovando to resign and turn his powers over to a triumvirate of the three service chiefs. Apparently there was considerable private negotiation with Ovando before the situation became known publicly, and it is not certain that General Sattori of the air force and Admiral Alberracín of the navy were fully committed to Miranda's plans. The latter barricaded himself in the Miraflores compound with the loyal "Ingaví" regiment and operated from there during most of the critical week after October 1. Some officers in the La Paz garrisons rallied to Ovando's defense, and others sought a compromise by urging both Ovando and Miranda to resign in favor of an officer the army could agree upon. Ovando did resign on October 5, but all indications are that he threw his support to the forces Torres was now mobilizing and neutralized the junta by persuading General Sattori to announce publicly his withdrawal. Miranda, having access to the military communications center at Miraflores, decided that he lacked sufficient personal support and resigned the following day, turning the headquarters over to General Guachalla, the armed forces chief of staff. The junta had tried to form an all-military cabinet by naming, without their knowledge in some cases, several popular officers from the elite and, in an obvious bid for support, most of the key unit commanders. In its only published bulletin, the junta promised elections within two years and a return of the armed forces to the barracks. It also reappointed the popular General Escobar, who had been sacked by Ovando as one of his first acts after taking power, as mayor of La Paz.[24]

Access to the pocket where La Paz nestles is by a narrow and precipitous road that crosses the altiplano rim at El Alto, site of the international airport and an air force garrison. If reinforcements can be blocked there—be they regular forces or irregular bands—the fate of the government palace lies in the hands of the units stationed in the city. This strategic location, rather than the 1940 vintage Mustang or two it can employ, probably constitutes the major card the air force can play in power struggles centered on La Paz. Torres mustered his forces there, and called upon the entrenched Ingaví regiment to surrender and avoid a fratricidal bloodbath. Miranda's departure undermined the resolve of many of the junior officers, despite announced support from the Colegio Militar, and, when the presidential guard unit (Colorados) adopted a neutral stand, the garrison found itself isolated.

General Torres was in possession of the Palacio Quemado by October 9, and, with a few exceptions, the key unit commanders pledged support to the new Torres-appointed army commander.

The confusion and indecision that reigned when Miranda finally made his move in October can probably best be understood in light of the great authority that Ovando continued to enjoy throughout the military institution. He had become army chief of staff in 1957, army commander in 1960, armed forces chief in 1963, and had actively encouraged an almost mythical image of himself as the rebuilder of an institution destroyed and degraded by the 1952 revolution. He had, in fact, been for almost a decade the dispenser of promotions and choice assignments. Practically all the colonels and many of the generals were in his debt, and to the more junior officers he was a revered, if distant, father figure. Many were genuinely disturbed by the move against him, and the issues, except to a small circle, were not clear.

Torres had to have army support or neutrality to stay in power and benefited largely from the latter. There were a few officers who shared his ideological convictions, and they were placed quickly into key, if second-echelon, positions in La Paz units and in the government. There were many officers who were personally loyal to Ovando and who accepted Torres as his heir when Ovando failed to make a fight of it. And there were the majority of career-minded officers who did not want to risk their futures in the confused high command in-fighting. A mixture of the two latter motives probably prompted General Reque Terán, comptroller in Ovando's cabinet and one of the army's most respected officers, to accept the army commander's post. General David La Fuente was carried over temporarily as minister of defense in the new cabinet, helping to maintain the impression of uninterrupted transfer of authority at the top.

Torres promised "a popular, nationalist government resting on four pillars–the peasant farmers, the workers, the students, and the armed forces." The level of revolutionary rhetoric increased perceptibly, and contacts with the Soviet Union and Eastern European countries took an increasing trend. Anti-United States sentiment showed a marked upswing, culminating in expulsion of the Peace Corps from Bolivia. Torres acquiesced in the convocation of a popular assembly in La Paz that sparked an increasingly strong reaction from middle-class groups and the military. There are some indications that he attempted to bypass the military hierarchy and establish cells of support among enlisted men and noncommissioned officers.

Despite a shift of units and commanders, Torres was not able to gain control of the army. The officers who shared his ideological beliefs were simply too few in number and too low in rank to allow him to control even those positions of great weight in the "political order of battle" that had formed since 1964. He threatened occasionally to rearm the irregular peasant and miner militias, but knew from his own long years of service that even sympathetic officers would not stand for it. He resurrected a noncontroversial pre-1952 general to head the defense ministry and tried to concentrate control of the superior council in the latter's hands; all to no avail. He weathered several coup attempts, the most serious coming in January 1971, when Colonel Hugo Banzer Suárez, military academy commander, apparently planned to kidnap him at the graduation ceremonies. Torres had been tipped off and failed to appear. Banzer, a military intellectual and one of the most respected young colonels in the army, had been kept on after the 1969 coup despite complicity with the Miranda group, probably at the insistence of the three service commanders. Following the January plot, however, he and several other officers were discharged from the army and exiled (New York Times, 1971a).

The 1971 Coup[25]

Banzer's second attempt was a masterpiece of planning that reflected a thorough knowledge of military sentiment within the institution and an appreciation for broader political considerations. He fashioned an unlikely political alliance with fellow exiles in Argentina representing the old MNR and their blood enemies of yore, the Bolivian Socialist Falange (FSB). He chose the eastern lowland province of Santa Cruz–whose economy had been drastically crippled by the reduction in Gulf Oil's activities following its nationalization and by state takeover of private sugar mills–as the focal point of his movement. It has long been an FSB stronghold, and the commanders of the two divisions in the province apparently were in on the plans from the beginning. The tough ranger regiment of Colonel Andrés Selich provided the muscle to overcome the limited opposition. (Selich was named minister of interior in the new government.) Within two days after the rangers took control of the seat of provincial government in Santa Cruz on August 19, every important garrison in the country had announced for the rebels and most had made overt moves to take control of key facilities in their respective areas. The key Cochabamba garrison was controlled by the commander of the Seventh Division, General Florentino Mendieta, who became minister in the new government. In La Paz, the military academy, the Castrillo regiment which Torres had brought in to replace the banished Ingaví, and the motorized battalion at nearby Viacha declared for the rebels. Only the presidential guard unit, the Colorados, stuck by Torres, and when the air force joined the bandwagon his last hope was gone and he sought diplomatic asylum.

Banzer consolidated his position with dispatch. He made no glowing promises and promised considerable austerity. With the exception of the two military men mentioned above, his first cabinet was made up of MNR and FSB civilians. The professional elite was called home from diplomatic and punitive exile, or resurrected from relative obscurity. General Miranda became head of the mining commission (COMIBOL). General Iriarte Paz, former ambassador to Argentina, was first named armed forces commander, but in a dispute that bodes ill for future military unity was replaced in October by General Zenteno

Anaya, recalled from an ambassadorship in Peru. General Vásquez was reinstated with rank and seniority. The new service commanders and their staffs are from Colonel Banzer's age group (he is 49), with academic and professional credentials similar to those described for older members of the professional elite.

Summary and Reflections

The MNR did not destroy the old army after its 1952 victory, nor was it able to establish what Samuel Huntington (1964: 80-85) has defined as "subjective" control over it.[26] For the first few years, the army was politically neutralized and rendered militarily impotent by a starvation budget and the maintenance of strong revolutionary militias. Relieved of any real responsibilities or capabilities, the army hibernated for some years within its surprisingly complete institutional structure, nurturing a "professional" elite and seeking its role in the revolutionary society. Changing politicoeconomic orientations by the MNR after about 1958 and subsequent power shifts within the party nucleus alienated leaders of the armed irregulars, which now included strong peasant bands, and a long-term effort to regain control of the state's coercive power by concentrating it in the regular armed forces was begun. Cold War tensions brought sharply increased U.S. assistance for counter-insurgency capabilities and civic action programs. Taking advantage of their increasing influence and affluence, military officers reentered the policy-making councils of the government after 1960. Objective control waned, and subjective control was never established. There are indications that almost complete institutional autonomy obtained during the early sixties, facilitating the decision made in 1964 by the top-level leadership, largely in pursuance of personal ambitions, to take advantage of the MNR's disarray and a legitimacy crisis to overthrow the civilian government. The army finally gained a measure of dominance over the irregular militias in the mid-sixties and was successful in putting down a Cuban-sponsored insurgence in 1967. The scandals that followed in the wake of that victory and the low-key but festering rivalry between the president and ambitious armed forces commander alienated influential members of the professional elite that reached general rank in the late sixties. Their attempt to limit Ovando's ambitions was a factor in his adoption of a populist-leftist stance in his search for alternative sources of support. His obvious lack of popular appeal following the 1964 coup probably convinced him that a more "political" image was necessary, although it went against his nature. Barrientos' death in 1969 propelled Ovando to power earlier than he had anticipated and before he could neutralize his opposition in the officer corps hierarchy. His attempts to placate them weakened his hand, but the officer corps was sufficiently divided that the elite move against Ovando in 1970 by another ambitious officer and associate of the latter was able to preempt the coup with an appeal to the radical left.

Graduates of the 1941-1944 military academy classes *(promociones)* have been most visible and influential in the events of the last few years. It can be safely assumed, however, that other promociones of the forties will reflect generally similar views. All are products of a school system with a strong professionalist orientation during a decade of general political impotence on the part of the military, and a majority have attended foreign schools, particularly U.S. courses.

Since 1960, they have become increasingly politically sensitized. Attendance at the school of higher military studies—opened in 1960—has no doubt influenced their views on domestic policies, as have the correlations between national security and economic development growing out of U.S. and other foreign internal security doctrines.

The military rationale could be summarized as follows: insurgence and subversion grow out of underdevelopment. National security demands economic development. The armed forces are responsible for security, and development is an implied mission. There is a divergence of views about the forces that impede development and the military's role in achieving it. One school that could be labelled "populist-developmental" defines the internal enemy as that sector of society allied with foreign and international markets and the external enemy as economic imperialism, which not only controls prices for exports and imports but also manipulates domestic policies in furtherance of global objectives. The role of international communism in insurgence is overstated by the United States for the latter reason. Neither the old liberal political system nor its permutation under the MNR can provide true sovereignty to the nation. Only the defeat of economic imperialism and its domestic allies will produce that end. A populist coalition of students, workers, peasants, and soldiers, headed by an enlightened elite, is the political answer.

The vast majority of the officer hierarchy would appear to be committed—for diverse motives—to what could be called a modified-traditional liberal view. This dominant element favors economic *growth* without the sweeping structural revisions of socioeconomic patterns that *development* has come to connote in Latin American developmental doctrines. The MNR revolution is seen as having provided the politicosocial reforms necessary to support economic growth with the addition of some measure of discipline (in the labor sector), rectitude (in the public and private sectors), and national planning. Attitudes toward state enterprises are ambivalent but generally favorable.

Traditionalists view the insurgence threat as rising more from communist-inspired subversion than from socioeconomic grievances and favor a foreign policy generally in consonance with U.S. views on the interdependence of the free world in the long-term struggle.

Industrialization and local processing of tin, zinc, and petroleum are goals, but foreign participation in the processes of growth is acceptable. There is an underlying commitment to some form of representative government in an undefined future. The military's role is seen as that of a moderator of the process. The institution would provide technicians (i.e., engineers and administrators) but generally avoid direct involvement in the day-to-day political process, expressing its opinions only on policies of great import to "national security."

If one accepts the thesis, as does the author, that General Ovando's choice of the populist-developmental line was largely opportunistic rather than ideological, it can be seen as a circumstantial or accidental factor.[27] One cannot, however, lightly turn aside the fact of Torres' successful preemption of the traditionalist coup in 1970, and the subsequent military support, albeit minor, and neutrality that he enjoyed. Torres, a 1942 academy graduate, is a product of the same experiences that formed the more traditional elite and is one of its most brilliant members. He was promoted ahead of his contemporaries and was only 46 when he became armed forces chief of staff in 1967. He found his greatest military support among the younger officers; the major who commanded his presidential guard accompanied him into exile.

Torres is the only general officer of the professionalist-oriented generation openly to opt for the leftist-populist orientation. The experiences and education of the majority have led to a preference for what we have described as a more traditional approach to national development. They have reasserted control, but there are many structural factors within the society and the military institution, as well as exogenous pressures, that will influence their ability to impose their model on the country.

Total withdrawal of the army from politics is not possible in the Bolivian context; even withdrawal in the degree apparently sought by the professional elite may not be possible. Its strength is to a large degree a function of the disarray of the political system and the weakness of other institutions. The strong institutional motivations for progressive study and schooling, the technical education offered at the engineering school, the international contacts afforded officers by the military apparatus of the inter-American system, all contribute to the formation of a pool of talent that looms large in the Bolivian society. That society is not yet so complex that there are great role differentiations between military administrators and technicians and those of the civilian sector.

The sense of discipline that exists in the army—imperfect as it may be—stands in stark relief to the virtual anarchy that obtains in political parties and even among civil servants. In a word, no resource is in shorter supply in Bolivia than disciplined administrative talent, and the officer corps provides an immediately available pool.

The military cannot escape the political implications of its role as the sole important national presence in immense areas that lie outside the La Paz-Santa Cruz-Oruro triangle that comprises the vital center. No other institution reaches these peripheral areas in an important way, and the combination of a weak center and primitive communications leave their administration largely in the hands of the local commander.

The ethos of the military is also greatly influenced by Bolivia's powerful neighbors. Officers who attend command and staff schools in Argentina, Brazil, and Peru are prime candidates for the elite nucleus, and usually serve one or more tours in the Bolivian career school system. They are enormously influenced by the sophistication of the doctrines they encounter in these foreign schools and frequently become ardent spokesmen for them upon return. All three countries maintain contact with graduates from their schools, and strong ties are frequently established.

There are also complications involved. Differences in philosophy that have divided the Argentine and Brazilian officer corps in recent years are reflected to some extent in the Bolivian army. This subject is deserving of further analysis, particularly if one accepts the view that U.S. influence is faced with a decline in southern South America. Ovando was obviously influenced by the Peruvian experience and once spoke of "ideological confederation" between the Bolivian and Peruvian armed forces. It is beyond doubt that whatever the tenor of their future governments, Argentina and Brazil will maintain a keen interest in Bolivia and will attempt to influence political developments there. Judging from recent history, the effort will be made principally through the military establishment, particularly if the Andes Pact results in a Bolivia aligned economically with the west coast nations. In geopolitical terms, Bolivia is viewed as the subcontinent's heartland in strategic studies in the higher military schools of Argentina, Brazil, and Peru. (MacKinder is still very much in vogue in Latin American military geopolitical thought.) Argentina's long-term interest in the natural gas of Santa Cruz and Brazil's interest in the Mutun iron deposits on its western border with Bolivia are frequently mentioned in strategic writings.

The absence of a dominating leader of Ovando's prestige and stature at the top of the military hierarchy could lead to corrosive in-fighting for power in the military hierarchy, and, unless the president can muster considerable support from his civilian supporters, that office would not be exempt from the struggle. Banzer revived the post of commander in chief of the armed forces, which, as mentioned earlier, has the effect of dividing the army's power between two leaders. Significantly, he replaced his first appointee in the post in less than three months.

The political sentiments of enlisted men and noncommissioned officers are difficult to discern. Soldiers are in the majority Indian conscripts with a tradition of sullenness and docility. Since 1967, they can be legally held for up to two years on active duty, but funds seldom permit even a full year's service. Noncommissioned officers are trained in the "Sargento Parades" *Escuela de Clases* in Cochabamba, where sixty to seventy graduate yearly as corporals after a three-year course. The career noncommissioned officers have never played an independent political role. During the Torres regime, there appeared some manifestos allegedly emanating from an "NCO vanguard" which provoked considerable concern in the army general staff. Radicalization, or any type of political activism, among noncommissioned officers would introduce a new element that probably could not be accommodated within the institution as it is now structured.

Probably the greatest potential for change in political orientation lies with the middle-level officers who will move into the elite circle during the seventies. Their relationship to the society is not a symbiotic one despite the high degree of institutional socialization inherent in the career system. Young officers relate to the students and increasingly to radical intellectuals, although they still have few common bonds with the miners or urban workers. The potential for cooperation with the campesinos is particularly high. The curricula of the military schools and nation-building studies abroad give them a politicosocial sensitivity and outlook that varies significantly from the experience of the current dominant elite that formed its philosophy in the relative isolation and apolitical environment of the fifties.

The depth of ideological division within the officer corps is not clear, but the recent experiences leave no doubt that the institution is vulnerable to radical doctrines. And one comes away from La Paz with the impression of a highly radicalized society being propelled by its raging young toward a still unforeseeable destination, seeking change without thought or fear of consequences.[28] Both Ovando and Torres tried to harness this pell-mell rush and ride it to power. If the essentially middle-class coalition now in power fails to hold together and rally substantial popular support, the radicalized sectors of the society will find support in the military for another attempt at mobilization politics.

NOTES

1. Information on the academy (Colegio Militar) and its history appears from time to time in the *Revista Militar,* but data vary and must be cross-checked. A fairly accurate historical sketch appears in the July/September 1958 issue, pp. 73-77.

2. A brief history of the command and general staff school appeared in the *Revista Militar* of October/December 1969, pp. 63-70. The organic law of the armed forces limits certain command and staff positions to *diplomados de estado mayor.*

3. An eyewitness account of the 1943 coup by a German adviser to the Bolivian army may be found in Arnade (1950). The MNR side is explained in Verlarde (1955: 117-133).

4. Valle (1957) says that by mid-1950 over 260 MNR militants and officers had been tried by military courts for their parts in the 1949 uprising, and notes that 53 discharged officers were reincorporated by the government after the MNR victory of 1952. Velarde (1955) says that the army lost over 300 field grade officers to exile or

discharge between 1946 and 1949 and that most of them joined the MNR. An Argentine border police officer told the author that as a young agent in August of 1949 in La Quiaca, the Argentine border town, he was with a party that apprehended Paz and about a dozen followers who planned to capture the village of Villazon on the Bolivian side. Included were a few professional officers.

5. Two officers who were captains at the time told the author that Seleme's participation led many of the interior garrisons to believe that the 1952 revolution was just another palace revolt. Such a conviction probably contributed to the general absence of army resistance in the hinterland.

6. Gutierrez (1956), among others, holds that about 80% of the officer groups were discharged or exiled. However, General Alfredo Ovando Candia, armed forces chief in later years, estimated that no more than 250 were dismissed (see Brill, 1966: 81-83). There was, however, a general housecleaning of senior officers; only 2 of the 26 officers promoted to brigadier general or colonel in the annual promotions of 1949 played any role in the post-1952 army. The list appeared in *Revista Militar* of January/March 1949.

7. This is taken from *Revista Militar* of August/September 1954, pp. 131-135. The Colegio resumed its regular cycle and, in the graduation speech of 1955, in the presence of Paz and party dignitaries, the director of studies charged the new officers to serve the revolution "like the sons of the middle class, to which we all belong." The quote comes from *Revista Militar* of January/April 1956, p. 68.

8. For budget information, see Loftus (1968: 37); Wilkie (1969: 60-61); Anderson (1967: 330-331), using Bolivian Central Bank statistics, indicates that 24% of the public budget was devoted to defense in 1951, 14% in 1952, and 7% in 1957.

9. This is taken from *Revista Militar* of April/June 1968, pp. 151-152. Many officers have given the author similar accounts.

10. The school of arms had about twenty graduates from its ten-month advanced course in 1955, the command and general school ten from its two-year course. The widow of Villarroel spoke at graduation ceremonies of the latter, for which we used *Revista Militar* of January/April 1956, p. 38.

11. Officers who studied in Panama or the United States told the author they received $5.00 (U.S.) before leaving Bolivia, and thereafter were completely dependent on the small per diem paid by the U.S. government. Among the trainees of those years was the current president, then captain, Hugo Banzer Suarez, who stood at the top of his motor transportation officer's course in Panama in 1956.

12. Most sources indicate a rise in the percentage of government expenditures devoted to the military from about 7% in 1957 to between 12 and 13% in 1963. Wilkie (1969: 60-61) gives 12.6 for 1962 and 12.4 for 1963; Loftus (1968: 11) shows a rise in absolute terms from $2.4 million (U.S. 1960) in 1958 to $6 million in 1963. Colonel Julio Sanchez, ambassador to Washington, is quoted as saying that the army got $7.5 million, or about 13% of the national budget in 1963 (Brill, 1966: 83).

13. The Escuela de Altos Estudios Militares is a nine-month series of morning lectures and seminars conducted for selected superior officers from all services and distinguished civilians with an interest in security affairs. The course usually consists of about 25-30 students evenly divided between officers and civilians. The class also takes tours to key frontier points and other strategic areas. Through 1967, 93 officers and 58 civilians had completed the course, which is a prerequisite for promotion to general.

14. CITE was formed in 1963 with officers trained by an Argentine advisory group according to an anniversary article appearing in the *Revista Militar* of July/August 1968, p. 222. The acronym came to refer to both the training center and its operational parachute battalion.

15. Ronant Monje Roca, an MNR militant from his junior officer days, was the first commander. Monje was prominent in the "military cell" of the MNR and used the *Revista de la Fuerza Fluvial y Lacustre* to push the party line. After the ouster of Paz in 1964, Ovando replaced Monje and his entire staff, who had adopted naval titles, with army colonels. The river and lake force was subsequently rechristened the Bolivian Navy, and the officers again used naval titles.

16. Linares, president of Bolivia from 1857-1861, is described by Osborne (1964: 57) as "a capable and upright administrator who carried autocracy to the point of fanaticism and suppressed every stirring of opposition with no less ruthless ferocity than his predecessors."

17. Promotion lists appear in the La Paz newspapers and in *Los Tiempos* of Cochabamba. Fairly complete biographical data, particularly on career patterns, appeared in the *Revista Militar* of January/March 1968 for the promotion list of that year. Other information in this section comes from interviews with the principals or acquaintances. The officers involved are Generals Hugo Ortiz Mattos, Remberto Iriarte Paz, Alberto Guzman Soriano, Eduardo Mendez Pereyra, Efrain Guachalla Ibanez, Cesar Ruiz Verlarde, Juan Lechin Suarez, Marcos Vasquez Sempertegui, Jesus Via Solis, David La Fuente Soto, Sigfredo Montero Velasco, Luis A. Reque Teran, Gonzalo Guzman Agudo, Hector Fuentes Ibanez, Eufronio Padilla Caero, Jaime Flores Becerra, Jaime Paz Galarza, Rogelio Miranda and J. Zenteno Anaya.

18. That the Bolivian army survived 20 years of cataclysmic change to emerge as a fairly cohesive institution of national scope is due in great part to its educational system. Although the schools themselves are of inferior quality when judged against those of larger neighbors, the structure is probably the most elaborate to be found in any of the lesser developed countries of equal size in the world, and the system's socialization function cannot be exaggerated.

19. One exception was Juan Lechin Suarez, who served for four years as chief of the Bolivian Mining Commission (COMIBOL) during its most productive period 1964-1968. He graduated second in the 1942 *Colegio* class, and is a graduate of the U.S. Army Artillery School and the Command and General Staff College at Ft. Leavenworth, Kansas.

20. The acronym refers to the state oil monopoly. There is a similarity here to the programs and speeches of Peru's President Velasco, but Ovando's article preceded the Peruvian coup of October 3, 1968 by some months. He was, however, familiar with developmental philosophies being taught in the Peruvian army's Center for Higher Military Studies (for an analysis of the latter, see Einaudi, 1971).

21. The Interior Minister, Antonio Arguedas, fled Bolivia after admitting that he had sent the diary to Castro, and later charged that he had been forced to act as a CIA agent for over four years. He returned voluntarily to face a military trial. See the analysis by Malcolm Browne in the *New York Times*, September 17, 1968 and November 8, 1968. The trial records by some fluke fell into the public domain, and the La Paz newspaper *Presencia* published a series on the whole affair during the first week of April 1969 that revealed publicly for the first time how severely the scandals had shaken the government.

22. The interview also appears in *Christianismo y Revolucion* of April 23, 1970.

23. The speech was partially reproduced in *Estrategia* (Buenos Aires) of November/December 1969, pp. 22-24.

24. A copy of this bulletin is in the hands of the author. The *New York Times* was carrying a running account of the coup in its editions of October 5-9, 1970.

25. This account is taken from Latin American and U.S. newspaper sources, read carefully between the lines, and conversations with two eyewitnesses to the events in La Paz (see New York Times, 1971b).

26. "Subjective" control is achieved by causing military officers to identify with the political group in control of the state; "objective" control is achieved by turning the military inward to its specific duties and competence (Huntington, 1964: 80-85).

27. Nún (1969) points out that structural factors generate a chronic tendency toward instability, while circumstantial factors are accidental, operate at short term, and tend to stem from structural factors.

28. Over half the population is under 20; only 19% is over 40 (Agency for International Development, 1968: 8).

REFERENCES

Agency for International Development (1968) Economic Data Book: Latin America. Washington, D.C.: Government Printing Office.

ALEXANDER, R. A. (1956) The Bolivian National Revolution. New Brunswick, N.J.: Rutgers Univ. Press.

ANDERSON, C. W. (1967) Politics and Economic Change in Latin America. Princeton: D. Van Nostrand.

ARNADE, K. C. (1950) "The technique of coup d'état in Latin America." United Nations World (February): 21-25.

BARBER, W. F. and C. N. RONNING (1966) Internal Security and Military Power: Counterinsurgency and Civic Action in Latin America. Columbus: Ohio Univ. Press.

BEDREGAL, G. (1966) "El problema militar en Bolivia." Politica 5 (October).

BRILL, W. H. (1967) Military Intervention in Bolivia: The Overthrow of Paz Estenssoro and the MNR. Washington, D.C.: Institute for the Comparative Study of Political Systems.

--- (1966) "Military civic action in Bolivia." Ph.D. dissertation. University of Michigan.

EINAUDI, L. (1971) Untitled essay in L. Einaudi and A. Stepan, Latin American Institutional Development: Changing Military Perspectives in Peru and Brazil. Santa Monica, Calif.: RAND.

GUTIERREZ, A. O. (1956) The Tragedy of Bolivia. New York: Devin-Adair.

HUNTINGTON, S. P. (1964) The Soldier and the State. New York: Vintage.

LOFTUS, J. E. (1968) Latin American Defense Expenditures: 1938-1965. Santa Monica, Calif.: RAND.

MALLOY, J. M. (1970) Bolivia, the Uncompleted Revolution. Pittsburgh: Univ. of Pittsburgh Press.

New York Times (1971a) January 11.

––– (1971b) August 20-25.
––– (1969) September 27.
NUN, J. (1969) Latin America: The Hegemonic Crisis and the Military Coup. Berkeley: University of California Institute of Internal Studies.
OSBORNE, H. (1964) Bolivia: A Land Divided. London: Oxford Univ. Press.
PATCH, R. W. (1969) "American universities field staff reports." West Coast South America Series 12 (December).
––– (1960) "Bolivia and U.S. assistance," pp. 119-142 in Social Change in Latin America Today. New York: Vintage.
POTASH, R. (1969) The Army and Politics in Argentina, 1928-1945. Stanford: Stanford Univ. Press.
ROCA, R. M. (1968) Letter in Los Tiempos (July 2).
SILVA, C. M. (1968) "La justicia militar y las guerrillas." Revista Militar (January/March): 81-82.
VALLE, N. P. (1957) Calendario Historico de la Revolucion. La Paz: E. Burrillo.
VELARDE, J. F. (1955) Victor Paz Estenssoro, el Hombre y la Revolucion. La Paz: E. Burrillo.
WILDE, C.M.F. (1963) "Historia militar de Bolivia." La Paz. (private publication)
WILKIE, J. W. (1969) The Bolivian Revolution and U.S. Aid since 1952. Los Angeles: Univ. of California Press.

JAMES M. MALLOY
Department of Political Science
University of Pittsburgh
Pittsburgh, Pennsylvania

PERU BEFORE AND AFTER THE COUP OF 1968

In October of 1968, in what appeared to be the typical and time-honored fashion of Latin American military establishments, the Peruvian Army unseated the constitutionally elected government of Fernando Belaunde Terry. To many in the United States and elsewhere who saw Belaunde as a dedicated reformer in the best tradition of the Alliance for Progress, the *golpe* represented yet further evidence of the Peruvian military's determination to remain the "watchdog of the oligarchy." However, the new government, headed by General Juan Velasco Alvarado, declared from the first that, far from being an attempt to defend the oligarchy, their action represented the firm intention of the Peruvian military to carry out the basic reforms that previous civilian governments had been either too weak or too corrupt to effect. Indeed, the new government Velasco promised would be nothing short of nationalist and revolutionary. At first skeptical, outside observers were soon

AUTHOR'S NOTE: This is an article stemming from José Carlos Mariátegui's *Seven Interpretative Essays on Peruvian Reality,* translated by Marjory Urquidi, published by the University of Texas Press in 1971; and Anibal Quijano's *Nationalism and Capitalism in Peru: A Study in Neo-Imperialism,* translated by Helen R. Lane, published by Monthly Review Press in 1971.

taken aback as the new government, true to its word, seized the holdings of the U.S.-owned International Petroleum Company, decreed an extensive agrarian reform, and then instituted a myriad of other basic reforms influencing many spheres of Peruvian life.

Once over the initial shock, observers both within and outside Peru, began to declare that the new government, for good or ill depending on one's point of view, was truly a new phenomenon. The generals vigorously pursued their new reforms internally, challenged the United States on a number of fronts and sought to broaden their points of contact in the international sphere. In response, journalists, social scientists, and others began to pour forth a plethora of news accounts and articles seeking to explain and predict, as well as to defend or condemn, the new regime. To this date, the generals have largely managed to confound their would-be interpreters and continue to follow their often erratic and, thus far at least, unpredictable course. Nonetheless, a number of those who have followed the Peruvian scene remain convinced that Velasco and his colleagues represent not only a new role for the military man, but, perhaps, a whole new approach or model to the problems of development in Latin America.

Given the new interest and fascination with Peru, it is particularly fortuitous that 1971 has seen the publication, in English, of two important books on Peru written by Peruvians: the publication, in English for the first time, of José Carlos Mariátegui's *Seven Interpretative Essays on Peruvian Reality,* and the simultaneous publication, in English and Spanish, of Anibal Quijano's *Nationalism and Capitalism in Peru: A Study in Neo-Imperialism.*

Mariátegui's work, first published in 1928, is a, if not the, classic diagnosis of the ills of Peruvian society in the twentieth century. Since it first appeared, this collection of essays has had a tremendous impact in Peru and the rest of Latin America as well. Most would-be Peruvian reformers or revolutionaries from the 1930s on have read either his work or interpretations of it or have followed men influenced by his ideas. Thus, it would be no exaggeration to say that, by reading Mariátegui, one gets a good sense of the reality Velasco and his colleagues are reacting against, as well as a feeling for the mood of reformism building in Peru since the thirties and culminating, perhaps, in the present regime. This is not to say that, by reading Mariátegui, we get a direct key to the thinking of the Velasco regime; for José Carlos was an avowed Marxist while the generals are self-declared anti-Marxists. By reading Mariátegui, we get rather a specific vision of the problems of Peru and, above all, a taste of the mood of those who would deal with them. In short, in these essays, we get at least a partial picture of Peru before the generals decided to adopt the role of reformers.

Anibal Quijano, on the other hand, is a contemporary Peruvian sociologist. In his short but powerful book, we get the first extensive and serious attempt, by a social scientist, to sort out and evaluate the new regime's performance thus far and to project the general lines of its future development. Like Mariátegui, Quijano writes from a Marxist perspective. Unlike many contemporary Marxists both in and out of Peru, who have yet to come to a definite position on the regime, Quijano has defined his position and set it forth clearly. His evaluation is, to say the least, negative.

Aside from giving a picture of Peru before and after the generals, a reading of these two works is instructive for at least one other reason: Both authors approach Peru from a Marxist perspective, and it is therefore interesting to compare Mariátegui's Marxist vision of the 1920s with that of Quijano's contemporary stance. In my view, Quijano comes out the worse in comparison.

Perhaps such a comparison is unfair because, although both are Marxists, they do approach the problem from different intellectual perspectives: Quijano, from a more modern empirical social scientific view and Mariátegui, from the more classic literary-journalistic tradition. The fact remains that, although stimulating, Quijano's work comes off as the product of a man with economically dominated tunnel vision when compared to the forceful breadth of Mariátegui's essays. One would expect a Marxist, whatever his intellectual style, to emphasize economic factors in his interpretation. Both authors do just that; but, whereas Quijano focuses on the economic and only the economic, Mariátegui weaves a more complex fabric, in which he tries to show how the economic dimension relates to other social dimensions, such as race, culture, religion, national identity, and so on, and how they, in turn, relate back to and affect the economic. Mariátegui gives us a more complete understanding of how sub- and superstructures interrelate to create a whole.

The stark contrast between the broadness of the two men's vision is not simply the result of different intellectual styles, tastes, or methods, but is instead indicative of an important development in contemporary approaches to the question of underdevelopment, its causes and solutions. Within contemporary social science, one can, without setting up straw men, delineate two broad and mutually antagonistic schools of thought on the question of underdevelopment. One, formulated by established North American academics, tends to focus on underdeveloped countries as isolated systems located at fixed points on a developmental continuum with positions on the continuum determined mainly by dominant cultural values. In recent years, this establishment position has been challenged strongly by a revisionist school of both North and South American (other third world areas as well) social scientists, who charge the former with developing a conservative ideology, designed to mask the role of the United States and Europe in causing underdevelopment in Latin America. To this group, underdevelopment is an economically determined phenomenon, created by the realities of the international capitalist system, which locks the Latin countries into a permanent position of inferiority and external dependence, while simultaneously causing a similar internal fission within each country between a dominant, modern, urban sector tied to the international capitalist system and a dependent, exploited, rural hinterland. In any event, although the picture is cloudy, there is a tendency toward a division between those who emphasize the casual force of values and those who emphasize economic factors.

There is little doubt that the latter group has launched an important and essentially correct critique of the former established theories. However, in their desire to demolish all aspects of the previous theories, they appear to have relegated questions of values, identity, and the like to an at best extremely marginal position in social analysis. Mariátegui's work demonstrates clearly that, even for a Marxist, such a position is tenuous and essentially false. Moreover, his essays demonstrate that, while one must examine and unearth the economic structure of the international system as such, one must also pay heed to the peculiarities of the specific national units of the system—peculiarities shaped not only by universal economic laws but by the specific historical, racial, and cultural composition of the respective nations. Mariátegui's book makes clear that, for the moment at least, the problem of development will have to be approached within the framework of the nation state and on a state-by-state basis. Thus, for Mariátegui, it is essential that each nation form an identity and a national purpose, based not only on an understanding of its position in the international system, but also of its own economic and cultural evolution.

Aside from its intellectual content, this edition of Mariátegui's seven essays stands out due to an excellent translation by Marjory Urquedi, and a most useful introduction by the distinguished Peruvian historian, Jorge Basadre. Basadre's introduction traces Mariátegui's intellectual and political development up to his untimely death at the age of 35. Basadre's introduction has the merit of placing Mariátegui within the intellectual and ideological context of his time, a period characterized, above all, by ideological effervescence and confusion as populist, anarchist and various Marxist lines vied with one another for public attention. Basadre recognizes the basic Marxism of Mariátegui, but challenges the usual image of him as a founder of the Peruvian communist party, which was actually formed on May 20, 1930, shortly after his death. Basadre argues that the question is beside the point, as Mariátegui was still in the process of ideological and political development and, therefore, like many Marxists in Peru and elsewhere, might have evolved along many different lines.

Aside from the arcane historical dispute of Mariátegui's relationship to the Peruvian communist party, Basadre's point is important for any contemporary reading of this book. As Mariátegui's specific political line was as yet incomplete and evolving, so was his vision of Peruvian society. Moreover, as the title of the work indicates, this is not a coherently planned book, but rather a collection of essays written at different times for different purposes. These two facts account for both the air of incompleteness, which hangs about the work, and the oftentimes superficiality of some of its passages.

As Basadre notes, it should also be kept in mind that Mariátegui was not an academic scholar but a self-trained journalist and activist. Thus, again as the title indicates, these are not works of research, but of interpretation and ideological exhortation. Like any such work, it overemphasizes some factors, slips over others, and is ultimately dependent on the quality of information available for analysis, which, in that day, was not always the best. Nonetheless, this is a major work by a major writer who, if he had lived longer, might well have achieved the stature of a Peruvian *Gramschi*.

Mariátegui's essays touch on seven themes: economic evolution, the Indian, land, education, religion, regionalism versus centralism, and literature. It is not possible here to review his thoughts on all these themes or to present an in-depth critique of his views. Let me instead simply try to whet appetites by indicating some of his major lines of analysis.

The underlying theme of the book is that contemporary Peru is the product of two major historical developments:

(1) the subjugation of a highly developed indigenous civilization by the Spaniards and their imposition on the Indians of an essentially feudal system and

(2) the later integration of part of Peru (i.e., the coast) into the world capitalist system.

From these developments emerges a situation similar to what many contemporary authors refer to as "dependence" and "internal colonialism"; that is, a backward rural hinterland dominated by the more advanced coast which, in turn, is dominated by foreign capitalist powers.

The essentially feudal forms and values of the Spanish colonial epoch survived into the twentieth century, especially in the rural highlands: the key to their dominance is the latifundia (large estate) ruled by the *gamonales* (large land owners).[1] Thus, despite the emergence on the coast of more modern capitalist-like forms (introduced mainly by foreigners), Peru has never experienced a full-blown capitalist stage of development, the primary reason being that the Peruvian elite has not had "the same entrepreneurial temperament" as foreign capitalists, and, hence, the "moral, political, and psychological elements of capitalism" never found a favorable climate in which to flourish. In short, for Mariátegui (p. 21): "Capitalism is not just a technique: it is also a spirit. This spirit, which reaches its heights in the Anglo-Saxon countries, is weak, incipient, and rudimentary in Peru."

Thus, Mariátegui sees the problem of Peru as one of both economic forms and moral, psychological, and spiritual values.

It is evident that the first part of his analysis (i.e., the dual nexus of internal and external economic colonialism) informs, to a large degree, the thinking and actions of the present government, its advisers, and many of its critics–Quijano, as well. The Velasco government has declared its intention, backed by such actions as agrarian reform and nationalization, to break both forms of dominance and thereby, spur industrial development and establish national autonomy. What the new form of society will be has been undefined, except to say it will be Peruvian *sui generis,* neither capitalist nor socialist. To critics such as Quijano, the notion of a Peruvian "third way" is camouflage for the real intention–to establish a "national-capitalist" system. To him, the new regime may be nationalist and reformist, but it is by no means socialist and, therefore (by definition perhaps), not revolutionary. For him, the generals have clearly demonstrated that their primary goal is to liberate the energies of a retarded capitalist system, so as to realize the capitalist promise in Peru. Given this fact, the generals, Quijano argues, are, at best, limited nationalists, in that capitalist development in Peru is predicated upon a restructuring rather than a breaking of the international capitalist system of domination. Thus, even if successful, the generals are, of necessity, condemning Peru to a–perhaps new but nonetheless subservient–role in the international capitalist order.

Quijano's small but useful book is a point-by-point, factual, and almost exclusively economic analysis of how the new system of national capitalism is being constructed in Peru and then how this system is being subjected to a new form of external domination. He does so by analyzing the implementation of regime policies in a number of spheres–e.g., agrarian reform, petroleum, mining, banking, industrial, external finance, and so on. Quijano stresses that his analysis is preliminary, but he feels confident enough to predict, at the end of his book, that the new system is doomed to failure.

In the long run, he argues, the system of national capitalism cannot solve the basic contradictions of Peru. The fundamental contradiction emerges from the fact that the workers have paid and will continue to pay the heaviest price for the implementation of the new system. This deprivation will give rise to increased class consciousness among the workers. When this consciousness develops, the other contradiction will come into play–namely, that Peru does not have a strong "nationalist anti-imperialist bourgeoisie" capable of asserting either its local or international autonomy. The political weakness of the workers and its nationalist posturing have bought the regime time, but as the contradictions become more apparent and the workers more conscious, the demise of national capitalism will be inevitable.

> It may be these regimes who propose, but their contradictions and the workers dispose. Latin America in the coming decade cannot help but be the scene of the greatest and most profound revolutionary movements, and it will not be long before Peru steps out from the wings onto this fiery stage [Quijano, p. 119].

Mariátegui would agree with a good deal of Quijano's analysis. His view was that, although Peru is backward because of the failure of capitalism to develop, the day of a capitalist solution in Peru is long since past. Although he gives little in the way of a project of how it is to come about, Mariátegui, like Quijano, saw socialism as the only solution for Peru.

Yet there is a dimension of Mariátegui's analysis which is starkly absent in Quijano's book and, rhetoric notwithstanding, from the actions of the present regime as well. This dimension again springs from Mariátegui's sensitivity to questions of culture and identity—a sensitivity which is thus far not evident in the actions of the Velasco government and not at all evident in the economically bounded analysis of its critics such as Quijano.

This dimension, which is most powerfully explored in Mariátegui's essays on education, regionalism, and literature, is the cultural identity of Peru—a reality which, for Mariátegui, will not be found in the modern industry of the coast favored by the generals nor in the workers of the same coast, to whom Quijano looks, but rather in the Sierra, in the Indian. Again, for Mariátegui, the issue is not simply one of forms, but of "mentalities."

Spanish colonial and international capitalist exploitation are only one side of the Peruvian problem; the other face of the problem is the Indian, who does not simply represent a social type, but "a people, a race, a tradition and a spirit." In my view, Mariátegui's position on the Indian is, at times, confused and somewhat naive. For example, he alludes to a "socialist" spirit in Inca civilization and intimates that it survives in the Indian and could be the basis of a contemporary socialism. This idealized view of the Inca empire was quite common in Mariátegui's day and inflamed the imagination of many Latin American writers, such as the Bolivian Tristan Marof in his *Justicia del Inca.* The great bulk of recent anthropological studies, not to mention the experience of both the Mexican and Bolivian agrarian reforms, have effectively demolished the myth of some inherent or culturally derived inclination on the part of the Indian toward harmonious collectivism.

But even if one rejects this particular idealization of the Indian, one cannot escape the question posed by Mariátegui. He is no simple nativist who wants to return to some glorified Indian past; he notes, simply, that as it stands, there is no

Peruvian identity and, without forging such an identity, Peru can never become master of its own fate. Peruvian identity cannot be found in the criollo (Spanish-American) or the mestizo (mixed race and culture); for both these types are formed out of the colonial experience and are, thus, part of the problem.

Nor does the solution lie in integration, which, in contemporary parlance, means nothing more than the incorporation of the Indian into the extant and dominant criollo and the mestizo cultural forms, both of which are predicated on the exploitation of the Indian. As it stands, the Indian in Peru is confronted with one of two choices: remain an Indian (i.e., culturally and economically isolated and exploited) or begin acculturation (as defined by his exploiters–mestizo, criollo). The latter course of action needs the Indian's denial of who he is, or, to put it more bluntly, its needs begin with an act of self-denial and, therefore, self-hatred on the part of the Indian. He must remake himself in someone else's image and likeness. The recent experience of the United States attests to the moral bankruptcy and political weakness of such a policy of benign neglect toward exploited racial groups.

Yet I think that most observers would agree this is exactly the solution being adopted by the present government. The agrarian reform, in the Sierra, is primarily an economic program which, while it unseats the gamonal, installs in his place mestizo technicians and administrators who, as heads of the new cooperatives, have the power to define the purposes and goals of the new units. In any event, the life situation of the Indian remains much the same; his life is controlled by others, unless he takes the crucial steps away from being an Indian. The present government is clearly nationalistic and oriented toward modernization, but it is also an expression of mestizo Peru: thus it says to the Indian, "Accept the modern world as we define it for you."

But, in relationship to this problem, Quijano also has little to offer. In his book, there is virtually no discussion of the problem of the land and no analysis at all of the Indian's role in Peru's future. Indeed, as I noted before, there is no discussion of Peru's racial and cultural complexity and the attendant issue of national culture and identity. To be sure, there are some references to peasant discontent, but Quijano devotes only three pages to the present regime's agrarian policy; even then, he focuses exclusively on the agroindustrial complexes of the coast. It is as if the Indian—over one-third of the population—did not exist.

When he focuses—and I think correctly—on the question of who is paying the price of the new order, Quijano ignores the Indian peasant and focuses on the plight of the worker and other city folk. In the same vein, when he paints an apocalyptic picture of Peru's revolutionary future, he looks to the worker and intellectuals to be its authors and, again, ignores the mass of Indian peasants. In confronting this lopsidedness, one feels compelled to question both his fairness and his judgment. Quijano wants to avoid the fact that Peru's urban working class has never been very revolutionary. Moreover, he ignores the fact that, in the late 1950s and 1960s, when the spark of revolution appeared to be ignited in Peru—precipitating in large part the coup of 1968—it was not due to an uprising of revolutionary workers, but to widespread uprisings in the Sierra of Indian peasants. Many recent studies of the Peruvian working class (see, for example, Aportes, 1972) have shown that the Peruvian worker, his unions, and many of the parties which seek to represent him follow a mainly bread-and-butter form of activism, designed to consolidate past gains and make new advances on a particularistic basis.

These remarks are not made to denigrate the Peruvian worker, belittle his plight, or ignore his potential role in Peru's future. They simply seek to point out the tremendous gap in Quijano's analysis and to suggest that neither he nor the generals have, as yet, come to terms with the fundamental questions posed by Mariátegui concerning the cultural and racial complexity of Peru. Before his death, Mariátegui posed questions that still remain unanswered. Can Peru, he asked, achieve the autonomous and just society that both reformers and revolutionaries claim to seek unless the Indian is viewed as more than a passive instrument to be manipulated by mestizo and criollo society? Unless the Indian is given or takes the role of a self-moving and creative force in defining a new Peruvian reality, can he truly see a societal manifestation of himself? In grappling with the question of identity and, particularly with the relationship of coastal Peru, epitomized by the hegemony of Lima, and the Sierra, Mariátegui (p. 181) posed a prior tactical question, which should continue to vex all would-be reformers and revolutionaries:

> It [Lima] is the capital today, but will it be the capital tomorrow? This is not an irrelevant question in terms of a bold search into the future. The answer depends on whether first place in Peru's social and political reform is given to the rural indian masses or to the coastal proletariat. The future of Lima, in any case, is inseparable from the mission of Lima, or even the will of Lima.

Although I find Quijano's factual description of the policy lines of the present regime persuading and agree with his argument that the elite of the modern private sector will benefit to the detriment of lower social groups, and that Peru's external dependence will be restructured but not broken, two final questions occur to me regarding his study. First is Quijano's concept of national capitalism an adequate tool to grasp the reality that is emerging in Peru? Second, is his prediction of the ultimate failure of the new system and an inevitable worker-based revolution realistic?

An answer to the first question depends, to a large degree, on whether one believes that the only available routes to modernization are some variants of capitalism and socialism. This is, no doubt, the generally held view, particularly, by many on the left. In recent years, however, many analysts, from within and outside Latin America, have begun to suggest the utility of reviving the concept of "corporatism" as a more adequate analytical category to grasp the reality of Latin America. As an offshoot, in part, of the Iberian Peninsula, corporatist legal, political, and economic concepts are obviously an important part of the Latin American heritage. Moreover, it is evident that, not only is corporatism far from dead in Spain but, under the present Spanish regime, a concerted effort is being made to modernize within a corporatist framework. Although the concept of the corporate state is a premodern concept, can we conclude that it cannot adapt to the pressures of the modern industrial world? If we cannot so conclude (I think we cannot), then may it not be that some modern form of the corporate state could well emerge in many Latin American countries?

There are many dimensions to the corporate state concept. Among the most salient are: society viewed as a functionally integrated organism, with each part, from the lowest to the highest, performing an assigned role; from this, a concept of a fixed hierarchical division of power, status, and wealth; and, from the above, the notion that central authority is to be valued over the particular interests of any parts of the social organism. A corporate state is, therefore, authoritarian and elitist. Corporatism rejects the liberal atomistic concept of society and its belief in an unfettered individualistic competition in an unregulated market. Corporatism—as expressed in both Spanish and Catholic philosophy—sees conflict as the major social evil, and the root of social conflict lies in the extreme economic deprivation caused by an unregulated market. Thus corporatism councils policies that alleviate the material plight of the lower orders without changing the basic hierarchical structure of the social organism—e.g., paternalism. In the corporate scheme, the state is charged with the task of maintaining social order and controlling conflict by regulating, but not absorbing, the social and economic dimensions of society—in the totalitarian state, they are absorbed. In sum, the corporate state is authoritarian, elitist, paternalistic, and state-regulated.

In the case of Peru, it is evident that some changes are taking place and that the Velasco government is devoted to the pursuit of economic development by means of industrialization. In the overall Latin American context, however, the orientation of the Velasco regime is hardly new or unique to Peru. Since at least the 1930s, political movements, such as the MNR in Bolivia, AD in Venezuela, and Peru's own APRA have proposed similar approaches to Latin America's problems. Many of the ideas associated with these so-called "populist" movements have been codified in Latin American constitutions, such as the Mexican of 1917, the Cuban of 1940, and the Bolivian of 1938. And the fact that the governments of Arbenz in Guatemala, Perón in Argentina, and Busch and Villarroel in Bolivia demonstrate the idea that military government is the best means to impose such reforms is also hardly new. The present Peruvian government is directly linkable to this reformist tradition: a tradition which proposed change, but not a total restructuring of Latin American society. There were limits to the changes that the so-called populists sought. These limits were transcended by the Cuban revolution of 1959, and, as many of their own statements indicate, the Peruvian generals sought to forestall such a radical outcome in Peru by imposing timely reforms in the long-established populist tradition. This fact has led observers, such as the Peruvian sociologist Julio Cotler (1970-1971), to refer to the Velasco regime as a system of "military populism."

Cotler's concept of military populism comes closer to describing the emerging system in Peru than Quijano's concept of national capitalism, but I think it is still not close enough. This is not the place for a detailed analysis of Latin American populist programs, but if one examines those programs, constitutions, and, more to the point, the actions of so called populist governments, such as Mexico's PRI and Bolivia's MNR, one will note a decidedly elitist and, at best, paternalistic, rather than populistic orientation. The concept of the state enshrined in these programs and constitutions reads as an updated, modernized version of the classic Hispanic corporate state. The changes sought by Latin America's populists have not been in the spirit of Marx, nor of some capitalist counterpart but, rather, in that of the nobleman in Giuseppe di Lampedusa's novel, *The Leopard,* when he said: "If we want things to stay as they are, things will have to change."

At times, things got out of hand and went too far, as in the early stages of the Mexican and Bolivian revolutions, but the limited reformist orientation remained firm, and both countries veered back to a more elitist and authoritarian model based upon a revised hierarchical division of wealth, status, and power. Velasco's regime, cognizant of the Mexican and Bolivian experiences, does not intend to let things get out of hand. The Peruvian military clearly intends to orchestrate a series of timely adjustments within a rigidly authoritarian mold. To put it in Peruvian military parlance, "Sectarianism of either the left or the right will not be tolerated."

To this date, we have seen a number of important developments in Peru. The state has taken on the task of regulating the economy, and the public sector has expanded considerably. Certain economic activities have been put outside the private sphere (for example, the agro-industry of the coast) but private local and foreign investors have been invited to exploit opportunities in manufacturing, mining, and petroleum, as long as they conform to governmental guidelines. Indeed, the government has provided significant incentives for the establishment of modern, technologically oriented business, such as immediate compensation for expropriated lands if the capital will be invested in the industrial sector. To be sure, elements of the old, so-called oligarchy have been unseated, but the previous elite has been far from eliminated. In numerous speeches, Velasco has made clear that those elite groups willing to adapt and cooperate with the new developmental scheme will not only survive, but prosper. As the new system rolls into gear (presuming it does), the expansion of administrative and technical jobs will benefit the middle class, but, at least in the short run, it is hard to see any significant payoff for the masses of workers, peasants, and urban marginals, with the probable exception of skilled workers in strategic industries.

Concomitant with these developments, the Velasco regime has sought to incorporate the bulk of the population into a centrally directed administrative structure. The regime has sought to bypass the established political parties and unions and involve people in government-sponsored cooperatives, neighborhood committees, the new industrial communities, and the like. The task of coordinating these residentially and occupationally based organizations has gone to a new state mobilization agency (SINAMOS). Established corporate groups, such as the church, and professional associations remain intact, and the regime seeks, and in the main has received, their cooperation. Some established business groups have complained about some of the government's reformist measures, but business associations have gone largely unmolested, and there are increasing signs of a growing coordination between organized business and government planners. In sum, recent developments in Peru smack heavily of an updated form of corporatism. Indeed, one might say Peru resembles a new form of fascism, in which the more atavistic characteristics of German and Italian fascism have been pruned.

Seen in this light, the Peruvian approach is not really unique in the Latin American scene; Peru can be grouped with other authoritarian regimes that are attempting to spur development, such as Brazil, Argentina, Bolivia, and Mexico. There are obvious differences among these regimes, but I would argue that these are superficial and fluctuate with circumstances. If and when, for example, the Peruvian government is challenged, like the Brazilian regime was, I expect it would react every bit as repressively as the Brazilians have done. There is a fundamental developmental theme upon which these regimes have variations. In my view, that theme is best described as national corporatism—a system that attempts to grapple with the problems of development and modernization by fusing modern economic forms with traditional corporate values and institutions.

In ideal-typical terms, the national corporate model can be defined as follows: The state is based on a mixed economy with large private and public sectors existing side by side—the nature of the mix can vary from time to time as policies shift. Power, status, and wealth are concentrated in the hands of a plural elite of modern entrepreneurs, technocrats, bureaucrats, and military officers. The power of the elites is grounded in an alliance of powerful modern corporate interests in the public and private sectors. These interests are coordinated by an authoritarian state, controlled by a nationalistic military, or a single dominant party, which seeks to regulate the private and public corporations, cooperatives, and so on, so that their activities feed national economic growth. The "costs" of the new system will fall on those least able to bargain in the limited nationally regulated market; that is, those who do not control powerful corporate organizations, such as peasants, urban marginals, and the less-well-organized workers. Social conflict will be regulated by the time-tested Mexican methods of repression or, when groups demonstrate power, by cooptation. Thus, the leaders of well-organized worker groups, for example, may achieve semi-elite status, while their followers will be somewhat better off than other lower groups, thereby dividing the lower orders and halting class-based action. Foreign private and public interests play an important role in this process, and, therefore, the basic structure of external dependence may change and even weaken, but it will not be abolished.

The question remains of whether the emergent Peruvian system and others like it can survive into the foreseeable future. Quijano thinks not; but I think he is being unrealistic when he predicts its imminent downfall, particularly at the hands of the workers. The early 1960s saw a spate of books which painted vivid portraits of the inevitable, imminent revolution in Latin America. For various reasons, the expected revolutions failed to materialize. Rather the 1960s witnessed a complex and contradictory series of political patterns that ranged from apparent counter-revolution in Brazil, to possible ballot box socialism in Chile, to military reformism in Peru, while a variety of countries continued to simply muddle through. With the notable exception of the *tupamaros,* the much-heralded guerrilla movements were either contained or destroyed. Cuba, the symbol of the revolution to come at the beginning of the decade, had by its end lapsed into a bureaucratized form of state socialism, more concerned with its own economic problems than in fomenting revolution in the rest of the continent.

Given the experience of the 1960s, the only realistic thing one can say about Latin America as a whole, in the 1970s, is that it will continue to manifest many different and contradictory patterns of change. One fact is clear, however; there are more military-dominated authoritarian regimes in Latin America today than there were in 1960. Indeed, the vast bulk of the population of the region now lives under the tutelage of such regimes. If one classifies Mexico as an authoritarian–if not military–regime, it is also clear that the existence of nonsocialist forms of authoritarian states is the major characteristic of contemporary Latin America.

One may wish to reject the label of national corporatism, but there is no gainsaying the fact that authoritarian regimes such as Mexico and Brazil—despite their internal contradictions and the continuance of massive injustices within their borders—have demonstrated a remarkable capacity for survival. There is also no escaping the fact that the Latin American working class has not been a major focal point of resistance to these regimes. In fact, many of the most advanced sectors of the working class have made their peace with these regimes at the expense of other workers, urban marginals, and peasants.

If we look for indicators of weakness or strength in these regimes hitherto, the only indicator appears to be economic success. Where regimes of this type have been successful economically, they have been rather stable politically—e.g., Mexico and Brazil; where they have been unsuccessful economically, they have been rather unstable—e.g., Bolivia and Argentina. Even in the latter cases, however, instability has manifested itself mainly in the form of a game of musical chairs among factions of the military.

Regimes such as the current government in Peru cannot be simply wished or predicted away. In the short run, at least—which is the reality in which most people live out their lives—the longevity of the emergent system in Peru will turn on its gross economic success, even if that success is at the expense of many in the lower social orders.

NOTE

1. In Colombia, a gamonal is the local political boss or what would be one *jefe politico* in other Spanish-American nations. It is not a common term outside the Andean nations.—Ed.

REFERENCES

Aportes (1972) Number 24 (April).

COTLER, J. (1970-1971) "Political crisis and military populism in Peru." Studies in Comparative International Development 6: 95-113.

THOMAS I. DICKSON, Jr.
Department of Political Science
Auburn University
Auburn, Alabama

AN APPROACH TO THE STUDY OF THE LATIN AMERICAN MILITARY

Political scientists today are deeply engaged in the search for better ways to study the phenomena within their purview and for more insightful characterizations of political processes. Examination of the politically active military in developing countries has not escaped the trend. Yet this remains a segment of the discipline where impressionism and conjecture still are much in vogue. Indeed, the state of the art of analysis of the military role in less-developed areas is discouraging to some (Nordlinger, 1970). Even without taking a glum view, however, there is ample room to hold that more precise and structured studies of the politicomilitary phenomenon are much needed. The approach to the study of the Latin American military suggested here, which has possible applications to other geographic sectors of the underdeveloped world, is not intended to substitute for, but rather to complement forms of analysis that customarily have been followed.

The assumption is, however, that data employed and methods used presently provide inadequate bases for explaining or even satisfactorily identifying some of the phenomena that can be observed in military rule in Latin America. A further assumption is that this does not derive from the fact that the data are unobtainable but, in part, from the fact that the more common analytical perceptions do not lead to exhaustion of potential resources.

As used here, approach does not imply detailed schemata for analysis, nor does it specifically include or exclude certain analytical tools. While some hypotheses will be put forward, they are hypotheses associated with justification for the suggested approach, and they would be subject to a degree of verification or disproval by the approach. Approach, then, refers to an orientation toward the study of the Latin American military; an orientation, it should be noted at the outset, that only can be applied in certain, but important, sets of circumstances.

The idea is to start with the contents and timing of economic policies adopted by ruling military regimes, and their performances in carrying out those policies. From thence, although this need not be an invariable data collection sequence, attention would be given to the decision-making processes that result in adopting certain economic policies and rejecting others, noting differences of opinion that arise within the councils of military governments. From economic output factors–regulative, extractive, and distributive–the effort would be made to work through the decision-making processes to identify individuals and groups associated with opposing identifiable points of view and the balancers and to deduce factors that impel the courses of action taken. If a total decision-making diagram cannot be drawn in every case, all would not be lost. Something should be learned from the output analysis alone, although the premise here is that it is primarily a launching pad, even though one that would involve substantial preliminary effort to construct.

There is nothing extremely innovative in this suggestion insofar as its basic component elements–output and decision-making analyses–are concerned. Groth (1971) has argued in a broader context the case for output analysis, and it is inherent in the functionalism of Almond and Powell (1966). In like manner, decision-making case studies are well known to political scientists and have been employed to some degree in studies of less-developed countries (see, for example, Paige, 1968; Stern, 1970; Pye, 1970).[1]

Some Hypotheses

A review of the recent experiences with military governance in four Latin American countries–Argentina, Bolivia, Brazil, and Peru–indicates that the following three hypotheses, although not necessarily only these, are worthy of attention:

Hypothesis 1–That the immediate (ostensible) causes for military coups and the conditions of their effectuation have little explanatory or anticipatory value with regard to the economic policies of the regimes resulting from the coups.[2]

Hypothesis 2–That the economic policies of military regimes are not carried in with the coup but develop subsequently as the leadership takes hold of the process of governing.

Hypothesis 3–That military regimes are not monolithic but are split within themselves on economic policies and, thus, policies adopted, sometimes falteringly, may well reflect the outcomes of factional conflicts within the officer corps rather than being "institutional" products.[3]

With regard to hypothesis 1, that the causes for coups have little predictive value insofar as subsequent military-sponsored economic policies are concerned, the case of Argentina is illustrative (Argentinian military government information is based on news sources and Alexander, 1969; Cohen, 1967; Craig, 1967; Goldwert, 1966; Jordan, 1970; Lee, 1969; Thompson, 1970). A plethora of causes have been cited for deposing the Illia government and starting an extended period of the military in power. Included are basic orientations ascribed to the military, such as its patriotic bent and attendant distrust of civilian politicians and their corrupt ways, and a belief by armed forces officers that their technical training and technocratic outlook better qualify them for rule. More immediately to the point, however, are the weak and unstabilizing performance of the Illia administration and Congress, a conflict with Illia over control of the armed forces, and the fear of a growing *peronismo*. This last motive is viewed by some observers as having been the most influential. Mismanagement by the civilian government, as seen by military leaders, did extend to the economic sphere, encompassing such items as inflation and the burden of support of the railroads, the ports, and the sugar industry. So it could be assumed that these problems would occupy the military regime, but this did not foretell the nature of the policies to come.

Peru yields a somewhat similar picture (Peruvian military government sources include news sources and Astiz, 1969; Bourricaud, 1970; Clark, 1971; Clinton, 1971; Cotler, 1971; Einaudi, 1969; Estep, 1970; Grayson, 1971, 1970; Yglesias, 1969). Among causes cited for the October 1968 coup are: Military fear that the APRA was reestablishing a position of strength on the Peruvian political scene; political, social, and economic ineffectiveness of the Belaunde regime and the belief that a sellout was under way on the IPC issue; scandals in the administration; conflict between Congress and the military; the personal ambitions of General Velasco. Here again, economic considerations weighed on the officers making the coup, but it appears there was little more than a sense of malaise. No precise design for economic rehabilitation was discernible this early. While certain economic problems obviously had to be dealt with, the coup arose from a number of other factors of equal or greater importance, and the nature of the economic program instituted by the military was not predictable from the causes for the coup. Accepting Almond's (1969) proposition that prediction in political science is probalistic in nature, it would be unfair to task observers of Peru for their almost universally erroneous expectations on the economic course the Peruvian military would follow. But the fact that it happened, coupled with the degree of conviction evinced by some soothsayers about the course of the revolution, indicates difficiencies in some of the assumptions that are frequently made about military rule.

Similar cases can be built for Bolivia and Brazil; the causes of the coups are inconclusive with regard to prospective economic policies. In effect, many of the causes were not economic at all, and, where they impinged on the economic sphere, they were likely to be little more than vague perceptions that the civilian leadership was doing poorly and somehow the military could handle these matters more efficiently.

If hypothesis 1 is true, hypothesis 2 follows. The military government, unless it serves merely as a caretaker awaiting the return of civilian rule (which did not occur in any of the cases used as examples), must somehow attempt to deal with economic issues, if for no other reason but that they are there. Hypothesis 3, of course, is concerned with the way this comes about.

Nevertheless, the theory that military regimes develop their economic policies while in power does not depend for demonstration exclusively on the premise that they come to power without having already developed such policies. Hypothesis 2 need not depend for its proof on being a residual. The timing, the piecemeal nature of economic actions, and the evident influence in some instances of outside advisers strengthen the assumption. While the Castelo Branco regime in Brazil moved with remarkable suddenness, the rapid creation and implementation of economic policies seems to have derived in important part from the early appointment of the civilian economist Roberto de Oliveira Campos as Minister of Planning (information concerning the sequence of Brazilian military governments beginning with the coup of March 1964 are drawn from news sources and Evans, 1968; Graham, 1967; Poppino, 1971, 1969; Roett, 1970; Rosenbaum, 1970, Schneider, 1971; Tuthill, 1969). In Argentina, the Ongania government created a development council for economic planning but may not have gotten under way in vigorous form until the major devaluation and import policy changes of March 1967, nine months after the coup, and then under the influence of the civilian Minister of Economy, Dr. Adalbert Krieger Vasena. In the period of uncertainty after ascension to power, some labor leaders are reported to have believed that the new government might be Nasserist.[4] In Peru, the nationalization of the IPC followed hard on the heels of the coup. While some commentators regarded this as evidence of radicalism, for most the IPC affair was a special case that proved no such thing, even though nationalization was accompanied by a rhetoric of revolutionary intentions. Some nine to eleven months later, concrete evidence of a strong reform orientation came with the passage of the agrarian reform law and the expropriation of the largest sugar plantations.

Bolivia provides highly visible evidence of the core element of the third hypothesis, that the military is internally split on economic issues, and situations of conflict exist within the bosom of the institution (information on the Bolivian military government sequence since September 1969 comes primarily from news sources; also see Cohen, 1971). The nationalization of Gulf immediately caused some erstwhile adherents of General Ovando to withdraw support. Rumors of possible counter-coups proved founded a year later when a "rightist" coup was followed immediately by a "leftist" coup, and then the leftist leaders succumbed within a year to another rightist coup. The socioeconomic orientation that goes with shorthand popular referents like right and left is not always very clear in the context of Bolivian politics, but dissension within the military was abundantly evident. While not so spectacular, differences of opinion among officers in the Argentine, Brazilian, and Peruvian armed forces also have been related. A "Peruanist" element is reported in the Argentine military. A split is often referred to in Brazil's military, and observers of Peru have undertaken to divide military leaders along a line of degree of enthusiasm for reformist measures by the regime, even identifying the role players by name.

That the divisions are there does not tell us how they influence the decision-making process in military regimes. It is likely that the impact is different in different instances, with reactions ranging from compromise to repression or some combination of both. But, that military regimes formulate policy as a segmented association of power holders does seem a reasonable proposition and should be in the foreground of analyses of the military and military rule.

This brief presentation possibly has slighted a number of factors; however, the three hypotheses presented do not seem exceptional. That the Argentine military is divided, for instance, is no new bit of information: It frequently has been noted (see especially Goldwert, 1966). But this fact tends to be glossed over and the military treated as if it were a coherent, homogenous whole when its governmental policies are recounted. An argument of this article is that these hypotheses deserve to be treated as fundamental in such reviews.

Applying the hypotheses to a mythical case might illustrate them more clearly. Let us imagine a country in which political forces are more or less equally divided among left, progressive center, and right political parties. The left wins a plurality and gains control of the executive. Over time, in order to effectuate radical reforms promised, the government becomes repressive of the opposition, which then provokes the military to act. In addition, some of the more radical left-wing elements are getting out of hand, requiring use of the relatively apolitical military to maintain order. The economy becomes less productive, and inflation grows. There is some civilian effort to meddle in internal military affairs. Finally, the situation develops to where an element of the military, fronted by a highly respected general officer, becomes sufficiently motivated and strong to take control. This group, especially the army members who predominate, are of the usual middle- and lower-middle-class social background.

The hypothetical example to this point is a classic case of military intervention to protect the country and the constitution, as well as the sanctity of the military institution. We might reasonably posit that the officers would set up a careholder government, soon turning control back to the civilians. But in the fractionated circumstances described, this might prove difficult to do, and recent examples of the continuance of Latin American military regimes in power might have an influence. So our coup makers hang on. Having done so, they have to rule.

Since the constitutionalist-type coup was against the left, we might anticipate a major swing back to the right. However, in a country with one-third leftist voters and another third progressive center, given the origin of the officer corps, the rightist orientation probably would not be the only one found in the officer class. Now the officers, who earlier could concentrate on their military roles, have to make political decisions. Their predispositions, possibly ranging the economic policy spectrum, come to the fore, and intragroup conflict becomes the mode of conducting public affairs, even if not publicly.

The Suggested Approach and Some Considerations

The mythical coup described above brings into the discussion two popular theories about military-political action that serve to demonstrate the analytical gap remaining. One is the "swing man" concept (Needler, 1966). While valuable for certain purposes, we might note that in two classic instances–Naguib of Egypt and Castelo Branco of Brazil–the prominence of the least committed in the coup did not result in a "soft line" return to civilian rule. Also, the two military regimes in question have evolved economic policies that are regarded as quite different. The other is the middle-class social composition of the officer corps, some of the implications of which presumably are mitigated, in that the "military phenomenon has a relative consistency of its own" (Nún, 1968).[5] But, again, neither middle classism nor military consistencyism seems to adequately explain the differing sets of actions of military regimes in Latin America.

Latin Americanists delight in arguing the issue as to whether the military is retarding or fostering socioeconomic progress. Lyle McAlister (1965: 85) wrote of this argument:

> Both traditional and revisionist views, however, are based on inadequate data and are generally expressed in continental-wide generalizations which do not apply to specific situations. Careful

> studies of individual countries are needed as bases for a truly comparative evaluation of the role of the military in Latin America.

This situation seems to have changed little. A recent article arguing the issue again was based on highly impressionistic responses to very generalized data (Needler, 1969). If competent scholars settle for no greater precision, possibly it is, as McAlister stated, a problem of an inadequate data base.

Approaching the problem through individual case studies of military regimes focusing on economic policies and decision-making seems to have a variety of advantages.

The time selected for detailed analysis is the period of highest visibility of military role players. The military, as rulers, must act. While in their "barracks," currents and views within the institution will be difficult for the scholar to plumb and might not even come to light. As already suggested, many of the political, social, and economic views of military officers could be latent, be little more than predispositions toward certain philosophies, until they are forced to the surface through the need for practical application. A number of scholars have commented on the difficulty of collecting information on the Latin American military (for mention of several, see McAlister, 1966). This problem does not dissolve when military officers come to power, but conflicts among them become more important for policy, and the press and other observers do seem to hear of differences. Moreover, decisions have to be made and policies announced and implemented. Many of these things are not secret and can be read in newspapers, public pronouncements, and decrees.[6] Case studies like William Brill's (1967) excellent work on the Barrientos coup in Bolivia, based in large part on interviews, shows that it is not always impossible to gather firsthand information on and even from the military in power.

Admittedly, the collection of information on decision-making still is skimming off the top, but the top is the leadership element, and this is a legitimate vein of analysis in political science.[7] In addition, this approach might be criticized as pragmatic in the pejorative sense: It does not tell us where we are going, nor does it tell us when we have arrived. To this the plea is "Guilty!" But we lack a map, our knowledge of the area is limited, and the road signs are few and far between, so we must wander a bit to seek our bearings and make our finds. At least we can attempt to do our wanderings according to an ordered pattern, like the reconnaissance pilot who flies predetermined azimuths that yield coverage of an area, even though he does not know precisely what the terrain is like nor what he might find hiding in it.

Stress has been placed on building a data base of economic output factors. This is not to argue that a similar effort could not be undertaken for political factors. However, economic ones seem to be better adapted to a first try. It might be noted initially that economic policy considerations are not alien to the concerns of political scientists assaying the military in Latin America and other developing countries. Much of the progressive-reactionary argument derives from varying perceptions of the economic efforts of military regimes. Second, economic aspects are possibly less difficult to classify, sort, and manipulate according to schemes that will attract fairly wide acceptance than are political aspects. Even so, the task would be difficult, particularly in areas like categorizing policy decisions rather than measuring items subject to monetary or other ordinal measures. A third consideration is that the economic side offer greater prospects for developing models that synthesize the policies themselves and their implementation, rather than expressing the viewers' opinions about those policies. Much of the writing on the military in politics in Latin America tells us almost as much about the emotional reactions of the authors to military regimes as it does about the military regimes themselves. Bias and ethnocentrism cannot be weeded out altogether, but some diligent gardening is in order.

Logically, the work of producing a format for implementing this approach would be shared among political scientists and economists with knowledge of the developing world in general and Latin America in particular. But some characteristic features can be foretold. Any format should be value-free (not concerned with good and bad) insofar as possible. It should identify time sequences, since these are important to identifying, for cross-national comparisons, the ways in which policies develop and are crucial to decision-making analyses. It should be broad enough to fit a variety of samples if the greatest benefit is to be obtained from the comparative analysis of multiple cases.[8]

Many other considerations would also enter into creating a scheme whereby the Latin American military could be studied following the lines indicated in this paper. However, no effort is made here to establish such a format. Rather, the purpose is to loft the idea that a combination of economic policy output and decision-making analyses would constitute a reasonable and rewarding approach. While aloft, the idea might be shot at and even brought down. But it can be hoped, instead, that the proposal will gain adherents to help carry it forward.

NOTES

1. While methodologically not the most elegant, case studies of the decisional process apparently still are most common (Robinson, 1968: 60). That they are rare on a cross-national basis is indicated by their omission, except, possibly, in the context of political anthropology, from the methods recounted by Merritt (1970).

2. This observation relates only to immediate observable factors without attempting to preempt the area of more basic analysis such as Taylor (1970).

3. This hypothesis is not intended to imply that the officers acquire nothing from the military experience itself. The influence of military schools has been cited by observers of Peru and Brazil; discussions of the effects of "professionalization" are common in the literature; Price (1971) argues the case for what he calls "reference-group theory."

4. The term Nasserism often has been used in Latin America to describe social reformers and promoters of economic development in the military (McAlister, 1965: 90). In connection with the hypothesis under consideration here, it is interesting to note that Nasser himself was a slow starter. Much of what we today call Nasserism dates from the late 1950s and early 1960s, not from the 1952-1955 period when Nasser established himself as the military ruler of Egypt (see, e.g., Peretz, 1959; Lenczowski, 1966). As late as 1958, the subsequently radical regime of Qasim in Iraq, although inspired by the Egyptian model, came into power with vague feelings of social injustice, but no clear aims or programs (Marr, 1970). Of course, the prototypes that have been developed may speed the processes of military reformism in the future, something that case studies would help determine.

5. Sloan (1971: 941) takes a strong stand for the view that institutional loyalty is probably more pervasive than class allegiance.

6. Luckham (1971: 10-11) recounts the case of Nigeria in 1966-1967 where circumstances following a coup resulted in a rich flow of published information (not all reliable) about events involving the military.

7. Obviously, it is not the only vein. However, the present state of groping for data to make deeper analysis is illustrated by Ropp's (1970) article using bibliographic data of cadets at the School of the Americas in the Canal Zone to attempt to define the socioeconomic orientation of the Latin American military.

8. Although Anderson's (1967) categories are placed in a broader, longer-range framework, they could generate ideas for the form of analysis suggested here. Anderson also sketches factors influencing the politicoeconomic decision-making framework.

REFERENCES

ALEXANDER, R. J. (1969) An Introduction to Argentina. New York: Frederick A. Praeger.

ALMOND, G. A. (1969) "Political development: analytical and normative perspectives." Comparative Pol. Studies 1 (January): 447-470.

--- and G. B. POWELL, Jr. (1966) Comparative Politics: A Developmental Approach. Boston: Little, Brown.

ANDERSON, C. W. (1967) Politics and Economic Change in Latin America. Princeton: D. Van Nostrand.

ASTIZ, C. A. (1969) Power Groups and Power Elites in Peruvian Politics. Ithaca: Cornell Univ. Press.

BOURRICAUD, F. (1970) "Los militares: ¿por que 'y paraque?' " Aportes 16 (April): 14-55.

BRILL, W. H. (1967) Military Intervention in Bolivia: The Overthrow of Paz Estenssoro and the MNR. Washington, D.C.: Institute for the Comparative Study of Political Systems.

CLARK, P., Jr. (1971) "Military government in Peru, 1968-1971." South Eastern Latin Americanist 14 (March): 1-5.

CLINTON, R. L. (1971) "The modernizing military: the case of Peru." Inter-Amer. Economic Affairs 24 (Spring): 43-66.

COHEN, A. (1971) "Bolivia: internal instability and international dependence." Current History 60 (February): 78-83.

--- (1967) "Revolution in Argentina?" Current History 53 (November): 282-290.

COTLER, J. (1971) Political Crisis and Military Populism in Peru. New Brunswick, N.J.: Rutgers Univ. Press.

CRAIG, A. (1967) "Argentina: the latest revolution." World Today 23 (May): 206-215.

EINAUDI, L. R. (1969) The Peruvian Military: A Summary Political Analysis. Santa Monica, Calif.: RAND.

ESTEP, R. (1970) The Role of the Military in Peruvian Politics. Montogomery, Ala.: Maxwell AFB Aerospace Studies Institute.

EVANS, R. D. (1968) "Brazilian revolution of 1964: political surgery without anaesthetics." International Affairs 44 (April): 266-281.
GOLDWERT, M. (1966) "Dichotomies of militarism in Argentina." Orbis 10 (Fall): 930-939.
GRAHAM, R. (1967) "Brazil's dilemma." Current History 53 (November): 291-297, 308.
GRAYSON, G. W., Jr. (1971) "Peru's military populism." Current History 60 (February): 71-77, 116.
--- (1970) "Peru's military government." Current History 58 (February): 65-72.
GROTH, A. J. (1971) Comparative Politics: A Distributive Approach. New York: Macmillan.
JORDAN, D. C. (1970) "Argentina's new military government." Current History 58 (February): 85-90, 116-117.
LEE, M. (1969) "Argentine political instability." J. of Inter-American Studies 11 (October): 558-570.
LENCZOWSKI, G. (1966) "The objects and methods of Nasserism," pp. 197-211 in J. H. Thompson and R. D. Reischauer, Modernization of the Arabic World. Princeton: D. Van Nostrand.
LUCKHAM, R. (1971) The Nigerian Military: A Sociological Analysis of Authority and Revolt, 1960-67. Cambridge, Eng.: Cambridge Univ. Press.
McALISTER, L. N. (1966) "Recent research and writing on the role of the military in Latin America." Latin Amer. Research Rev. 2 (Fall): 5-36.
--- (1965) "Changing the concepts of the role of the military in Latin America." Annals of Amer. Academy of Pol. and Social Sci. 360 (July): 85-98.
MARR, P. A. (1970) "The Iraqi revolution: a case study of army rule." Orbis 14 (Fall): 714-739.
MERRITT, R. L. (1970) Systematic Approaches to Comparative Politics. Chicago: Rand McNally.
NEEDLER, M. C. (1969) "The Latin American military: predatory reactionaries or modenizing patriots." J. of Inter-American Studies 11 (April): 237-244.
--- (1966) "Political development and military intervention in Latin America." Amer. Pol. Sci. Rev. 60 (September): 616-626.
NORDLINGER, E. A. (1970) "Soldiers in mufti: the impact of military rule upon economic and social change in the non-Western states." Amer. Pol. Sci. Rev. 64 (December): 1131-1148.
NUN, J. (1968) "A Latin American phenomenon: the middle-class military coup," pp. 145-187 in J. Petras and M. Zeitlin (eds.) Latin America: Reform or Revolution. New York: Fawcett.
PAIGE, G. D. (1968) The Korean Decision. New York: Free Press.
PERETZ, D. (1959) "In search of a doctrine: a study of the ideology of the Egyptian revolution." Middle East Forum 35, 13-17, 33.
POPPINO, R. E. (1971) "Brazil's third government of the revolution." Current History (February): 102-107, 115.
PRICE, R. M. (1971) "A theoretical approach to military rule in new states: reference-group theory and the Ghanaian case." World Politics 23 (April): 399-430.
PYE, L. W. [ed.] (1970) Case Studies in Comparative Politics–Asia. Boston: Little, Brown.

ROBINSON, J. A. (1968) "Decision-making: political aspects," p. 60 in Volume 4 of International Encyclopedia of the Social Sciences. New York: Macmillan and Free Press.

ROETT, R. (1970) "A praetorian army in politics: the Brazilian military, 1946 to the present." Presented at the annual meeting of the Southern Political Science Association, Atlanta, November.

ROPP, S. C. (1970) "The military and urbanization in Latin America: some implications of trends in recruitment." Inter-Amer. Economic Affairs 24 (Autumn): 27-36.

ROSENBAUM, H. J. (1970) "Brazil's military regime." Current History 58 (February): 73-78, 115-116.

SCHNEIDER, R. M. (1971) The Political System of Brazil: Emergence of a "Modernizing" Authoritarian Regime, 1964-1970. New York: Columbia Univ. Press.

SLOAN, J. W. (1971) "Three views of Latin America: President Nixon, Governor Rockefeller, and the Latin American consensus of Vina del Mar." Orbis 14 (Winter): 941.

STERN, R. W. (1970) The Process of Opposition in India: Two Case Studies of How Policy Shapes Politics. Chicago: Univ. of Chicago Press.

TAYLOR, C. L. (1970) "Turmoil, economic development and organized political opposition as predictors in irregular government change." Presented at the annual meeting of the American Political Science Association, Los Angeles, September.

THOMPSON, J. (1970) "Argentine economic policy under the Ongania regime." Inter-Amer. Economic Affairs 24 (Summer): 51-71.

TUTHILL, J. W. (1969) "Economic and political aspects of development in Brazil and U.S. aid." J. of Inter-American Studies 11 (April): 186-208.

YGLESIAS, J. (1969) "Report from Peru: the reformers in brass hats." New York Times Magazine (December 14): 58-59.

JOHN M. BAINES
Department of Political Science
University of Wyoming
Laramie, Wyoming

U.S. MILITARY ASSISTANCE TO LATIN AMERICA
An Assessment

This paper examines the nature of the U.S. Military Assistance Program (MAP) to Latin America and the historical development of the Military Assistance Program in the hemisphere. It further analyzes this program with regard to the two major criticisms levelled at it:

(1) that Military Assistance Programs have perpetuated "militarism" in the form of military coups and strong-man military regimes; and

(2) that Military Assistance Programs have encouraged large military forces where they are not needed.

Changes in U.S. policy toward Latin America are noted as they affect MAP–i.e., the shift in U.S. policy from one of fostering hemispheric defense to one of promoting internal security and economic development. Finally, an assessment of the impact of this change in U.S. military assistance policy forms the conclusion of this paper.

AUTHOR'S NOTE: The author would like to acknowledge the assistance of Lt. Col. Roger L. Crump (USA) in the research of this article.

The entire question of military assistance to developing countries has generated considerable debate in recent years. It has been charged that military assistance programs furnish support for military dictators and strong men and thus diminish the chances for the survival of civilian-led democratic regimes.

In addition to having encouraged large military forces where they are not needed, it is further alleged that military assistance programs have perpetuated militarism—especially in Latin America, where the military coup has long been utilized as a means of changing governments (see Hahr, 1969: 15). However, before analyzing these objections to MAP, it is first necessary to view the background and nature of the Military Assistance Program.

Background of U.S. Military Assistance

Historically, the interests of the United States in Latin America have been to develop and preserve the security of the Western hemisphere, promote trade, extend democratic concepts, and foster democratic governments throughout the area. This was particularly true of U.S.-Latin American policy during the period 1889 to 1932. However, the period 1933 to 1939 showed a marked shift in U.S. policy toward Latin America. The Good Neighbor Policy, and the efforts of the United States to disengage itself from the internal affairs of the Latin American states by withdrawing from its protectorates and renouncing its right to intervene, created an increased confidence and trust in the United States and its policies. This trust and confidence was to endure throughout World War II.

Prior to 1938, European countries were the primary source of military assistance to Latin America. German and French missions were most active. The German influence was particularly strong in Argentina and Bolivia, while the French operated most actively in Peru and Chile. The Italians engaged in similar activities in Ecuador. The German and French missions stressed the importance of the military not only as the traditional defender of the nation, but military academies staffed by French and German officers also stressed engineering and management (see Dame, 1962: 32-33).

Although the United States sent several military missions to Latin America prior to 1938, it was not until that year that the United States became actively engaged in building the military forces of the hemisphere. In 1938, the United States embarked on a program of attempting to undercut Axis influence in Latin American military establishments. U.S. military missions began to be established, and the training of Latin American officers in U.S. military schools was increased (see Hovey, 1968: 49).

By 1940, Latin American military forces, largely functionally dependent on European sources of supply, began to look to the United States as a major arms supplier. In return for these arms shipments, the United States negotiated for base facilities (see Lieuwin, 1965: 76). Throughout World War II, the United States attempted to enlist the aid of the Latin American states in a supporting role as allies. Some states, notably Chile and Argentina, were reluctant to do so; while others exhibited varying degrees of cooperation. The most active allies were Brazil, which sent an infantry division to Italy, and Mexico, which sent a fighter squadron to the Pacific. In 1942, the Inter-American Defense Board was established to deal with matters of hemispheric defense. However, a multilateral defense arrangement proved impossible to obtain, and the United States had to rely heavily upon bilateral defense arrangements.

During World War II, bilateral lend-lease agreements were concluded with eighteen Latin American states. Under these agreements, military equipment was provided in exchange for commitments from contracting countries that they would assume specific hemispheric defense reponsibilities. Approximately $500 million was provided in the form of lend-lease grants, equipment, and economic assistance (see McArdle, 1964: 46). By 1945, the United States had acquired a monopoly in military assistance to Latin America.

The elements of wartime cooperation between the United States and Latin America were continued, and the United States attempted to maintain its monopoly in the area of military assistance through the emphasis on inter-American military cooperation. The foreign ministers directed the Inter-American Defense Board to plan for the defense of the hemisphere, and further recommended (United States[9]: 574):

> That the American Republics, in accordance with their capabilities and constitutional processes, should so direct their national military policies that, through self-help and mutual aid:
>
> I. Each will strengthen those armed forces and resources best adapted to the collective defense and maintain those armed forces in such a status that they could be deployed promptly in defense of the hemisphere and:
>
> II. Each will cooperate with the others in military matters to the end that the necessary collective strength of the hemisphere is developed to combat aggression.

The adoption of this resolution was largely the result of the U.S. desire to obtain Latin American support for the Korean War effort, and its perceptions of the threat of Communist penetration of the hemisphere.

In order to assist the Latin American states in meeting these responsibilities, the U.S. Congress appropriated $38,150,000.00 for direct military assistance to Latin America through the Mutual Security Act of 1951 (see Mutual Security Act, 1951: section 105). Under this act, states receiving military assistance had to agree to specific terms and conditions. Aid was to be granted only for specific programs consistent with the defense plans drawn up by the Inter-American Defense Board. The Latin American states receiving military assistance had to agree to use the arms and equipment furnished "exclusively for missions important to the defense of the hemisphere" (United States[8]: 2-3). In addition, U.S. military advisers were to determine the military requirements of each of the recipient countries.

Acceptance of the terms of assistance took the form of bilateral agreements between the United States and the contracting Latin American countries. The first of these agreements was concluded with Ecuador in January of 1952. Also in 1952, agreements were concluded with Chile, Colombia, Cuba, and Peru. These were followed in 1953 by agreements with Brazil, the Dominican Republic, and Uruguay. Nicaragua and Honduras concluded agreements with the United States in 1954, with Haiti and Guatemala in 1955, and with Bolivia in 1958. All these bilateral arrangements took the form of executive agreements and thus did not require the consent of two-thirds of the U.S. Senate before becoming effective.

Through fiscal 1959, military assistance was extended only to the thirteen countries listed above. Three types of assistance were offered:

(1) *direct* grants of equipment;

(2) opportunities to purchase U.S. weapons and equipment at low prices;

(3) provisions for the establishment of U.S. Army, Navy, and Air Force missions to assist in the training of the recipient Latin American military forces.

Throughout the 1950s, the primary goal of the Military Assistance Program was improving the capability of the Latin American states to aid in the defense of the hemisphere from external attack.

Beginning in 1960, the scope and nature of the Military Assistance Program underwent significant change and redefinition. U.S. policy makers realized that the nature of the threat to the hemisphere had changed. The emergence of Castro's Cuba stimulated indigenous Latin American Communist parties, and the Cuban revolutionary example stirred insurgency throughout the hemisphere. During its first years in office, the Kennedy Administration took another look at the concept of hemispheric defense and concluded that internal Communist subversion and guerrilla warfare were the real threats to U.S. security interests. In 1961, the Kennedy Administration "decided to shift the basis of its military policy in Latin America from hemispheric defense to internal security, from protection of the hemisphere's coastline and sea lanes to internal defense of Latin American governments against Castro-communist subversion, terrorism, and guerrilla warfare" (see Lieuwin, 1965: 101-102).

As a result of this shift in military policy, the nature of U.S. military assistance changed significantly. This change was from a policy of encouraging external defense to one of promoting internal security and, concomitantly, social and economic development programs. This emphasis required that military assistance programs concentrate on the development of small, mobile forces trained in the techniques of counter-insurgency. U.S. anti-guerilla advisory teams began instructing Latin American military forces in these techniques. In addition, Latin American states were urged to equip their forces with small arms, helicopters, and trucks, rather than heavier armaments such as tanks, jet aircraft, and large warships.

A major emphasis of the counter-insurgency program was placed on "civic action." Civic action is basically the use of military forces on projects useful to the local population in such areas as education, public works, public health, and agriculture. This program was to contribute to economic development and deny the insurgents a political base for their operations. The emphasis on civic action stems in large measure from studies made by the Draper Committee in 1959, which concluded that

> the military establishments of our own and friendly nations have the human and material resources for making important contributions to economic as well as to military phases of our foreign aid program particularly in the underdeveloped areas [President's Committee To Study the Military Assistance Program, 1959: Annex D].

Advocates of a civic action role for the military forces of Latin America considered that such a role would lessen the likelihood of three types of military activity that were considered detrimental to U.S. interests:

(1) First, civic action involvement will motivate the military to assist rather than veto political and economic reform. If South American armies are given extensive civic roles, they will

TABLE 1
MILITARY ASSISTANCE DELIVERIES TO LATIN AMERICA
(in millions of dollars)

Fiscal Year	*Amount*	*Fiscal Year*	*Amount*
1952	.2	1962	54.3
1953	11.2	1963	51.8
1954	34.5	1964	62.9
1955	31.8	1965	51.3
1956	23.5	1966	80.7[a]
1957	27.1	1967	56.4[a]
1958	45.6	1968	27.2[a]
1959	31.5	1969	22.7[a]
1960	32.3	1970	21.4[a]
1961	45.0		

SOURCE: Hovey (1968: 51).
a. Figures for 1966-1970 were taken from United States [5]: 703-707.

expedite reform rather than staging coups d'état against their authors.

(2) Second, civic action involvement will motivate the military to give priority to domestic development rather than to external ventures.

(3) Third, civic action involvement will motivate the military to acquire economic and managerial skills and multiply their commitment to mass modernization (see Bobrow, 1966: 101).

The shift in U.S. military assistance policy was clearly evidenced by Secretary of Defense Robert S. McNamara when, in 1965, he stated that 52% of military assistance to Latin America was for internal security, while 15% of the total was spent for civic action programs (see Hovey, 1968: 60). Although appropriations for military assistance to Latin America have been reduced in the last three years, the emphasis is still upon internal security and civic action (see Table 1).

Some Major Criticisms of the
U.S. Military Assistance Program

Criticisms of military assistance programs have usually arisen in connection with congressional consideration of military aid programs. The Congress has been concerned that the Department of Defense has undue control of these programs, thus diminishing the influence of the Department of State in this area of foreign policy. In addition, Congress has been concerned about the use of executive agreements in concluding military assistance pacts. While these criticisms may be important, they do not represent congressional disenchantment with the Military Assistance Program as an instrument of policy. Two other critical charges levelled against the Military Assistance Program are, in my view, more serious, since they question the entire program. Primarily, it is charged that military assistance programs increase the likelihood of military coups and overt military interference in civil politics and the political process in general. An example of this charge is the following statement by Senator J. William Fulbright (United States[6]: 610-612):

> It is true, is it not, that three of the countries which have received the largest amount of our military aid–outside of the Western European countries–Turkey, Pakistan and Korea, have all had military coups supplanting a civilian government, and now are under what could be called a military dictatorship.
>
> I was wondering whether there is any relationship here between these events and the extent of our military aid.

One method of determining the validity of this charge that military assistance increases the likelihood of military coups is to compare the number of coups that occurred before the program was extended to the number of coups after the program was under way. In testimony before a congressional committee in 1969, the Department of Defense presented comparative figures on the number of coups that took place before and after the initiation of direct military assistance programs in the early 1950s. The testimony revealed that since the authorization of military assistance to Latin America in 1950 through 1969, there were 39 coups. Yet over the 19 years preceding 1950, there were 42 coups in Latin America (United States[5]: 666-667). Clearly, the military coup had been a major instrument for effecting political change long before the advent of the Military Assistance Program, sponsored by the United States. Indeed, the evidence suggests no direct correlation between military assistance and the incidence of coups (see Table 2).

A further indication of this lack of direct correlation between military coups and the Military Assistance Program may be obtained by comparing the relationship between the number of military coups and the Military Assistance Program worldwide. Between January 7, 1961, and June 5, 1969, there were 50 military coups and 28 attempted coups (see Tables 3 and 4). These figures do not include the 8 coups in South Vietnam and Laos, which stemmed from conditions of continuous open warfare in those countries. Countries with moderate or large military assistance programs ($1 million or more) experienced 24 military or attempted coups; while countries with small military assistance programs (under $1 million) or no programs at all experienced 54 military or attempted coups. These data further indicate no direct correlation between military coups and the Military Assistance Program (see Tables 5 and 6).

TABLE 2

TOTAL MILITARY ASSISTANCE PROGRAM AID TO SELECTED LATIN AMERICAN STATES (U.S. fiscal years–millions of dollars)

Country	*1968*	*1969*	*Total (MAP) 1946-1969*
Argentina	13.7	17.7	129.1
Bolivia	3.5	1.6	22.6
Brazil	26.8	19.0	350.7
Chile	7.6	4.6	143.2
Colombia	12.2	6.7	106.2
Dominican Republic	2.3	2.2	25.0
Ecuador	2.8	2.6	52.0
Guatemala	2.3	1.1	16.6
Honduras	1.0	0.6	7.7
Mexico	0.1	0.1	10.5
Panama	0.3	0.4	3.2
Paraguay	1.8	1.0	10.4
Peru	9.9	2.9	141.0
Uruguay	2.0	1.7	41.4

SOURCE: Agency for International Development (1971).

TABLE 3

MILITARY COUPS AND MILITARY ASSISTANCE PROGRAMS (MAP)

In Nations With:	*1961*	*1962*	*1963*	*1964*	*1965*	*1966*	*1967*	*1968*	*1969*	*Totals*
moderate or large MAP[a]	2	3	3	2	3	1	1	1	0	16
very small MAP or none[b]	2	1	7	2	2	9	5	5	1	34
Totals	4	4	10	4	5	10	6	6	1	50

SOURCE: United States [5] : 667.
a. Value of military assistance averaged more than $1,000,000 per year.
b. No military assistance or value of military assistance averaged less than $1,000,000 per year.

TABLE 4

ATTEMPTED MILITARY COUPS AND MILITARY ASSISTANCE PROGRAMS (MAP)

In Nations With:	*1961*	*1962*	*1963*	*1964*	*1965*	*1966*	*1967*	*1968*	*1969*	*Totals*
moderate or large MAP[a]	0	3	3	0	0	0	1	1	0	8
very small MAP or none[b]	2	3	1	3	2	3	2	4	0	20
Totals	2	6	4	3	2	3	3	5	0	28

SOURCE: United States [5] : 667.
a. Value of military assistance averaged more than $1,000,000 per year.
b. No military assistance or value of military assistance averaged less than $1,000,000 per year.

A similar conclusion was reached by Charles Wolf, Jr., in a study prepared for the Assistant Secretary of Defense for International Security Affairs. The Wolf (1963: 28) study concluded that

> dictatorships, military and otherwise, are a frequent and disturbing phenomenon in Latin America. But their occurrence and recurrence is not properly attributable to simple causes like military aid or defense programs. Indeed, these factors do not appear to play a significant role in the process at all. Rather, the explanation lies in a complex set of influences rooted in Latin American history, social structure, and political tradition.

Military involvement in the Latin American political process has been a political tradition in most Latin American states since the wars of independence in the early nineteenth century. Armies, both public and private, have often been the final arbiters in the political process. Traditionally, Latin American military forces have been viewed as elites that have acted as a brake on rapid social and economic change. The military has been identified as representing entrenched conservative interests, rather than as instruments of social change in their respective societies. However, in the 1960s, due in part to changing recruitment and socialization patterns within the military, and the threat of Castro-Communist subversion, the military has become increasingly identified with the need for social change. Indeed, in countries such as Peru and Bolivia, the military is seeking to become the agent of this change by promoting gradual reforms that avoid the stagnation of the conservative right, and the violent upheaval of the radical left.

Increasingly, one of the factors that has recently led to military coups has been the failure of civilian regimes to move rapidly and effectively enough to solve pressing national problems. In growing numbers and with greater frequency, Latin American military forces are becoming identified with those civilian elements of society that support economic development and technological progress. This changing attitude of the military results more from internal social and political

TABLE 5

MILITARY ASSISTANCE PROGRAM–VALUE OF GRANT AID DELIVERIES: 1950 TO 1970 (in millions of dollars)

Area and Country	*1950-1963*	*1964-1967*	*1970*
Worldwide	*28,016.0*	*6,355.7*	*521.6*
East Asia and Pacific[c]	7,209.2	3,108.2	281.8
Cambodia	83.2	8.7	4.8
China, Republic of	1,960.3	567.9	37.9
Indochina	709.6	–[a]	–
Indonesia	53.3	21.3	4.0
Japan	772.1	83.1	.6
Korea	1,706.3	1,224.0	216.3
Philippines	268.4	139.6	15.7
Thailand	415.0	173.9	–
Vietnam	846.6	629.8	–
Near East and South Asia[c]	4,349.3	1,680.9	164.6
Afghanistan	2.3	1.7	.2
Greece	1,044.9	441.3	30.2
Iran	556.0	264.3	15.2
Iraq	46.1	.5	–
Jordan	20.6	32.4	1.0
Lebanon	8.4	.6	.1
Saudi Arabia	28.8	6.4	.5
Turkey	1,994.2	795.2	116.6
Europe[a]	13,542.8	703.5	12.8
Belgium	1,189.6	48.0	–
Denmark	530.0	87.9	–
France	4,144.5	8.5	–
Germany	900.4	.4	–
Italy	2,160.0	130.3	–
Luxembourg	8.2	b	–
Netherlands	1,153.7	63.3	–
Norway	701.1	187.3	.3
Portugal	293.9	24.0	1.3
Spain	436.4	141.9	10.9
United Kingdom	1,034.0	.5	–
Yugoslavia	693.9	–	–
Africa[c]	92.8	168.2	21.8
Congo, Dem. Rep.	.1	24.9	3.1
Ethiopia	62.3	78.2	11.2
Liberia	2.0	5.1	.4
Libya	4.4	11.2	.3
Morocco	10.1	26.4	1.2
Tunisia	10.7	16.4	5.4
Latin America[c]	388.8	363.6	27.4
Argentina	2.8	39.8	2.4

Table 5 (Continued)

Area and Country	*1950-1963*	*1964-1967*	*1970*
Latin America (Continued)			
Bolivia	5.4	16.8	1.2
Brazil	150.6	67.1	4.3
Chile	52.0	39.4	2.0
Colombia	39.4	51.0	3.9
Cuba	10.6	–	–
Dominican Republic	8.2	14.4	2.1
Ecuador	22.2	18.9	2.0
Guatemala	5.3	10.9	2.0
Honduras	2.6	4.6	.3
Nicaragua	4.5	7.5	1.1
Paraguay	.9	7.9	.8
Peru	41.1	45.6	1.9
Uruguay	27.5	13.6	1.7
Venezuela	1.6	7.7	.8
Nonregional	2,433.1	331.4	13.1

NOTE: For years ending June 30. Covers programs authorized and appropriated by the Foreign Assistance Act and the Foreign Assistance Appropriation Acts. Does not include military assistance to Thailand and the other countries in Southeast Asia, which was formerly a part of this program but which has been withdrawn and put in the Department of Defense appropriation. Represents military equipment and supplies delivered and expenditures for services. Includes (a) equipment and supplies procured for the Military Assistance Program; and (b) services, such as training, military construction, repair and rehabilitation of excess stocks, supply operations, and other charges.

SOURCE: United States [7].

a. – represents zero.

b. Less than $50,000

c. Totals include countries not shown separately.

conditions within each country, and the increasing awareness by the military of these conditions, than from the Military Assistance Program.

Generally, during periods of civilian rule, Latin American military forces have assumed an ambivalent role in the political process. The military will usually support a civilian president as long as he does not tamper with the military budget or perquisites and as long as he can maintain civil peace without undue reliance on the military as an internal police force. Yet the spectre of military intervention has always loomed in the background; and with few exceptions civilian rulers are aware of

TABLE 6

MILITARY ASSISTANCE PROGRAM FOREIGN MILITARY SALES DELIVERIES: 1950 TO 1970 (in millions of dollars)

Area and Country	*1950-1963*	*1964-1970*	*1970*
Worldwide	*2,885.4*	*6,775.9*	*1,429.8*
East Asia and Pacific[c]	183.6	811.0	124.8
Australia	113.8	491.3	52.5
China, Republic of	1.1	68.0	36.9
Indochina	7.9	–[a]	–
Japan	51.2	146.3	19.4
Korea	.3	4.2	1.9
Malyasia	b	15.1	2.7
New Zealand	3.4	62.0	10.1
Singapore	–	19.9	.2
Near East and South Asia[c]	161.4	1,297.1	537.8
Greece	.9	28.2	10.9
Iran	1.0	449.7	189.7
Iraq	.6	12.3	–
Turkey	.2	5.0	3.4
Europe[c]	1,688.5	4,057.3	639.4
Belgium	53.3	61.7	7.9
Denmark	15.6	53.7	10.9
France	94.5	217.8	12.4
Germany	1,323.6	1,815.2	226.2
Italy	58.4	316.4	50.4
Netherlands	31.5	68.9	6.4
Norway	4.0	142.1	40.4
Portugal	3.7	4.2	1.1
Spain	1.1	70.9	8.6
Sweden	21.3	9.2	.5
Switzerland	12.4	91.4	43.7
United Kingdom	58.1	1,151.4	221.5
Yugoslavia	8.5	3.1	.3
Africa[c]	5.2	50.8	17.7
Libya	.1	23.4	6.1
Morocco	–	21.0	11.3
American Republics[c]	200.8	194.4	36.6
Argentina	44.9	34.5	8.1
Brazil	16.9	68.0	11.7
Chile	12.8	20.0	10.0
Colombia	9.9	1.4	.2
Cuba	4.5	–	–
Ecuador	2.5	1.8	.5
Mexico	7.1	3.6	.4
Peru	35.9	13.8	2.0
Venezuela	56.0	47.0	3.0

TABLE 6 (Continued)

Area and Country	*1950-1963*	*1964-1970*	*1970*
Canada	578.1	219.2	49.7
Int'l. organizations	67.9	146.1	23.8

NOTE: For years ending June 30. Covers sales authorized and appropriated under the Foreign Military Sales Act. Includes deliveries of equipment, supplies, and services purchased for cash, U.S. government-financed credit, and U.S. government guaranty of privately financed credit.
SOURCE: United States [7].
a. –represents zero.
b. Less than $50,000.
c. Totals include countries not shown separately.

this fact. Indeed, the military has often ousted a military president when such action was considered necessary. Given the nature of most Latin American constitutions, the relative weakness of democratic processes, and the professional socialization of military officers, the military views itself not only as the embodiment of nationalism, but the moral and juridical guarantor of the constitution and civil order as well. It is doubtful that military assistance programs have fostered these anti-democratic sentiments on the part of the military. Nor have military assistance programs altered these views.

Military assistance represents only a small part of the total military expenditures of most Latin American states. As Wolf (1963: 20) has noted:

> for 14 of the Latin American countries for which unclassified data are available on domestic defense budgets, during the 1950-1960 period, total defense expenditures annually averaged about 25 times more than the average annual amount of military aid to these countries.

It is clearly reasonable to conclude that military coups would occur without U.S. military assistance. General Andrew F. O'Meara, Commander-in-Chief for the Caribbean, expressed a similar view in testimony before the House Foreign Affairs Committee in 1964. He stated that: "There are plenty of arms in Latin America to overthrow any number of governments if we had never given them one rifle, if we had never given them one truck" (United States[1]: 425). Military assistance, therefore, cannot be simplistically viewed in any way as the single causal factor in the incidence of coups.

The force-level requirements of the Latin American armed forces vary from country to country. This is especially true in the area of internal security and counter-insurgency–now the primary mission of military forces in many Latin American states. Mexico and Costa Rica, for example, have achieved a high level of political stability and have made substantial progress toward meeting the economic and social demands of their people. Therefore these countries have had little need for large armed forces or for military assistance. On the other hand, countries such as Colombia, Bolivia, and Peru have had long traditions of political violence. These states clearly require substantial internal security forces in order to maintain political stability and civil order.

Under such diverse circumstances, it is difficult to generalize about the types and sizes of force levels required by the Latin American states. Generally, it is recognized that it is in the best interests of the Latin American states *and* the United States that Latin American governments not maintain forces that place excessive demands on their resources, thus diverting these scarce resources from sorely needed developmental programs. However, Latin American governments have resented any attempt by the United States to dictate appropriate and justifiable military force levels. They insist on making their own determination as to what armed forces they need and how they should be organized and equipped. Indeed, when the United States has attempted to halt sales of military equipment to Latin American countries–equipment that the United States believed unnecessary–these states have simply sought alternative sources of supply. The example of the purchase of British-made jet fighters by Venezuela and Peru is a case in point.

Given the independent attitude of the Latin American states regarding the determination of necessary force levels and the fact that annual military assistance programs have been relatively small and widely diffused throughout the hemisphere, there seems little substance to the argument that U.S. military assistance has encouraged large military forces where they are not necessary.

Conclusions and Comments

It is evident that the shift in U.S. policy from one of fostering hemispheric defense to one of promoting internal security and economic development has created problems for the Military Assistance Program in the 1960s. While counter-insurgency, civic action, and the promotion of economic development more closely approximate Latin America's needs, such a program has proven very difficult to administer. One of the major problems centers around the traditional role of the Latin American military as the arbiter of the political process. As long as the military can effectively determine who shall govern, there is the danger that democratic civilian regimes may be toppled. In addition, the non-Communist left may feel forced to side with the Communists should the military choose to act as a conservative restraint on the process of social change.

Clearly, the development of a strong internal security capability not only increases the military's ability to deal with insurgency, but also raises the possibility that *any* opposition to the military may be suppressed as well. In order to counter this, the United States should encourage Latin American military forces to seek broader bases of support for their modernizing goals—especially among the non-Communist civilian elements of the left. (This is precisely what the military regime of General Juan Velasco Alvarado is attempting in Peru.) Furthermore, Latin American military forces should consistently be supported and encouraged to increase their role in civic action programs.

In terms of the criticisms levelled at the Military Assistance Program, it has been demonstrated that military assistance has not been a direct cause of anti-democratic military coups or of militarism in general in Latin America. Rather, the major causal factors are bound up in the complexities of Latin American social and political traditions. Likewise, the assertion that military assistance encourages large, unnecessary armed forces has little validity. The amount of military assistance provided by the United States to Latin America has not been of the magnitude that would enable any one country to build or sustain its forces solely on this aid. This is in clear contrast to the case of Cuba, where available evidence indicates that the Cuban military establishment is being almost wholly sustained by Soviet military assistance.

The Latin American states themselves have determined the appropriate and necessary military force levels and will continue to do so. They will sustain these force levels with or without U.S. military assistance. Withdrawal of U.S. military assistance would merely encourage the Latin American states to purchase arms or accept assistance from Europe or, in some cases, from Communist states. An example of this is the Chilean regime of Salvador Allende, which has recently shifted from the United States to the Soviet Union as the major supplier of arms and assistance to the Chilean military.

In the final analysis, the U.S. stake in Latin America is too important for it to abdicate its interests and responsibilities in the hemisphere. Part of this responsibility and interest has been implemented and protected by the Military Assistance Program. What is required of military assistance is that it continue to attempt to meet the needs of the Latin American states in the areas of social and economic development. Admittedly, the Military Assistance Program has not met these needs. Yet as long as the military forces in Latin America continue to operate as arbiters of the political process and, in some cases, as agents of social change, there is no reason to discontinue the Military Assistance Program. Despite its obvious shortcomings, the Military Assistance Program can be a valuable tool to both aid in the resolution of the vast social and economic problems that plague the hemisphere, and to advance U.S. strategic interests as well.

REFERENCES

Agency for International Development (1971) Economic Data Book. Washington, D.C.: U.S. Department of Commerce.

BOBROW, D. (1966) "The civic role of the military: some critical hypotheses." Western Pol. Q. Volume 19 (March): 101-111.

DAME, H. (1962) United States Military Assistance and Latin American Relations. Washington, D.C.: American University Center for Research in Social Systems.

HAHR, J. (1969) "Military assistance to Latin America." Military Rev. 49 (May): 12-21.

HOVEY, H. (1968) United States Military Assistance: A Study of Policies and Practices. New York: Frederick A. Praeger.

LIEUWIN, E. (1965) U.S. Policy in Latin America. New York: Frederick A. Praeger.

LOFTUS, J. (1968) Latin American Defense Expenditures, 1938-1965. Santa Monica, Calif.: RAND.

McARDLE, C. (1964) The Role of Military Assistance and the Problem of Arms Control. Cambridge, Mass.: Center for International Studies.

Mutual Security Act (1951) Washington, D.C.: Government Printing Office.

President's Committee to Study the Military Assistance Program (1959) Report. Washington, D.C.: Government Printing Office.

United States

[1] Congress, House of Representatives, Foreign Affairs Committee (1964) Foreign Assistance and Related Agencies Appropriations for 1965 Hearings, Eighty-Eighth Congress. Washington, D.C.: Government Printing Office.

[2] --- Subcommittee (1971) Military Assistance Training. Ninety-First Congress. Washington, D.C.: Government Printing Office.

[3] --- (1970) Military Assistance Training and Developmental Television. Ninety-First Congress. Washington, D.C.: Government Printing Office.

[4] --- (1970) Military Assistance Training Hearings. Ninety-First Congress. Washington, D.C.: Government Printing Office.

[5] Congress, House of Representatives, Subcommittee of the Committee on Appropriations (1969) Foreign Assistance and Related Agencies Appropriations for 1970 Hearings. Ninety-First Congress, First Session. Washington, D.C.: Government Printing Office.

[6] Congress, Senate, Committee on Foreign Relations (1961) International Development and Security. Eighty-Seventh Congress. Washington, D.C.: Government Printing Office.

[7] Department of Defense, Office of the Secretary (1971) Military Assistance and Foreign Military Sales Facts. Washington, D.C.: Government Printing Office.

[8] Department of State (1953) Military Assistance to Latin America: Background. Washington, D.C.: Government Printing Office.

[9] --- (1951) "Inter-American military cooperation." Department of State Bull. 24 (April 9).

WOLF, C. (1963) The Political Effects of Military Programs: Some Indications from Latin America. Santa Monica, Calif.: RAND.

SAGE RESEARCH PROGRESS SERIES ON

WAR, REVOLUTION, & PEACEKEEPING

SPONSORED BY THE INTER-UNIVERSITY SEMINAR ON ARMED FORCES AND SOCIETY

Series Editor Charles C. Moskos, Jr., *Professor of Sociology, Northwestern University*

THE MILITARY-INDUSTRIAL COMPLEX: A Reassessment

Edited by **SAM C. SARKESIAN**, *Loyola University (Chicago)*

Produced in cooperation with the Center for Policy Study at the University of Chicago

CONTENTS

Sam C. Sarkesian, INTRODUCTION

I. CONCEPTS AND REALITIES

Charles C. Moskos, Jr., THE MILITARY-INDUSTRIAL COMPLEX: THEORETICAL ANTECEDENTS AND CONCEPTUAL CONTRADICTIONS

Charles Wolf, Jr., MILITARY-INDUSTRIAL SIMPLICITIES, COMPLEXITIES AND REALITIES

Stanley Lieberson, AN EMPIRICAL STUDY OF MILITARY-INDUSTRIAL LINKAGES

Albert D. Biderman, RETIRED SOLDIERS WITHIN AND WITHOUT THE MILITARY-INDUSTRIAL COMPLEX

II. STRATEGIC ALTERNATIVES

Morris Janowitz, STRATEGIC DIMENSIONS OF AN ALL VOLUNTEER ARMED FORCE

Seymour Melman, ALTERNATIVE STRATEGIES AND BUDGETS FOR MILITARY SECURITY

Bruce M. Russett, A COUNTERCOMBATANT DETERRENT? FEASIBILITY, MORALITY, AND ARMS CONTROL

III. ARMS AND CONFLICT CONTROL

K. Wayne Smith and J. N. Merritt, SOME COMPLEXITIES OF ARMS CONTROL PLANNING

IV. DECISION-MAKING AND POLITICAL LEADERSHIP

Adam Yarmolinsky, THE PRESIDENT, THE CONGRESS, AND ARMS CONTROL

Lawrence J. Korb, THE SECRETARY OF DEFENSE AND THE JOINT CHIEFS OF STAFF: THE BUDGETARY PROCESS

ISBN 0-8039-0134-8 (C)
0-8039-0135-6 (P)
L.C. 78-183960

1972
352 pages

$12.50 (Cloth)
7.50 (Paper)
Market: World

SAGE PUBLICATIONS, INC.
275 S. Beverly Dr. / Beverly Hills, CA. 90212

SAGE PUBLICATIONS LTD
44 Hatton Garden, London E C 1

REVIEW ESSAY

CULTURE AND COLONIALISM IN THE WEST INDIES

Salmon, C. S., THE CARIBBEAN CONFEDERATION. London: Frank Cass & Co., Ltd., 1971 (Original London: Cassell & Co., Ltd., 1888). Preface, map, 175 pp. $9.50.

Braithwaite, Edward, CREOLE SOCIETY IN JAMAICA 1770-1820. London: Oxford University Press, 1971. Introduction, maps, appendices, bibliography, index, xvi + 374 pp. $16.00.

Moore, O. Ernest, HAITI, ITS STAGNANT SOCIETY AND SHACKLED ECONOMY. New York: Exposition Press, 1972. Preface, notes, x + 281 pp. $8.00.

de Kadt, Emanuel, Ed., PATTERNS OF FOREIGN INFLUENCE IN THE CARIBBEAN. London: Oxford University Press, 1972. Preface, introduction, index, map, 188 pp.

Szulc, Tad, ed., THE UNITED STATES AND THE CARIBBEAN. Englewood Cliffs, N.J.: Prentice-Hall, Inc., 1971. The American Assembly Series. Preface, introduction, index, map, 212 pp. $5.95.

A subtle shift has developed recently in the academic study of West Indian societies. There has been a move away from traditional historical and sociological accounts in which the region is viewed largely as an extension of European and North American political history and cultural

EDITOR'S NOTE: A companion review to this one will be published in the *Journal of Interamerican Studies* of February 1973.

norms. Increasingly, scholars have been turning to what has been loosely termed the "internal history" of Caribbean societies. What this phrase means varies from author to author, but in general it suggests greater attention to the internal structure of island societies—class groups, social relations, and life styles. In some important respects, each of the books under review reflects this internal point of view.

The internal focus is not new, however; it is only its academic respectability which is becoming more apparent. To historians, the drama of slavery and slaving, the foibles of the planters, and the acts of governors and admirals have been traditionally more interesting than the rise of free peasantries, the folklore of the slave barracks, or the inter-island movement of cane-cutting labor gangs. This is consistent with the view residents of the metropole have often taken toward their distant island colonies. In the late nineteenth century, when Jamaica and other British colonies in the Caribbean were popularly known as the "slums of the empire," it was common among writers such as Carlyle, Froude, and Trollope to dismiss the painful development of indigenous Creole institutions as nothing more than deviations from preferred English norms. The decomposing present was simply a foil for their imaginings of a glorious past. Subsequent writers took not the West Indies as their topic, but rather the interest and activities of metropolitan powers in the region. British, French, or American concerns, expressed in the tropical West Indian setting, were the dominant theme.

But the hegemony of colonialist power and ideology was not complete, even in the economic trough of the latter nineteenth century. C. S. Salmon, a high colonial administrator whose experience included residencies in West Africa, the Seychelles Islands, and the island of Nevis, challenged what he saw as the unholy alliance of Colonial Office bureaucracy and West Indian planter-merchant interests. Even in the 1880s, he recognized as the issue of his times local self-government through island assemblies occupied and run by black West Indians. He specifically rejected the "merchant monopoly" which strangled island economic life, as well as James Anthony Froude's infamous remark on island political autonomy: "govern them as we govern India." This froudacity, as Salmon called it, was typical of metropolitan views of the time. It was based on a virulent racism which denied that black West Indians were capable of self-government. It assumed that only through close ties to the superior civilization of the "mother country" could the benefits of Western culture and Western Christianity trickle down to the ignorant West Indian masses.

Perhaps inevitably, Salmon's political liberalism and his humanitarianism were tainted by similar assumptions of European cultural superiority. His style is rambling and tedious, with lengthy asides on the morals (or lack of them) among white West Indian residents. He saw life in the colonies leading to corruption of the Western European work ethic and to habits and preferences which were distinctly "un-English."

But for black West Indians, significantly referred to as "British black men," the touch of British culture has been uplifting, the more so the lighter the hand of metropolitan institutions. Salmon believes in the manifest loyalty to England of black West Indians, and their latent attachment to the English belief in progress through hard work and diligence. Therefore he is incensed at the crudities of Froude and those who think like him. Salmon's model for West Indian development is one of assimiliation to English culture. He cannot conceive of other historical possibilities. Only the bureaucratic bungler and the greedy planter-merchant groups impede what to even an enlightened nineteenth-century figure was the only logical social development.

Brathwaite clearly shares in this ideological dislike of immobile bureaucracies and stultifying provincialism. But he is more willing to view West Indian societies in their own terms—that is, as having histories in their own right. Brathwaite examined Jamaica at an earlier period, before the end of slavery, but the problems are the same as those which challenged Salmon. In the balance between external colonial pressures and internal adjustments to slave-based plantation agriculture, what arises that can be labeled as authentically indigenous to the society? What is it that we can call Creole society, which is distinguishable from colonial polity and economy?

Brathwaite's approach is sociological as well as historical; it is "an attempt to examine the nature of a society, based on slavery, from the point of view of its institutions, its social groupings, and the attitudes of individuals and groups to each other." It is an attempt which largely succeeds through a most impressive use of thoroughly documented historical materials. There cannot be much of significance in any relevant archives that Brathwaite has overlooked or failed to use.

To the extent that Jamaica became a distinctively Creole society, Brathwaite sees two major causes: The American Revolution and what he calls an ongoing "humanitarian revolution." The former isolated Jamaica from its previously close ties, both economic and social, with the Atlantic seaboard colonies and the American North and South. The United States then developed without any strong Caribbean interest. The latter, a less clear or analytically successful concept in the book, was marked by the anti-slavery crusade, emanicipation, and the emergence of a distinctive Creole culture. Presumably, although he does not elaborate the point, that revolution is still unfolding, as much in the struggles of the Ras Tafarians or Black Power enthusiasts as during the Maroon wars or the rise of the Garveyites.

The most interesting portion of this excellent study is that in which Brathwaite attempts to deal with two major points: what is meant by creolization, and why the process of creolization was so consistently subordinate to the perpetuation of colonialization. Here, creolization and colonialization refer not only to groups, classes, and formal institutions in island society, but to attitudes and states of mind as well. Brathwaite has dug deeply into the historical materials which would illuminate these points. His chapters on whites, enslaved blacks, and free coloreds provide fascinating views of daily life in Jamaica at this time. The documentation is rich, and the author's handling of it is both deft and informative. (Only the chapter on the folk culture of the slaves is a disappointment, relying as it does on an outmoded concept of African "survivals" and resulting in a trait list compiled in order to make the point.) As worthy as these chapters are, however, they appear to stand independently of the humanitarian revolution schema in which the formal argument of the book is cast. Indeed, the humanitarian revolution argument seems at best superfluous, at worst an ideological distraction. I say this because Brathwaite is asking some very fundamental and important questions about West Indian societies. His data go a long way, much further than those of most historians of the region, in illuminating those questions. But the ideal of humanitarian revolution is not in any sense an adequate device for clarifying the creolization process as described in Brathwaite's pages, nor does it encapsulate any central tendencies in Jamaica's historical development. We are left convinced by the thorough and expert handling of much historical data that something called creolization was indeed going on. But a more adequate concept of culture is required to finally bring all the threads together.

After a fine history such as this, one which recognizes and utilizes much from sociology and anthropology in the interpretation of long-term historical processes, it is indeed a drab and flat performance which greets us in Moore's book on Haiti. This is too bad, since Haiti is certainly the seedbed of West Indian nationalism, and the imposition of colonial forms on the development of Creole society were thrown off early. But Moore is a technician of "development," having twice served as an economic adviser to the Haitian government. His book is well larded with statistics, many of them useful and culled from little-used sources. The whole is receded by a brief but interesting history of Haiti from the Arawak Indians to Jean-Claude Duvalier. But Moore's purposes in Haiti were singular, as on page 3, where he writes, "For one thing is certain: we would be foolish to leave next-door Haiti to wallow indefinitely in extreme poverty and misery and thus constitute a standing invitation to communist infiltration and control." And how is one to react to a characterization of "the Haitian peasant," 88% of the population, such as the following:

> When well nourished and free from illness, he reveals himself as intelligent and capable of hard work. However, he has little foresight, and no conception of such terms as 'progress' and 'development.' If he can eke out a bare subsistence for himself and family, he is satisfied (p. 143).

Amid the choppy style of Moore's writing and the narrowness of his appreciation of Haitian society, one is suspicious of a lurking froudacity against which Salmon invoked a far more generous vision of island society almost a century ago.

The last two books bring us to the present, but they deal with the same pernicious problem–the tension between indigenous Creole culture and the imposition of external restrictions and control. Internal history must still be reconciled, to one degree or another, with forces and agencies external to the region. Both books are edited volumes, and the papers are generally good, although those of the de Kadt collection are more uniform in quality. Since it would be impossible here to review every contributor's paper and unfair to single out one or two for extensive comment, we will list the contributors and then consider some general themes common to both books.

The Szulc volume contains papers by Gordon K. Lewis, Anthony Maingot, Ben Stephansky, George Volsky, Frank McDonald, Juan De Onis, Gerard Latortue, and Kalman Silvert. Those of Lewis, Maingot, McDonald, and De Onis are particularly interesting.

The contributions assembled by de Kadt are generally more detailed and, as in the Szulc collection, contain extensive background information on their respective topics. They include an introduction by the editor and articles by Peter Odell, Douglas Hall, Colin Henfrey, Guy Lasserre and Albert Mabileau, Harry Hoetink, Robin Blackburn, Bryan Roberts, and Lincoln Gordon.

The title of each book indicates the problem area: foreign influence. This has become particularly acute where it concerns the United States, for, as de Kadt indicates in his introduction (p. 2), American public opinion accepts the Caribbean as a legitimate sphere of influence, and this view has been "much strengthened by the ideology of the cold war, which helped to convert considerations about the internal socio-political structure of nations swiftly into quasi-military ones." Where once buccaneers colonial governors, planters, and merchants jostled for the control of island territories in order to secure the claims of European governments, now all manner of hucksters, island bureaucracies, monopolies, and international corporations scrounge what they can from the few available resources to assure for themselves a favorable place under the North American economic and political shield. The protective self-interest of superpowers is evident from the Canal Zone to Anguilla.

But fortunately, neither of these books is limited to rehashing policy decisions of colonial and colonial-like powers. Considerable attention is given to sociological and political conditions peculiar to each Caribbean society and the way these conditions are modified as well as how they modify foreign influence. The emphasis in Roberts' paper on Guatemala and Blackburn's on Cuba is in the nature of internal conditions in those countries. They show that the purposes of foreign powers—the United States in the former case and Russia in the latter—are modified and even reversed when internal conditions are taken into account. They imply that the pessimism of many of the other contributors in giving island societies little credit for having a positive role in the expression of colonial influence may be somewhat overdrawn. In his typically provocative style, Gordon Lewis has indicated that anti-colonialist and pronationalist sentiments are growing throughout the region. Although he is dubious as to what the new nationalist groups may be able to accomplish, he is insistent that someone must undertake "the historically determined task of black militancy in the area." It is just this militancy, as an expression of island (as against metropolitan) cultural and social values, with which the representatives of foreign influence will have to increasingly deal in the future.

Many of the papers, like that of Maingot, give us an excellent survey of the structural and political divisions within their respective societies and describe the historical development of class interests and class antagonisms. Some, like him, do not see in the near future a resolution of the problems created by the colonial balkanization of the Caribbean. They echo the pessimism of the Trinidadian novelist and essayist, V. S. Naipaul, who once wrote, "these islands, black and poor, are dangerous only to themselves."

But others are more hopeful. They point to a rising sense of cultural self-identity in the islands. That identity takes various forms, ranging from the "February Revolution" of early 1970 in Trinidad to the trenchant economic-political analyses conducted by the New World Group of Jamaica. Increasingly, these expressions of discontent will have political repercussions and, to the extent they do, the political interest in the Caribbean of large foreign powers will have to be modified. The Szulc and de Kadt volumes show the rising interest of historians, sociologists, and social planners in the internal conditions of Caribbean societies. Like Brathwaite and Salmon, they are looking increasingly at the sources of and obstacles to indigenous social and political development.

Whatever creolization of these societies may mean, there are still to be faced hard questions about how change is to be brought about through reliance on internal rather than external resources. To what extent, for instance, can West Indian activists and intellectuals, socially isolated as they have often been, form a working alliance with the poor? Can the long history of inter-island jealousies be overcome, jealousies which separate "big islanders" from "little islanders," Spanish from English speakers? Can the enthusiasm and excitement of dramatic public events and encounters be sustained and turned to the more tedious job of basic community organization? Salmon had hope over a century ago, and Brathwaite clearly believes a humanistic revolution is a continuing reality. The contributors to the edited works are not quite as confident. But all are looking to West Indian societies themselves as their own ultimate best hope.

–James W. Green
College of Community Sciences
University of Wisconsin–Green Bay

BOOKS RECEIVED

GENERAL AND REGIONAL LATIN AMERICA

Clissold, Stephen, LATIN AMERICA: NEW WORLD, THIRD WORLD. New York, Washington, London: Praeger Publishers, 1972. Acknowledgments, table of basic data, main events 1945-1971, abbreviations, glossary, bibliography, index. ix + 394 pp. $13.50.

de Kadt, Emanuel, ed., PATTERNS OF FOREIGN INFLUENCE IN THE CARIBBEAN. New York: Oxford University Press, 1972. Abbreviations, preface, contributors, index, map. viii + 188 pp.

Johnson, Charles W., INDICE DE CUADROS ESTADISTICOS SOCIO-POLITICOS SOBRE AMERICA LATINA 1946-1969. Volume I. Mexico: Instituto de Investigaciones Sociales, 1972. Agradecimientos, advertencia y guía para el manejo del índice. iii + 701 pp.

Johnson, Charles W., INDICE DE CUADROS ESTADISTICOS SOCIO-POLITICOS SOBRE AMERICA LATINA 1946-1969. Volume II. Mexico: Instituto de Investigaciones Sociales, 1972. 907 pp.

Katz, Friedrich, THE ANCIENT AMERICAN CIVILIZATIONS. Translated by K. M. Lois Simpson. (Praeger History of Civilization.) New York: Praeger Publishers, 1972. Foreword, notes, bibliography, glossary, maps, index. xvi + 386 pp. $15.00.

Lowenthal, David, WEST INDIAN SOCIETIES. New York: Oxford University Press, 1972. Foreword by Philip Mason, acknowledgments, preface, abbreviations, sources and bibliography, index, table, map. xvii + 385 pp.

NATIONAL DIRECTORY OF LATIN AMERICANISTS, Second Edition. (Hispanic Foundation Bibliographical Series No. 12.) Compiled by the Hispanic Foundation Reference Dept., published by the Library of Congress, Washington, 1971. Introduction, list of abbreviations, bibliographies, indexes of subject and area specialties. 684 pp. $4.25.

Rivera, Julius, LATIN AMERICA: A SOCIOCULTURAL INTERPRETATION. New York: Meredith, 1971. Acknowledgments, introduction, glossary, index. xvi + 204 pp.

Theberge, James D., ed., SOVIET SEAPOWER IN THE CARIBBEAN: POLITICAL AND STRATEGIC IMPLICATIONS. (Praeger Special Studies in International Politics and Public Affairs.) New York: Praeger Publishers, 1972. Acknowledgements, list of tables, list of figures and maps, introduction, notes, selected bibliography, about the editor and contributors. xv + 175 pp. $13.50.

COUNTRIES OF LATIN AMERICA

Argentina

Goldwert, Marvin, DEMOCRACY, MILITARISM, AND NATIONALISM IN ARGENTINA, 1930-1966: AN INTERPRETATION. Austin, Texas: The University of Texas Press, 1972. Preface, introduction, bibliographical essay, sources, index. xx + 253 pp. $8.00.

Brazil

de Vasconcelos Cavalcanti, Clóvis, MERCADOS PARA A PESCA EM ARACAJU. Brasil: Instituto Joaquim Nabuco de Pesquisas Sociais-IJNPS, 1971. Nota explicativa, índice das ilustrações. 119 pp.

Freyre, Gilberto, Estevão Pinto, Renato Campos, Francisco Julião, Pe. Antonio Melo E Outros, CANA E REFORMA AGRARIA. Brasil: Instituto Joaquim Nabuco de Pesquisas Sociais-MEC, 1970. Indice, prefácio à 2a edição (pelo sociólogo-anthropólogo Gilberto Freyre), anexos. 369 pp.

Mota, Mauro, HISTORIA EM ROTULOS DE CIGARROS. Brasil: Instituto Joaquim Nabuco de Pesquisas Sociais-MEC, 1971. 131 pp.

Quartim, João, DICTATORSHIP AND ARMED STRUGGLE IN BRAZIL, translated by David Fernbach. New York: Monthly Review Press, 1972. Publisher's note, chronology, historical introduction 1930-64, appendix: Parties and Organizations, index. 250 pp. $6.95.

Ribeiro, René, VITALINO, UM CERAMISTA POPULAR DO NORDESTE. Brasil: Instituto Joaquim Nabuco de Pesquisas Sociais, 1972.

Roett, Riordan, ed., BRAZIL IN THE SIXTIES. Nashville, Tennessee: Vanderbilt University Press, 1972. Introduction, index. xviii + 434 pp. $15.00

Trigueiro Mendes, Durmeval, TOWARD A THEORY OF EDUCATIONAL PLANNING: THE BRAZILIAN CASE. (Monograph Series, No. 7). East Lansing, Michigan: Michigan State University, 1972. Foreword. iv + 125 pp.

Colombia

Reichel-Dolmatoff, Gerardo, SAN AGUSTIN: A CULTURE OF COLOMBIA. (Arts and Civilizations of Indian America, General Editor: Michael D. Coe.) New York: Praeger Publishers, 1972. Preface, selected bibliography, table of radio-carbon dates, notes, list of illustrations, index. 163 pp. $12.50.

Caribbean Region

Hurwitz, Samuel J. and Edith F., JAMAICA: A HISTORICAL PORTRAIT. New York: Praeger Publishers, 1971. Preface, selected bibliography, index, illustrations. xii + 273 pp. $9.50.

Mexico

Heath, Shirley Brice, TELLING TONGUES: LANGUAGE POLICY IN MEXICO, COLONY TO NATION. New York: Teachers College Press, Columbia University, 1972. Editor's note, foreword, preface, acknowledgments, appendixes, notes, bibliography, index. xx + 300 pp. $10.00.

Peru

Stein, William W., CHANGING VICOS AGRICULTURE. Buffalo, New York: Council on International Studies, State University of New York at Buffalo, 1972. Footnotes. iv + 69 pp.

Venezuela

Burggraaff, Winfield J., THE VENEZUELAN ARMED FORCES IN POLITICS, 1935-1959. Columbia, Missouri: University of Missouri Press, 1972. Acknowledgements, preface, appendixes, glossary, bibliography, index. 241 pp. $10.00.

INTERAMERICAN RELATIONS

Crassweller, Robert D., THE CARIBBEAN COMMUNITY: CHANGING SOCIETIES AND U.S. POLICY. (Published for the Council on Foreign Relations.) New York: Praeger Publishers, 1972. Acknowledgments, introductory note, notes, bibliographic note, index, maps. x + 470 pp. $13.50.

Lopez Urrutia, Carlos, LA ESCUADRA CHILENA EN MEXICO-1822. Buenos Aires-Santiago de Chile: Editorial Francisco de Aguirre, 1971. Indice de ilustraciones, dedicatoria, presentacion, prologo, bibliografia, index. xxi + 135 pp.

Sharp, Daniel A., ed., U.S. FOREIGN POLICY AND PERU. Austin, Texas: The University of Texas Press, 1972. Preface, acknowledgments, notes on contributors, project participants and sponsoring organizations, index. xxv + 485 pp. $10.00.

MISCELLANEOUS

Hinton, William, TURNING POINT IN CHINA: AN ESSAY ON THE CULTURAL REVOLUTION. New York: Monthly Review Press, 1972. Author's note. 112 pp. $1.75.

Horowitz, Irving Louis, THREE WORLDS OF DEVELOPMENT: THE THEORY AND PRACTICE OF INTERNATIONAL STRATIFICATION. New York: Oxford University Press, 1972. Preface to first edition (1965), name index, subject index. xxx + 556 pp. $15.00.

Klare, Michael T., WAR WITHOUT END: AMERICAN PLANNING FOR THE NEXT VIETNAMS. New York: Alfred A. Knopf, 1972. Acknowledgements, foreword by Gabriel Kolko, introduction, appendixes, notes, research guide, research bibliography, index. xx + 464 + xvii pp. $10.00.

Medina, Pedro, de. A NAVIGATOR'S UNIVERSE: THE LIBRO DE COSMOGRAPHIA of 1538. (Translated and with an introduction by Ursula Lamb.) Chicago: The University of Chicago Press, 1972. Acknowledgements, notes on the translation, bibliography, index. 224 pp. $18.50.

Myint, H., SOUTHEAST ASIA'S ECONOMY: DEVELOPMENT POLICIES IN THE 1970s. (Penguin Modern Economics–A study sponsored by the Asian Development Bank.) Middlesex, England: Penguin Books 1972. Editorial foreword, Pote Sarasin foreword, preface, introduction, table of currency equivalents, map of Southeast Asia, references, further reading, index. 189 pp. $1.95.

Richardson, Ken and David Spears, RACE, CULTURE, AND INTELLIGENCE. (Penguin Education.) Middlesex, England: Penguin Books, 1972. Editorial foreword, context of debate, conclusions, index. 205 pp. $1.65.

Wilson, Carter, A GREEN TREE AND A DRY TREE. New York: Macmillan, 1972. Notes. 300 pp. $7.95.

JOURNAL OF INTER-AMERICAN STUDIES and WORLD AFFAIRS

INDEX

to

JOURNAL OF INTERAMERICAN STUDIES AND WORLD AFFAIRS

VOLUME 14

Number 1 (February 1972) pp. 1-128.
Number 2 (May 1972) pp. 129-268.
Number 3 (August 1972) pp. 269-372.
Number 4 (November 1972) pp. 373-500.

SAGE PUBLICATIONS, INC.
275 South Beverly Drive
Beverly Hills, California 90212

SAGE PUBLICATIONS LTD
St George's House / 44 Hatton Garden
London E C 1

INDEX

to

JOURNAL OF INTERAMERICAN STUDIES AND WORLD AFFAIRS

VOLUME 14

Number 1 (February 1972) pp. 1-128.
Number 2 (May 1972) pp. 129-268.
Number 3 (August 1972) pp. 269-372.
Number 4 (November 1972) pp. 373-500.

Authors:

ADAMS, RICHARD, "New Lands and Old Traditions; Ketchi Cultivators in the Guatemalan Lowlands" [Book Review] 120.
BAINES, JOHN M., "U.S. Military Assistance to Latin America: An Assessment," 469.
BARBER, WILLIAM F., "Guerrillas in Latin America" [Book Review] 255.
BLOUGH, WILLIAM J., "Political Attitudes of Mexican Women: Support for the Political System Among a Newly Enfranchised Group," 201.
CORBETT, CHARLES D., "Military Institutional Development and Sociopolitical Change: The Bolivian Case," 399.
COY, PETER E. B., "Social Anarchism: An Atavistic Ideology of the Peasant," 133.
DESSAINT, ALAIN Y., "Ixil Country, a Plural Society" [Book Review] 260.
DICKSON, THOMAS I., Jr., "An Approach to the Study of the Latin American Military," 455.
EBEL, ROLAND H., "Governing the City-State: Notes on the Politics of the Small Latin American Countries," 325.
GARDINER, C. HARVEY, "The Japanese and Central America," 15.
GLADE, WILLIAM, "Latin American Peasant Movements" [Book Review] 251.
GONZALEZ, NANCIE L., "The Mexican-American People" [Book Review] 118.
GREEN, JAMES M., "Culture and Colonialism in the West Indies" [Review Essay] 489.
GREER, THOMAS V., "The Mercantile Potpourri Called Panama," 347.
HASSAN, M. F., "The Communist Party of Venezuela" [Book Review] 262.
KEARNS, KEVIN C., "The Andean Common Market: A New Thrust at Economic Integration in Latin America," 225.
KOLINSKI, CHARLES J., "Politics of the Chaco Peace Conference, 1935-1939" [Book Review] 257.

KOSSOK, MANFRED, "The Armed Forces in Latin America: Potential for Changes in Political and Social Functions," 375.

KRESL, PETER KARL, "The United States, Canada, and the 'Market Mentality,' " 3.

LEONARD, THOMAS M., "Yanqui Politics and the Isthmian Canal" [Book Review] 259.

LIEBMAN, SEYMOUR B., "History of the Jews of the Netherland Antilles" [Book Review] 113.

MAEYAMA, TAKASHI, "Ancestor, Emperor, and Immigrant: Religion and Group Identification of the Japanese in Rural Brazil (1908-1950)," 151.

MALLOY, JAMES M., "Peru Before and After the Coup of 1968," 437.

MESA-LAGO, CARMELO, "Ideological, Political, and Economic Factors in the Cuban Controversy on Material Versus Moral Incentives," 49.

PREMDAS, RALPH R., "Elections and Political Campaigns in a Racially Bifurcated State: The Case of Guyana," 271.

RANDALL, STEPHEN JAMES, "Colombia, the United States, and Interamerican Aviation Rivalry, 1927-1940," 297.

VINCENT, JON S., "The Brazilian Novel: Some Paradoxes of Popularity," 183.

WRIGHT, IONE S., "Editorial Note," 131.

Articles:

"Ancestor, Emperor, and Immigrant: Religion and Group Identification of the Japanese in Rural Brazil (1908-1950)," Maeyama, 151.

"The Andean Common Market: A New Thrust at Economic Integration in Latin America," Kearns, 225.

"An Approach to the Study of the Latin American Military," Dickson, 455.

"The Armed Forces in Latin America: Potential for Changes in Political and Social Functions," Kossok, 375.

"The Brazilian Novel: Some Paradoxes of Popularity," Vincent, 183.

"Colombia, The United States, and Interamerican Aviation Rivalry, 1927-1940," Randall, 297.

"Editorial Note," Wright, 131.

"Elections and Political Campaigns in a Racially Bifurcated State: The Case of Guyana," Premdas, 271.

"Governing the City-State: Notes on the Politics of the Small Latin American Countries," Ebel, 325.

"Ideological, Political, and Economic Factors in the Cuban Controversy on Material Versus Moral Incentives," Mesa-Lago, 49.

"The Japanese and Central America," Gardiner, 15.

"The Mercantile Potpourri Called Panama," Greer, 347.

"Military Institutional Development and Sociopolitical Change: The Bolivian Case," Corbett, 399.

"Peru Before and After the Coup of 1968," Malloy, 437.

"Political Attitudes of Mexican Women: Support for the Political System Among a Newly Enfranchised Group," Blough, 201.

"Social Anarchism: An Atavistic Ideology of the Peasant," Coy, 133.

"The United States, Canada, and the 'Market Mentality,' " Kresl, 3.

"U.S. Military Assistance to Latin America: An Assessment," Baines, 469.

Book Reviews

"The Communist Party of Venezuela," Hassan, 262.
"Guerrillas in Latin America," Barber, 255.
"History of the Jews of the Netherland Antilles," Liebman, 113.
"Ixil Country, a Plural Society," Dessaint, 260.
"Latin American Peasant Movements," Glade, 251.
"The Mexican-American People," Gonzalez, 118.
"New Lands and Old Traditions; Ketchi Cultivators in the Guatemalan Lowlands," Adams, 120.
"Politics of the Chaco Peace Conference 1935-1939," Kolinski, 257.
"Yanqui Politics and the Isthmian Canal," Leonard, 259.

Review Essay:

"Culture and Colonialism in the West Indies," Green, 489.

EUS | EDUCATION AND URBAN SOCIETY

. . a new independent quarterly journal of social esearch with implications for public policy.

ditor: JAY D. SCRIBNER, *Graduate School of ducation, University of California at Los Angeles*

rovides a multidisciplinary forum for studies which oncentrate on the role of education in a society vhich is urban—including research on educational nnovations on education as a social institution, and ne politics of education, as well as explorations of ducational institutions and processes as agents of ocial change.

ublished quarterly in November, February, May, and ugust.

'early rate: $15.00 (£7.00); $10.00 (£4.70) to profes- onal individuals; $8.00 to full-time students in U.S. nd Canada only.

UE | URBAN EDUCATION

. . . exists to improve the quality of education in the city by making the results of relevant empirical and scholarly inquiry more generally available. Contributions are invited from education, jurisprudence, the behavioral sciences, medicine, philosophy, history, and administration.

Editor: WARREN BUTTON, *Department of Social Foundations of Education, State University of New York at Buffalo*

Published quarterly in April, July, October, and January.

Yearly rate: $15.00 (£7.00); $10.00 (£4.70) to professional individuals; $8.00 to full-time students in U.S. and Canada only.

PSR | PACIFIC SOCIOLOGICAL REVIEW

Official Journal of the Pacific Sociological Association

. . a forum for articles which attempt to contribute o the literature of sociology—whether they be sub- tantive or methodological, theoretical or empirical.

:ditor: JOHN MacGREGOR, *Oregon State University*

'or membership information, contact Dr. Leonard Gordon, Acting Treasurer, PSA, Department of Sociology, Arizona State University, Tempe 85281, U.S.A.

Published quarterly in January, April, July, and October.

Yearly rate: $15.00 (£7.00); Individual (non-member) subscriptions are available at a professional discount of one-third ($10.00/£4.70).

■ ORDER FORM ■

☐ **Please enter my subscription to:** OR ☐ **Please send more information about:**

- ☐ American Behavioral Scientist
- ☐ American Politics Quarterly
- ☐ Comparative Group Studies
- ☐ Comparative Political Studies
- ☐ Criminology
- ☐ Education and Urban Society
- ☐ Environment and Behavior
- ☐ International Studies Quarterly
- ☐ Journal of Black Studies
- ☐ Journal of Comparative Administration
- ☐ Journal of Contemporary History
- ☐ Journal of Interamerican Studies
- ☐ Pacific Sociological Review
- ☐ Political Theory
- ☐ Poverty and Human Resources Abstracts
- ☐ Public Finance Quarterly
- ☐ Professional Papers in Administrative Sciences
- ☐ Professional Papers in American Politics
- ☐ Professional Papers in Comparative Politics
- ☐ Professional Papers in International Studies
- ☐ Sage Urban Studies Abstracts
- ☐ Simulation and Games
- ☐ Sociological Methods and Research
- ☐ The New Atlantis
- ☐ Urban Affairs Quarterly
- ☐ Urban Education
- ☐ Urban Life and Culture
- ☐ Urban Research News
- ☐ Youth and Society

☐ Check enclosed

☐ Bill me at: ☐ Institutional ☐ Professional ☐ Student rates

NAME ______________________________

ADDRESS ______________________________

CITY ______________ STATE ______________ ZIP ________

Students indicate

Prices valid until 12/31/72